Envision

Envision

Envision

WRITING AND RESEARCHING ARGUMENTS

Envision

WRITING AND RESEARCHING ARGUMENTS

FIFTH EDITION

Christine L. Alfano and Alyssa J. O'Brien
Stanford University

PEARSON

Boston   Columbus   Indianapolis   New York City   San Francisco
Amsterdam   Cape Town   Dubai   London   Madrid   Milan   Munich   Paris   Montreal   Toronto
Delhi   Mexico City   São Paulo   Sydney   Hong Kong   Seoul   Singapore   Taipei   Tokyo

Senior Acquisition Editor: Brad Potthoff
Development Editor: David Kear
Marketing Manager: Allison Arnold
Content Producer: Laura Olson
Media Editor: Kelsey Loveday
Media Producer: Elizabeth Bravo
Program Manager: Lauren Finn
Project Manager: Denise Phillip Grant

Project Coordination, Text Design, and Electronic
    Page Makeup: Lumina Datamatics, Inc.
Program Design Lead/Designer: Barbara Atkinson
Cover Photos: WIN-Initiative/Getty Images
Senior Manufacturing Buyer: Roy L. Pickering, Jr.
Printer/Binder: R.R. Donnelley/Crawfordsville
Cover Printer: Phoenix Color/Hagerstown

Acknowledgments of third-party content appear on pages 341–343, which constitute an extension of this copyright page.

PEARSON, ALWAYS LEARNING, and MyWritingLab are exclusive trademarks owned by Pearson Education, Inc. or its affiliates in the United States and/or other countries.

Unless otherwise indicated herein, any third-party trademarks that may appear in this work are the property of their respective owners and any references to third-party trademarks, logos, or other trade dress are for demonstrative or descriptive purposes only. Such references are not intended to imply any sponsorship, endorsement, authorization, or promotion of Pearson's products by the owners of such marks, or any relationship between the owner and Pearson Education, Inc., or its affiliates, authors, licensees, or distributors.

Library of Congress Cataloging-in-Publication Data

Names: Alfano, Christine L., author. | O'Brien, Alyssa J., author.
Title: Envision in Depth : Reading, Writing, and Researching Arguments/Christine L. Alfano and Alyssa J. O'Brien.
Description: Fourth edition. | Boston : Pearson, 2016.| Includes bibliographical references and index.
Identifiers: LCCN 2015039727 | ISBN 9780134093987
Subjects: LCSH: English language—Rhetoric. | Persuasion (Rhetoric) | College readers. | Report writing. | Visual communication. | Visual perception.
Classification: LCC PE1431 .E56 2016 | DDC 808/.0427--dc23
LC record available at http://lccn.loc.gov/   2015039727

10 9 8 7 6 5 4 3 2 1—DOC—19 18 17 16

www.pearsonhighered.com

Student Edition ISBN 10: 0-13-407176-X
Student Edition ISBN 13: 978-0-13-407176-3
A la Carte ISBN 10: 0-13-406353-8
A la Carte ISBN 13: 978-0-13-406353-9

CONTENTS

Chapter 3   Composing Arguments   89

PART III: DRAFTING AND DESIGNING ARGUMENTS   211

Chapter 6   Organizing and Writing Research Arguments   212

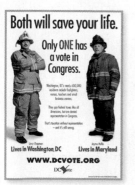

PREFACE

The Story of This Book

Several years ago, we (the authors) met as colleagues in the Program in Writing and Rhetoric at Stanford University. Our shared focus on teaching writing through attention to both written and multimedia texts led us to look for materials we could use in the classroom that would provide both excellence in pedagogical instruction—attending to such essentials as thesis statements, style, integrating sources, and avoiding plagiarism—along with cutting edge and even *fun* examples that offer sound rhetorical models for analysis and research. While we were able to gather materials from a variety of sources, our students wanted more than a collection of handouts: they wanted a textbook that they could use to guide and inspire their development as writers.

The result was *Envision*, an argument and research guide designed from the ground up to serve the needs of real student writers. In fact, throughout the many editions, students remain an indispensable part of the process, reading our drafts in progress, offering suggestions, and submitting their own writing as examples. Now in its fifth edition, *Envision* has expanded and changed over time, but remains true to its original vision: guiding students through the processes of analysis, argument, source evaluation, and research-based essay writing while keeping the examples fresh and relevant to student lives. Students learn to analyze both written texts and a range of visual texts, from cartoons and ads to websites and film, while working through the nuts of bolts of writing thesis statements, titles, introductions, conclusions, in-text citations, and MLA-style bibliographies. Additional writing lessons focus on diverse modes of argument, plagiarism, academic document design, and multimodal production.

As we now finalize the fifth edition of *Envision* and the fourth edition of *Envision in Depth* (with readings), our continued hope is that this textbook might help students develop the skills, confidence, and enthusiasm for writing, researching, and communicating effectively about issues that matter to them.

What's New in This Edition

Feedback from our insightful reviewers as well as suggestions from the many students and instructors who have used *Envision* and *Envision in Depth* in the classroom have been indispensable in guiding our most recent revisions. In this new edition, you'll find the same commitment to supporting our readers in developing critical competencies in analysis, argumentation, and research as in prior editions. However, you'll also find increased attention to helping students accomplish the following learning outcomes:

- **Learn from Model Writing:** New and updated annotated articles and student writing show readers exactly how to move from invention to argument, whether they are analyzing a written text, a visual text, or developing a research-based argument.
- **Experiment with Different Modes of Argumentation:** The refreshed section in Chapter 3 on classical argumentation, Toulmin logic, and Rogerian argument offers students guidance in exploring different strategies of arrangement to construct effective arguments.
- **Explore Contemporary Issues:** New readings and examples have been integrated into *Envision*, focusing on relevant and timely cultural issues: the BlackLivesMatter movement, the Charlie Hebdo shootings, the "cult" of Apple products, fast-food marketing, the influence of online social networks, photo manipulation in teen fashion magazines, women in computer science, the addictive properties of sugar, vegetarianism, and texting and driving.
- **Understand Advanced Concepts in Rhetoric:** In addition to the focus on rhetorical appeals and the canons of rhetoric found in prior editions, this new edition features expanded coverage of *ethos* and *logos*, as well as more detailed examination of persona and rhetorical stance.
- **Focus on the Writing Process:** Expanded sections on invention in Chapters 3, 4, and 6—complete with additional student samples— encourage students to find modes of prewriting that best suit their learning style, writing habits, and the parameters of their writing tasks.
- **Develop Strategies for Analyzing Arguments in Diverse Media:** Student writing in the chapters showcases ways to analyze a variety of types of argument, from written to visual arguments. In addition to guided instruction in the body of each chapter, the Spotlighted Analysis feature offers students the opportunity to apply strategies of rhetorical analysis to a diverse range of texts, from traditional written

arguments, to political cartoons, advertisements, photographs, posters, Websites, and even film trailers.

■ **Engage Deeply with the Research Process:** A refreshed section on search methodologies includes discussion of adapting search methodology to different search engines (i.e., Google vs. academic databases) and how to effectively conduct Boolean searches. In addition, the streamlined discussion of evaluating sources is designed to provide students with a useful process for assessing materials for their own research once they find them. Lastly, a brief introduction to Joseph Bizzup's BEAM approach to research encourages students to move beyond categorizing sources in terms of primary and secondary materials to considering how to use those sources to produce effective research-based arguments.

The Substance at a Glance

From the very beginning, our philosophy in *Envision* has been to teach students about writing, rhetoric, and research by considering the different modes of argument that operate in our culture every day. Each chapter uses interactive and engaging lessons, and focuses both on analyzing and producing words (print materials, articles, blog posts, and even tweets) as well as on writing *about* images and other contemporary media (cartoons, ads, photographs, films, video games, and websites, to name a few). In this way, the book teaches *critical literacy* about all kinds of texts. Moreover, we provide numerous student writing examples and professional, published readings—both with annotations—in order to reinforce the writing lessons in each chapter and to demonstrate how students might successfully implement such strategies in their own texts. Our aim is to help students accomplish specific writing tasks for your courses as they encounter, analyze, research, and produce a range of compositions.

We have designed *Envision* to be flexible enough to adjust to different curricula or teaching styles. You can either follow the chronological sequence of chapters—moving from analysis to argument, bringing in research, and then considering design and presentations—or you can consult the chapters and assignments in any order that meets the needs of your course and curriculum. More specifically, we have organized *Envision* into three parts:

Part I: Analysis and Argument

Chapters 1 through 3 encourage students to become proficient, careful readers of rhetorical texts and to learn practical strategies for crafting thesis statements, rhetorical analysis essays, and position papers incorporating various perspectives. Students learn how to analyze the forms of persuasion in verbal and visual texts—from short articles and essays to political cartoons, ads, and photos—with an emphasis on rhetorical conventions. At the same time, we teach students key rhetorical concepts for effective communication, such as attending to audience, understanding rhetorical appeals and fallacies, and attending to exigency and motive.

Part II: Planning and Conducting Research

Chapters 4 and 5 focus on strategies of research argument for sustained writing projects. The lessons in this section of the book take students through key writing practices: writing a research proposal, keeping a research log, locating sources, and understanding the complexities of evaluating and documenting sources. Students have sample proposals, outlines, and annotations to consult as well as articles, propaganda posters, and websites to analyze.

Part III: Drafting and Designing Arguments

Chapters 6, 7, and 8 teach students how to write and deliver an effective research-based argument, with a focus on the process of drafting and revising. Students learn how to identify, assess, and incorporate research into their own arguments, while avoiding plagiarism and accomplishing successful documentation of sources. They learn to present their writing effectively through a discussion of document design—both for academic papers and for visual and multimodal arguments. They also gain important skills in practicing the canons of rhetoric and differentiating among levels of decorum.

Meeting WPA Outcomes for Writers

Each chapter offers specific activities and assignments designed to help students meet the WPA Outcomes for First-Year Composition. The following table indicates the chapter's specific learning goals as they are aligned with the WPA outcomes statement, the major assignments offered in each chapter, and the media focus.

Online Resources

The Instructor's Manual

The Instructor's Manual for *Envision* provides teachers with pedagogical advice for each chapter, including conceptual overviews, teaching tips for working with the main concepts and reading selections in the chapter, and suggestions for classroom exercises and writing assignments. The Instructor's Manual also offers ideas for organizing the reading and exercises according to days of the week. For access to the Instructor's Manual, please contact your Pearson representative.

MyWritingLab for Composition

MyWritingLab is an online practice, tutorial, and assessment program that provides engaging experiences for teaching and learning.

MyWritingLab includes most of the writing assignments from your accompanying textbook. Now, students can complete and submit assignments, and teachers can then track and respond to submissions easily—right in MyWritingLab—making the response process easier for the instructor and more engaging for the student.

In the Writing Assignments, students can use instructor-created peer review rubrics to evaluate and comment on other students' writing. When giving feedback on student writing, instructors can add links to activities that address issues and strategies needed for review. Instructors may link to multimedia resources in Pearson Writer, which include curated content from Purdue OWL. Paper review by specialized tutors through Smart-Thinking is available, as is plagiarism detection through TurnItIn.

Respond to Student Writing with Targeted Feedback and Remediation

MyWritingLab unites instructor comments and feedback with targeted remediation via rich multimedia activities, allowing students to learn from and through their own writing.

MAJOR ASSIGNMENTS AND LEARNING OBJECTIVES

CHAPTER TITLE	WPA OBJECTIVES MET BY THIS CHAPTER	MAJOR ASSIGNMENTS	MEDIA FOCUS
1: Analyzing Texts and Writing Thesis Statements	■ Understanding the rhetorical situation ■ Considering relationships among audience, text, and purpose ■ Textual analysis ■ Developing thesis statements	■ Personal narrative essay ■ Rhetorical analysis essay	■ Cartoons, comic strips, and editorial articles
2: Understanding Strategies of Persuasion	■ Strategies of argumentation ■ Understanding rhetorical appeals: *logos, pathos,* and *ethos* ■ Fallacies or exaggerated uses of rhetorical appeals ■ Importance of *kairos* and *doxa*	■ Contextual analysis essay ■ Analysis of rhetorical appeals and fallacies ■ Comparison/contrast essay	■ Advertisements and written analysis of ads
3: Composing Arguments	■ Introductions and conclusions ■ Arrangement and structure of argument ■ Considering various modes of argument: Toulmin, Rogerian ■ Developing persona and rhetorical stance ■ Addressing opposing opinion in an argument ■ Writing with style	■ Position paper ■ Classical argument assignment ■ Toulmin and Rogerian argument analysis ■ Synthesis essay	■ Photographs, newspaper articles and images, opinion pieces, visual analysis essays
4: Planning and Proposing Research Arguments	■ Generating and narrowing research topics ■ Prewriting strategies ■ Developing a research plan ■ Drafting a formal proposal	■ Visual brainstorm ■ Research log ■ Informal research plan ■ Research proposal	■ Propaganda posters, historical images, rhetorical analysis essay

CHAPTER TITLE	WPA OBJECTIVES MET BY THIS CHAPTER	MAJOR ASSIGNMENTS	MEDIA FOCUS
5: Finding and Evaluating Research Sources	■ Research strategies ■ Evaluating sources ■ Distinguishing between primary and secondary sources ■ Locating sources ■ Conducting field research, interviews, and surveys ■ Best practices for note taking	■ Critical evaluation of sources ■ Annotated bibliography ■ Field research ■ Dialogue of sources	■ Magazine and journal covers, Websites, and annotated bibliographies
6: Organizing and Writing Research Arguments	■ Organizing and outlining arguments ■ Multiple drafts and revision ■ Integrating research sources: summary, paraphrase, and quotations ■ Writing and peer review	■ Formal outline ■ Peer review and response ■ Integrating sources ■ Writing the research argument	■ Film and movie trailers, film review and critique, drafts and revisions
7: Documenting Sources and Avoiding Plagiarism	■ Understanding intellectual property ■ Best practices in documenting sources: in-text citation and notes ■ MLA-style rules and examples	■ Working with multimedia sources ■ Ethical note-taking ■ Citation practice ■ Producing a Works Cited list	■ Documentation examples, MLA-style essay
8: Designing Arguments	■ Understanding the conventions of academic writing ■ Writing an abstract and bio ■ Decorum: appropriate voice and tone ■ Relationship between rhetorical situation and types of argument ■ Formatting and genre considerations ■ Transforming written arguments into visual or spoken texts	■ Writing an abstract ■ Constructing a bio ■ Integrating images in academic writing ■ Creating electronic arguments using multimedia (audio and visual) ■ Considering different delivery techniques	■ Academic design examples, abstracts, bios, op-ads, photo essays, Websites, posters, slidedecks, and multiple media

Writing Help for Varying Skill Levels

For students who enter the course at widely varying skill levels, MyWritingLab provides unique, targeted remediation through personalized and adaptive instruction. Starting with a preassessment known as the Path Builder, MyWritingLab diagnoses students' strengths and weaknesses on prerequisite writing skills. The results of the preassessment inform each student's Learning Path, a personalized pathway for students to work on requisite skills through multimodal activities. In doing so, students feel supported and ready to succeed in class.

Learning Tools for Student Engagement

Learning Catalytics   Generate class discussion, guide lectures, and promote peer-to-peer learning with real-time analytics. MyLab and Mastering with eText now provide Learning Catalytics—an interactive student response tool that uses students' smartphones, tablets, or laptops to engage them in more sophisticated tasks and thinking.

MediaShare   MediaShare allows students to post multimodal assignments easily—whether they are audio, video, or visual compositions—for peer review and instructor feedback. In both face-to-face and online course settings, MediaShare saves instructors valuable time and enriches the student learning experience by enabling contextual feedback to be provided quickly and easily.

Direct Access to MyLab   Users can link from any Learning Management System (LMS) to Pearson's MyWritingLab. Access MyLab assignments, rosters, and resources, and synchronize MyLab grades with the LMS gradebook. A new direct, single sign-on provides access to all the personalized learning MyLab resources that make studying more efficient and effective.

Visit www.mywritinglab.com for more information.

Acknowledgments

Our work with *Envision* and *Envision in Depth* has spanned many years, students, writing classes, and colleagues. However, one element remains constant: It started out inherently collaborative and remains so. The revisions we have made in this edition and our ongoing work in this field could only have been accomplished through the ongoing support and guidance from others. For that reason, we'd like to offer our deepest thanks to all those who helped us with the book over the years, and in the revision of this edition in particular.

We've been fortunate to have a particularly helpful group of reviewers provide us guidance for this revision: John Aramini, Erie Community College; Diana Bell, University of Alabama–Huntsville; Shannon Griffin Blair, Central Piedmont Community College; Ronald Brooks, Oklahoma State University; Linsey Cuti, Kankakee Community College; Trevor Dodge, Clackamas Community College; Susanna Kelly Engbers, Kendall College of Art and Design; Rachel McKenny, Iowa State University; Patrick T. Niner, Florida Gulf Coast University; Jenny Rice, University of Kentucky; Elizabeth Rollins, Pima Community College; Matthew Schmeer, Johnson County Community College; Andrew Scott, Ball State University; and Kay Siebler, Missouri Western State University.

In addition, we are grateful to our other "reviewers"—our students who use our textbook in the classroom and who are always happy to share praise—or suggestions—about Envision. In particular, we are grateful for the students who played a concrete role into shaping this new revision by contributing their own writing to serve as models to inspire our readers: Oishi Banerjee, Ali Batouli, Tucker Burnett, Vincent Chen, Clare Conratto, Molly Fehr, Will Hang, Savi Hawkins, Samantha Kargilis, Lucas Lin, Catherine Mullings, Emmanuel Omvenga, Ryan O'Rourke, Wanjin Park, Stephanie Parker, Trevor Rex, Claire Shu, Ada Throckmorton, Miranda Alfano-Smith, Jared Sun, Michael Vela, and Thomas Zhao.

We'd also like to express our gratitude to our colleagues at Stanford who have supported our revisions to *Envision* and *Envision in Depth* and whose commitment to pedagogy and to their students inspires our own. In particular, we'd like to thank Julia Bleakney, Karli Cerankowski, Erica Cirillo-McCarthy, Annelise Heinz, Donna Hunter, Kiersten Jakobsen, Raechel Lee, Kimberly Moekle, John Peterson, Emily Polk, Carolyn Ross, Felicia Smith, and Trisha Stan, whose advice, scholarship, and inspiring pedagogy helped enrich our work in this text. In addition, we'd especially like to recognize those colleagues who provided us with particular guidance or graciously allowed us to include versions of their exemplary class-tested activities in this new edition: Mary Stroud, who contributed the Twitter dialogue of sources activity in Chapter 5; Marvin Diogenes and Ethan Plaut, who permitted us to use a version of their Accordion prewrite activity in Chapter 4; Russ Carpenter and Sohui Lee, whose scholarship on poster design informed our section on that topic in Chapter 8; Sarah Pittock, whose activity on titles inspired our own expanded section; and Jennifer Stonaker, who provided insight and guidance on the rhetoric of podcasting. So much of what we've accomplished over our years of work on the *Envision* series has been possible by the supportive atmosphere found in our academic home in Stanford's Program in Writing and Rhetoric; the people and the program continually remind us of the importance of providing the best resources and instruction to students and of fostering a culture of intellectual curiosity, sharing, and collegiality among our teaching faculty.

We'd also like to extend out thanks to our expert team at Pearson, the dedicated drivers of the *Envision* series: Joe Opiela and Brad Potthoff; our development editor David Kear; Katy Gabel and her staff at Lumina; our contract support Jim Miller; and Michael Greer, who went from guiding the drafting of the first edition of *Envision* to now helping us refresh and reinvigorate the reader section of the most recent edition of *Envision in Depth*.

Of course, there's another expert team to thank as well: Our friends and family who keep life running smoothly even amid the creative chaos of writing and revision. Without their love, support, and expansive understanding, this revision would never have been transformed from a marked-up manuscript to the bound copy that now sits before you.

Lastly, thank you, our readers, for your interest in *Envision*; we hope you find the book as useful to your teaching as it has been rewarding for us to work on and use with our own students over the years.

Christine L. Alfano and Alyssa J. O'Brien

Envision

WRITING AND RESEARCHING ARGUMENTS

Part I

ANALYSIS AND ARGUMENT

CHAPTER 1

Analyzing Texts and Writing Thesis Statements

Chapter Preview Questions

1.1 How do we read and analyze texts rhetorically?
1.2 How do we define the rhetorical situation?
1.3 How do exigence and purpose affect persuasion?
1.4 What are effective strategies for analyzing rhetorical texts?
1.5 How should I brainstorm parts of an essay, including the thesis statement?

Everywhere around us, words and images try to persuade us to think about the world in certain ways. We can see this persuasive power at every turn: from newspaper articles to television broadcasts, blog posts, advertisements, political campaign posters, Facebook status posts, tweets, and even video footage circulated online. In each case, such texts—whether verbal, visual, or a combination of the two—try to move us, convince us to buy something, shape our opinions, or make us laugh.

Consider the text in Figure 1.1 by Mike Luckovich, a Pulitzer Prize–winning cartoonist who publishes in the *Atlanta Journal Constitution*. Luckovich created this cartoon after the 2011 assassination attempt on Gabrielle Giffords, a member of the U.S. House of Representatives, outside a Safeway store in Tucson, Arizona. Six people were killed, including a 9-year-old girl. Giffords herself was critically injured, along with 12 other people. The incident raised concerns over political speeches and Website images that had used gun metaphors to target Democrats such as Giffords in upcoming elections. Some feared that such language and imagery might have contributed to the attack. In response to the controversy, Luckovich composed a cartoon as a persuasive text indicating his view. How does his text use both words and images to persuade audiences to think a certain way about the top term: "Violent Rhetoric"? Look at the hierarchy of values, beginning with "happy talk" at the bottom, moving through "warm conversation" and "friendly debate" to a more vigorous "spirited discussion." Notice how the words then become more negative, including "angry discourse" and "hateful speech." While we usually consider "hateful speech" to be the worst form of communication, Luckovich places "violent rhetoric" above it, as the very apex of dangerous discourse. The cartoon is ironic since when most people think of *rhetoric*, they often think of political rhetoric, which they perceive as either empty and meaningless (all talk, no action) or worse, as negative: harmful to the reputation of others, fear-mongering, and even hateful. The cartoon emphasizes this common view placing the words "violent rhetoric" at the top.

FIGURE 1.1 Mike Luckovich's political cartoon demonstrates through words and images how people commonly view "rhetoric" as a negative and dangerous form of communication.

But understanding this cartoon depends not just on analyzing the words. The location of words in particular places within the visual—and the visual elements themselves—also contribute in crucial ways to the meaning of the text. The lowered flag, for instance, might indicate that Giffords nearly died from her critical injuries, and indeed six people did die. The purposeful lowering of the flag to half-mast is itself a form of visual communication, well understood across America; it represents the nation's act of honoring a deceased person. The dome of the Capitol Building in the background suggests that the government has lowered the flag and wants people to move from "violent rhetoric" to "spirited discussion." In this way, the cartoon combines words and visual details to suggest both a tribute to Giffords and the need for calmer, gentler political communication. That is our understanding of the cartoon's argument when we **analyze the text rhetorically**. As you develop your skills of critical thinking and rhetorical analysis, you will also learn how to interpret and write your own arguments about such texts.

At the same time, you will learn how to apply your skills of analysis across a range of media, including printed or spoken words. With regard to the assassination attempt, many writers commented on the event through newspaper articles, on blogs, via email, and on social media. In a post on the political blog *Daily Kos*, for example, Barbara Morrill used the term *rhetoric* right in her title: "Violent Rhetoric and the Attempted Assassination of Gabrielle Giffords." While the title seems objective in tone, the writer draws on very strong language in the opening paragraph in order to connect the two parts of the title:

> In the two days since the attempted assassination of Rep. Gabrielle Giffords, the debate has been raging over the culpability of the violent rhetoric that is so commonplace in today's political climate. Which of course has led to the rapid-fire peddling of false equivalencies by the right, where now, saying a congressional district is being targeted is the same as actually putting cross-hairs on a district and saying it's time to "RELOAD."

By accusing the right of "rapid-fire peddling," the author frames words through a gun metaphor in a way that creates a vivid image in the reader's mind. She also refers to the metaphoric language that politicians had used—targeting a district, crosshairs, and "reload"—as evidence for her claim. The details of her written text parallel the elements of the cartoon (Figure 1.1). As you develop your skills of analysis about texts, keep in mind that you can understand them better if you look closely at all the specific elements, whether verbal or visual. Once you recognize how texts function *rhetorically*—that is, how texts try to persuade you and shape your opinion about the world around you—then you can decide whether or not to agree with the many messages you encounter every day. To grasp this concept, let's follow one hypothetical student—we'll call her Alex—as she walks across campus and note the rhetorical texts she sees along the way.

1.1 How do we read and analyze texts rhetorically?

UNDERSTANDING TEXTS RHETORICALLY

By shadowing Alex and noticing what she notices, you can construct her **personal narrative**, or written account of her journey, about the rhetorical texts she sees along the way.

Let's begin in her dorm room, which Alex and her roommate have decorated with a concert tour poster, an artsy map of New York City, a poster for the women's basketball team, and a photo collage of pictures from their spring break cross-country trip. As she prepares to leave, she smiles as she glances at a meme she's printed and taped over her desk: the black-turtleneck-wearing Hipster Barista, with the caption, "$120,000 Art Degree … Draws faces in latte foam."

As Alex walks down the hall, she pauses when a friend calls her into the lounge to watch a brief clip from a rerun of *Last Week Tonight with John Oliver* on his laptop. Oliver is in top form, providing a satirical critique of the militarization of American police forces, and Alex and her friend laugh for a few minutes about the sketch before she heads out. Walking down the stairwell, she glances briefly at the flyers that decorate the walls—for a charity dance for the victims of a recent earthquake, a dorm meeting about a ski trip, and a rally against immigration laws. She does a double-take to look at the clever design of a flyer for the Zen club (see Figure 1.2), making a mental note about the meeting time, and then walks into the cool autumn air.

FIGURE 1.2 A flyer that Alex notices on her way to class.

Outside, Alex looks down at her smartphone, scrolling through recent Instagram posts as she walks along. She sees one friend's updated profile photo, another's pictures from a recent trip to New Orleans, and a third's reposting of a link to a parody video of a Taylor Swift song. She stops at the outdoor café and checks her Twitter feed while waiting for her coffee, amused by her favorite celebrity's posting about the Academy Awards. As her coffee arrives, her phone buzzes, and she opens a funny Snapchat photo from her younger sister, pausing for a moment to send a selfie of her own, which she captions with the phrase, "Must have coffee." Looking at the time, she realizes she's running late and hurries off to class.

FIGURE 1.3 A snapchat from Alex's younger sister.

Now Alex has only 2 minutes before class starts, so she takes the shortcut through the student union, past a sign advertising the latest Apple laptop, and then heads outside and crosses in front of an administration building where a group of student protestors are chanting and waving signs demanding that the university divest from fossil fuels. She weaves alongside a cluster of gleaming steel buildings that constitute the engineering quad and passes the thin metal sculpture called *Knowledge* that guards the entrance to the library.

Finally she reaches her destination: the Communications department. Walking into the building, she stops to glance at the front page of the school newspaper, stacked by the door; intrigued by the headline, "Greek Life Claims University Targets Them," she grabs a copy to read later. She slips into the classroom for her Com 101 class on Media and Society and realizes that the class has already started. Ducking into the back row, Alex watches the professor advance his PowerPoint slides to one containing key questions for that day's class (see Figure 1.4). As she sits down, the TA passes her a handout, and she opens her laptop to take notes. She's immediately distracted by posts on the social media sites that pop up, calling for her attention: targeted advertisements, viral videos, even Buzzfeed quizzes. Ignoring them, she opens a blank document instead and then turns to examine the handout, which includes an editorial about a tragic shooting at the offices of a French satirical magazine.

With Alex safely at her seat, think about how many texts you noticed along her journey. Flyers, ads, posters, videos, Websites, newspapers, television shows, photographs, memes, sculpture, signs, PowerPoint slides, even architectural design: each is an example of rhetoric. Why? Because each text offers a specific message to a particular audience. Each one is a persuasive act. Once you begin to look at the world rhetorically, you'll see that just about everywhere you are being persuaded to agree, act, buy, attend, or accept an argument: rhetoric permeates our cultural landscape. Just as we did above, you might pay attention to the rhetorical texts that you find on your way to class and then construct your own personal narrative consisting of words and images. Learning to recognize the persuasive power of texts and read them rhetorically is the first step in thinking critically about the world.

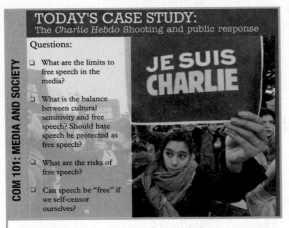

FIGURE 1.4 PowerPoint slide from Alex's class.

WRITER'S PRACTICE   MyWritingLab

Look back at the texts that Alex encountered in Figures 1.2, 1.3, and 1.4. How do they attempt to persuade their audience? For each one, jot down some notes about each text's message and the different ways the texts try to make their arguments. Consider how they use words and images, alone and in combination, to convey their message.

UNDERSTANDING THE RHETORICAL SITUATION

1.2 How do we define the rhetorical situation?

In one of the earliest definitions, the ancient Greek philosopher Aristotle characterized **rhetoric** as *the ability to see the available means of persuasion in any given situation.* While Aristotle's lessons in rhetoric emerged in the fourth century BCE as a form of instruction for oral communication—specifically, to help free men represent themselves in court—today, the term *rhetoric* has expanded to include any verbal, visual, or multimedia text that aims to persuade a specific audience in a certain place and time. More generally, you can understand rhetoric as the strategies people use to convey ideas; in the words of scholar and rhetorician Andrea Lunsford, "Rhetoric is the art, practice, and study of human communication."

To understand how a rhetorical text works, you need to analyze how it targets a specific **audience**, how it has been composed by a specific **author**, and how it conveys a particular **argument**. This dynamic relationship is called the **rhetorical situation**, and we have represented it with a triangle in Figure 1.5.

As a writer, when you compose persuasive texts, you need to determine which strategies will work to convince your audience in a particular situation. There are many different choices to consider, and that is why rhetoric is both a dynamic and a practical art. Imagine, for instance, that you are involved in the following rhetorical situations and have to decide which strategies would be most persuasive for each case.

- **Attend to *audience.*** If you were a politician writing an editorial for a newspaper or speaking at an interview on CNN about your definition of marriage, you would use strikingly different metaphors and statistics depending on which constituency (or *audience*) you are addressing.
- **Attend to *author.*** If you wanted to publicize a

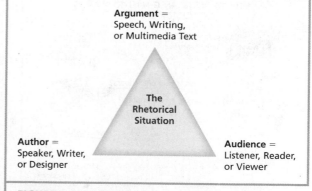

FIGURE 1.5 The rhetorical situation is dynamic and governs all communication, whether oral, written, or multimedia.

message against drug use to local middle school students, you might compose pamphlets, emails, presentations, or posters with information graphics, and each one would be designed based on your position as *author*—teacher or police officer? student or parent?—while trying to reach that teenage audience.

■ **Attend to *argument*.** If you were fashion industry intern updating the company's social media marketing campaign, you would revise the message (or *argument*) of the advertisements to fit the media, whether Facebook posts, tweets, or even Internet videos.

Cartoonist Jorge Cham offers us an example in Figure 1.6 of how the rhetorical situation affects persuasion in relation to a communicative act that might be even more familiar to you: a students' email to the instructor. In a panel for his series *PhD comics*, he shows how a misunderstanding of the rhetorical situation can sabotage successful communication.

What the comic illustrates is the instructor's analysis of the student's communication and his implicit criticism that the student misreads his *audience* and therefore composes an ineffective *argument*. The agitated arrows point us to evidence for this interpretation: misspellings, punctuation mistakes, jargon, and an uninformed message (the answers to the email apparently are all in the syllabus). However, the comic also invites us to critique the instructor's assessment of the rhetorical situation. On the one hand, the fictional instructor has treated the email communication like an essay, scoring it with red-inked annotations; on the other, he uses an angry voice that seems inappropriate to the instructor–student relationship ("OMG, what are you, 14?"; "we are not friends"). In both cases, he fails in the same way as his student to create a moment of effective communication.

In fact, there are two layers to this cartoon, two rhetorical situations that we can explore (see Figure 1.7): the fictional situation of the email, where the relationship is between student (writer), instructor (audience), and

FIGURE 1.6 This comic from *PhD comics* offers a pointed analysis of a hypothetical student's misjudging of the rhetorical situation in emailing his instructor.

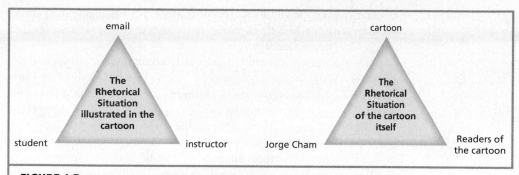

FIGURE 1.7 The cartoon's two rhetorical situations.

email (argument), and then the rhetorical situation of the editorial cartoon itself, which triangulates the relationship between Jorge Cham (writer), the cartoon's readers (audience), and cartoon (argument). Cham encourages us to engage with both levels explicitly by including the asterisk and footnote. In his qualifier, "No offense to those actually called 'Hey,' 'Yo,' 'Sup,' or 'Dude,'" he differentiates his own voice from that of the fictional instructor, helping us remember there are dual levels at work in the cartoon.

UNDERSTANDING EXIGENCE AND PURPOSE

1.3 How do exigence and purpose affect persuasion?

As you move toward better understanding rhetoric, another important concept to consider is **exigence**—the *urgent demand* that writers feel to respond to a situation, his or her motive for writing. Have you ever seen a news article or heard about an event on campus that prompted you to respond strongly? When this happens, in rhetoric, we call this the **exigencies of a situation,** or the demands put on a writer to respond immediately and urgently in the attempt to take action or raise a concern about a specific problem or issue.

Think about tweets sent out in response to a sports team winning a championship, a flash of celebrity gossip, a political debate, or a crisis on campus. These are all contemporary instances of exigency. The scholar who gave us the rhetorical situation shown in Figure 1.5, Lloyd Bitzer, emphasized that *rhetorical exigency* happens when change is possible: "An exigence is rhetorical when it is capable of positive modification and when positive modification *requires* discourse or can be *assisted* by discourse." That is, rhetorical exigency exists when there is the possibility that **discourse** (i.e., forms of communication) can effect change. For instance, policies regulating parking on campus can potentially be modified through discourse or language, but drought and death cannot.

Understanding exigence can help us likewise understand an author's **purpose**. Whether that purpose be internal and emotional or more objective—for instance, seeking to affirm or reaffirm the status quo—*motive* and *purpose* shape the way authors write texts across media. Many rhetoricians identify three broad types of possible purposes for communication: to entertain, to inform or explain, or to persuade. However, purpose can be more nuanced. An author's purpose might be to describe, to define, to influence, or to call to action, for instance; in fact, an author might have complementary purposes in crafting a text. By examining an author's *motive* or *purpose*—what he wanted to accomplish with the text—we can get a better understanding of the rhetorical choices he made in communicating with his audience.

Let's look at a contemporary example to see how rhetorical exigency combines with purpose to create persuasive texts. When Disney announced its acquisition of the *Star Wars* enterprise from George Lucas in 2012, people were shocked and even outraged. Many felt the need to respond through discourse—by tweeting, writing blog posts, composing articles in popular online magazines, and even drawing cartoons. In each case, the author felt prompted to respond urgently and immediately to what was widely viewed as a problem situation.

Consider, for instance, the cartoon in Figure 1.8 by Nate Beeler, an award-winning editorial cartoonist for the *Columbus Dispatch*, which he created in response to the merger. Entitled, "Disney Acquires 'Star Wars,'" the cartoon demonstrates the exigency that caused so many Americans to speak out or write about this surprising amalgamation between two enormous entertainment companies.

FIGURE 1.8 Nate Beeler's cartoon uses humor in response to Disney's purchase of Star Wars.

The giant head of Mickey Mouse, floating in space toward the galactic fleet, has an ominous look to it, creating a sense of foreboding. It suggests the *motive* of the cartoonist might have been to criticize this acquisition. In fact, this critique is further amplified by the way Mickey's head has been transformed into a version of the iconic Death Star, threatening to supplant the original space station/super weapon, which seems small and less imposing by comparison. Beeler is clearly presenting Mickey (and, by association, Disney) as the new "bad guy" of the Star Wars universe.

Moreover, the words emerging from the space station, "I sense a great disturbance in the force," echo Obi-Wan Kenobi's classic line from *Star Wars Episode IV*, "I felt a great disturbance in the force, as if millions of voices suddenly cried out in terror and were suddenly silenced." In the original context, Obi-Wan refers to the destruction of an entire planet and the death of its inhabitants; here the fleet makes a similarly ominous pronouncement about the impact of the Disney acquisition on the Star Wars franchise. Putting the visual and the verbal together, we perceive that Beeler exploits the imagery and lexicon of Star Wars fans themselves for a specific *purpose*: to persuade his audience of the negative implications of Disney's acquisition of Star Wars. It is a comic argument, to be sure, but it is an important position that arises from the exigencies of the situation.

Some writers opted for a different mode of editorial commentary, turning to Twitter to offer their perspective on the acquisition. As urgent responses to the deal, the tweets demonstrate how authors react in an attempt to use discourse to voice a personal position or in the hopes of modifying the situation. For instance, writer Andrés de Rojas, who goes by the Twitter handle @aderojas, tweeted the following:

> May the Force be with … Mickey Mouse?

He plays on the iconic phrase, "May the Force be with you," using ellipses and substituting Mickey Mouse for "you" to create a humorous tone. The final question mark, too, functions rhetorically, to convey his uncertainty over the implications of the acquisition. Raymond Kemp (@RaymondKemp) similarly responded to the exigence of the situation, composing a tweet that, like Nate Beeler's cartoon, adapts Obi-Wan's famous line:

> There was a disturbance in the force like the voices of a million nerds were silenced.

His tweet would have greatest resonance with readers familiar with the Star Wars series, but his critique would be evident even to a broader audience. By stating that "the voices of a million nerds were silenced," he demonstrates his motive or purpose: joining the outcry against the way in which the "nerdy" series of Star Wars might change under the ownership of the more pop culture-oriented vision of Disney.

Clearly, although tweets are brief, they still function as rhetorical acts. Authors who recognize the unique rhetorical situation of the tweet can turn these concise epithets into powerful editorial commentaries. Even the hashtags that writers append to their tweets add a layer of argument. Consider how a tweet about the Disney-Star Wars acquisition becomes more powerful when tagged with a hashtag such as #Depresseddarth, #Darthgoofy, #Don'tpanic, or #awholenewworld. In addition, some authors take advantage of the viral nature of Twitter to punctuate their tweets by attaching pictures, often mash-ups of popular images. For instance, over the first week after the acquisition announcement, scores of images spread through Twitter: photoshopped pictures of Mickey Mouse in Darth Vader's robes, saying, "Luke, I am now your father"; visual remixes of a Disney poster with the caption, "When you wish upon a Deathstar"; a photo of R2D2 wearing mouse ears; a still from *A New Hope* showing the three suns of Luke Skywalker's planet aligned to resemble Mickey Mouse's head. One of the most widely re-tweeted images was originally posted by Eric Alper (@ThatEricAlper): a photoshopped version of a popular image of the Disney princesses with a cartoon version of Princess Leia from Star Wars, wielding her blaster rifle, inserted in the middle. Re-tweeted over 200 times to an ever-broader circle of audiences, the image makes a pointed argument about how it might be the Disney world—not the Star Wars universe—that would change most because of the merger. In each of these examples, the author was responding to the exigence of the situation, using the best available means of persuasion to make his argument to a broad audience.

Considering the concepts of rhetorical exigence and purpose reinforces the fact that rhetoric, since Aristotle, has been linked to *action*. It is far from "empty" but rather can motivate audiences to produce particular outcomes. As Bitzer has argued: "Rhetoric is a mode of altering reality [...] by the creation of discourse which *changes reality* through the mediation of thought and action."

STRATEGIES FOR ANALYZING RHETORICAL TEXTS

1.4 What are effective strategies for analyzing rhetorical texts?

As we turn to discussing practical strategies for analyzing texts, it's important to understand how these can contribute to helping you develop **critical literacy**—a life skill that entails knowing how to read, analyze, understand, and even create texts that function as powerful arguments about culture and the world around us. In fact, some have argued that writing itself no longer refers just to words on a page, but that writing, redefined for the twenty-first century, invites us to express ourselves and make arguments across media and genres—whether in a book chapter, a podcast, a blog post, a video, or comic. In fact, in many cases, the most powerful arguments are those that combine word and image, the verbal and the visual; such multimedia texts often have greater persuasiveness and reach a broader audience than words alone.

This is the argument made by Scott McCloud in his groundbreaking book, *Understanding Comics*, one of the first texts to use graphic novel form to help readers understand visual rhetoric:

> When pictures are more abstracted from "reality," they require greater levels of perception, more like words. When words are bolder, more direct, they require lower levels of perception and are received faster, more like pictures.

McCloud tells us we need to develop "greater levels of perception," or *critical literacy*, in order to read with greater levels of perception. In fact, we can look to the brief passage quoted here as an example of persuasive written rhetoric, in which McCloud makes very deliberate choices to strengthen his point. Notice how his words use comparison–contrast (pictures versus words), qualified language ("reality"), and parallel structure (both sentences move from "When" to a final phrase beginning with "more like") in order to convince his audience that images and words operate in similar ways. Such attention to detail is the first step in *rhetorical analysis*—looking at the way the writer chooses the most effective means of persuasion to make a point.

What is interesting about McCloud's piece is the way in which he uses both words and images to make his point. To fully appreciate McCloud's rhetorical decisions, we need to consider the passage in its original context. As you can see in Figure 1.9, McCloud amplifies his argument about comics by using the form of the graphic novel itself.

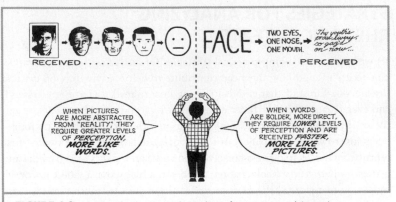

FIGURE 1.9 Scott McCloud writes in the medium of cartoons to explain comics.

Source: Courtesy of Scott McCloud

This complex diagram relies on the visual–verbal relationship to map out the complicated nature of how we understand both written text and images. The repetition and echoes that we found in the quoted passage are graphically represented in Figure 1.9; in fact, translated into comic book form, the division between word and image becomes a visual continuum that strongly suggests McCloud's vision of the interrelationship between these rhetorical elements. The power of this argument comes from McCloud's strategic assessment of the rhetorical situation: he, the *author*, recognizes that his *audience* (people interested in visual media) would find an *argument* that relies on both visual and verbal elements to be highly persuasive.

McCloud's example is also instructive for demonstrating the way in which authors can strategically adapt their argument to different media. More than ever, rhetoric operates not just through word choice but also through choice of multimedia elements—images in a commercial, the audio of a viral ad on the Internet, the design choices of a website or flyer, even the layout strategies of your textbook. Therefore, we need to develop skills of analysis for all rhetorical texts. We need to understand argument *as writing across diverse media* and we need, therefore, to develop *critical literacy*, or a careful way of reading, analyzing, and understanding media (visual, verbal, and other rhetorical texts).

Understanding how rhetoric works across different media will give you the ability and confidence to analyze and produce texts of your own. That is, these skills of analysis will help you approach other kinds of texts rhetorically: scholarly articles, books, editorials, letters to the editor, political speeches, and—as writing continues to evolve into new forms—blog posts, memes, mash-ups, and more.

Analyzing Visual Rhetoric

When persuasion—discourse or communication intended to change— happens through visual means, we often look to investigate its *visual rhetoric*. As we saw earlier in the chapter, such visual arguments surround us constantly in our everyday lives. We can use them as a starting point for developing strategies for analysis that we can then transfer to how we approach analysis of written rhetoric.

Editorial cartoons offer a rich resource for this sort of work since, as cultural critic Matthew Diamond asserts, they "provide alternative perspectives at a glance because they are visual and vivid and often seem to communicate a clear or obvious message." Those messages might be powerful, but they sometimes might offend, as Pulitzer Prize–winning cartoonists Doug Marlette has suggested: "[T]he objective of political cartooning 'is not to soothe and tend sensitive psyches, but to jab and poke in an attempt to get at deeper truths, popular or otherwise.'" Marlette's words confirm what you probably already know—that cartoons are not just humorous texts but rather, as we have seen, they are rhetorical—they intend to persuade, and sometimes even to provoke.

Let's begin with the editorial cartoon in Figure 1.10 by Bill Bramhall. Originally published in the *Daily News* on December 4, 2014, the cartoon represents a pointed response to the news that a grand jury declined to bring charges against a New York police officer for the death of Eric Garner, a 43-year-old black man, who died after being put in a chokehold during his arrest. In Bramhall's cartoon, "I can't breathe"—Garner's last words—take on greater resonance when uttered by Lady Justice, shown sprawled on the sidewalk.

FIGURE 1.10 Bill Bramhall composed this powerful cartoon to comment on the 2014 death of Eric Garner.

By replacing Garner with the symbol of Justice, Bramhall is making a much stronger argument than just that Garner's death was tragic: his cartoon suggests that justice itself has been laid low by the grand jury decision and that the American people can no longer look to the justice system to defend their rights (with its sword and balancing scales).

Keeping this analysis in mind, consider the different rhetorical effect the cartoon would have had if it had been drawn differently. What if the central figure speaking the words "I can't breathe" were the Statue of Liberty? What if she were represented as African American? What if instead of being laid out on the sidewalk, she was shown crushed to her pedestal under three police officers, actively trying to restrain her? How would these changes alter the way you understood the cartoon's argument? This is, in fact, the composition of a different cartoon created by editorial cartoonist Steve Benson. In both Bramhall's and Benson's cases, the text was generated out of the same exigence—the grand jury decision—but made different claims about the implications of the event.

Let's look at another example of how a cartoonist uses visual rhetoric to make a powerful cultural critique on a similar theme.

Appearing days after the Bramhall cartoon we examined above, this cartoon by Adam Zyglis (Figure 1.11) moves beyond the specifics of the Garner case to address the tense U.S. conversations over race prompted by the deaths of Michael Brown (which catalyzed riots in Ferguson, Missouri,

FIGURE 1.11 Adam Zyglis's 2014 cartoon addresses larger issues of race relations in America.

in late summer 2014) and Eric Garner. Notice the ways in which Zyglis uses seemingly simple rhetorical elements to convey a multilayered message:

- He heads the cartoon with a powerful title that plays on the word "color" both to refer to how we "fill in" or "shade" our conversations on race (the way a child would color in a picture in a coloring book) and also to allude to the issue of "color" that in itself underlies many discussions of race relations.
- He features an iconic image of a crayon box, replacing the trademark Crayola symbol with an American flag to make the symbolic force of his argument clearer to the audience.
- Instead of filling the box with a multitude of crayon colors, he simply draws one black and one white crayon, underscoring how all other variations, shades, and hues (i.e., racial and cultural identities) are absent from the "conversation."

Looking at these elements, we can see his message: that conversations about race in America seem limited to a Caucasian-versus-African-American perspective. However, we can push this analysis even further. In choosing a crayon box, Zyglis seems to be indicating that we take a somewhat childish approach to these conversations. Additionally, if we consider the crayon colors to represent argumentative stances rather than symbols of racial identity, he also seems to be arguing against a "black versus white" approach to the issue, that is, an approach to an argument that relies on extreme oppositional stances rather than looking at the complexities or nuances of the issue.

As a final example, let's turn to a visual argument that responds directly to an event very appropriate to the focus of this chapter: the *Charlie Hebdo* shootings. On January 7, 2015, two Al-Qaeda gunmen entered the offices of the French weekly newspaper, Charlie Hebdo, known around the world for its provocative and satirical articles, jokes, and political cartoons. By the time the shooting spree was over, 12 people were dead and 11 injured. Charlie Hebdo had long been a target of criticism from many groups, offended by their risqué portrayal of different cultural icons and customs; Muslim readers in particular often expressed displeasure at its irreverent caricatures of the Prophet Mohammed. However, despite the newspaper's notoriety, the actions of the terrorist extremists were completely unanticipated and sent shock waves across the world.

As might be expected, the editorial cartoonist community in particular responded immediately to this assault on their French colleagues, and

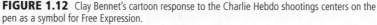

FIGURE 1.12 Clay Bennet's cartoon response to the Charlie Hebdo shootings centers on the pen as a symbol for Free Expression.

newspaper columns and Internet websites were flooded with editorials—in words and images— reacting to this tragedy. Many of them relied on a central symbol to catalyze their argument: the pen or pencil as a symbol for free speech. One example can be found in Figure 1.12. This image by cartoonist Clay Bennett makes a powerful argument of resilience echoed by many of the other editorial cartoonists who responded to the incident. Notice the way that even with an extremely simplistic design, it articulates a powerful position: the pen, labeled "free expression," takes center stage on the white background; broken in half and yet mended hastily with string, it suggests that free speech might have been damaged by tragic events, but it has not been destroyed and is ready to be wielded again by the next author who picks up the pen.

Bennett's cartoon was one of many such visual responses to the tragedy. Graphic designer Lucille Cleric circulated a similar image on social media. Her cartoon featured three pencils stacked on top one another: on top, a sharpened pencil (labeled "yesterday), in the middle, a broken pencil (labeled "today"), and, on the bottom, the broken pencil, resharpened to form two smaller pencils (labeled "tomorrow"). In its original version, Cleric reinforced her visual message with the caption, "Break one, thousand will rise." She further punctuated her point by circulating it with the hashtag #raiseyourpencilforfreedom.

Her graphic accumulated over 100,000 "likes" almost immediately after its release, demonstrating its resonance with the "Je Suis Charlie" (I am Charlie) movement that swept the world within hours after the attack, as cartoonists, journalists, and citizens offered a hydra-headed expression of solidarity with those who had died in the service of free expression of ideas. In an interview with the website Mashable, Cleric made her motive for creating the cartoon clear, saying, "I can only hope [the cartoon] will inspire people to use their pencils too and that there will be thousands of drawings like this very soon." This purpose—to inspire, to move others to action— speaks once again to the power of rhetoric, visual and verbal, not only influence people's ideas but, in some cases, to call them to action.

WRITER'S PRACTICE   MyWritingLab

Look at this editorial cartoon created by Adam Zyglis (Figure 1.13). Practice your own skills of rhetorical and critical analysis by analyzing the editorial cartoon, taking into account color, composition, characters, and action. Then, try to answer the following questions:

- Who is the audience for the cartoon? How can you tell?
- What is the argument? What elements of cartoon contribute to this message?
- What is the exigency of the cartoon?
- What was the author's motive or purpose for creating the cartoon?

Consider carefully how the artist uses words, images, and elements of composition to convey his message.

FIGURE 1.13 by Adam Zyglis

Analyzing Written Rhetoric

As we turn to developing your own analytical skills with regard to written rhetoric, you might find encouragement in Scott McCloud's point from *Understanding Comics* that "Writing is perceived information. It takes time and specialized knowledge to decode the abstract symbols of language." The purpose of this book is to help you develop the tools and acquire the knowledge to understand—or decode—the symbols we use to communicate with each other, including visual images but also written rhetoric in all its complexity. The strategies of rhetorical analysis that we discussed above—considering the rhetorical situation, exigence, and the motive and purpose behind a text—will serve you well as you examine communication in its many different forms. However, while with visual rhetoric we layered in more detailed examination of image, layout, color, and composition, as we move to more conventional written forms, you'll correspondingly need to take into account additional rhetorical elements: word choice, word usage, structure, rhetorical devices (such as symbolism, metaphor, and allusion), and tone, to name just a few.

Let's look at an article that derives from the same exigency as the cartoon in Figure 1.1: the assassination of Gabrielle Gifford. If we return to the blog post by Barbara Morrill that we looked at earlier in the chapter, we can see how the genre of the blog affords her different rhetorical opportunities than those presented to editorial cartoonists. In her piece, Morrill writes:

> And while there are many examples of the violent language employed by the right: "Second Amendment remedies," "resorting to the bullet box," calls to be "armed and dangerous," to name just a few, it's more than that. [...]
>
> Because since the election of Barack Obama, the right, both elected Republicans and their minions in the media, have pounded the non-stop drumbeat that Obama/Democrats/liberals want to destroy the country, they want to kill your grandmother, they're shredding the Constitution, they're terrorist sympathizers, they're going to take away your guns, that they're ene- mies of humanity, that the government is the enemy ...
>
> And that, as much as the obvious examples of violent rhetoric, can appeal to the extremist, the mentally unstable, or the "lone nut," to act. And last Saturday, one of them did.

The same way an editorial cartoonist sketches his argument with differ- ent shades, shapes, and strokes, so Morrill as an author powerfully draws her points through language. Consider some of the rhetorical techniques she uses:

- Morrill includes direct quotations of phrases used during the con- gressional election, listing them in a way that generates intensity and a sense of escalation (similar to the how the hierarchy of words on the flagpole operated in Figure 1.1).
- In the second paragraph, she switches to a set of images that attack the character of elected Republicans through criticizing their "minions in the media" and asserting that they have "pounded the nonstop drumbeat" as if at war with Democrats. This condemning language produces a strong animosity in the writing that might also sway a reader toward condemning the Republicans.

- Morrill uses a strategy called *anaphora*—deliberate repetition for rhetorical effect—by repeating "they're" at the end of the second paragraph to create a powerful rhythm and build emotional energy.
- The list itself relies on hyperbole and exaggeration ("destroy the country," "kill your grandmother," "shredding the Constitution," and so on) to present Morrill's version of what Republicans tend to suggest in their media statements.
- She concludes by reminding the reader of the exigence of the situation—how the "violent rhetoric" she has critiqued produced tragic action: the shooting of Giffords.

As you can see, such details can deeply move an audience. What we learn from reading this blog post rhetorically is that when you analyze written texts, you can apply similar strategies to those you use when reading visual texts: look for the vivid details, which in the case of language might include repetition, concrete metaphors, emotional phrases, and characterization of others that together act as what Aristotle would call "available means of persuasion" in writing. In this way, such written rhetoric, even while it disparages "violent language," is actually also forceful, even violent in its emphasis. It, too, is a form of communication that has as its purpose the goal of persuading audiences.

Let's consider a longer passage of writing. Remember Alex and her walk across campus? When she arrived at her Communication 101 class on "Media and Society," her TA gave her a handout containing an editorial about the *Charlie Hebdo* attack from the news site *Humanosphere*. Back in her dorm room, Alex sits down to read the article, writing **annotations** in the margins that indicate brief points of analysis or observation about the strategies of persuasion at work in each part of the article. As you read the article and Alex's accompanying commentary, add your own marks on points that you find provocative or interesting. Use the strategies of *critical literacy* that we've been developing throughout this chapter and ask yourself:

- Who is the main *audience*?
- How does David Horsey position himself as *author*?
- What is his *purpose* or *motive* in response to the *exigency* of the situation?
- Where and what is his *argument*?
- What rhetorical strategies does Horsey use to persuade the audience?
- What is your response to the text?

The title captures my attention—what does he mean by *obnoxious freedom?*

Interesting to read an article by an author who usually expresses his opinions in cartoons.

Sets up context right away. Also, the *Charlie Hebdo* shooting clearly is the exigence for this article.

His emphasis here indicates that this is the driving point of his essay. It echoes his title somewhat, too.

"My career of giving offense" and the story at the end of the paragraph seem both blunt and cynical—sounds like the voice of an editorial cartoonist!

Repetition here ("sometimes") is very powerful.

Makes an assumption about his audience here.

OBNOXIOUS FREEDOM

David Horsey

I have received many messages of solidarity from friends and readers in the couple of days since Islamic terrorists stormed into the Paris office of the satirical magazine *Charlie Hebdo* and murdered 12 people, including several cartoonists.

One friend—a prominent officeholder who, despite getting his share of barbs from reporters, nevertheless understands the absolute necessity of maintaining an unfettered news media—wrote in an email, "I am thinking of you following the France assault on journalists. It follows the loss of something like 40 journalists in the Mideast. Freedom cannot exist without people willing to ferret out the truth."

I appreciated his words, but I responded with a crucial caveat:

"Not only can freedom not exist without truth tellers, freedom cannot exist without obnoxious expressions of opinion, no matter who is offended."

Throughout my career of giving offense, I have received an unending stream of comments from people who disagree with what I draw or write. Sometimes they are rude. Sometimes they are insulting. Sometimes they are seriously angry. And sometimes they are just having fun sparring with me. Only once have I gotten anything like a death threat, which was unsettling, but quickly forgotten. One guy offered to fight me, but he lived 3000 miles away, so the bout never happened.

Love or hate the way I think, though, just about everyone would agree my right to free speech is unassailable. That's what makes America great, of course, and why there is near unanimous shock about the attack on the cartoonists in Paris. But, as people get a closer look at the kinds of images those French satirists were publishing, some are having second thoughts about all this freedom.

Editorial cartoonists in the United States are an essentially tame species. Traditionally part of the establishment media,

American cartoonists mostly poke fun at obvious targets. Even when the cartoons my ink-spewing compatriots and I produce are sharply barbed and a little bold, they stay within fairly tight boundaries of social responsibility and good taste. I do not think that's a terrible thing—even though it encourages too many bland cartoons with elephants and donkeys and labels galore—but it does mean we very seldom really test the limits of what our readers will tolerate.

The martyred cartoonists at *Charlie Hebdo* were different. Unrestrained mockery, not reasoned commentary, was their raison d'etre. Page after page, week after week, they turned out scatological, simplistic images attacking not only the political figures everyone picks on, but the cherished images and idols of organized religions. There were cartoons of Christ partaking of three-way sex with God and the Holy Spirit; nasty cartoons of the pope that got the magazine sued numerous times by Catholics; images of Orthodox Jews reminiscent of the anti-Semitic art of Nazi Germany; and, of course, caricatures of Mohammed doing all manner of disgusting things, sometimes with his genitals exposed.

It is those images that outraged the Parisian Muslim community and brought the cartoonists into the extremists' line of fire. The magazine office was firebombed in 2011 and the publication's editor, Stephane Charbonnier, received enough death threats to justify hiring a bodyguard. The editor and the bodyguard are now among the dead.

Even with all our proud proclamations in favor of free speech, would a wildly iconoclastic magazine like *Charlie Hebdo* be tolerated in the United States? Conservative religious people would be deeply offended, of course, but neither would such a publication fare well on liberally minded university campuses. Given the social sensitivities in the academic world, a student cartoonist who drew even one cartoon of the type regularly produced by the *Charlie Hebdo* crew would be pilloried and run off campus.

My take? Most of the *Charlie Hebdo* cartoons I have seen are crudely drawn, crass, and juvenile. Giving offense simply for its

---

Great word choice here!

Paragraph topic: state of U.S. editorial cartooning. Interesting that it ends in a critique of American editorial cartoons. Is he asking if these cartoons achieve their rhetorical purpose?

Now he moves to French cartooning practice. Effective comparison/ contrast move.

These examples are really important given that many websites and newspapers refused to publish these cartoons.

Sets up background for the attack. So this wasn't the first time that Charlie Hebdo suffered for its "unrestrained" cartoons.

Great question. I think he must assume his audience is predominantly American readers.

I'm thinking that this essay is getting at a comparative between U.S. editorial practices and French ones ...

Nice move here—says they're crude, but then praises the principle behind them.

Powerful way to show multiple perspectives.

"Terror" is a charged word. Great ending line; echoes "Je Suis Charlie." He is Charlie, though he says he wouldn't cartoon that way.

own sake has never been my style. Yet, I appreciate the principle on which Charbonnier took a stand. He kept publishing outrageous depictions of Mohammed mostly because people kept insisting he had no right to do it.

Religious fundamentalists may believe limits to free expression are what the Deity demands. College administrators may think it is the politically correct thing to do. Politicians may believe it will keep their constituents calm. But, without the freedom to offend—even in the most outrageous way—freedom is circumscribed and tepid. The French cartoonists were constant offenders and most people would not like their work, but they believed in freedom with a dedication few of us can match. And they died for it.

As Parisians are now saying in response to the terror, "Je suis Charlie."

By annotating the essay, Alex acts as an *active reader* and begins to identify which aspects of the article's written rhetoric interest her most. Her analysis evokes the *rhetorical situation* (see Figure 1.5): she analyzes the way the writer (or *author*) uses language (or *argument*) to persuade the reader (or *audience*) of the article (or *text*). She also noted the rhetorical moves of the author: word choice, structure, style tone, voice. She could then use those points in order to formulate her own argument about Horsey's article.

As you develop your own skills of analyzing written rhetoric, you can also use annotations to help you identify and track your observations on how rhetoric works; these notes, gathered together, will enable you to generate your own interpretation and, ultimately, a persuasive argument. In fact, Sir Francis Bacon, the great philosopher, politician, and scientist from the Age of Enlightenment, developed a system of logical "inductive" reasoning based on the very practice of gathering observations and using them to construct knowledge, a new conclusion, or an argument. Echoing the position of Aristotle, he also saw rhetoric as that which moves others. Bacon asserted: "The duty and office of rhetoric is to apply reason to imagination for the better moving of the will."

The varied ways that you and your classmates might read and respond to this editorial depend on both *audience* and *context,* bringing to light again the importance of the *rhetorical situation.* Differences in your interpretation also reveal the importance of learning effective means of persuading others to see the text through a certain lens or way of reading and analyzing the text. That is, your task as a reader and a writer is both to study a text carefully and to learn how to persuade others to see the text as you see it. In order to learn how to do so, we will turn next to the key elements in writing an argumentative essay about your interpretation of a text, so you, too, can "apply reason to imagination" to persuade others.

WRITER'S PRACTICE   MyWritingLab

Practice your skills of rhetorical analysis on this 2014 editorial by Chris Baker, also known as "Angry Nerd," who critiques Disney's decision to "destroy" what Star Wars fans call the "Expanded Universe canon"—including comic books, video games, and hundreds of pieces of fan fiction and unauthorized Star Wars–derivative texts—as part of creating continuity in the new Disney version of the Star Wars saga. Annotate like Alex did in the example above, looking for elements of the piece that make it particularly persuasive. Consider how Baker takes into account the rhetorical situation as well as exigency and purpose through style and composition. For added challenge, consider analyzing the video version of this editorial, available through YouTube.

"IS DARTH DISNEY DESTROYING STAR WARS' EXPANDED UNIVERSE?"
By Chris Baker

Help me, George Lucas, you're my only hope. Darth Disney is destroying the Expanded Universe. Please come back, George Lucas; this is our most desperate hour.

I felt a great disturbance in the force as if thousands of storylines cried out and were suddenly silenced. The Star Wars franchise is committing "canon-icide." The fate of an entire universe is at stake. You've understand: the Star Wars movies are the barest fraction of star war stories out there.

The so-called "Expanded Universe" has existed in comic books and novels and games for decades, and Lucas film is now air-locking it all. The Thrawn trilogy novels; *Shadow of the Empire* for Nintendo 64; the Tattoine manhunt module for the Star Wars RPG; the holiday special: erased from existence. Only a Sith Lord would decree that everything except the Star Wars films and the Clone Wars series did not happen. All future tie-in cartoons and novels—everything—will be forced to march in lockstep with the JJ Abrams sequel films. You know who else marched in lockstep? [The storm troopers.] And a new story group inside Lucasfilm will make sure that all elements in the Star Wars continuity fit together.

Normally I approve of an orderly and cohesive continuity, but this crisis on infinite Endoors is deleting incidents that are more interesting than almost anything that happened in the movies. No Expanded Universe means Boba Fett never escaped from the Sarlacc Pit, Luke Skywalker never flirted with the dark side, and Han Solo never befriended … Jackson Starhopper… .

Oh, Darth Disney, only you could be so bold! To think that I was cautiously optimistic about your stewardship of Star Wars. I was far too trusting.

The survival of the Expanded Universe is now in the hands of Star Wars fans. Fan fiction kept Star Trek alive through the lean years. We can do with the same for Star Wars. The more you tighten your grip, Darth Disney, the more Expanded Universe stories will slip through your fingers. You may control the canon, but you will never control the Fan-on. Your tightly controlled continuity can't handle the pulse-pounding exploits of Pedanticus Nitpickser, a bald bespectacled jedi, who lectures the entire galaxy about how lightsabers are scientifically impossible and how you couldn't actually hear explosions in the vacuum of space.

Strong he is in the force … of logic.

WRITING A RHETORICAL ANALYSIS

1.5 How should I brainstorm parts of the essay, including the thesis statement?

We've seen that rhetoric works as a means of persuading an audience to accept the argument of the author. This is also true for the argument you make about a text. When you write an analysis essay for class, you are crafting a rhetorical text in order to persuade your readers (the instructor and your peers) to accept your interpretation. In some cases, your instructor might ask you to select your own text for analysis; in others, you may be assigned a particular text. In either case, ask yourself the following questions:

- What elements stand out that you might analyze in your essay?
- What do you know about the author or the intended audience?
- What do you know about the timing or context of this text?
- What is your interpretation of the meaning or message of this text?

As you work through the questions above, you can see that your task as a writer is to argue convincingly for your audience to see the text the way you yourself see it. In the case of Figure 1.14, what is the cartoon's argument about the NFL's response to recent allegations of domestic violence among the players? What details could you discuss in order to support your interpretation?

FIGURE 1.14 Gary Markstein's comic humorously tackles the sensitive issue of domestic violence in the NFL.

Your challenge as a student of writing and rhetoric is not only to identify the argument contained by a text but also to *craft your own interpretation of that text*. This involves careful assessment of the ways in which the elements of the rhetorical situation work together to produce meaning in a text.

In looking at Markstein's comic, you may notice many details—the uniforms, the hand gestures, the captions, the facial expressions, the shading on the referee's pants, the use of black shadows, and the fact that the lettering on the hats is yellow. However, when crafting your own argument, it's valuable to remember that a successful rhetorical analysis does not need to discuss every component in the source text, only those relevant to supporting your interpretation. In fact, it's also important to tailor your analysis itself to prioritize a particular approach. You might decide to focus on any one of these elements as you shape your overall interpretation:

- **Argument:** What is the text's argument, and is it persuasive? How does the author use evidence to support his interpretation?
- **Audience:** How did the author compose the text to persuade a particular audience? How did he take into account their context and predispositions to try to create a convincing argument?
- **Genre:** How did the author either trade on or depart from the conventions of a particular genre (such as the conventional essay, blogging, twitter, even email as we saw in Figure 1.6)? How did that decision influence the persuasiveness of the argument?
- **Style:** How did the author use style as a persuasive tool? How did he use symbol, metaphor, word choice, voice, and other stylistic devices?
- **Exigence and Purpose:** How does the cartoon respond to a pressing need? What is the author's purpose, and to what extent does he accomplish it?

AT A GLANCE

Selecting and Evaluating a Text for Rhetorical Analysis

When choosing a text for analysis, ask yourself the following questions:

- What is the text's purpose? To entertain? Educate? Persuade?
- Are there sufficient elements in the text to analyze?
- What do you know about the author, the intended audience, and the context?
- What's your interpretation of this image? Can you develop a strong claim that you can support with evidence from the text?

Ultimately, your analysis might touch on aspects of the different approaches; however, it is important to try to achieve a unified interpretation, so you probably will need to focus on one more than the others. To help you through this process, we recommend writing out your answers to the questions above. Many times it is through writing itself that we can access—and create—our best ideas.

Developing a Thesis Statement

In brainstorming your essay, you need to determine your interpretation of the meaning or message of a specific text (whether written, visual, or a combination of the two). In writing studies, we call this interpretation your **thesis,** or *the concise statement of your claim or interpretation about a particular text, issue, or event.* A thesis should be more than a statement of observation or a fact. It should also be more than merely your opinion. It needs to combine **observation + evidence** (based on the elements of the text).

To understand how to generate a *thesis statement* using your skills of critical analysis, let's work through an example. Imagine that you want to write an argument about the cartoon in Figure 1.15, a commentary on recent debates about immigration policy. How might you develop a thesis statement that persuasively conveys your interpretation of how this cartoon contributes to the debate surrounding the status of undocumented immigrants?

Start by jotting down what you see; make *close observations* about the text. Then use questions to bring your argument into focus and to make a specific claim. The end product will be a *working thesis.* The process of developing your thesis might look like this:

1. **Write down your observations.**

   Close observations: The cartoon focuses on the border between the United

FIGURE 1.15 This cartoon by Daryl Cagle uses engaging visuals and well-chosen words to make an argument.

Source: Daryl Cagle, Cagle Cartoons, Inc.

States and Mexico and on the way that we set up fences to keep illegal immigrants out. A key element is the gap in the fence that people are crawling through to get into the United States. The contradictory messages are interesting, too. The big sign says "Keep out," while the smaller signs are designed to draw people in.

2. **Work with your observations to construct a preliminary thesis statement.**

   First statement: The cartoon focuses on the contradiction in American border policy.

3. **Refine your argument by asking questions that make your statement less general.**

   Ask yourself: How? What contradiction? To what effect? How do I know this?

4. **Revise your preliminary thesis statement to be more specific; perhaps include specific evidence that drives your claim.**

   Revised statement: The cartoon in Figure 1.15 focuses on the contradictions in American border policy by showing that, on the one hand, the American government wants to keep illegal immigrants out, but, on the other hand, economic forces encourage them to enter the United States illegally.

5. **Further polish your thesis by refining your language and asking questions about the implications of your working thesis statement.**

   Ask yourself: What do you find interesting about this observation? How does it tap into larger social or cultural issues?

6. **Revise your working thesis to include the implications or significance of your claim. Sometimes we call this the "So what?" point.**

   Working Thesis: The political cartoon in Figure 1.15 offers a sharp commentary on the recent immigration debate, suggesting that official government policies against illegal immigration are undermined by economic forces that tolerate, if not welcome, the entry of undocumented workers into the United States. Yet the added detail of the hole in the fence suggests that such entry comes at great cost to immigrants who enter illegally.

In the working thesis, the significance appears as the final point about "great cost"—that is, the cartoon indicates that current immigration policies have serious consequences for undocumented laborers entering the United States. From this example, you can tell that a strong argumentative thesis does more than state a topic: it makes a claim about that topic that you will develop in the rest of your paper.

Let's look at one more example to further consider ways to produce sharp, clear, and persuasive thesis statements. For her rhetorical analysis assignment, Alex decided to write about David Horsey's editorial from earlier in the chapter. As we saw in her annotations, she had already noted several elements that struck her about the text: the comparison between the United States and France, the word choice, and Horsey's unique position as an editorial cartoonist/author. While drafting her essay, she experimented with a variety of different thesis statements before arriving at a strong claim:

Thesis 1: David Horsey's article offers a powerful perspective on the *Charlie Hebdo* shooting and free speech.

Assessment: This thesis statement relies too heavily on subjective opinion: the author offers no criteria for evaluating the cartoon. What does it mean to be "powerful"? Moreover, the author does not include any elements of analysis or use evidence.

Thesis 2: David Horsey's article makes an argument about free speech.

Assessment: This thesis statement is too much of a broad generalization and offers no critical interpretation of the meaning of the text. It does not make a claim as to what Horsey's opinion is, and it relies too heavily on vague language.

Thesis 3: According to my analysis, David Horsey, a well-known editorial cartoonist, discusses both American and French approaches to editorial cartoons in this article.

Assessment: While this thesis is promising in that it offers some more detail, it nevertheless only describes the content of the essay rather than offering a focused interpretation, despite the writer's claim to be making an argument.

Thesis 4: In the article, Horsey, a well-known editorial cartoonist, uses an underlying compare-and-contrast strategy bolstered by strong word choice to make the argument for solidarity with *Charlie Hebdo* in defense of all levels of free speech.

Assessment: While a bit long, this working thesis statement does combine observation and significance. Of the four examples, it provides the most specific and argumentative articulation of Alex's interpretation of Horsey's editorial.

As the examples above demonstrate, a strong thesis is characterized by a specific and contestable claim. This central claim in turn functions as the heart and driver of a successful rhetorical analysis essay.

AT A GLANCE

Testing Your Thesis

- Does your thesis present an interesting angle on your topic?
- Does it avoid being overly obvious or a commonplace statement? Is it nuanced?
- Does it present a debatable point? That is, could someone argue against it?
- Is it too dense (trying to compact the entire paper into a single sentence)? Conversely, is it overly simplistic or general (neglecting to adequately develop your claim)?
- Does it use concrete and vivid language?
- Does it suggest the significance of your topic?

Analyzing Student Writing

Let's look at how Alex combines effective strategies of analysis with her carefully crafted thesis statement to compose her rhetorical analysis of the David Horsey article that she read for class. As you read through this selection, consider how she analyzes "Obnoxious Freedom" as well as the ways in which she herself uses rhetorical strategies to make her own argument persuasive.

Alex crafts a title that refers to the article but also hints at her own thesis.

Ramirez 1

Alexandra Ramirez
Rhetorical Analysis Essay
Comm 101

"Obnoxious Freedom":
A Cartoonist's Defense of the Freedom to Be Crass

On the morning of January 7, 2015, two brothers entered the Paris office of *Charlie Hebdo*, a weekly satirical newspaper. Armed with assault rifles and other weapons, the pair of brothers

Ramirez 2

killed 12 people in the office that day: cartoonists, writers, maintenance workers, editors, and a bodyguard. The brothers, who identified as members of the Yemeni branch of Al Qaeda, took issue with cartoons published in *Charlie Hebdo* that they considered disrespectful to Mohammed and to Islam as a whole (Smith-Spark, Ford, and Mullen).

Following the attack, there was both great mourning for the victims and outrage at a terrorist strike against the freedom of press. In days following the attack, the *Charlie Hebdo* shooting caught the international media by firestorm and sparked a new conversation (and controversy) on freedom of speech. One article contributing to the conversation is David Horsey's "Obnoxious Freedom." In this article, Horsey, a well-known editorial cartoonist, uses an underlying compare-and-contrast strategy bolstered by strong word choice to make the argument for solidarity with *Charlie Hebdo* in defense of all levels of free speech. As he does so, however, Horsey also makes a subtle criticism of the status of American free speech as well, adding another dimension to the debate surrounding the *Charlie Hebdo* tragedy.

At a basic level, Horsey made a very significant choice in choosing to publish an article expressing his opinion about the *Charlie Hebdo* tragedy. Indeed, as a two-time Pulitzer Prize–winning cartoonist speaking about a retaliation to cartoons, it might be expected that Horsey would choose to express himself via a cartoon ("David Horsey"). Yet in this case, Horsey

She designs her opening paragraph to set up context for her essay, drawing on a source that she found through a quick Google search. Note how she makes sure to cite the source from which she got her information, even though she doesn't use a direct quotation here.

Alex places her thesis statement near the end of the introductory section.

In writing her essay, Alex adds a layer of complexity to her preliminary thesis statement (which we saw on p. 31).

Her thesis implies levels of interpretation, so Alex begins her main body by referring to the most basic level, implying that she will engage with the more complex aspects of Horsey's argument later in her essay.

Even from the beginning of her essay, she grounds her analysis in terms of the rhetorical situation—the relation of the audience and author to the argument.

Her transition here demonstrates that she's moving from the "basic" to more nuanced elements of Horsey's essay.

Alex cites specific examples from the text to support her points and also explains their significance.

chose prose. To some extent, this choice alone sets a tone of seriousness; it is as though the jokester has finally learned to be serious. The effect of this is ultimately that the audience is forced to take the article—and the argument within—more seriously.

Beyond just setting the serious tone for the argument, however, the prose format also allows for Horsey to demonstrate both more nuance and voice, and even include his own credentials as an author. For example, the extensive discussion of both Horsey's own cartoon style and that of the works published in *Charlie Hebdo* allows Horsey to make multilevel arguments such as the idea that although more tame cartoons can sometimes be more effective, the crass ones must be allowed to exist as well in order to not give in to a sliding scale of censorship. Along with this substance, however, Horsey expresses a strong, humorous voice using asides such as a story about a guy that "offered to fight [Horsey], but he lived 3000 miles away, so the bout never happened." Ultimately, the serious arguments in tandem with witty humor are an effective method of capturing the audience's attention while capitalizing on the author's strengths. It is also significant to note that the longer form also allows Horsey to introduce himself more to the reader. In some ways, Horsey relates himself to the cartoonists at *Charlie Hebdo* by, for example, referencing his "career of giving offense." At other points in the article, Horsey chooses to distance himself more, stating that "giving offense simply for its own sake" isn't his

Ramirez 4

style. This creates a sense of impartiality on the part of the author, which makes him appear more trustworthy to the reader.

And yet, at the same time that Horsey works to appear impartial in some ways such as his relation to the *Charlie Hebdo* cartoonists, he also actively plays upon almost nationalistic, patriotic writing he presumes to resonate with his audience. This strategy is first capitalized on by a comparison of French and American culture and cartoons. For example, when describing American cartoons, Horsey paints the pictures of "tame species" that only criticize targets that are well-accepted as targets and can become "bland."

By comparison, Horsey describes the *Charlie Hebdo* cartoons as "unrestrained mockery" that go after widely idolized figures. While this might seem to equally criticize both cartoon cultures for their shortcomings, when paired with the rest of the article, Horsey's feelings about both cultures become more clear. First, the buildup to this portion of the article features rather dramatic and even patriotic word choice such as "unassailable" free speech as well as cartoonists that are both "compatriots" and martyrs (Horsey). Evoking these images prime the audience, reminding them how great the foundation of American society (freedom) really is. But through the comparison to French cartoons, Horsey implicitly asks the reader a new question: how free *are* American cartoons?

As he more directly begins his conclusion by asking the rhetorical question ("My take?"), Horsey clearly delineates the

Alex continues her emphasis on how Horsey constructs himself as an *author* in his article and how that relates to the strength of his argument.

In this paragraph, Alex shows her powers of critical thinking and analysis in the way she interprets specific elements of the text.

Alex pauses here to clarify her interpretation of Horsey's argument.

argument that he builds up to throughout the rest of the piece: Americans need to be supporting *Charlie Hebdo*, and American free speech might not represent pure freedom any more. Indeed, as Horsey lists what he considers to be opposing groups to free speech in America—religious fundamentalists, college administrations, and politicians—he attaches them with somewhat stigmatized or less-than-altruistic goals such as political correctness or just trying to assuage constituents. Further capitalizing on American readers raised hearing the "give me liberty or give me death" battle cry, Horsey praises the *Charlie Hebdo* cartoonists as having the utmost dedication to freedom, ultimately making the victims into martyrs. As just another subtle touch of preference for the French culture of freedom, Horsey ends his argument with a resounding phrase of solidarity with the French, "Je suis Charlie," or *I am Charlie*.

Could this support and solidarity with the French be felt without a sense of the author's giving a warning about American culture? Perhaps, but throughout the piece Horsey leaves subtle indicators that in the very system he publishes in everything isn't perfect, such as hinting that the fear of offending is creating "bland" cartoons or that politicians pressure media to produce cartoons that will keep people "calm." These insinuations, in combination with the overall comparison to the French, allow for Horsey to not only stand in solidarity with *Charlie Hebdo* but also make a commentary on the true meaning of free speech. Perhaps Horsey meant his signatory "Je suis Charlie" merely as solidarity with fellow cartoonists. However, perhaps he felt his cautionary piece alerts Americans to guard their

---

Alex draws attention to how Horsey devises his argument to appeal to his specifically American audience.

Note how Alex includes a translation of the French phrase here for clarity.

Alex uses a question here to transition into her own conclusion, mirroring the question-asking strategy that Horsey used in the original essay.

Alex concedes here that not all might agree, but then reaffirms her own claim.

Ramirez 6

freedoms just as the cartoonists of *Charlie Hebdo* remind the people of France to do so with each of their "obnoxious" cartoons.

Alex designs a conclusion that again plays off of Horsey's, leaving her audience to interpret as they will.

Ramirez 7

Works Cited

"David Horsey." *Los Angeles Times*. Los Angeles Times, Jan. 2015. Web. 28 May 2015.

Horsey, David. "Obnoxious Freedom: Editorial Cartoonist David Horsey on the Charlie Hebdo Murders." *Humanosphere*. Tom Paulson's Humanosphere, 9 Jan. 2015. Web. 28 May 2015.

Smith-Spark, Laura, Dana Ford, and Jethro Mullen. "Charlie Hebdo Attack: What We Know and Don't Know." CNN.com. Cable News Network, 21 Jan. 2015. Web. 26 May 2015.

Alex includes a Works Cited that lists not only the original article that she was analyzing but also the two texts she used for background on the *Charlie Hebdo* shooting.

THE WRITER'S PROCESS

As you turn now to write your own rhetorical analysis of a text, you'll be putting into practice all the skills you've learned in this chapter. You'll need to write down your observations of the text, spend time analyzing them in detail, and use these points of analysis as *evidence* to make an argument that will persuade others to see the text the way you see it. In other words, when composing your own rhetorical analysis, you need to use the same process we have worked through when analyzing different texts in this chapter:

- First, look carefully at all the elements in the text. Create a list of your observations to help you analyze the text more closely.

■ Then, consider the argument of each element. How does it contribute to the text as a whole?

■ Next, complete the rhetorical triangle (see Figure 1.5) for the text, identifying the author, the intended audience, and the argument, based on your observations of the details. In addition, identify the rhetorical exigence and the author's purpose or motive in creating the argument.

■ Finally, put all these elements together and develop your thesis statement about the argument and significance of the text.

It's crucial to remember that when you write a rhetorical analysis, you perform a rhetorical act of persuasion yourself. Accordingly, you need to include the key elements of analytical writing: (1) have a point of interpretation to share with your readers, (2) take time to walk readers through concrete details to prove your point, and (3) lead your readers through the essay in an engaging and convincing way. But of all these, the most important is your thesis, your interpretation of or position on the text—your *argument*.

Spend some time working on your thesis before composing the entire draft. Make sure your angle is sharp and your interpretation takes into

AT A GLANCE

Composing Rhetorical Analysis Essays

• Do you have a sharp point of interpretation, or *thesis*, to make about the text?

• Have you selected key elements or details to analyze in support of your thesis?

• Do you lead readers through your interpretation of the text by discussing important aspects in sequence? These might include:

   ○ Verbal elements in the text (words, font, quotes, dates)

   ○ Visual composition, layout, and images

   ○ Framing words for the text (article title, cartoon caption)

   ○ Color, arrangement, and meaning of items

• Can you include information about the author, intended audience, or context?

• Have you drafted a title for your own essay?

• Does your introduction name the author, date, and rhetorical situation for your text?

• Do your paragraphs build and progress through the essay using transitions?

• Have you offered a summary and a larger point or implication in the conclusion?

• Can you insert the image right into the essay and label it?

account audience, author, and argument as well as concrete points of visual and verbal composition.

Moreover, keep in mind the need to begin with observations, but avoid simply describing the elements you notice. Instead, zoom in on specific details and think hard about their meaning. Make a persuasive argument by using *specific* evidence to support your analysis of how the text succeeds at convincing an audience to perceive an issue in a particular way. These writing strategies will enable you to craft a persuasive and effective rhetorical analysis essay.

Seeing Connections
See Chapter 7 for more instructions on integrating images in your writing and referring to them correctly.

SPOTLIGHTED ANALYSIS: EDITORIAL CARTOONS

MyWritingLab

Pick a cartoon to analyze from a news magazine such as *Time*, a newspaper, a Web comic collection such as *xkcd* or *Penny Arcade*, or an online archive such as Daryl Cagle's political cartoon Website. Using the skills of analysis you have learned in this chapter, work through the questions below to guide your analysis.

- **Audience:** Who is the audience for this comic? How does it address this audience? In what country and in what historical moment was the cartoon produced? In what type of text did it first appear? A journal? A newspaper? Online? Is this text conservative? liberal? How does it speak to this audience?

- **Author:** What do you know about the artist? What kinds of cartoons (or other types of texts) does he or she regularly produce? Where does he or she live and publish?

- **Argument:** What issue does the cartoon address, and what is the cartoon's argument about it? Is there irony involved (does the cartoon advocate one point of view, but the cartoonist wants you to take the opposite view)?

- **Composition:** Is this political cartoon a single frame or a series of sequential frames? If the latter, how does the argument evolve over the series? How do elements like color choices, layout, and style shape its impact on the audience?

- **Imagery:** What choices of imagery and content does the artist make? Are the drawings realistic? Do they rely on caricatures? How are character and setting portrayed? Does the artist include allusions or references to past or present events or ideas? How do images and words work together in the cartoon?

- **Tone:** Is the cartoon primarily comic or serious in tone? How does this choice of tone create a powerful rhetorical impact on readers?

- **Cultural resonance:** Does the cartoon implicitly or explicitly refer to any actual people, events, or pop culture icons? What sort of symbolism is used in the cartoon? Would the symbols speak to a broad or narrow audience? How does the cultural resonance function as a rhetorical strategy in making the argument?

WRITING ASSIGNMENTS

1. **Rhetoric Practice:** Experiment with the scenarios below in order to understand the power of rhetoric as a persuasive act. In each case, first write down your ideas. Then, following the directions, write, speak, design, or present your own rhetorical text. Keep in mind that the success of your argument will depend on your choice of media (verbal plea, written email, cover letter, visual poster, etc.) in relation to the specific audience you are addressing (coach, professor, potential employer, or peers).

   - Scenario 1: When you realize that you will never finish an essay on time because of your heavy work schedule, you decide to ask for an extension on the paper's deadline. Craft an argument asking for extra time on the assignment that would appeal to the personality of your teacher; compose it in a way appropriate for an email communication.

   - Scenario 2: Imagine that you have a conflict with your practice schedule for your sport—a midterm, interview, or visit from your parents. Compose an oral argument that persuades your coach to let practice out early. After you write out your ideas, make your case face-to-face through in-class role-playing.

   - Scenario 3: When applying for a summer internship, you are asked to submit a formal résumé in order to indicate your qualifications for the position. As you design your résumé think about how to most persuasively present yourself: What content will you include? How will you describe yourself, your goals, and your duties in past positions? How will you organize it and lay it out? What font will you use? Consider taking your résumé to your Writing Center or Career Center for expert feedback.

   - Scenario 4: As Social Chair for your Greek House, you need to advertise an upcoming charity event: create an effective flyer and also a brief paragraph for email and social media distribution. Consider how you'll need to adapt your rhetorical techniques to adjust to the different media.

2. **Personal Narrative Essay:** Recall Alex's observations of rhetoric on her way to class; conduct a similar study of the rhetoric in your world. Write your reflections into a *personal narrative essay.* Discuss which types of visual, verbal, bodily, or architectural rhetoric were most evident, which were most subtle, and which you found the most persuasive. Conclude with a statement or argument about these texts—what do they collectively say about your community or culture? How do these texts try to shape the views of audiences through specific messages or arguments?

3. **Rhetorical Analysis:** Using the At a Glance box on p. 28 as a starting point, develop your analysis of a text of your choice into a full *rhetorical analysis*, complete with a persuasive thesis statement. Make sure that your writing supports a thesis about elements and messages of all the texts you are analyzing.

4. **Comparative Rhetorical Analysis:** Refer back to the article by David Horsey included in this chapter. Now search online for his editorial cartoon on the same subject, entitled "The Death Cult." Write a comparative rhetorical analysis of these texts that examines the similarities and differences in their arguments and composition. (If you prefer, choose two texts of your own—whether two visual texts, two verbal texts, or a visual and a verbal text—that address the same issue to analyze instead.) What rhetorical strategies does each one use to make an argument? How do their arguments about the issue in question differ, and how is each composed to convey that argument? Include a persuasive thesis statement and specific supporting details about each text. Don't forget to take into account your own rhetorical situation (the relationship between your audience, your argument, and your own identity as a writer) in composing your essay.

MyWritingLab Visit Ch. 1 Analyzing Texts and Writing Thesis Statements in MyWritingLab to complete the Writer's Practices, Spotlighted Analyses, and Writing Assignments, and to test your understanding of the chapter objectives.

CHAPTER 2

Understanding Strategies of Persuasion

Chapter Preview Questions

2.1 What specific strategies of argumentation can I use to write persuasively?

2.2 What role do the rhetorical appeals of *pathos*, *logos*, and *ethos* play in persuasion?

2.3 How can I shape my argument based on time, place, and shared values?

What convinced you to buy that new smartphone, to try that new sports drink—or even to decide which college to attend? Chances are that your decision was influenced by a moment of persuasive communication—whether that was a pitch from a college recruiter, a brochure, a printed ad, commercial, product review, or even a billboard. Any time someone tries to market or sell us something, he or she is acting as a rhetorician, carefully assessing the *rhetorical situation* and crafting arguments designed to persuade the target audience. In this chapter, we'll turn our attention to analyzing advertisements as a way to help us discern specific strategies of argumentation that you can use to convince others in your own persuasive writing.

For instance, while walking down a city street, you might cross under billboards such as the one for a clothing store in Figure 2.1, positioned strategically alongside the busy Manhattan sidewalks. Look carefully at its design: what strategies of persuasion does it use to engage the passersby? Does it make a logical argument about its clothing line? Does it appeal to the audience's emotions? How much does it rely on the product's reputation to market its products? How might this ad be revised to provide an even more persuasive argument that would convince a consumer not only to stop and enter the store but also to purchase a piece of clothing? As you can see,

FIGURE 2.1 This New York City street scene presents a typical example of how the rhetoric of advertising looms over our every day lives.

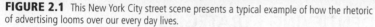

even a seemingly simple advertisement like this one is a carefully composed text, constructed to make a particular argument about a product.

Think of how other ads you've seen make you pause and pay attention. Much like the billboard in Figure 2.1, ads in fashion or sports magazines often feature a photo of a celebrity or an attractive person to try to get their readers to connect emotionally with their products. Commercials often use compelling stories or memorable examples to hook their audiences. Brochures tend to incorporate impressive statistics or factual evidence to support their claims. Targeted ads on social media sites draw on information from your personal profile and search history to connect to you through customized product suggestions. Often, in fact, it is not one but a combination of factors that we find persuasive—and many times these factors are so subtle that we hardly recognize them. Such techniques that are used to move and convince an audience are called **rhetorical strategies**.

While such strategies are a vital part of any successful persuasion, advertisements offer us a particularly productive means of analyzing them because they represent arguments in compact forms. An ad has to be quite efficient; it has to convey its message persuasively before its audience flips the page, fast forwards, hits mute, or scrolls further down the page. Ads also provide us with a particularly effective example of contemporary argument through their sheer ubiquity. Consider all the places ads appear nowadays: not just in magazines or on the television or radio, but also (as we saw in Figure 2.1) on billboards, the sides of buses, trains, and buildings; in sports stadiums and movie theaters; on T-shirts and baseball hats; as banners on Webpages and sidebars on social media sites; even spray-painted on sidewalks or integrated into video games.

By analyzing advertisements, we can detect the rhetorical strategies writers select to make their points and convince their audiences. More importantly, by using advertising as a way to understand persuasion, we can take away lessons that apply to the composition of all sorts of texts, including those that you will produce in academic situations. In this way, you'll gain a working vocabulary and learn specific principles that you can use both to become a savvy reader of advertisements and also to produce your own persuasive written texts.

2.1 What specific strategies of argumentation can I use to write persuasively?

IDENTIFYING STRATEGIES OF ARGUMENTATION

Like more traditional writing, advertising often deploys **strategies of argumentation** to persuade. These can be used effectively to structure either a small unit (in an essay, a paragraph or section of the argument; in an ad, a small subset of the text) or a larger one (the argument as a whole). Let's look at how such strategies might operate in both advertising and academic texts:

- **Narration:** Using a story to draw in the audience.

    The Budweiser, commercial, "Brotherhood," for example (see Figure 2.2), tells the story of a man who raises a foal, sells it so it can become one of the Budweiser Clydesdales, and then is unexpectedly reunited with it after a city parade.

    Similarly, a writer might use narration to hook her reader by telling a story that illustrates a key point of her argument or predisposes them to her line of thinking. For instance, in writing about the ethical implications of marketing fast-food to children, you might open your essay with the story of how a young child watches a McDonalds commercial, is drawn in by its cheerful music, appealing colors, and product information, and then begs his mother for a Happy Meal for lunch.

FIGURE 2.2 The Budweiser "Brotherhood" commercial relies on narration to hook its audience, using the reunion of the man and his horse as the emotional climax of the story.

■ **Comparison-Contrast:** Making a point through showing the similarities or differences between two or more items.

> For instance, soap manufacturer Olay ran a comparison-contrast ad campaign arguing the superiority of its product due to how much moisturizer it contained; it juxtaposed a picture of Dove soap next to a measuring cup marked "1/4 moisture" with a picture of Olay soap next to a measuring cup "1/3 moisture" to support this claim.

> In an essay, relatedly, a writer might contrast two different texts as a way that gives the reader a better understanding of a larger claim. For instance, if you were writing an essay that argued that a famous *New York Times* columnist's approach to an issue had become more conservative over time, you might compare one of her articles from the 1990s with one that she wrote within the last five years.

■ **Example/Illustration:** Focusing on a specific, representative example to persuade your reader.

> We can see this strategy at work in the Lego ad in Figure 2.3, which spotlights a smiling girl, holding her Lego creation, as an example of who might use the new Lego Friends products and what she might build.

> In a similar way, writers often help readers understand a larger issue by exploring one or more example. In an essay on nationalism in advertising, for example, you might examine the commercials with a patriotic theme

It's as one of a kind
as she is.

It's a garden, a rocket ship, a castle, an island, an enchanted forest and an epic adventure. It's exactly what she wants it to be.

She's an explorer, a builder, a designer, a creator and an inventor. She's every child that ever spilled a bucket of LEGO® bricks onto the carpet and made them her own.

She's not just showing you what she made. She's showing you what she's made of.

It's a LEGO® thing.

LEGO Friends

FIGURE 2.3 This Lego ad speaks to the target audience for the Friends line by showing the types of creations that can be made with that product.

that were broadcast during the 2002 Superbowl, shortly after the 9/11 terrorist attacks.

■ **Cause and Effect:** Structuring an argument around the causal relationship between two elements, considering why something occurred or happened.

Acne face wash companies and weight loss programs such as Jenny Craig are famous for cause-and-effect arguments, organizing their commercials around the idea that using their facial scrub or following their diet (cause) helps their customers achieve a clear complexion or lose weight (effect).

Many writers find cause and effect a powerful way to argue for the logical consequences of an action, event, or phenomenon. For instance, a cause-and-effect essay might argue how the rise of DVR and online subscription services for television shows (cause) has changed the marketing strategies and design of commercials (effect).

■ **Definition:** Defining a term, concept, or theoretical premise for your reader.

Advertisers for the search engine Bing used definition to drive their 2009 marketing campaign through a series of commercials that defined "search overload syndrome," which they claimed was the tendency of Google users to succumb to spontaneous verbal outbursts of unrelated information as a result of their unfocused Internet searches.

Often in assessing their audience's understanding of concepts fundamental to their argument, writers will take time to define an important term or idea to make their claims more persuasive. For instance, if you were writing an essay on emergent forms of online advertising, you might devote a paragraph to defining the term "advergaming" before moving on to examine examples of this new genre of interactive games designed to promote a product or company.

- **Analogy:** Using a simpler or more familiar concept or metaphor to help an audience understand a complicated idea.

    Consider how analogy works in an ad series from the pharmaceutical company, Elter Drugs. In 2007, it created several magazine ads, sponsored by its "Gastric and Antibacterial Therapy Divisions," with the slogan "An Unwashed Vegetable Can Become a Deadly Weapon" and the tagline "Always wash your vegetables to win the battle against foodborne illnesses such as amoebiasis, dysentery, and cholera." What made the ads so powerful was the way the imagery built on the slogan's metaphor. One ad featured a close up of a tomato, against a red background, with a lit fuse on its top stem, turning it into a bomb; another transformed an artichoke into a grenade by replacing its stalk with a fuse and safety pin; a third ad stood a mushroom on a base of billowing smoke, turning it into a visual equivalent of a mushroom cloud. In each case, the ad used analogy to drive home its argument about the potential dangers of eating unwashed vegetables.

    Analogies found in essays are often not as heavy-handed as those found in this ad series, but they can be very persuasive in establishing a rich correlative that helps the reader better understand the argument. In an essay analyzing social media marketing, for instance, you might find it useful to employ a Cinderella analogy throughout the essay to persuade your reader that the seemingly insignificant strategy of Twitter advertising actually just needs the right "fairy godmother" to usher it into prominence and power in the marketing scene.

- **Description:** Describing an element, event, or idea in detail so as to set up background or create an impression on your reader.

    Advertisements for resorts and tropical getaways generally paint a picture of the destination they are promoting, using vivid, descriptive language and beautiful images to motivate audiences to choose that locale for their next vacation.

    When analyzing texts, writers often use descriptive language to paint a picture for their readers to make a stronger point. For instance, if you were to write a rhetorical analysis about a commercial, you probably would include a detailed description of the commercial—which your readers might not have seen; alternately, if you were writing an essay about a place that had had a profound impact on you, you would describe the location in vivid detail. In both cases, you would be helping your reader "see" something in a way that would incline them be more persuaded by your claim.

a) log in

b) open a Merrill Edge® IRA
and fund it from my bank
account

c) there is no c

Welcome to Merrill Edge®. It's online investing, streamlined.
Open a Merrill Edge IRA or roll over your 401(k) with one-on-one support
from a specialist. Get a full range of investment offerings. Log in once to
see investing and banking on one page. **merrilledge.com/simplified**

MERRILL
EDGE®

Bank of America Corporation

Bank of America

Bank with Bank of America. Invest with Merrill Edge.

Are Not FDIC Insured   Are Not Bank Guaranteed   May Lose Value

FIGURE 2.4   This ad for Merrill Edge shows the simplicity of the investment process to persuade readers to try out its services.

■ **Process:** Persuading through showing a series of sequential steps.

The ad in Figure 2.4 relies on a process-based argument; it argues that Merrill's IRA is easy to use by showing the simple a-b-c steps the woman follows to invest her money.

Process can be extremely effective in a written text to advocate for a certain course of action. If you decided to write an article presenting what you thought was the best way to navigate the college admissions process, you could use this strategy to move your readers step-by-step from campus visits, to standardized test-taking, interviewing, composing a strong application essay, and finally to deciding which school to attend.

■ **Classification and Division:** Helping the reader understand either how individual elements fit into a larger category or set of ideas or how a larger category breaks down into component parts.

We can see classification and division at work in many car ads; automobile manufacturers like Honda and Toyota often run ads that promote their entire product line—from SUVs to compact cars—to show the variety of models they produce and invite their audience to select the one that best suits their needs.

In an essay, classification and division can help your reader understand the complexities of what you're discussing and better understand the differences between a set of items. Think how useful this strategy might be in an essay about celebrity endorsements. Rather than discussing all types of spokespersons, you might formulate categories to help your reader understand the different ways such advertising is structured: for instance, expert ads (ads based on the expertise of the celebrity); reputation ads (ads that draw on the celebrity's overall public status, not necessarily related to the product); and parody ads (ads that mock the celebrity's character or actions as a selling point). Using this technique could help you produce more sophisticated and nuanced analysis.

Let's now turn to a more extended analysis of a text to see the way in which you can combine multiple strategies of argumentation to make your own writing more persuasive. Consider this excerpt from Ian Bogost's discussion of advertising in his book *Persuasive Games*, in which he sets up a theoretical foundation that he will later use in his discussion of "persuasion games" (short interactive games designed to advertise a product). As you read this selection, look carefully for the strategies Bogost uses to support his analysis.

PERSUASIVE GAMES
Ian Bogost

There are three important types of advertising that can participate in such persuasion games: *demonstrative, illustrative,* and *associative* advertising.

    Demonstrative advertising provides direct information. These ads communicate tangibles about the nature of a product. This type of advertising is closely related to the product as commodity; demonstrative ads focus on the functional utility of products and services. Among this category of advertisements, one might think of the "sponsor messages" of the golden age of television, ads that featured live demonstrations of detergent or "miracle" appliances. Also among this category are the copy-heavy print ads of the 1960s–1980s (examples abound in back issues of magazines like *National Geographic*), as well as modern-day television infomercials.

    Ads like these focus on communicating the features and function of products or services. Consider [a] magazine ad for

Here Bogost uses **classification/division** to taxonomize different types of advertising: he takes a larger category (advertising) and breaks it into component parts.

Having established the different parts, he now moves to **definition**.

To clarify his definition of demonstrative advertising, Bogost gives a brief list of **examples**.

He follows up with a more detailed **example** that relies on more detailed **description** to help the reader understand his point.

As he moves to the second category of advertising that he has identified above, he once again leads with **definition** and follows up with **example** and **description**.

Notice the use of **comparison-contrast** here to promote dialogue between the different terms and help his reader better understand how each of these types of advertising works.

In the paragraph that follows in the original chapter, Bogost proceeds to use the same structure to explore the concept of associative advertising.

a Datsun hatchback [from the 1970s]. In the aftermath of the oil crisis of the 1970s, the ad foregrounds the car's focus on fuel economy, a tangible benefit, with the large headline "Nifty Fifty." Additional copy at the bottom of the ad further rationalizes and defends this position, citing a five-speed transmission with overdrive as a contributor to the car's increased fuel economy.

Illustrative advertising communicates indirect information. Illustrative ads can communicate both tangibles and intangibles about a product, with a focus on the marginal utility, or the incremental benefit of buying this product over another, or over not buying at all. These ads often contextualize a product or service differently than demonstrative ads, focusing more on social and cultural context. Consider another automobile ad, this one for a Saab sedan [...]. Unlike the Datsun ad, which depicts the vehicle in an empty space, the Saab ad places the car on a road and uses photographic panning to telegraph motion. No additional copy accompanies the ad, but the vehicle in motion serves to illustrate speed. The ad makes a case for the liveliness of the vehicle despite its "practical" four-door sedan frame, which is clearly visible in the center of the image.

2.2 What role do the rhetorical appeals of *pathos*, *logos*, and *ethos* play in persuasion?

UNDERSTANDING THE RHETORICAL APPEALS

The rhetorical strategies we've examined so far can be filtered through the lens of classical modes of persuasion dating back to 500 BCE. In writing about persuasion, Aristotle differentiated between **inartistic** and **artistic proofs**. He defined *inartistic proofs* as elements available to the writer but not created by the writer. Statistics, laws, quotations from others, facts: these all fall under the category of inartistic proofs. *Artistic proofs*, conversely, comprise arguments that the speaker constructs through rhetorical strategies. The strategies and structures of argumentation analyzed above are examples of artistic proofs; they might leverage facts or external evidence, but the arguments themselves are designed by the author. For the rest of this chapter, we'll continue to focus on artistic proofs and how you can learn to wield such strategies of argument effectively in composing your own persuasive texts.

From Aristotle's perspective, artistic proofs were derived from one of three rhetorical appeals: the formal terms are *pathos*, *logos*, and *ethos*. You might recognize them more readily by how they work: *pathos* operates through developing an emotional connection with the audience; *logos* persuades through facts and reasoning; and *ethos* functions as an appeal to the authority or credibility of a person's character.

Since, as we discussed in Chapter 1, rhetoric involves careful and strategic assessment of the rhetorical situation in constructing persuasive arguments, let's look carefully at each of the appeals in turn to help you understand how you might use them in your own writing.

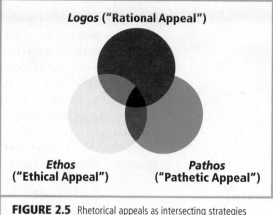

FIGURE 2.5 Rhetorical appeals as intersecting strategies of persuasion.

AT A GLANCE

Rhetorical Appeals

- *Pathos*, or "the pathetic appeal," refers to an appeal to the emotions: the speaker attempts to put the audience into a particular emotional state so that they will be more receptive to the speaker's message. Inflammatory language, sad stories, appeals to nationalist sentiments, and jokes are all examples of *pathos*.

- *Logos* entails rational argument: it appeals to reason and persuades the audience through clear reasoning and evidence. Statistics, facts, definitions, and formal proofs, as well as interpretations such as syllogisms or deductively reasoned arguments, are all examples of "the logical appeal."

- *Ethos* is an appeal to authority or character; according to Aristotle, *ethos* means the character or goodwill of the speaker. Today we also consider the speaker's reliance on authority, credibility, or benevolence when discussing strategies of *ethos*. Although we call this third mode of persuasion the "ethical appeal," it does not strictly mean the use of ethics or ethical reasoning. Rather, *ethos* is the deliberate use of the speaker's character as a mode of persuasion.

Appeals to Emotion: *Pathos*

Roughly defined as "suffering" or "feeling" in its original Greek, the term *pathos* actually means to put the audience in a particular mood or frame of mind. Modern derivations of the word *pathos* include *pathology* and *pathetic,* and indeed we speak of *pathos* as "the pathetic appeal." But *pathos* is more a technique than a state: writers use it as a tool of persuasion to establish an intimate connection with the audience by soliciting powerful emotions.

We encounter ads that rely on *pathos* all the time, and, indeed, the composition of an ad often taps our emotions in ways that we barely recognize. Many use description or an analogy to set the mood, such as displaying an idyllic landscape scene to serve as the backdrop for a commercial for engagement rings or retirement funds or choosing a color scheme (bright primary colors or muted pastels) to create a specific effect. The music in the commercials, whether on television or radio, also produces a *pathos* effect on the audience, from the catchy, up-beat jingles that create a positive association with a product to well-known songs that are repurposed to appeal to a particular generation, demographic, or type of consumer. For instance, when Hyundai filmed a commercial for its Sonata model car using Mozart's playful Piano Sonata #11 as the score, their message was clear: this car is sophisticated, classic, and yet still embodies a sense of lively fun.

Even more blatant examples of *pathos* in advertising abound: from an Iams dog food commercial showing an Irish Wolfhound exuberantly greeting his owner just home from a military tour abroad; to a Subaru commercial where a mother looks into her car and sees not her teenager, but a 5-year-old version of her, getting ready to drive off in the car by herself for the first time; to the previously mentioned Budweiser "Brotherhood" example (Figure 2.2), where a man is reunited with a horse he had sold. In each case, the advertisement relies on creating an emotionally laden narrative to sell its product. The power of such stories is perhaps no better used than in commercials that sell life insurance or property insurance. The formulaic, yet powerful template for these types of *pathos*-infused ads are no doubt familiar to you: show images of devastated homes and families, especially small children; lead the audience step by step through the story of destruction or death; offer up the product (insurance) as a way to mitigate the depicted tragedy.

However, *pathos* does not only operate through triggering the highs and lows of sentiment in audiences. Sometimes the *pathos* appeal is more subtle, operating by evoking deep feelings such as patriotism, indignation, even hope or fantasy. Consider the Porsche commercial showing a sleek red car speeding along a windy mountain road, the Jeep "beautiful lands" commercial that shows the Renegade crisscrossing breath-taking landscapes in the United States and abroad, or the Fiat ad playing on the car's unique, quirky design. Each of these ads uses *pathos* to produce a specific feeling in viewers: I want to drive fast, wind in my hair; I want to explore and see the world; I want to stand out in a crowd and have fun.

You are probably even more familiar with another type of *pathos* appeal—the appeal to sexuality. Clearly, sex sells. Look at Victoria's Secret models who posed in near nudity or at Abercrombie & Fitch or Hollister poster displays featuring models more likely to show off their toned abs than a pair of jeans, and you can see how advertisers tend to appeal more to nonrational impulses than to our powers of reasoning. Perfume and cologne advertisers in particular often use the rhetoric of sexuality to sell their products, whether it be Calvin Klein's Eternity Aqua, Ralph Lauren's Polo Black, or even Axe's cologne commercials, which demonstrate the "Axe effect" by showing cologne-wearers being mobbed by bikini-clad women. Such ads work cleverly to sell fragrance, not on the merits of the scent or on its chemical composition, but through the visual rhetoric of sexuality and our emotional responses to it.

Yet there is an even more powerful *pathos* appeal: what some students refer to as *humos*. Humor remains one of the most effective forms of persuasion; against our more rational impulses, the ads that make us laugh are usually the ones we remember. To prove this point, you need only think back to last year's Superbowl ads: Which ads do you remember? Which ads did you talk over with your friends during and after the game? Probably most of the ones you recall relied on humor. In fact, some of the most memorable—and at times controversial ads—combine a *pathos* appeal to sexuality with humor. Case and point? Carl's Juniors long-lasting ad campaign showing a scantily clad woman messily eating a burger. The arguments such ads make may not always be the most logically sound, but the way they foster a connection with the audience makes them persuasive nonetheless.

Many of these same *pathos*-based strategies can be used in academic writing to foster a connection with your audience. You might use the **first-person perspective** to invite your readers into your point of view or, in some cases, use **second-person direct address** to speak to them directly. You might include vivid **description, narration,** or **example** to draw them in, supplemented with careful attention to powerful **word choice** and **figurative language** (such as using metaphor, analogy, or personification). Depending on your rhetorical situation and purpose, you might even experiment with **tone** and **humor** as a way to get your readers to engage with your argument.

Consider, for instance, the way in which pop culture critic Doug Barry increases the persuasiveness of his analysis by using *pathos* to connect with his audience in his analysis of a Tide laundry detergent commercial below:

Ah, the American father—that beer-guzzling, football-watching, hamburger-grilling lump of a human who so often prostrates himself on the family couch before his stupefied children like a sedated gorilla has been soundly mocked as a hapless oaf since, well, General Yepanchin in *The Idiot*. Then, of course, there's *every sitcom father ever*, even lumpy dinosaur Earl Sinclair, whose mere presence in the sitcom-dad pantheon suggests that working and middle class fathers have been supreme idiots since human fathers even existed.

It's refreshing, then, to see a dad not play the dumb-dad clown every now and then. When Stereotypical American Clown Father appears in a commercial for some housekeeping chemical, it's usually to demonstrate his utter incompetence (dads don't clean, silly! they spill rib juice all over the couch as they slip into a meat stupor over the course of a lazy Sunday afternoon) and promptly exit stage right, a freshly chastised goon. A (relatively) new Tide commercial, however, doesn't rely on goon-father to hawk its detergent—Tide Dad is just a normal parent having a blast playing-pretend with his daughter. And what do they play in this blissful domestic imaginarium? Everything from fairy tale princess to wild west sheriff (hint: dad has to stay in a jail made of chairs until his power-drunk daughter decides to free him).

Many authors use narrative as a *pathos* device since readers tend to react powerfully to storytelling; however, here we see Barry relying on alternative methods to produce a similar effect. He uses rich imagery and word choice to paint an engaging description of the American father's typical pop culture incarnation: notice how he employs unusual and catchy modifiers ("beer-guzzling," "football-watching," "hamburger-grilling"); how he integrates striking imagery ("sedated gorilla," "hapless oaf," "dumb-dad clown"); how his allusions anchor his description in other cultural texts (General Yepanchin, Earl Sinclair). Even his strategies of emphasis—from italics for highlighting a point to rhetorical questions and his comical parenthetical asides—foster his connection with the reader by capturing his voice vividly. In its original online version, Barry's analysis was accompanied by a link to the commercial itself, which offered yet another mode of engaging the audience on an emotional level. In your own writing, you might similarly use *pathos*-driven language and images to solidify your argument and persuade your reader.

Exaggerated Uses of Pathos.   Although writers often use pathos to move their audiences, sometimes they exaggerate the appeal to emotion for dramatic effect. While the intention might be to enhance persuasion, this misuse of pathos can significantly undermine an argument's effectiveness. Let's look at some of the most typical emotional fallacies:

- **Scare tactic:** In this case, *pathos* capitalizes on the audience's fears, sometimes unreasonably, to make a point. For instance, Allstate Insurance's recent Mayhem commercials—with actor Dean Winter personifying different types of "mayhem" (from heavy snow that collapses your garage roof, to a screaming toddler in the backseat, to a raccoon in your attic)—employ this sort of tactic to prompt viewers to update their insurance coverage.
- **Slippery slope:** This variation of the *scare tactic* suggests that one act will lead to a chain of events that results in an unforeseen, inevitable, and (usually) undesirable conclusion, without providing any evidence to support the claim. An AT&T smartphone commercial put a positive spin on this fallacy, demonstrating how the simple act of being able to check a train schedule on his smartphone led a man to meet his future wife, and then experience a series of positive life events that culminated in his son becoming the president of the United States.

- **Oversentimentalization:** The overabundant use of *pathos* can outweigh a focus on relevant issues. Occasionally, for instance, organizations like PETA overreach in their emotional appeals, showing the results of animal abuse in such graphic detail that audiences actually tune out in horror rather than take action.

- **Bandwagon appeal:** Sometimes called the *ad populum* argument, this emotional fallacy hinges on the premise that since everyone else is doing something, you should too. Pepsi's campaign "The Choice of a New Generation" used the bandwagon appeal to argue that if you wanted to be identified with part of the new, hip generation, you needed to drink Pepsi.

- **False need:** In this fallacy, the author amplifies a perceived need or creates a completely new one. Companies market their products based on false needs all the time: think of the commercials you've seen advertising men's or women's razors, transparent Band-Aids, cinch-tie garbage bags, "smart" water, or lash-curling mascara. How many of those products reflect actual *needs*, and how many rely on a false need that has been constructed by the company or advertiser?

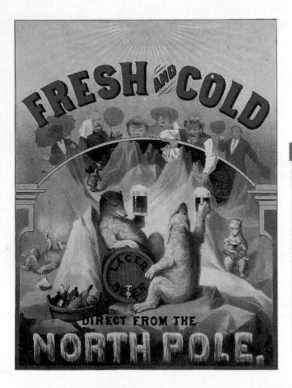

WRITER'S PRACTICE   MyWritingLab

Consider how the nineteenth-century advertisement in the figure uses *pathos* to make its argument. What is its main pitch about why the consumer should buy Lager Beer, and how does it back that up with visually and textually? What other strategies of argumentation do you see it at work in the ad? Write down some notes and compare your analysis with a partner's. For added challenge, compare this marketing strategy to that currently used by twenty-first beer and soft drink companies to sell their products. What similarities and differences do you see?

Appeals to Reason: *Logos*

Although some call *logos* the "logical appeal," it pertains to more than just formal logic. While *pathos* moves an audience on a nonrational level, *logos* engages our critical reasoning faculties to make a point. As a writer, you use *logos* when you construct an essay around facts and reason. That is, you provide both a solid line of reasoning as well as evidence to support it.

A *logos*-based argument can take many forms. You might use:

- **Inductive reasoning,** a line of argument that moves from specific examples to a generalized conclusion. For instance, if you reflect on all the times that you pulled all-nighters and ended up falling asleep in your afternoon classes, you might inductively reason that pulling all-nighters have a negative effect on your grade (generalized conclusion). In an inductive essay, you might open with a question or general statement, then move through specific examples to arrive at a statement of your argument in your conclusion; alternately, you might closely examine a particular case study and specific example and then draw a broader, more general conclusion from it.

- **Deductive reasoning,** a form of logic that bases argument on how premises (often unstated assumptions) work together to prove the argument. The idea behind deductive reasoning is that if the premises are accepted as true, then the argument must be true. For instance:

    Premise 1: A college degree helps students find a fulfilling career.

    Premise 2: Everyone wants a fulfilling career.

    Argument from premises: University students, by virtue of being enrolled in college, do so to position themselves to have a fulfilling career.

  In essays, this form of argument often means you lead with a strong thesis statement, which you then support with examples to arrive at a conclusion.

- **A cause-and-effect strategy of development** that demonstrates logically how one idea, event, or element caused another. As we've discussed earlier in this chapter, the logic of causality can be a strong support for an argument.

- **A reliance on example** to support claims. By providing evidence—whether in the form of statistical evidence, empirical data, proven facts, testimony, or quotations from authorities or experts—you can demonstrate that abstract concepts and generalizations have a grounding in concrete example. For instance, while the statement "Companies rely too heavily on ethnic stereotype in their marketing campaigns" might seem an interesting claim, it becomes much more persuasive when supported by examples from recent commercials that illustrate this point.

Let's build on this last example and get look more carefully at how *logos* works by turning our attention once again to advertising. In that medium, the mode of persuasion we call *logos* often operates through the written text; significantly, the Greek word *logos* can be translated as "word," indicating the way in which we, culturally, often look to words as repositories of fact and reason. However, in advertising, just as in academic writing, *logos* also emerges through the use of quantifiable data, statistics, and facts. The type of *logos*-based reasoning found in the Chevrolet Volt marketing display in Figure 2.6 appears in many ads that you may also be familiar with: think, for instance, of a computer ad that juxtaposes a striking photo of a laptop

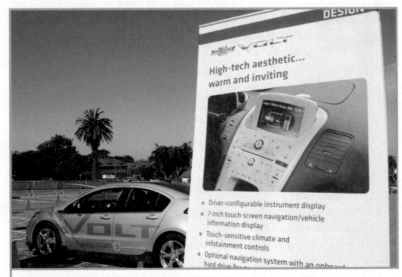

FIGURE 2.6 This Chevrolet Volt promotional display is designed to persuade its reader through *logos* by listing the car's various features.

with a chart detailing its processor type, memory capacity, screen size, and graphics features; a commercial for a bank that features a smiling agent listing the reasons to open a checking account at that branch; the smartphone commercial that rattles off facts about its data plan, wireless coverage, and contracts terms. In each case, the advertisement drives its point through facts, evidence, and reason.

Some might even argue that *logos* as an appeal underlies almost all advertising, specifically because most advertising uses an implicit *causal argument:* if you buy this product, then you or your life will be like the one featured in the ad. Often the associations are explicit: if you use Pantene shampoo, then your hair will be shinier; if you buy Tide detergent, then your clothes will be cleaner; if you buy a Subaru, then your family will be safer driving on the road. Sometimes the *cause-and-effect* argument is more subtle: buying Sure deodorant will make you more confident; drinking Coke will make you happier; wearing Nikes will make you perform better on the court. In each case, *logos*, or the use of logical reasoning, is the tool of persuasion responsible for the ad's argumentative force.

In academic situations, writers often privilege a *logos*-based approach to persuasion because many scholarly claims draw on evidence from research to substantiate assertions. Consider the way Laurence Bowen and Jill Schmid use *logos* as a strategy of argumentation in this passage from "Minority Presence and Portrayal in Mainstream Magazine Advertising: An Update":

> Some might argue that the small number of minorities featured in mainstream magazine advertising may be due to a very deliberate media strategy that successfully targets minorities in specialized and minority media. However, each of the magazines analyzed does have a minority readership and, in some cases, that readership is quite substantial. For example, according to *Simmons 1993 Study of Media and Markets*, the Hispanic readership of *Life* is 9.9%, yet the inclusion of Hispanics in *Life's* advertisements was only .8%. *Cosmopolitan* has a 11.3% Black readership, yet only 4.3% of the advertisements included Blacks; 13.3% of the magazines' readership is Hispanic and only .5% of the advertisements use Hispanics.

Notice how the authors drive their point home through reference to their research with mainstream magazines as well as to statistical data that they have both uncovered and analyzed. Their use of such concrete information and examples makes their argument much more convincing than had they provided a more general rebuttal to the statement that begins their paragraph. In this way, appeals to logic can take on many forms, including interpretations of "hard evidence," such as found in syllogisms (formal, structured arguments), reasoned arguments, closing statements in law, inferences in the form of statistical models, and appeals to "common sense" or cultural assumptions.

Logical Fallacies. As with *pathos, logos* can be susceptible to misuse. Such mistaken or misleading uses of *logos*, commonly called **logical fallacies,** often involve faulty reasoning that undermines the validity of an argument.

- **Post hoc ergo propter hoc fallacy:** This fallacy confuses *cause* and *effect*, namely, the idea that because something happened first (showering with an aloe-enhanced body gel), it causes something that happened afterward (getting a person you like to ask you out on a date).

- **Cum hoc ergo propter hoc fallacy:** A variation of the *post hoc fallacy*, this type of argument is often called a *correlation-causation fallacy* because it suggests that since two unrelated events happen at the same time (are correlated), they should thus be interpreted as *cause* and *effect*. For instance, the following syllogism is an example of a *cum hoc fallacy*: (1) a teenager plays his varsity basketball game wearing his new Air Jordans; (2) the teenager makes many key rebounds and jump shots while playing the game; (3) the Air Jordans caused his success in the game.

- **The hasty generalization:** Writers who use *hasty generalizations* draw conclusions too quickly without providing enough supporting evidence or considering all the nuances of the issue. A comic example of this type of argument can be found in a commercial for the Taco Bell bacon club chalupa taco: a young woman confides to her friend that she's carrying a chalupa tucked in her purse because "guys love bacon," a generalization the ad attempts to substantiate by showing her, moments later, surrounded by men who had been drawn to the woman by the "intoxicating" smell.

- **The either-or argument:** This fallacy involves the oversimplification of a complicated issue, reducing it to a choice between two diametrically opposed choices that ignore other possible scenarios. We see this fallacy often in commercials that compare a pair of competing products (iPhone versus Android, McDonalds versus Burger King, Verizon versus AT&T) without taking into consideration the other alternatives available to the consumer.

- **Stacking the evidence:** An argument that *stacks the evidence* presents only one side of an issue. Political candidates frequently use this strategy in their campaign ads by stating facts and data that support only their policy platform, without presenting an issue in its full complexity.
- **Begging the question:** This form of circular logic uses an argument as evidence for itself, thereby evading the issue at hand. For instance, consider the conversation between a mother and her six year old daughter in a commercial for the Wannabee-Mommy doll:

  > Mother: So I guess it's that time again – time to start your birthday list. What do you want for your birthday?
  >
  > Daughter: The Wannabee-Mommy doll, of course! I don't need anything else.
  >
  > Woman: Really? That's it? That's all you want?
  >
  > Daughter: Yup. Everyone wants the Wannabee-Mommy doll. Jessica want it. Kirsten wants it. Maria wants it …
  >
  > Woman: [interrupting] Really? Why does everyone want the doll so badly?
  >
  > Daughter: Mommy, don't you know anything? Because it's the most popular doll of the year!

  In this quick exchange, the daughter "begs the question" by using the fact that the doll was popular (i.e. many children want it) to argue for why so many children want it. The commercial could have avoided this fallacy simply by changing its line of reasoning, linking the toy's popularity to its design, quality, marketing or even its price.
- **The red herring or non sequitor:** Some arguments employ unrelated information or a *non sequitor* (in Latin, literally meaning "does not follow") in order to distract the audience's attention from the issue at hand. A sudden shift of topic or focus in an ad can function as a *red herring*. Dow Chemical's ad "The Human Element" shows a plethora of artistic and ecofriendly scenes that make the logical argument that the company relates to human connection and nature, but in fact serve as a red herring to distract the viewer from Dow's massive industrial production of oil, gas, and electronic products.
- **Straw man argument:** The visual metaphor of the *straw man* effectively represents this fallacy; the writer sets up a fake or distorted representation of a counterargument so as to have something to easily argue against and to present the writer's own position in a more favorable light. Here's one example: during the 2012 presidential

campaign, vice presidential candidate Paul Ryan accused President Obama of using *straw man* tactics, citing the way the president characterized Republicans as anti-government and pessimistic about the country in his speeches. According to Ryan, in doing so, Obama was misrepresenting the opposing party's stance so as to ingratiate himself with the American people.

■ **Equivocation:** Arguments that fall prey to this fallacy use ambiguous terminology that misleads the audience or confuses the issue. For instance, a 2008 commercial for California's Proposition 8 undermined its argument for marriage equality by using the term "rights" indiscriminately to refer to both legal rights and moral rights.

■ **False analogy:** While an *analogy* can be a powerful strategy of argumentation, a *false analogy* claims that two things resemble each other when they actually do not. For instance, one Mercedes-Benz commercial suggested that refraining from eating ice cream is like refraining from buying one of their cars, when in fact there is very little connection between the two actions.

WRITER'S PRACTICE   MyWritingLab

Look carefully at the hypothetical advertising pitches below, each one of which represents a flawed use of *logos* as a marketing strategy. For each one, identify which type of logical fallacy it contains: *post hoc ergo propter hoc*, *cum hoc ergo propter hoc*, hasty generalization, either/or, stacking the evidence, begging the question, red herring, straw man, equivocation, or false analogy. Then, consider ways in which the pitch might be revised so as to make a more solid *logos*-based argument.

• Buy American because our products are made right here in the United States!
• In these increasingly complex financial times, if you try to manage your finances without a trained professional advisor, you could well find your life savings wiped out. Protect your savings: contact your local GoodCents agent today for a full portfolio review.
• Corey uses Sparkle Fresh mouthwash every morning and recently received a promotion at work. If you start using Sparkle Fresh, your career will take off too!
• Other paper towel companies don't care about global warming or climate change. Use Greener World paper towels: there's always 100% recycled paper on every roll.

- Buying the right car is like choosing the right spouse: you need to find one perfect for you. So choose a What-a-Catch-Car: it's dependable, affordable, and built to last.

For added challenge: find your own examples of writing that display logical fallacies; identify the fallacy and consider how to revise it in a way that eliminates the problematic use of *logos*.

Appeals to Character and Authority: *Ethos*

The last of the three classical appeals that we'll learn in this chapter is *ethos*—literally, "character." Perhaps you have used *ethos* in other disciplines to mean an argument based on ethical principles. But the *rhetorical* meaning of the term is slightly different: according to Aristotle, *ethos* works as a rhetorical strategy by establishing the goodwill or credibility of the writer or speaker. Based on the Aristotelian model, we can distinguish between three different operations of *ethos*:

1. *Ethos* based on practical skills and wisdom
2. *Ethos* based on virtue and goodness
3. *Ethos* based on goodwill toward the audience

When conceived in this way, the *ethos* appeal clearly functions as a very powerful persuasive tool by establishing a bond of trust with the audience. In fact, almost more than with any other appeal, *ethos* involves a critical awareness of audience. It is the audience who evaluates your "good character" or credibility as a writer and, therefore, the persuasiveness of your argument.

Another way to understand *ethos* is to think about it in terms of two different types: *situated ethos* and *invented ethos*. The first form refers to the credibility you possess because of your expertise (i.e., how you are *situated*) in a field; it is an authority you bring to your argument because of your own experience. For instance, when Nike signed Michael Jordan as a spokesperson for their basketball shoes, they were counting on his fame as an NBA player to sell their product; likewise, Gatorade traded on Jordan's career as an athlete to argue that he knew a good sports drink when he drank one.

Invented ethos, conversely, refers to the authority you create for yourself through rhetorical strategies rather than through situated expertise.

Namely, it is the way that an author or speaker persuades the audience of his trustworthiness on a subject that seems unrelated to his area of expertise. Advertising occasionally trades on the *invented ethos* of a spokesperson rather than expertise: when we are persuaded by the Geico's talking gecko lizard to consider buying insurance from the company, for instance, it is not because we recognize the lizard as an authority on car insurance; it is because his monologue in the commercial develops his likeability, his sincerity, and clear goodwill toward the audience.

As a writer, you rely on the *ethos* appeal at the most basic level every time you pick up a pen, open a blank document on your laptop, or proofread your essay—that is, you construct your *ethos* through your word choice, your tone, your grammar, your punctuation, and the way your present your argument. However, as our discussion above suggests, you can establish *ethos* in other ways as well. By establishing your authority in relation to the topic—whether because of your depth of knowledge or your close engagement with the subject—you help your readers trust your claims. By constructing a sense of **common ground** with your audience, you can invoke shared values to draw more of a connection with your audience. By using **credible sources** in your research, you attest to the quality of your argument and analytic methodology. Likewise, by respectfully acknowledging **other arguments**, you establish yourself as fair-minded and well-informed on your topic; whether you ultimately concede a point or refute the counterargument, your willingness to entertain alternative positions increases your *ethos*. Consider one more characteristic of *ethos*: while your *situated ethos* rarely changes, your *invented ethos* can fluctuate and shift depending on how effectively you construct your sense of credibility in your text.

The example that follows demonstrates how one writer uses *ethos* to set up the foundations for a complex argument. In this excerpt from her famous piece, "Sex, Lies, and Advertising," Gloria Steinem, founding editor of the feminist magazine *Ms.*, deliberately builds her *ethos* through an opening narrative. Her decision is strategic: she anticipates that the issue itself—the constraints that advertisers put on the content of women's magazines—might produce a skeptical reaction from her readers. Accordingly, she devotes her opening paragraphs to establishing both the validity of the problem and her own qualifications in terms of addressing it.

About three years ago, as *glasnost* was beginning and *Ms.* seemed to be ending, I was invited to a press lunch for a Soviet official. He entertained us with anecdotes about new problems of democracy in his country. Local Communist leaders were being criticized in their media for the first time, he explained, and they were angry.

"So I'll have to ask my American friends," he finished pointedly, "how more subtly to control the press." In the silence that followed, I said, "Advertising."

The reporters laughed, but later, one of them took me aside: How dare I suggest that freedom of the press was limited? How dare I imply that his newsweekly could be influenced by ads?

I explained that I was thinking of advertising's media-wide influence on most of what we read. Even newsmagazines use "soft" cover stories to sell ads, confuse readers with "advertorials," and occasionally self-censor on subjects known to be a problem with big advertisers.

But I also explained, I was thinking especially of women's magazines. There, it isn't just a little content that's devoted to attracting ads, it's almost all of it. That's why advertisers—not readers—have always been the problem for *Ms.* As the only women's magazine that didn't supply what the ad world euphemistically describes as "supportive editorial atmosphere" or "complementary copy" (for instance, articles that praise food/fashion/beauty subjects to "support" and "complement" food/fashion/beauty ads), *Ms.* could never attract enough advertising to break even.

"Oh, *women's* magazines," the journalist said with contempt. "Everybody knows they're catalogs—but who cares? They have nothing to do with journalism."

I can't tell you how many times I've had this argument in 25 years of working for many kinds of publications. Except as moneymaking machines—"cash cows" as they are so elegantly called in the trade—women's magazines are rarely taken seriously. Though changes being made by women have been called more far-reaching than the industrial revolution—and though many editors try hard to reflect some of them in the few pages left

To build her *ethos*, Steinem first mentions that she was invited to a lunch with a political figure, indicating her importance in journalistic circles.

Next, after humorously introducing her main argument (that freedom of the press is curtailed by advertising), she demonstrates how she gracefully addresses counterarguments.

Then, she utilizes the discourse of magazine publishing ("supportive editorial atmosphere" and "complementary copy") to remind her audience of her insider status in the industry.

Lastly, she informs the reader directly about her long professional history working in media ("… in 25 years of working for many kinds of publications"). In this move, she situates her *ethos* not only in the current moment of her opening narrative but also in her continued involvement in the publishing field.

> to them after all the ad-related subjects have been covered—the magazines serving the female half of the country are still far below the journalistic and ethical strands of news and general interest publications. Most depressing of all, this doesn't even rate an exposé.

Having established her *ethos* in this opening section, Steinem can then move forward with her argument, which is driven largely by an accumulation of examples designed to further underscore her expertise and authority. Thus, *ethos* is a driving force in the persuasiveness of her writing.

To continue our exploration of the complexities of *ethos*, let's look to advertising once again and see how companies have long recognized the persuasive power of *ethos*. In fact, a brand logo is in essence *ethos* distilled into a single symbol: it transmits in a single icon the entire reputation of a company, organization, or brand identity. From the Nike swoosh to McDonald's golden arches or the Apple computer apple, symbols serve to mark (or brand) products with *ethos*. When Apple began construction on a new store in Madrid, for example, the iconic Apple logo itself was all the marketing it needed to publicize its new store (see Figure 2.7).

FIGURE 2.7 Apple used its logo on a billboard surrounding its construction site to advertise a new store in Madrid.

Yet the power of the brand logo as a seat of *ethos* relies on the company's overall reputation with the consumer—a reputation that the company carefully cultivates through advertising campaigns. Many companies, for instance, trade on *ethos* by using spokespeople in their advertising campaigns. You've probably seen ads that invoke the practical skills or knowledge (*situated ethos*) of the celebrity to sell a product: basketball superstar LeBron James selling basketball shoes or Martha Stewart selling linens, towels, and dishware. Sometimes companies even rely on this strategy when using a less famous spokesperson; for instance, we trust Flo from the Progressive commercials because of her clear, empathetic personality (*invented ethos*) and the expertise and information she shares during their commercials (*situated ethos*).

However, many campaigns rely not only on the spokesperson's expertise, but also on the person's star appeal, character, and virtue. Consider the power of the billboard shown in Figure 2.8. On display during the summer of 2012, this billboard used gold-medalist Cullen Jones's fame to vouch for Citibank's reputation and quality of services. We might not believe that

FIGURE 2.8 A Citibank billboard in New York City leverages Olympian Cullen Jones's *ethos* to draw in new customers.

Jones knows much about banking, but we trust him as a recognizable and admirable public figure. We find his argument persuasive because of our "knowledge" of his character and his willingness to put his reputation on the line to promote a product. Of course, ad campaigns based on celebrity endorsements—specifically those based on Aristotle's categories of virtue and goodness—can backfire. Lance Armstrong's 2012 confession about his steroid use left advertisers from Nike to Giro and Radioshack scrambling to distance themselves from their endorsement deals with the world-class cyclist.

Clearly, *ethos* matters to companies because so much of their business relies on their reputation. For this reason, we often come across ads that market not a product but a corporate *ethos* intended to establish that company's credibility. One recurrent example of this appears in various oil company ads that have emerged over the last few years. Battling the perception that Big Oil, heedless of its role in global warming, is motivated only by ever-increasing profits, these ads inform us endlessly of each company's "green" policies and efforts to give back to the earth. In addition, *ethos* can be used as a tool in attack ads. Often, companies deliberately attempt to undermine the *ethos* of their competition as a way of promoting their own products. You probably have seen ads of this sort, perhaps a DIRECTV ad that criticized cable providers or a Pepsi commercial that suggested their beverage was more refreshing than Coke. You might have even seen one of the Samsung smartphone commercials that targeted Apple—whether spots that mocked iPhone users standing in endless lines for the newest product release or commercials that demonstrated how the Samsung features easily trumped the capabilities of its Apple-brand competitor. In each case, the deliberate *comparison-contrast* builds up one company's *ethos* at another's expense.

Misuses of Ethos. Since *ethos* derives from credibility or trustworthiness, misuses of *ethos* tend to involve a breach of trust between the author and the audience. For this reason, you should take special care as a writer not to abuse this ethical contract with your reader. What follows are some of the most common misuses of *ethos*:

- ■ ***Ad hominem***: This strategy attempts to persuade by reducing the credibility of opposing positions through attacks on a person's character. Rather than focus on the argument itself, *ad hominem* criticizes the speaker or writer who makes the argument. We see *ad hominem* at work most often in political campaign advertisements, where candidates focus less on the issues at hand and instead emphasize their opponents' weaknesses. This misuse of *ethos* also happens in commercials where companies attack each other for the way they run their businesses rather than the quality of their products.

- *Argument from authority*: This type of argument involves a misrepresentation of skills and wisdom; the writer contends to be an authority—or holds another up to be an authority—based on an overinflated or fallacious suggestion of expertise. For instance, Oprah Winfrey came under fire in 2012 for tweeting an endorsement for the Windows Surface from her iPad; her credibility as a Surface user was immediately called into question.

- *Association fallacies*: This fallacy often takes the form of "guilt by association," where an argument is dismissed because it is associated with an undesirable person or position. Conversely, this fallacy can also unfairly promote or advocate an argument based on unrelated positive associations. We can find prominent examples of this technique at work in the political advertising during the 2008 presidential campaign: both Barack Obama and John McCain released commercials that used *guilt by association* to denigrate each other's characters.

- *Appeal to anonymous authority*: This type of argument references broad, unspecified groups as its authority. For instance, while the taglines "Four out of five dentists surveyed ..." or "Studies indicate ..." lend some credibility to advertising campaigns, unless the ads provide tangible references to *which* dentists, *which* studies, and *what* context, the argument is ultimately empty and unsupported.

- *Authority over evidence*: This mode of argument involves the practice of overemphasizing authority or *ethos* rather than focusing on the merits of the evidence itself. Celebrity endorsements based on goodwill can verge on this fallacy.

WRITER'S PRACTICE   MyWritingLab

Review the different fallacies and misuses of appeals and then, alone or with a group, draft your own advertisement or commercial that clearly hinges on a particular fallacy of argument. Look ahead to Chapter 6 and Chapter 8 for strategies for developing your visual argument, whether as a storyboard for a commercial (Chapter 6) or a mock-up of an ad (Chapter 8). Write a cover memo for your draft in which you define the fallacy that you're illustrating and provide a brief analysis to underscore your point for your readers.

Combining the Rhetorical Appeals

As we've seen, the rhetorical appeals provide writers with powerful modes of persuading their audience. However, while each appeal functions as an effective mode of persuasion alone, in most cases, successful writers and communicators use them in combination, depending on their understanding of the rhetorical situation. As you might imagine, a text may employ a combined mode of persuasion, such as "passionate logic" (a rational argument written with highly charged prose), "good-willed *pathos*" (an emotional statement that relies on the character of the speaker to be believed), or "logical *ethos*" (a strong line of reasoning employed by a speaker to build authority). Since they appear so frequently in combination, you might find that conceptualizing *pathos*, *logos*, and *ethos* through a visual representation helps you to conceptualize how they relate to one another (see Figure 2.5).

To better understand how this works, let's look at Derek Thompson's analysis of brand advertising, originally published in *The Atlantic*. As you read, consider not only how he examines the *ethos* of branding, but the way in which he draws on the rhetorical appeals and various strategies of development in his own writing.

TURNING CUSTOMERS INTO CULTISTS

Why many companies now take their cues from cults.

Derek Thompson

The very first sentence relies on a *pathos* appeal by using **description** to capture the reader's interest.

In the third week of September, thousands of people organized themselves into neat lines that snaked along the city blocks of New York, Seattle, London, and dozens of other cities around the world. Sleeping in cardboard boxes, or keeping wakeful vigil through the night, they were participants in a biennial ritual: waiting in line to buy the new iPhone. Like most quasi-religious ceremonies, this one made little sense to outside observers. But the iPhone isn't just another phone, and Apple isn't just another phone manufacturer. It's a brand with a cult following, whose new products inspire sane people to squat for hours outside the nearest Apple store like Wiccans worshipping before Stonehenge.

What is a brand, anyway? The word seems gaseous in its ability to expand or contract to fill any space. Is it a promise, a lie, a reputation, or just a TED Talk buzzword? To companies and consumers, it can be any of those things, but to economists, the definition is simple: a brand is a signal, good or bad, that influences a consumer's decision to buy a product. And according to some economists, this signal is now in danger of being drowned out by the sheer amount of competing information on the Internet.

Research shows that typically, the more information consumers have, the better they are at ignoring corporate iconography. One 2014 study, for instance, found that pharmacists and physicians are three times less likely than the typical customer to buy national brands of headache medicine when cheaper store brands are available. If all consumers became as informed as medical experts, the study concluded, national headache-remedy brands would see their sales cut in half.

An economy filled with product experts would wreck certain brands, according to Itamar Simonson, a marketing professor at Stanford. Advertising thrives in markets where consumers are essentially clueless, often because quality is hard to assess before you buy the product (medicine, mattresses, wine). But on sites like Amazon or eBay, and across social media, information from other sources—ratings, reviews, comments from friends—is abundant. We're more likely to trust these signals precisely because they aren't beamed from corporate headquarters.

The market for high-definition TVs shows how too much access to information can destroy the brand premium. A TV's two most salient features—its screen size and resolution—are easy to look up, which makes it difficult for companies to charge extra for

Thompson continues to build on *pathos* as he gently develops the **analogy** suggested by his title with words like "ritual," "quasi-religious" and "ceremonies" and by describing Apple customers as "Wiccans worshipping before Stonehenge."

Thompson devotes his second paragraph to **definition** to lay a foundation for his analysis of contemporary brand marketing.

He now amplifies the *ethos* of his argument by including an **example** from a 2014 study and, in the next paragraph, a reference to the work of a Stanford professor.

By **contrasting** sites like eBay and Amazon to "markets where consumers are essentially clueless," Thompson strengthens his point.

a logo. Making televisions is a notoriously low-margin business, and the price of TVs has declined 95 percent since 1994. Sony's TV unit had been in the red for 10 years when the company spun it of in July.

And yet Apple, among many other brands, still means a great deal to a great many people. There are at least two reasons to question the notion that we're evolving into a race of Homo economicus super-shoppers, or ever will. First, even with perfect information, consumers often make imperfect decisions. Sites like Amazon provide an exhaustive array of choices, but having too many options can make us feel both overwhelmed as we shop (the "paradox of choice") and less satisfied with the choices we make (buyer's remorse). Returning to an old brand is a mental shortcut that is not only simple but also, in its own way, blissful.

More important, in categories like cars or clothes, brands aren't just signals of quality; they also help us communicate our identities. When somebody totes a Fendi bag or drives a Harley-Davidson chopper, she is sending a message (particularly when doing both at the same time). "People are meaning-seeking creatures," says Susan Fournier, a professor of management at Boston University. "The brands we buy and wear and use are symbols to express our identities. I don't think any of that is diluted by the Internet."

As branding loses some of its influence as a marker of quality, savvy companies are shifting their marketing efforts ever more strongly to this other source of brand advantage—identity and community. Recently, many of the most successful new brands have been looking to an unusual but powerful source of inspiration: religious cults.

In 1984, the British sociologist Eileen Barker published *The Making of a Moonie*, a seven-year investigation of the Unification Church, based on interviews with members of one of America's most popular cults. While many cults are portrayed as preying on the poor and uneducated, and particularly people from broken homes, Barker discovered that Moonies tended to be middle-class, with college degrees and stable families. The cult inculcated new members through simple techniques: weekend retreats, deep conversations, shared meals, and, most seductive, an environment of love and support.

Cults like the Moonies are built on the paradox that we feel most like ourselves when we're part of a group, says Douglas Atkin, the global head of community at the room-sharing company Airbnb, and the author of the 2004 book *The Culting of Brands*. "The common belief is that people join cults to conform," Atkin wrote. "Actually, the very opposite is true. They join to become more individual."

A number of Bay Area companies have come to incorporate this insight into their marketing strategies. In 2004, shortly after launching the restaurant-review site Yelp, the founders were struggling to grow the company. They decided to convene a gathering of about 100 power-users. The get-together "was a big success," Ligaya Tichy, who later served as Yelp's senior community manager, told me. "Bringing users together to share what they loved about the site led to a huge spike in activity. What we realized is that people aren't really motivated by companies. They're motivated by other people. We needed to get the message across: you are what makes this product cool." The number of reviewers on the site grew from 12,000 in 2005 to 100,000 in 2006.

Even today, Yelp still holds exclusive events for its most prolific reviewers, the Yelp Elite Squad, which a 2011 *Bloomberg Businessweek* article noted for its "cult influence." "People have been thinking about the similarities between cults and brands for years," Tichy says. "Only now you're really seeing people start to codify these practices with evangelists and groups like Yelp Elite."

In 2009, the founders of Airbnb were facing a similar challenge. They had a product that wasn't growing and a customer base that wasn't talking. "I call this period the Midwest of analytics," says co-founder Joe Gebbia. "It was the fattest growth you've ever seen."

Encouraged by an early investor to "meet your customers," Gebbia and his team flew to New York to visit with users, take pictures of their living rooms, and gather feedback. The team quickly realized that it needed to bring users together to share

Notice the way he uses first person plural here (we) to help the reader connect more personally with Douglas Atkin's theory.

Thompson builds his point through a moment of **narration** that underscores the **cause–effect** relationship between developing the interpersonal connections between users and increasing the popularity of the product.

He follows the Yelp example with a moment of **narration**, once again both providing evidence while also helping readers connect more with his points, using examples from companies they probably would be familiar with.

their experiences and enthusiasm. They organized the first Airbnb meet-up, which has since been replicated more than 1,000 times around the world. "I don't think of it as a cult," Gebbia says. "We're a community- driven brand, but at the same time, we want every host in every home to recognize that they're all individuals, and to use Airbnb as an expression of their individuality."

One of the hallmarks of a cult is that members unite to oppose what they see as an oppressive or illegitimate mainstream culture. Collaborative-economy companies—from Airbnb to the ride-sharing service Uber—have proved particularly savvy at exploiting this sense, and in so doing converting both merchants and consumers (the line between which sometimes blurs). But companies like Apple show that the creation of a cult mentality can be just as powerful with customers of regular goods—even products that have grown so popular, they would seem to be poor markers of individuality or special identity.

"Apple was more of a cult in the 1980s, when it was the converted few supporting the company against Microsoft and IBM," says Jennifer Edson Escalas, an associate professor of marketing at Vanderbilt University. From its famous hammer-smashing "1984" ad against IBM to its 1998 commercial "Crazy Ones," Apple has been deliberate in reinforcing an us-against-the-world ethos. The fact that it has preserved its devoted following while becoming larger than its opponents "shows that culting is useful, even when it's misleading," Escalas says.

It might seem creepy that some successful marketers are taking their cues from cult theory. But all advertising is manipulation. This new wrinkle takes advantage of a particular vulnerability—our need to be unique and belong to a group at the same time. Even experts like Susan Fournier, who doubts that cults offer a relevant model for marketing, think that brands play an important role beyond the simple provision of economic information. "I'm more frightened by a world that assumes we are rational actors optimizing all the time, without a sense of emotional connection, comfort, stability, or belonging," she said. "Who would want that?"

---

*Thompson now returns to the cult comparison, reminding his reader of his **definition** of how a cult operates. This is an important paragraph for solidifying his argument, and transitioning back to Apple, the example he used in his introduction.*

He strategically inserts a direct quotation here from a source that explicitly connects a brand (Apple) with the cult phenomenon.

In his conclusion, he once again uses word choice ("creepy"; the use of first person) to solidify his pathos connection with the reader, while also addressing a possible counter argument. Notice also how the first sentence of his conclusion functions as a statement of his argument, showing his use of an inductive line of reasoning (many examples, leading to a specific conclusion). He ends with a provocative question from one of his sources that asks the reader to consider the interplay between logos, ethos and pathos in brand marketing.

CONSIDERING CONTEXT AND VALUES: *KAIROS* AND *DOXA*

2.3 How can I shape my argument based on time, place, and shared values?

As you can tell from the examples we've examined so far, a successful argument must take into account not only the *rhetorical situation* but also the context—or right time and place—as well as the values of an audience. That is why the Citibank billboard of Cullen Jones shown in Figure 2.8 had tremendous resonance when first displayed right after the London Olympics in 2012, but was passed over in favor of a more timely ad once "Olympics fever" had died down. In ancient Greece rhetoricians called this aspect of the rhetorical situation *kairos*—namely, attention to the right time and place for an argument.

In your own writing, you should consider *kairos* along with the other aspects of the rhetorical situation: audience, text, and writer. It is important to recognize the *kairos*—the opportune historical, ideological, or cultural moment—of a text when analyzing its rhetorical force. You undoubtedly already consider the context for persuasive communication in your everyday life. For instance, whether you are asking a friend to dinner or a professor for a recommendation, your assessment of the timeliness and the appropriate strategies for that time probably determine the shape your argument takes. In essence, by picking the right moment and place to make your case, you are in fact paying attention to the *kairos* of your argument.

Consider Coca-Cola's ad campaigns. Coke has exerted a powerful presence in the beverage industry for many years, in part because of its strategic advertising. During World War II, Coke ran a series of ads featuring servicemen and showing inspiring slices of Americana that built its campaign around the nationalistic sentiment of a specific cultural moment. Look at Figure 2.9, an advertisement for Coke from the 1940s. This picture

FIGURE 2.9 This Coca-Cola ad used *kairos* to create a powerful argument for its World War II audience.

uses *pathos* to appeal to the audience's sense of patriotism by featuring a row of seemingly carefree servicemen, leaning from the windows of a military bus, the refreshing Cokes in their hands producing smiles even far away from home. The picture draws in the audience by reassuring them on two fronts:

- It builds on the nationalistic pride in the young, handsome servicemen who so happily serve their country.
- It is designed to appease fears about the hostile climate abroad: as both the picture and the accompanying text assure us, Coca-Cola (and the servicemen) "goes along" and "gets a hearty welcome."

The power of this message relates directly to *kairos*. An ad such as this one, premised on patriotism and pride in military service, would be most persuasive during wartime when many more people tend to support the spirit of nationalism and therefore would be moved by the image of the young serviceman shipping off to war. It is through understanding the *kairos* of this advertisement that you can appreciate the strength of the ad's rhetorical appeal.

An awareness of *kairos* likewise helps us see how even more in a contemporary setting, companies can develop a marketing campaign whose success relies on its timeliness. For instance, in 2015, Lane Bryant launched its "I'm No Angel" campaign, which featured lingerie models staring provocatively from the pages of magazines, TV screens, and billboards (Figure 2.10).

On the surface, the campaign relies on a *pathos* appeal to sexuality, both in terms of the image and the provocative tagline. However, our analysis of the argument becomes sharper when we consider how *kairos* comes into play. Both the text and image implicitly are in dialogue with a *different* advertisement: Victoria's Secret's advertising for its "Angel" line. Often under fire for presenting a waif-like version of ideal feminine beauty, Victoria's Secret here suffers a pointed critique from Lane Bryant's campaign, as more realistically proportioned models set themselves up in direct opposition to the Victoria's Secret Angel image. While the power of the Lane Bryant marketing does not lie solely in its conversation with its competitor, the dialogue between the two campaigns undoubtedly makes it more resonant at that particular moment in time.

Our examples also call attention to the way in which ads appeal to an audience's values, or **doxa**. A crucial concept to the ancient Greeks, *doxa*

FIGURE 2.10 The Lane Bryant store supercharges its argument by implicitly criticizing the Victoria's Secret "Angels" campaign.

means "popular opinion" or "belief"—a learned value system—since it refers to those values or beliefs that are deeply held by a particular community at a particular place and moment in time. The term is related to a concept you may know, *dogma*—or unchanging doctrine—but importantly, *doxa* can and does change over time. When an author considers *doxa* while crafting a persuasive text, she constructs an argument based on her understanding of the values held in common by a group of people. The Victoria's Secret and Lane Bryant campaigns provide us with an interesting example of conflicting doxa. Both move beyond simple *pathos*-laden sex appeal to tap into cultural ideas about beauty. While Victoria's Secret's marketing trades on cultural assumptions that value extreme slenderness, the Lane Bryant campaign appeals to a rising contemporary sentiment that values more realistically proportioned ideals of beauty.

Likewise, in its recent campaign for its new beverage "Coke Life," Coca-Cola used *doxa* when tapping into the audience's commitment to healthy living. The selling point of the ads for this re-vamped beverage is that Coke Life uses only sugar and stevia extract as sweeteners, so the ads promise lower calorie "sweetness from natural sources." Replacing its signature red background with vivid green, the Coke ads reach out to a health-conscious populous who might be persuaded to indulge in a soft drink that uses only natural sweeteners. However, some critics have dismissed this campaign as an empty marketing gesture toward health rather than a concerted effort to promote healthier dietary habits, accusing the soft drink giant of "green-washing"—that is, using the rhetoric of environmental consciousness to distract from a less commendable agenda. Moreover, while the appeal to national health works for an ad in the United States today, a contemporary Coca-Cola ad in Lebanon, by contrast, appeals to the culture's celebration of voluptuous singing divas, such as Nancy Ajram, and therefore presents a video focused on romance among adults rather than nutrition and children. By invoking the cultural values of each location, Coca-Cola deliberately uses *doxa* as a rhetorical strategy. You can probably think of many other examples of how attention to *doxa* works in arguments aimed at a specific demographic, even within the United States (for instance, Diet Mountain Dew ads that target Nascar lovers versus Honest Tea ads targeting bicycling enthusiasts). Consider also how political ads appeal to popular opinion or deeply held values of a specific community (such as a depressed region needing manufacturing jobs or a rural constituency opposed to gun control).

Attending to *kairos* and *doxa* in these ways enables us to understand differences in context and values, to see how persuasion makes powerful use of the present place and moment, and finally, to learn how we can implement these rhetorical strategies when composing our own arguments.

READING AN AD ANALYSIS

Now that we've seen how strategies of argumentation and the rhetorical appeals operate in advertising, let's look at how they come together in a written analysis. As you read student Clare Conrotto's rhetorical analysis of a McDonald's commercial, consider not only whether you find her analysis persuasive, but also how she leverages different rhetorical strategies to make a compelling argument to her audience.

Clare Conrotto
Writing & Rhetoric 1

I'll Have the Lies on the Side, Please

Tranquil pastoral fields, waving peacefully in the breeze. Contented cattle, grazing freely under a delicate sunrise. A family tending happily to their beloved animals, smiling as they stroll alongside the cattle. These scenes from a recent McDonald's commercial is made all the more perfect by the viewer's desire to believe that such is the reality of our foodstuff before it is slaughtered, processed, packaged, and sold. But one must look beyond the polished images and ask the question, *Could this possibly be true?*

Current national sentiment in America yearns to answer this question with a resounding *yes*, but as public opinion scrutinizes the ever more attentively glossed-over and brushed-under culture in which advertising companies flourish, it soon becomes clear that many companies have merely exploited viewers' expectations. Indeed, McDonald's, keenly aware of modern Americans' hypersensitivity to issues regarding the food industry, seizes the opportunity to revitalize its reputation tarnished by decades of horrifying revelations; in one of McDonald's most recent advertising campaigns, the company attempts to assure viewers that the corporative giant has become both socially and ethically responsible, going so far as to paint a utopian portrait of the traditional American family farm in its video "Raising Cattle and a Family." However, McDonald's is largely unsuccessful in

Clare begins her essay with descriptive language that sketches some scenes from the McDonald's commercial to hook her audience and help them visualize the text she will be analyzing.

Clare uses a question-answer format to transition between her first and second paragraph.

Although Clare doesn't use the term *ethos*, her analysis focuses on the way in which the commercial fails to persuade the audience of McDonalds's credibility and integrity.

Conrotto 2

As she moves toward
her thesis statement,
Clare suggests how she
will push beyond a sur-
face reading of the com-
mercial to more in-depth
analysis.

The use of a charged
word like "pandering"
underscores Clare's critical stance in relation to
the McDonald's advertis-
ing campaign.

While *ethos* (McDonald's
credibility) is a founda-
tion for her argument, in
her thesis she indicates
that she also will exam-
ine *pathos* (connection
with audience) in her
essay.

In her first main body
paragraph, Clare begins
with an examination of
ethos, relying on strategies of description and
example to make her
point.

this endeavor, despite its intuitive awareness of the American social mindset. Although it may convince a passive audience that trusts the products it already consumes, for many more critical viewers, the company's rhetorical persuasive strategies fall short when the countless implicit and explicit assertions of the advertisement are compared with reality. Thus, despite evidence of McDonald's keen awareness of its audience's priorities and careful execution of a video pandering to these ideals, the company fails to establish a meaningful connection with the viewer and therefore fails to effectively convince its audience.

This disconnect between author and viewer is due largely to McDonald's inability to persuade the audience of its transparency and integrity. Although the entire advertisement indirectly boasts of McDonald's fine moral standing, the disparity between concrete reality and the impossible construction of reality as it is presented in the video is too large a gap to be ignored. That is, in "Raising Cattle and a Family," McDonald's effort to relate to the modern American public manifests itself most obviously in the deceivingly simplistic cinematographic techniques of the video. Indeed, at the very beginning of the advertisement, the viewer is immediately greeted by an idealized version of an American farm when the screen fades from black to the image of a lush field at dawn, the unbroken view of sky and grass only enhanced by cows standing happily within nature: all appears open, peaceful, and idyllic. Although this reveals McDonald's

Conrotto 3

intimate understanding of modern Americans' growing desire to
return to honesty and simplicity regarding the food industry, and
most certainly an appeal to *kairos*, the subtle techniques which
McDonald's employs focus primarily on the audience's unconscious
inclinations. In other words, McDonald's appeals to *pathos*, to
the emotional impulses of the audience. It is true that humans
respond to such quiet beauty and peacefulness strongly, especially
in an era overwrought by a constant influx of errands that must be
accomplished, emails which must be answered, and tasks that must
be finished by a looming deadline. Nonetheless, the argument
that McDonald's asserts with this technique is effective for a very
short time, if at all. As the video progresses, with continually
intensifying images of what appears to be a ranching utopia filled
with peaceful cattle and striking views of nature, analytical viewers
will soon begin to question the validity of this indirect claim. Could
it be true that McDonald's sources its beef only from local U.S.
farms that focus on sustainable and humane practices, allowing
the cattle to graze as happily as they do in the video?

   The short answer is, quite simply, no. With a few simple clicks
of the mouse, the audience finds that, according to McDonald's
own answer section on its website, all of the meat it purchases
"comes from cattle *corn-fed* [italics added] in the U.S." and that
"in order to keep up with demand, a small percentage of grass-fed
beef is imported from Australia and New Zealand" (McDonald's).
Thus are the viewers' misgivings proven true in an instant: not

Clare examines the interchange between the rhetorical appeals; while she uses rhetorical terminology here (*pathos*, *kairos*), she could have used less discipline-specific terminology if she wanted to present her argument to a more general audience.

Again, Clare considers the *kairos* of the commercial as a way of analyzing its influence on the audience.

She concludes this paragraph with a rhetorical question that she then answers as her transition into her next paragraph, indicating a shift to a more skeptical perspective.

Conrotto 4

Clare considers the commercial's impact on varying audiences—as she continues to scrutinize its *ethos.* She recognizes here the multiple, interrelated audiences for this text.

once does the audience see even one kernel of corn or the metal cages which inevitably accompany such fodder when it replaces the natural act of grazing. McDonald's idyllic American farm setting is therefore already established as a web of lies, immeasurably weakening any future arguments. As a result, actively thinking viewers will remain skeptical, and passive viewers will remain unaffected in their loyalty to the products they already consume at McDonald's; the ultimate purpose of the advertisement—to persuade its audience of its new reputation—will have failed.

Again, she weaves an understanding of audience and *kairos* into her analysis.

This lack of credibility continues to plague the video, even as McDonald's works desperately to seem more convincing. Already burdened by the weight of a tarnished status in the minds of millions of Americans, owed partially to such documentaries as the 2004 hit *Super Size Me* and celebrity chef Jamie Oliver's recent uncovering of the fast food industry's horrifying chemical-treated "pink slime" meat product (Reilly), McDonald's embarked on a new advertising style, determined to develop a similarly new reputation: the company well understood that the timing for its next move was ripe. Turning to the human instinct to trust familiar faces, the

Clare turns her attention at this point to the *situated ethos* of the spokesperson.

primary spokesperson in the advertisement is Steve Foglesong, former president of the National Cattlemen's Beef Association (Goodman), a fact that, one fancies, ought to lend immediate weight to any statement made during the video. Unfortunately, not even this appeal to *ethos* can persuade viewers—of any level of passivity, or, conversely, activeness in thought—that there is any

Conrotto 5

credibility to be found in this advertisement. McDonald's flails;

seeking to promote any fact about the Foglesongs that might help

its case, the company highlights the authority of Foglesong as a

father and grandfather whose family has owned a cattle ranch for

three generations (and who apparently enjoys McDonald's burgers

himself, as manifested by a scene in which he and his sons smilingly

eat McDonald's on a short lunch break) by indirectly likening time

spent on a project to quality. A failed attempt to appeal to *logos*

thus surfaces, one of many flaws in logic offered by McDonald's

largely emotion-driven video. Although there might be a correlation

between the implication that a man with the knowledge and

authority of decades of ranching ought to understand the farming

process and thus produce high-quality products, the claim that this

is of course the end result, and that McDonald's should be trusted

because of this conclusion, remains unproven.

   Finally, to continue the evaluation of such logical fallacies,

it is vital to understand that most viewers will be aware of the

fact that since this video is an advertisement, Foglesong may be

former president of the NCBA, a third-generation rancher, and

seemingly a strong voice to be trusted, but he is a *hired actor* and is

thus self-promoting. This consequently undermines any seemingly

rational argument offered by the spokesperson or his experience

with raising cattle. Even his manner of delivery—endearing and

informal—does little to move the viewer when she acknowledges the

fact that Foglesong is *paid* to speak in such a way. This might have

Clare moves to pointing to flaws in logic and reasoning to underscore the shortcomings of the commercial.

Here Clare points to what she sees as a correlation-causation fallacy.

Once again, Clare points to fallacies in the argument, this time questioning the *ethos* of the spokesperson.

Conrotto 6

been persuasive had the interview-like situation been genuinely spontaneous, due to its ability to transport the viewer to what feels like an intimate acquaintance with Foglesong and, by extension, McDonald's. Unfortunately, like most of McDonald's rhetorical appeals, this, too, fails to convince even the most inactive viewer due to the contrived nature of Foglesong's participation.

In her penultimate paragraph, Clare concedes that some of the commercial's techniques foster a connection with the audience, but then — at the end of the paragraph — reasserts her argument that more critical viewers will see past *pathos* appeals in a way that compromises McDonald's *ethos*.

Conversely, it must be noted that one of the more simplistic techniques in "Raising Cattle and a Family" proves to be one of the most effective in this largely insufficient attempt to revitalize McDonald's reputation. The audio of the advertisement, which serves chiefly the same purpose as the technical photographic angles and focuses, begins with the serene harmony of chirping birds and gently mooing cows. The suave vocals of Foglesong slide over the sounds of nature before an endearingly folksy guitar is heard strumming in the background of Foglesong's narration. Immediately the audience responds to these emotionally

Clare's use of vivid, descriptive language ("serene harmony," "endearingly folksy", "evocative stimuli") adds increased *pathos* appeal to her own writing

evocative stimuli—the audio is simple and peaceful, emphasizing the apparent tranquility to be found on McDonald's farms. To a certain extent, logic does take over to render even this attempt at persuasion somewhat irrelevant. The viewer grasps that, just as with the utopian visual scenes, the music is simply a ploy to force audiences to reassess their current view of McDonald's and connect the chain with the ever sought-after small business dream. However, most viewers will remain passive in this analysis of audio strategies and thus the unconscious appeal to *pathos* will have been more or less successful. Nevertheless, this small

Conrotto 7

victory in persuasion does little to improve the overall success of the advertisement and McDonald's aim of rebuilding its reputation in order to better relate to potential consumers. The other faulty attempts at persuasion outweigh the minor victory of the audio's appeal, and the advertisement remains, ultimately, ineffective.

> Claire moves into her conclusion paragraph by reasserting her argument in the opening sentence.

Encumbered with the insurmountable task of reworking its reputation, McDonald's simply cannot connect with its viewers on a level that encourages mutual respect and confidence. Despite the modestly successful audio and visual techniques utilized by the company, the advertisement still falls short of convincing: active viewers remains capable of examining such emotive appeals as defined by their allure, and passive viewers who do accept the advertisement's premise are typically already loyal to a company from which they have been purchasing for years. Ultimately, the seeds for a new reputation may have been planted, but most Americans are currently too suspicious of large corporations to uncritically accept concepts established in an advertisement overrun by sweeping generalizations and vague half-truths. By failing to foster trust between Americans and its company, McDonald's ultimately fails to win over its audience.

> Her own argument rests on the idea of *doxa* — that current, shared skepticism about Big Business influences how susceptible the audience is to the commercial's message.

> Her final sentence is a succinct and powerful reiteration of her main claim.

Conrotto 8

Works Cited

Goodman, Ryan. "McDonald's Launches Farmer Ad Campaign." *Agriculture Proud*, 10 Jan. 2012. Web. 1 Oct. 2012.

McDonald's Corporation. "Meats." McDonald's, n.d. Web. 1 Oct. 2012.

Reilly, Jill. "Victory for Jamie Oliver in the U.S. as McDonald's Is Forced to Stop Using 'Pink Slime' in Its Burger Recipe." *Mail Online*. Daily Mail, 7 Oct. 2012. Web. 1 Oct. 2012.

THE WRITER'S PROCESS

As you turn to write up your analysis of advertisements in the way that Clare did above, consider the ways in which your own writing can "sell" your argument to the reader. What is the rhetorical situation of your writing assignment? What *strategies of argumentation* and *rhetorical appeals* would be most effective in reaching your target audience? Do you want to use narration, a humorous analogy, or a stirring example to forge a connection with your readers based on *pathos*? Or is your written analysis better suited to *logos*, following the step-by-step process of reading an ad, drawing on empirical evidence, or looking at cause and effect? Perhaps you will decide to enrich your discussion through cultivating your *ethos* as a writer, establishing your own authority on a subject or citing reputable work done by other scholars. Finally, how can you make use of *kairos* and *doxa* as persuasive tools by evoking something from today's culture in your writing or appealing to the beliefs of your reader? In your essay, you certainly will use many of these strategies and a combination of rhetorical appeals; as we saw in the examples from this chapter, a successful argument uses various techniques to persuade its audience.

SPOTLIGHTED ANALYSIS: ADVERTISEMENTS   MyWritingLab

Use the following prompts to guide your analysis of the advertisement of your choice, focusing on how the ad relies on particular strategies of development and rhetorical appeals to persuade its audience.

- **Content:** What exactly is the ad selling? An object? An experience? An idea?
- **Argument:** How is the ad selling the product? What message is the ad sending to the audience?
- **Character and setting:** What is featured by the ad? An object? A scene? A person? How are these elements portrayed? How do these choices relate to the ad's intended audience and reflect deliberate rhetorical choices?
- **Rhetorical appeals:** Which rhetorical appeals does the ad rely on to persuade its audience? *Pathos*? *Logos*? *Ethos*? *Kairos*? *Doxa*? How do these appeals operate both through language and through imagery?
- **Strategies of development:** Which strategies of argumentation does the ad use? Narration? Definition? Comparison–contrast? Example or illustration? Classification? Process? Analogy? Cause and effect? How do these strategies contribute to the ad's persuasive appeal?
- **Word & image:** What is the relationship between the word (written or spoken) and the imagery in the ad? How does this relationship affect the persuasiveness of the advertisement?
- **Layout & design:** How are the elements of the ad arranged—on a page (for a print ad) or in sequence (for a television or Internet commercial)? What is the purpose behind this arrangement? How does the ad's organization facilitate its argument? How do elements like choice or coloring of typeface, filtering or cropping of photographs, or the overall tone of the advertisement (informal, personal, authoritative, technical, comic, serious) affect its persuasiveness?
- **Design:** What typeface is used? What size? What color? What tone do these choices create for the advertisement? How do these decisions reflect attention to the ad's rhetorical situation or use of rhetorical appeals?
- **Medium and context:** How was the ad distributed (i.e., television, Internet, radio, magazine, billboard)? In what country and at what historical moment was the advertisement produced? How does the ad reflect, comment on, challenge, or reinforce contemporary political, economic, or gender ideology?
- **Cultural resonance:** Does the ad use famous events or places or recognizable symbols to increase its persuasiveness? If so, how does that establish audience or a relationship to a cultural moment?

WRITING ASSIGNMENTS   MyWritingLab

1. **Rhetorical Analysis Brainstorm:** Review David Horsey's article "Obnoxious Freedom" from Chapter 1. Take notes on how he uses strategies of development and rhetorical appeals in constructing his argument. Then look at Alex's essay at the end of that chapter. Where is she addressing his use of these techniques during her analysis? Jot some notes down about what you would suggest that she add to her argument if she were to revise it to better feature how Horsey uses rhetorical strategies (such as rhetorical appeals and strategies of argumentation) in his essay.

2. **Rhetorical Analysis Essay:** Building from your own reading of Derek Thompson's article and the accompanying annotations, develop your thoughts into a cohesive rhetorical analysis essay, driven by a strong thesis statement and drawing on evidence from the article to support your claim. If you prefer, write instead on the article of your choice.

3. **Rhetorical Analysis of an Advertisement:** Using the analysis you started for the Spotlighted Analysis above as a starting point, write a rhetorical analysis of an advertisement, using a strong claim to guide your argument. Be sure to draw on evidence to support your claim, but be selective in which details you include in your essay: your goal is not to produce a list of all your observations but to produce a focused analysis that argues for how the advertiser used specific rhetorical appeals or strategies to produce a persuasive argument.

4. **Rhetorical Analysis—Fallacies:** Working alone or with a group, select an article, editorial, op-ed, essay, or even an advertisement that includes a misuse of either *pathos*, *logos*, or *ethos* as a persuasive strategy. Compose an essay (or a PowerPoint or Prezi) in which you define the fallacy and then analyze how it functions in the text. In your conclusion, suggest how the text itself could be altered to avoid this line of argument.

5. **Rhetorical Analysis—*Kairos*:** Working in groups, look at several ads from different time periods produced by the same company, such as ads for cigarettes, cars, hygiene products, or personal computers. Each member of your group should choose a single ad and prepare a rhetorical analysis of its persuasive appeals. Share your analyses to explore how this company has modified its rhetorical approach over time. Collaborate on a paper in which you chart the evolution of the company's persuasive strategies and how that evolution was informed by *kairos.*

6. **Reflection and Revision:** Select an essay that you have written, whether for one of the assignments above or that you have written for a class previously. Perform a rhetorical analysis on *your own essay*, taking notes in the margins to guide your thinking. When do you use *pathos*, *logos*, or *ethos* in your writing? Do you take into account *kairos* or *doxa*? Refer back to the strategies of development: to what extent do you use the strategies listed on pages 44–49? How do you take into account the concepts of rhetorical situation, exigence and purpose that we discussed in Chapter 1? Having completed this analysis, revise your essay in a way that more deliberately leverages the powers of rhetoric to persuade your reader. Remember that you don't need to use *all* the appeals or every strategy in your essay: the key is to use a strategic combination that will produce the most powerful effect. Finish the revision by drafting a memo in which you reflect on the process of rhetorical analysis and revision that you put into practice.

MyWritingLab Visit Ch. 2 Understanding Strategies of Persuasion in MyWritingLab to complete the Writer's Practices, Spotlighted Analyses, and Writing Assignments, and to test your understanding of the chapter objectives.

CHAPTER 3

Composing Arguments

Chapter Preview Questions

3.1 How do the Canons of Rhetoric determine the content, shape, and style of arguments?

3.2 What is the role of invention in creating persuasive arguments?

3.3 How does the canon of arrangement influence a reader's response to a text?

3.4 How can style be used to compose a powerful argument?

3.5 How can I write a persuasive position paper?

When you skim news stories online or watch media coverage of dramatic events, you are in fact reading about an issue through a filter: the newscaster's selection of images and quotations as well as the reporter's choice of words in composing a story about that event. Such writing aims to persuade you to read further—to stay on the Website, share the link with friends, or post a comment with your response—and in that way even the news functions as argument. Let's consider an example. Imagine that it is September 2005 and the United States is still reeling from the aftermath of Hurricane Katrina. As you click through several news sites, you pause to look at the images they display. One features a striking photo of a military helicopter dropping supplies to the citizens of New Orleans (see Figure 3.1). Another shows a mother clutching two small children and wading through waist-deep water. Yet another displays the image of a mob of angry people, packed together and arguing as they try to evacuate the city. A final site uses the picture of a child's dirt-smeared doll, swept

FIGURE 3.1 A photograph of supplies being dropped to survivors of a hurricane in New Orleans.

into a pile of debris on the road, as its poignant commentary on natural disaster.

Based on these images, which site would you visit? How does each image make a different argument about what happened? How might the words that accompany the photo shape your interpretation of the visual texts? How does the choice of a particular visual–verbal combination present a specific point of view or argument about an event in the news?

Photographs and their accompanying text on news sites or in newspapers rely on the same tools of persuasion that we examined in earlier chapters. In this chapter, we'll continue to explore how rhetoric shapes our reality. We'll become acquainted with the *Canons of Rhetoric*—five classifications of argument established by Aristotle—and we'll work through the process of composing an argument: coming up with ideas, structuring those ideas, and developing a style for your position, or stance, on an issue. We'll also explore how you can apply these lessons about arrangement and style through specific strategies for how you can write compelling titles, introductions, and conclusions for your own essays. Finally, we'll build on these lessons to consider how to craft a powerful position paper that takes into account counterarguments while persuasively articulating your stance on an issue.

3.1 How do the Canons of Rhetoric determine the content, shape, and style of arguments?

UNDERSTANDING THE CANONS OF RHETORIC

In ancient Greece, all communicative acts were classified into five categories, or what Aristotle called the **Canons of Rhetoric**:

- **Invention:** creating and constructing ideas and identifying the best modes of persuasion
- **Arrangement:** ordering and laying out ideas through effective organization
- **Style:** developing the appropriate expression for those ideas
- **Memory:** retaining invented ideas, recalling additional supporting ideas, and facilitating memory in the audience
- **Delivery:** presenting or performing ideas with the aim of persuading

Each one of these canons is necessary for persuasive communication, whether that be through spoken word, written discourse, or, more recently, multimedia texts. For our discussion of composing arguments in this chapter, we'll focus on the first three canons.

INVENTION IN ARGUMENT

3.2 What is the role of invention in creating persuasive arguments?

Aristotle defined *invention* as methods for "finding all available arguments." When you craft language with the purpose of persuading your audience, you are **inventing** an argument. That is, you are generating ideas about a topic and the ways to best persuade your audience. Classical rhetoricians recommended two systems for invention: *stasis*, a series of question that speakers could use to identify a point or topic for debate, and *topoi*, a set of categories or topics that help a speaker discern the relationships between ideas. In your own writing, you can draw from their central premise of categories and directed questioning to help you familiarize yourself with your topic and the options for argument available to you:

- **Fact:** What are you talking about, exactly? Is it a person, a text, an idea, an event? Is it in the real world or speculative?
- **Definition:** What does it *mean*? What are other examples?
- **Division:** What are its *parts*? What are its different features?
- **Comparison:** How does it *compare* to other topics or texts? Does it mean something new now versus years ago?
- **Purpose:** What is its *purpose*? To inform? Teach? Entertain? Persuade? Promote action? How does that purpose influence its structure?
- **Quality:** Is it possible to *evaluate* what you're talking about? Where does it fall into the categories of right/wrong, moral/immoral, important/insignificant? Does it resist such a binary interpretation?
- **Causes and Consequences:** What *causes* the issue or text? What are the *results* or consequences of it?
- **Testimony:** What do *others* say about it?

Some of these lines of questioning might be more applicable to your topic than others; however, taken in combination, they offer you a variety of strategies to help you generate the foundation for a persuasive argument.

To further develop ideas as you continue to "invent" your argument during the drafting stage, you can use a range of **rhetorical strategies**, including those you learned in the previous chapter: you might invoke *pathos*, use *ethos* or appeals to character, or employ *logos* to reason with your readers or listeners. Your task as a writer is to forge a powerful text that argues your point—the focus of your *invention*—and to convince others to agree with you. In composing arguments, you can look for examples in texts all around you and learn from them how *invention*—or the way the author chooses the most effective mode of persuasion—generates particular perspectives that the author wishes to convey to the audience.

Consider pictures. We might think that a photograph provides a window on another person's reality. But in fact photographs, like written works, are texts of *rhetorical invention*. The "reality" that photographs display is actually a version of reality created by a photographer's rhetorical and artistic decisions: whether to use color or black-and-white film; what sort of lighting to use; how to position the subject of the photograph; whether to opt for a panorama or close-up shot; what backdrop to use; how to crop, or trim, the image once it is printed. In effect, when we see photographs in a newspaper or art gallery, we are looking at the product of deliberate *strategies of invention.* In photography, these strategies include key elements of composition, such as selection, placement, perspective, and framing. So when we look carefully at the image shown in Figure 3.2, we can see that the photograph is more powerful because of its composition. The photographer deliberately maximized the power of both foreground (the doves in flight) and background (the advancing tank) to transform a photograph of a middle-eastern street scene into a commentary on peace and war. In written texts, the same elements—selection, placement, perspective, and framing—are critical to making an argument.

Let's consider another example, the photograph in Figure 3.3, an image captured by photojournalist Margaret Bourke-White, which shows a line of homeless African Americans, displaced by the 1937 Louisville flood, waiting in line to

> Invention is the "discovery of valid or seemingly valid arguments to render one's cause probable."
>
> —*Cicero*, De Inventione, I.vii

FIGURE 3.2 The powerful image of doves in front of a tank in the Middle East suggests the photographer's view on the tensions between foreign aid and military occupation.

FIGURE 3.3 Margaret Bourke "At the Time of the Louisville Flood," 1937.

receive food and clothing from a local Red Cross center. Does the photo merely document a moment in the history of Kentucky? Or have the choice of subject, the cropping, the angle, the background, and the elements within the frame been selected by the photographer to make a specific argument about race and American culture during the first half of the twentieth century?

In your own writing, you could use this photograph as a springboard for inventing an argument. Perhaps you would write a historically focused argument that examines the catastrophic 1937 Louisville flood and its impact on the local community. Or you could refer to this photograph as visual evidence in a paper that examines the link between social status, race, and disaster relief. Either argument could draw on the power of the photograph, which reveals the invention strategies of the artist.

Let's look more closely at how invention factors into the way photographers and writers compose arguments. Consider two famous photographs by Dorothea Lange (see Figures 3.4 and 3.5), which offer very different

FIGURE 3.4 Dorothea Lange's wide shot gives a stark sense of the experience of migrant farmers.

FIGURE 3.5 The close-up focuses on the struggles of the migrant mother.

representations of migrant workers during the Great Depression. In each case, we see a migrant family huddled inside a tent. The subjects seem to be poor, hungry, and struggling to make a living. Their material conditions are bleak.

But notice the effects of the different perspectives. In Figure 3.5, we get an intimate look inside this woman's eyes, where we can see her concern. The lines on her face, visible in this close-up, are evidence of her hard life and worries. The photograph in Figure 3.4 has a wider frame that encompasses the tent and the barren ground. This perspective makes a different kind of argument, one that addresses the condition of the soil, the landscape, and the living quarters. We can hardly make out the woman huddled in the darkness of the tent. When we look for visual evidence of the living conditions of migrant workers in the American West during the 1930s, each photograph offers different angles on our argument. Which one would we use to support a thesis about the labor conditions of migrant workers? Which one would we use to argue that the human body is scarred by hardship? Depending on our purpose, we would choose one photograph over the other to serve as evidence for our claims about the Great Depression. Each photograph demonstrates a particular strategy of invention, creating and constructing ideas in visual form about the "reality" of life for migrant workers. We, in turn, can invent different arguments based on our starting point: which photo do we use as evidence for our thesis?

Similarly, in written documents, divergent perspectives on the same topic can yield different arguments. Commentary on Lange's *Migrant Mother* photographs exposes the variety of perspectives not only on the photographs' status as "documentary" evidence from the Great Depression but also on the way our historical understanding of that period itself is constructed by the invention or arguments of others. For instance, the following excerpt from historian James Curtis's article "Dorothea Lange, Migrant Mother, and the Culture of the Great Depression" demonstrates the way in which Lange's photos are often interpreted as windows into that period:

> In addition to being a timeless work of art, *Migrant Mother* is a vital reflection of the times. Examined in its original context, the series reveals powerful cultural forces of the 1930s: the impact of the increasing centralization and bureaucratization of American life; the anxiety about the status and solidarity of the family in an era of urbanization and modernization; a need to atone for the guilt induced by the destruction of cherished ideals, and a craving for reassurance that democratic traditions would stand the test of modern times.

For Curtis, the images function both as what elsewhere in the article he calls "a timeless and universal symbol of suffering in the face of adversity" as well as the key to understanding Lange's relationship to the evolving genre of documentary photography. For journalist Geoffrey Dunn, however, Lange's series prompts a different response:

> The photographs taken by Lange and her colleagues at the Resettlement Administration (later to become better known as the Farm Security Administration) have been widely heralded as the epitome of documentary photography. The eminent photographer and curator Edward Steichen called them "the most remarkable human documents ever rendered in pictures."
>
> In recent years, however, the FSA photographs have come under a growing criticism. Many view them as manipulative and condescending, to the point of assuming a "colonialistic" attitude toward their subjects. Still others have argued that they are misleading and disingenuous, and in some instances, fabricated.
>
> In a compelling essay entitled "The Historian and the Icon," University of California at Berkeley professor Lawrence Levine has argued that the FSA

photographers focused their lenses on "perfect victims," and in so doing, rendered a caricatured portrait of the era.

"Americans suffered, materially and physically, during the years of the Great Depression to an extent which we still do not fully fathom," Levine asserted. "But they also continued, as people always must, the business of living. They ate and they laughed, they loved and they fought, they worried and they hoped ... they filled their days, as we fill ours, with the essentials of everyday living."

With the notable exception of FSA photographer Russell Lee, and later, Marion Post Wolcott, whose largely overlooked bodies of work actually capture the dimensions of "everyday living," Lange and her colleagues focused almost exclusively on human suffering. That is most certainly the reason that people like Florence Owens Thompson [the mother in these photographs]—and many others who appeared in FSA images—resented their photographic portrayal.

"Mother was a woman who loved to enjoy life, who loved her children," says Thompson's youngest daughter, Norma Rydlewski, who appears as a young child in Lange's classic photograph. "She loved music and she loved to dance. When I look at that photo of mother, it saddens me. That's not how I like to remember her."

Like Curtis, Dunn uses the photographs as the basis for an argument about Lange's practice of documentary photography; however, Dunn considers first-person accounts from other witnesses of that historical moment and arrives at a different argument. He concludes that the series exemplifies not reflection but misrepresentation.

All texts—whether written accounts or photographs—are actually shaped by individual perspective and point of view. Texts are "invented" for a specific audience. Your own writing is a text informed by your invention strategies, your purpose, your point of view, and the rhetorical situation of your argument. In your writing, you are like a photographer, making important compositional decisions: What will be the subject of your text: an individual, a group, an institution? How will you pose that subject to best convey your own perspective? Should you zoom in, focusing on one particular example as a way of addressing a larger concern? Or should you take a step back, situating your argument in relation to the broader context that surrounds the issue? The choices you make will determine the ultimate impact of your argument: like photographs, effective writing persuades the viewer to look at a topic through the lens of the author's interpretation.

WRITER'S PRACTICE   MyWritingLab

Examine the picture in Figure 3.6, taken by photographer Todd Heisler, of a soldier's coffin returning home on a civilian flight into Reno, Nevada, being draped with the American flag prior to being unloaded from the plane. What argument is Heisler making about Americans' response to the war and casualties? Now consider this image as the basis for inventing your own position: What types of arguments might you construct that would use this image as visual evidence? What other sorts of images or evidence would you use to develop your argument?

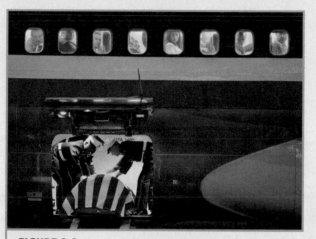

FIGURE 3.6 Photograph of the arrival of a soldier's coffin in Reno.

ARRANGEMENT IN ARGUMENT

3.3 How does the canon of arrangement influence a reader's response to a text?

After invention, the second canon of rhetoric, **arrangement**, becomes your key consideration because the way in which you present material on the page will shape a reader's response to your ideas. In many cases, attention to *arrangement* takes the form of the way you order elements in your argument—whether that be the layout of images and text on a newspaper front page or the way you structure a written argument in an academic paper. It is the arrangement of an argument that separates a spontaneous reaction or stream-of-consciousness freewrite from a carefully developed and argued essay on a specific issue or topic.

AN AMERICAN FAMILY, MRS. YAEKO NAKAMURA . . .

FIGURE 3.7

OLDER DAUGHTER, JOYCE YUKIKO NAKAMURA . . .

FIGURE 3.8

To return once again to our photography example, let's look at how award-winning photographer Ansel Adams approached the issue of arrangement in his 1944 photo essay, *Born Free and Equal*, which captures his impressions of the Japanese-American residents of the Manzanar internment camp during World War II. Adams explained his purpose for writing the book most clearly to his friend, Nancy Newhall: "Through the pictures the reader will be introduced to about twenty individuals . . . loyal American citizens who are anxious to get back into the stream of life and contribute to our victory." The work as a whole follows a *thematic structure*, moving the reader from "The Land" to "The Place," "The History," "The People," and finally "The Problem." On the surface, Adams seems to have arranged the sections to move from broader context, to the individuals, to the articulation of the social and political realities of the internment process. However, closer analysis shows that his strategy is much more complicated; he interweaves portraiture with his more panoramic, contextualizing photographs so as to constantly remind his audience of the fact that the people who have been imprisoned in this way are Americans—everyday people with everyday lives.

The selections gathered here are from the "People" chapter; note how the strategic arrangement amplifies many of the concepts that Adams stresses in his summary to Newhall. Figure 3.7 and Figure 3.8 first create an emotional connection with the reader by focusing on individual example.

By showing close-ups of mother and daughter, with the caption strategically emphasizing the fact that these are "An American Family," Adams suggests the unfairness of the relocation process. Subsequently, he widens his frame to show "A Manzanar Household" (Figure 3.9), portraying a quotidian family scene, little girl at her desk doing homework, family clustered around in a typical domestic setting. From here, we can see Adams' next move in strategic arrangement in Figure 3.10: the pair of adorable young boys eating at a mess hall. Having engaged the reader once more, Adams broadens his scope yet again to give us context for this scene. We are no longer inside the faux middle class home; we see the barracks, the food lines, and the unforgiving landscape. As we saw with Dorothea Lange's *Migrant Mother series*, Adams uses shifting perspectives rhetorically, and in tandem, in order to emphasize his argument about in the injustices of the internment process.

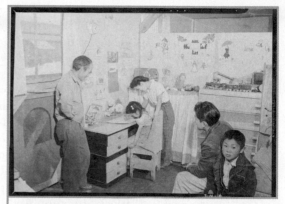

FIGURE 3.9

From this example we can see how, as a photographer, Adams made deliberate rhetorical choices in moving from capturing individual images to arranging them into powerful sequences and arguments on the page. Contemporary photojournalists have an even more expansive range of possibilities available to them through online publication, where modes of arrangement are designed to be versatile, flexible, and hyperlinked, often allowing the audience to customize their reading experience.

As a writer, you, too, need to assess the possibilities and limitations of the genre in which you're writing. In practical terms, this means that the way you organize your essay should be dictated by the conventions of the discipline or genre: a history term paper, for instance, will have a different structure from a lab report or a public policy white paper. In deciding which mode of arrangement might work best for your argument, you might decide to draw on one of these common structures that authors often use to organize their ideas into a convincing and well-organized written argument:

FIGURE 3.10

- **Chronological Structure:** Demonstrates change over time. Chronology relies on examples arranged in a temporal sequence, so it would be an effective structure, for instance, for an analysis of the changes in the rhetoric of the Black Panthers between their founding in 1966 and their peak influence in 1970.
- **Process or Narrative:** Arranges information sequentially, moving from beginning to end. If you were writing an essay proposing how activists could best leverage social media for their cause, you

might organize it to move from starting with the basics (setting up a Facebook page) to the more complex strategies such as customized messaging or integrating offline and online communications.

- **Cause–effect:** Shows how one event causes another. An essay confronting the issue of sexist language in rap music might start by exploring the words and allusions used to refer to women in popular rap music (*cause*) and then conclude by discussing the impact of this representation on the self-esteem of young girls (*effect*).

- **Problem–solution:** Defines the problem and then offers a solution. A paper about violence and video games might devote the first half of the paper to exploring the *problem* of desensitization and then focus in the second half of the paper on proposing a possible *solution*.

- **Block Structure:** Works systematically through a series of examples or case studies. For instance, in an essay about the underlying social and political themes in young adult fantasy literature, you might structure your essay to analyze first *The Lightning Thief*, then *The City of Bones*, and lastly *The Hunger Games*.

- **Thematic or Topical Structure:** Organizes by themes or subtopics. An essay on reality TV might include sections on voyeurism, capitalism, and Darwinism (*the themes*), integrating examples from *Survivor*, *American Idol*, and *So You Think You Can Dance* as evidence in each section.

- **Inductive Reasoning:** Begins with a guiding question and defers your thesis to your conclusion. For instance, an essay on media coverage of national disasters might contain a thesis question at the end of the introduction, such as "How do images featured in the news define our understanding of the impact of natural disasters on specific communities?", then synthesizing its evidence and building toward its claim at the end.

As you can see, you have many methods at your disposal to help you approach the question of arrangement strategically and deliberately. In the next sections, we'll examine a few organizational approaches you might emulate in your own writing and then suggest ways in which you can further customize your arrangement to best suit your individual assignment, purpose, and academic discipline.

Using Classical Strategies of Arrangement

In his *Rhetoric*, Aristotle proposed a relatively streamlined approach to arrangement, suggesting that an argument should be composed of two components: the statement of the case and the proof or support for that case. However, other rhetoricians, including Cicero and Quintilian, espoused a more complex approach. They maintained that persuasive speeches relied on a six-part structure:

I.   Introduction (or *exordium*). In this section, the orator states the topic and develops his *ethos* as well as a connection with the audience.

II. Statement of facts or background (or *narratio*). This section provides the audience with context and any key information.

III. Division (or *partitio*). The orator uses this section to summarize the different lines of argument he will present, providing an overview or road map of the *parts* of the argument to follow. Often what we would consider the "thesis" occurs in this section.

IV. Proof (or *confirmatio*). This section contains the heart of the argument; it is where the orator presents his central claims, supported by evidence, facts, and reasons. This section would comprise what we might consider the "main body" of the argument.

V.   Refutation (or *refutatio*). Once he has shared the argument, the orator then anticipates any objections to his claims and evaluates those counterarguments.

VI. Conclusion (or *peroratio*). In closing, the orator summarizes the strongest points of his claim and makes a final appeal to the audience.

Each of the parts could be comprised of a single paragraph or of several paragraphs. Notice how this structure moves from a firm grounding in the claim (I–IV) to a consideration of counterarguments (V) before reemphasizing the orator's position at the end (VI). The inclusion of step V might surprise you. Too often, when we present an argument, we're tempted to focus only on our own position, concerned that allowing other voices in the conversation might undermine our authority. However, classical rhetoricians recognized that this is not the case, that we build credibility as a writer or speaker by demonstrating that we have thought through alternate arguments and anticipated objections before arriving at our own claim.

It is worth noting that even in developing these models, classical scholars recognized that a formulaic approach to argument was limiting. They considered the orator's understanding of his rhetorical situation and the *kairos* of his argument to be of primary importance in determining the rhetorical arrangement of argument. In more modern times, contemporary rhetoricians have built on this principle to develop alternate models for argumentation that they considered best suited to the types of topics, situations, and audiences that writers and speakers address today.

Using the Toulmin Model to Analyze or Arrange an Argument

The Toulmin model of argumentation was developed by British philosopher Stephen Toulmin in 1969 as a way to define a system of persuasive reasoning. Toulmin found formal logic limited in its ability to apply to everyday, nonacademic issues and so decided to develop a structure that could have relevance to more common instances of argumentation and persuasion. At the most basic level, Toulmin identified three common features of argument: claims, warrants, and grounding.

The **claim** represents the writer's argument. It often manifests itself in the thesis statement, although many essays contain a series of linked smaller claims, or subclaims, which build together to the central thesis. One characteristic of a claim is that it is debatable, and so the burden is on the author to persuade his or her audience of its merit and validity.

That's where the **grounds** come in, which are comprised of the reasons and the evidence that support the claim. When an author doesn't back his claim with sufficient grounds, the claim can come off as unsupported opinion and be dismissed by his audience. In presenting their grounds, authors tend to draw on the *logos* appeal that we discussed in Chapter 2, supporting strong reasons with hard data, facts, testimonials, and even relevant personal experience.

The last feature, **warrants**, is an often unspoken element of the argument; it represents the unspoken assumptions that connect the claim to the grounds. Persuasion can easily be short-circuited if an author's audience doesn't agree with the warrants or the underlying ideas that support the argument.

Figure 3.11 lays out how these different elements work together to produce an argument, using the argument in favor of government-subsidized college education as an example. This model demonstrates the intricate relationship between the different elements of the argument: the claim itself is only as strong as the grounds (reasons and evidence) that support it and the degree to which the audience concurs with the warrant (assumptions or premises) that underlies it.

However, while the relationship between *claim*, *grounding*, and *warrant* provides the foundation for the Toulmin approach to argumentation, Toulmin himself expanded his model to account for the additional complexities

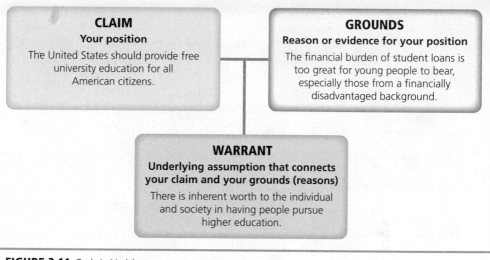

FIGURE 3.11 Toulmin Model

that often accompany everyday argument. The complete Toulmin model includes three additional elements:

- **Backing**: reasons, examples, or evidence that support the warrant. These may or may not also support the central claim.
- **Rebuttal**: a description and refutation of anticipated counterpoints and opposing claims. Keep in mind, it is important in this section to not only identify alternate perspectives and respond to them but also to do so in a fair, unbiased, and respectful way that enhances your *ethos*.
- **Qualification**: words or statements that adjust your claim to take into account counterarguments. These might be as subtle as hedging language that makes your claim more conditional (words like *perhaps*, *probably*, *in most cases*), or they might involve a separate sentence or point that softens or revises your original stance. Taking the time to adjust your claim based on alternate opinions demonstrates your willingness to consider the limitations to your position.

These additional features help us remember that arguments operate not in a vacuum but in dialogue with larger conversations, and that the most persuasive claims take into account other perspectives.

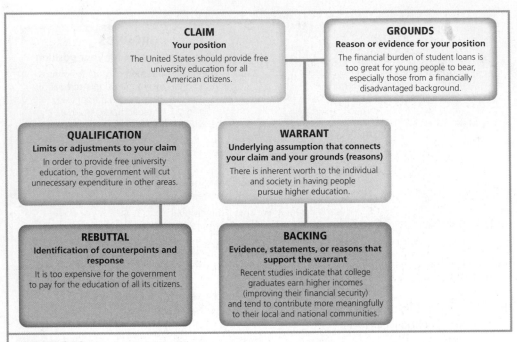

FIGURE 3.12 Complete Toulmin Model

In Figure 3.12, we can see the addition of *backing*, *rebuttal*, and *qualification* yield a more rigorous and persuasive treatment of the issue.

Developed as a paragraph, a draft of this argument would look something like this:

The financial burden of student loans is too great for young people to bear, especially those from a financially disadvantaged background. [grounds] Consequently, the United States should provide free university education for all Americans. [claim] This financial investment would be a worthwhile one for the government, since a higher education degree is valuable to both the individual and society. [warrant] As recent studies have shown, college graduates earn higher incomes and tend to contribute more meaningfully to their local and national communities. [backing] However, in order to afford such a program, the government would need to take a hard look at its other expenditures and streamline its budget for other programs. [qualifier] Without such careful auditing and reassignment of resources, the costs of universal education would be prohibitive, even for the government. [rebuttal]

In reading this paragraph, you can see how the Toulmin approach generates a reasoned and logical argumentative structure. However, you probably also can identify areas for expansion or elaboration: additional specific details needed to make the grounds and backing more persuasive; further counterpoints or opposing perspectives that need to be addressed; added adjustments to the claim or the qualification. You might even want to fine-tune the warrant further to make the underlying premise of the claim more persuasive. Expanding on the basic structure in this way would allow you to develop this idea into a more robust argument, one that could serve the foundation for a well-reasoned and persuasive essay. The At a Glance box offers a model for how you could use the Toulmin method for a full-length essay.

As you can see, the Toulmin model provides a framework that helps you think through the complexities of your claim and produce a more nuanced argument. You can rely on the Toulmin method to compose a claim of your own, support it with appropriate evidence, and explain clearly how and why that evidence does in fact prove, or support, your claim; you can use it on a small scale to build a well-reasoned paragraph or on a larger scale for an entire essay. In addition, keep in mind that Toulmin himself developed this structure as an analytic tool, so you can draw on it to help you further develop the way you critically engage with and assess the arguments made by others.

AT A GLANCE

Following the Toulmin Model

Rely on this structure to strengthen a claim by looking at unstated assumptions (warrants) and alternate viewpoints:

1. Introduction of topic
2. Thesis claim
3. Grounds (reasons and evidence to support the claim)
4. Warrants (connections between the grounds and the claim)
5. Backing (support for the warrants)
6. Rebuttals (including qualification)
7. Conclusion

WRITER'S PRACTICE   MyWritingLab

Select one of the topics below (or one of your own choosing) and use invention techniques to identify your stand on the issue:

- High school uniforms or dress codes
- General education requirements at colleges and universities
- Standardized tests and college admissions

Next, using the chart in Figure 3.12 as a model, diagram your argument to identify your *claim, grounding, warrant, backing, rebuttal,* and *qualification*. Afterward, follow the process showcased above and transform your diagram into a cohesive paragraph.

Considering Rogerian Arguments

An alternative mode of argumentation was developed by rhetoricians Richard Young, Kenneth Pike, and Alton Becker in 1970. Drawing from the communication practices of Carl Rogers—an influential psychologist—Young, Pike, and Becker modeled a process of persuasion based on a deep understanding and appreciation of an opponent's perspective. Their model of argumentation was empathic and conciliatory rather than adversarial, putting into practice Rogers's suggestion from 1951 that communication based on finding common ground can help resolve emotionally intense situations such as found in negotiations or diplomacy.

As a writer, you might wonder how the Rogerian approach differs from other types of argument. Consider this example from an argument about Instagram posts:

> Some media watchdog groups argue that parents should be able to arbitrarily override their teenagers' Instagram account settings so that the parents can remove any photos they deem objectionable, which is a clear violation of the right to free speech.

On the one hand, in this statement, the author clearly articulates her opinion. On the other hand, however, she offers only a dismissive and cursory glimpse of the opposing viewpoint, closing down any possibility of dialogue or negotiation. Notice how an exchange using a Rogerian approach fosters a greater possibility for a productive conversation on this issue:

> Some media watchdog groups worry that teenagers post pictures on Instagram without considering the future implications of the images. They believe that provocative photos (featuring teenagers in sexualized poses or engaged in reckless activities) might produce unforeseen results, such as limiting the Instagram user's college or employment prospects later in life, or even attracting sexual predators. For this reason, they argue, Instagram should put into place parental overrides to allow a parent to monitor and safeguard their children's well-being. This raises an important question: would this mechanism impinge on the teenager's right to free speech?

The revision does more than simply removing inflammatory or biased language; it offers acknowledgment and fair assessment of the counterposition. For this reason, a Rogerian argument hinges on establishing a sense of **common ground** between diverse opinions, and, as Douglas Brent has argued, necessitates "imagining [the counter-position] with empathy." By fostering more open and nonjudgmental dialogue, a Rogerian approach can help transform volatile exchanges into opportunities for productive consensus. To adopt this strategy in your own writing, incorporate the following steps into your writing process:

1. When you introduce the issue, be sure to restate your opponent's position in a respectful way that shows a rich knowledge and understanding of that stance.

2. In discussing the opposing opinion, elaborate on the contexts in which such a stance might be valid.

3. In stating your own position, likewise be sure to suggest the contexts in which your stance might be valid.

4. As the closing moment in your argument, move toward compromise or conciliation, suggesting how your opponent's stance might benefit from incorporating components of your own position. Ideally, you would demonstrate how the positions can complement each other, rather than showing which one "wins."

Keep in mind that while you can use a Rogerian method to shape your entire essay, you can also employ it in certain sections of your argument, such as when you are restating counterarguments to show your own nuanced understanding of your topic.

AT A GLANCE

Arguing from Common Ground with the Rogerian Approach

Center your argument on mutual understanding and common ground to make your audience more open to your position:

1. Introduction
2. Summary of opposing viewpoint
3. Statement of common ground or understanding
4. Statement of your claim and position
5. Statement of contexts
6. Conclusion (appealing to self-interests of the audience)

WRITER'S PRACTICE   MyWritingLab

Return to the chart and paragraph you composed for the Writer's Practice on page 105. Addressing the same topic, now draft a paragraph about it using a Rogerian structure (arguing from common ground). Compare your Toulmin paragraph to your Rogerian paragraph on the topic. Which seems to be the most effective way to make your particular argument? What type of audience would each resonate best with? Why?

Exploring Effective Modes of Arrangement

Whether you are working with the classical model of arrangement, the Toulmin method, or the Rogerian approach, each asks you to reflect on one key question: how can you best articulate your argument when taking into account your audience and alternate arguments on the topic? While you may choose to adopt one of these frameworks to organize your own writing or presentations, in most cases you need to do more than simply follow a rigidly defined structural paradigm. As we discussed above, even classical rhetoricians recognized that following a certain formula for structure was less important than reflecting on what would be most persuasive to a particular audience.

Consider the strategies represented in the Strategies of Arrangement table, which represent variations on the classical, Toulmin, and Rogerian structures discussed above. Notice the way these alternative modes of arrangement balance making your own argument with taking into account diverse perspectives on the issue.

Strategies of Arrangement

Leading with Your Claim

Use when you want to ground the reader in your argument before bringing up opposing perspectives:

1. Introduction, identification of rhetorical stance
2. Thesis
3. Statement of background, definition, or context
4. Evidence and development of argument
5. Opposing opinion, concession, qualification, refutation
6. Conclusion

Leading with Counterarguments

Establish opposing opinion up front so that the entire piece functions as an extended rebuttal or refutation of that line of argument:

1. Introduction and opposing viewpoint
2. Thesis and identification of rhetorical stance
3. Evidence and development of argument
4. Conclusion

Integrating Claims and Counterclaims

Treat diverse viewpoints as appropriate during the development of your argument and presentation of your evidence:

1. Introduction, identification of rhetorical stance
2. Thesis
3. Statement of background, definition, or context
4. Evidence, opposing opinion, concession, qualification, refutation
5. Conclusion

These models of arrangement are not designed to function as rigid templates for organization. Instead, they suggest possibilities and potentially effective strategies of arrangement. In your own writing, you will have to select the most productive way to lay out your argument, depending in part on your claim, your understanding of your audience, and your approach to alternate perspectives on your issue.

In considering these various modes of arrangement, first consider your audience:

- How much do they know about the issue? *Their level of familiarity with the topic will influence how much background information you incorporate into your essay and where you introduce it.*
- What is their rhetorical stance toward the issue? *If addressing a hostile or resistant audience, you might begin your essay by trying to forge a connection with your readers or trying to soften their stance.*
- What is their stance toward you as a writer or speaker? *If they already consider you credible, you do not need to do too much ethos-building in your essay; however, if you have not yet established your trustworthiness or expertise, you will need to organize your argument in such a way as to assert your authority on the issue.*

Second, take into account how you want to integrate diverse viewpoints, asking yourself:

- Do the alternate perspectives corroborate your argument? *If so, you could include them as supporting evidence.*
- Do they offer points of view that you can disprove? *If they do, you might present the opinion and provide a rebuttal, or refutation of the points, demonstrating why they are not valid.*
- Do they offer points of view that are irrelevant to your argument? *If so, you demonstrate that these perspectives, while perhaps salient in some situations, are not directly relevant to the issue as you define it.*
- Do they offer points of view that you can't disprove? *In this case, you might concede the validity of some parts of their argument but go on to qualify their points by showing why your own argument is nonetheless persuasive.*

The key is to treat these other voices with respect; always represent their points of view fairly and without bias, even if you disagree with them.

STYLE IN ARGUMENT

Inventing a thesis or main idea and *arranging* the elements of your writing are two steps in completing your task of written persuasion. You also need to spend some time considering what tone, word choice, and voice you will use in your writing. This is where **style**—the third canon of rhetoric—enters the scene. While "style" often suggests basic grammar or mechanical correctness, from the vantage point of classical rhetoric, style—according to the Roman rhetorician Cicero—concerns choosing the appropriate expression for the ideas of your argument; these choices relate to language, tone, syntax, rhetorical appeals, metaphors, imagery, quotations, level of emphasis, and nuance.

We often translate *style* into *voice* to indicate how a writer's perspective is manifested in word choice, syntax, pacing, and tone. To construct a successful argument, you need to be able to employ the voice or style that best meets the needs of your rhetorical situation. As Cicero famously stated: "I don't always adopt the same style. What similarity is there between a letter and an oration in court or at a public meeting?"

Now consider two contemporary examples of style, both focused on President Obama. The first is an excerpt from a *Sports Illustrated* piece:

> Obama's erect carriage and lefthandedness led me to think of Lionel "Train" Hollins, who commanded the Portland Trail Blazers' backcourt when the kid then known as "Barry O'Bomber" was making his way through high school.

Using basketball lingo ("backcourt") and casual vocabulary ("the kid" and "making his way"), the writer Alexander Wolff describes Obama as someone who speaks the language of popular readers—what Cicero would have called "plain style." Moreover, the naming of famous players gives credibility or *ethos* to Wolff himself as someone who knows the players and even their nicknames. In this way, his style or writing contributes to building his authority as an author.

In contrast, a writer from the academic journal *Rhetoric & Public Affairs* uses what Cicero called *high style*, or elevated diction, in making a critique of President Obama:

> While Obama's rhetoric of *consilience* approximates dialogic coherence, it nonetheless falls short of the discursive demands of racial reconciliation.

By using sophisticated concepts—such as "dialogic coherence" and "discursive demands"—familiar only to a highly educated academic audience, writer Mark McPhail uses the style of an erudite member of the intellectual class. His "backcourt buddies" can be understood as the colleagues who understand that "dialogic coherence" and "discursive demands" refer to ways of speaking and writing. While McPhail's style is radically different from Wolff's, it has a parallel function in that it builds his authority as a writer for those familiar with the journal's conventions.

Let's consider another case, this time examining how an author adjusts his rhetorical style when presenting the same material to two different audiences, in two different forms and contexts. Yale Professor Nicholas Christakis is well known in his field for his work on how social networks influence the behaviors of individuals; more specifically, he looks at how networks create behavior "clusters," that is, groups of people connected through social networks who exhibit similar inclinations, habits, or behavior patterns. As part of his exploration of this topic, Christakis examined how people's likelihood of becoming obese statistically increased in relation to the presence of other obese people in their social network, even at a remove (i.e., their friends, their friends' friends, and even their friends' friends' friends). When giving a TED talk on the topic in 2010, he adopted plain style, focusing on translating his scientific findings into a format that would be both engaging and clear for a public audience. Here he describes his three initial hypotheses for why he found obesity clusters in his research into social networks; Figure 3.13 shows the slide he used to accompany his description:

> Well, what might be causing this clustering? There are at least three possibilities: One possibility is that, as I gain weight, it causes you to gain weight. A kind of induction, a kind of spread from person to person. Another possibility, very obvious, is homophily, or, birds of a feather flock together; here, I form my tie to you because you and I share a similar body size. And the last possibility is what is known as confounding, because it confounds our ability to figure out what's going on. And here, the idea is not that my weight gain is causing your weight gain, nor that I preferentially form a tie with you because you and I share the same body size, but rather that we share a common exposure to something, like a health club that makes us both lose weight at the same time.

Notice his stylistic choices: his reliance on first and second person to personalize the three hypotheses, connecting them to ideas or experiences that

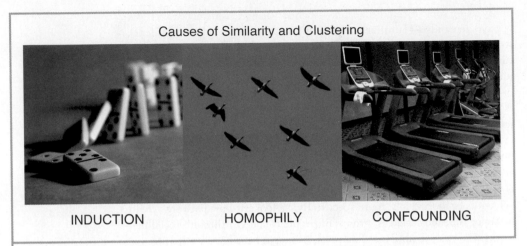

Causes of Similarity and Clustering

INDUCTION   HOMOPHILY   CONFOUNDING

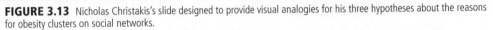

FIGURE 3.13 Nicholas Christakis's slide designed to provide visual analogies for his three hypotheses about the reasons for obesity clusters on social networks.

would be familiar to his audience; his integration of a common expression ("birds of a feather flock together") that translates the idea of "homophily" into more commonplace terms; his use of an analogy ("like a health club") to help his audience better understand his point; and his use of more informal sentence structures, contractions, and word choice ("to figure out what's going on"). Even the slide itself follows the same method, providing visual correlatives for the technical concepts that he's been describing to speak to an audience unfamiliar with network theory.

When addressing his academic peers, however, Christakis had to convey the same information, but in a way that would take into account their expertise and advanced understanding. Consider the way he shifted to a more elevated level of style in his article from *The New England Journal of Medicine* to describe the same three hypotheses:

We considered three explanations for the clustering of obese people. First, egos might choose to associate with like alters ("homophily").[21,23,24] Second, egos and alters might share attributes or jointly experience unobserved contemporaneous events that cause their weight to vary at the same time (confounding). Third, alters might exert social influence or peer effects on egos ("induction"). Distinguishing the interpersonal induction of obesity from homophily requires dynamic, longitudinal network information about the emergence of ties between people ("nodes") in a network and also about the attributes of nodes (i.e., repeated measures of the body-mass index).[25]

In reading the two paragraphs, you might think that they were written by two separate people because the style varies so greatly; in reality, what they showcase is the ability of a single author to accommodate different rhetorical situations through his stylistic choices. In the journal article, Christakis does not need define all his terms; he can use words like *egos* and *alters* without additional definition because he knows they would be familiar to the readers of *NEJM*. In addition, because this article is meant to be read silently (instead of listened to, as the TED talk was), he could use a different technique when he did decide to offer definitions, providing the definition first ("egos might choose to associate with like alters") and then glossing it with the term in parenthesis ("homophily"). That strategy would be hard to follow if you were listening to the paragraph, but is much easier to comprehend when reading. Even Christakis's use of footnotes presents a stylistic choice, one that indicates that he prioritized building his *ethos* with his colleagues through referencing his knowledge of other work in the field, a move he did not feel as necessary in his TED presentation. While the information in the *NEJM* paragraph is essentially identical to that found in the TED paragraph, it has been styled to better suit the discourse of Christakis's professional community.

Similarly, in your own writing, your choice of style should address a specific audience and can thus build your *ethos* with those readers. If you are wondering how to move from invention and arrangement to developing your own style, then it is time to learn about constructing a *persona* and developing a *rhetorical stance* in your writing.

Constructing Your Persona

The term *persona* has its roots in Latin word for "mask," referring to the theatrical masks worn by actors in ancient Greece. In more contemporary terms, we use persona to refer to *a deliberately crafted version of yourself* that you construct and project in response to a specific audience or context.

You probably are already practiced at the art of tailoring your persona for specific rhetorical situations. Think about how you represent yourself on different social media platforms. The persona you project—both in your profile picture and the written information you share online—on a platform like Facebook, Instagram, or Tumblr, is probably different than the one you would craft for a site like LinkedIn or a university department Webpage. Even the fleeting images you share on Snapchat might represent a different "you," one that you anticipate will last only a few seconds before disappearing into the ether. In each case, while attending to the type of *ethos* you want to cultivate, you make a series of strategic choices about what type of "mask" you want to show to the world.

We see the power of persona at play in the public sphere every day. Candidates for a presidential election might book appearances on late night TV to show their lighter side; Hollywood celebrities might appear at high profile charity events to overlay their glamorous image with one that shows they care deeply about important social issues. President Barack Obama might choose to give a speech about war flanked by a group of military men and women or a speech about health care surrounded by doctors, as we see in Figure 3.14. In each case, persona functions as a rhetorical construction of self-designed to present a certain argument about the individual that directly influences his *ethos*.

The same principle governs the writing process. When you compose a text (whether verbal, visual, or multimedia), you decide how to use language to shape your particular *persona* as a writer and rhetorician. That is, you create a portrait of yourself as the author of your argument through a number of stylistic choices:

- Tone (formal or informal, humorous or serious)
- Word choice and diction (academic, colloquial, technical, or clichéd)

FIGURE 3.14 When President Barack Obama talks about health care surrounded by white-coated medical personnel, he creates a persona for himself as a friend and supporter of physicians.

- Imagery (allusions, metaphor, vivid descriptions)
- Sentence structure (complex or simple and direct)
- Use of rhetorical appeals (*pathos*, *logos*, *ethos*, *kairos*, *doxa*)
- Strategies of persuasion (narration, example, cause and effect, analogy, process, description, classification, or definition)

Creating a persona requires care. A well-designed one can facilitate a strong connection with your readers and therefore make your argument more persuasive. However, a *poorly constructed persona*—one that is, for instance, biased, inconsistent, or underdeveloped—can have the opposite effect, alienating readers and undercutting your text's overall effectiveness. An additional challenge in constructing your persona lies in retaining a sense of authenticity—in your voice, your perspective, and your argument—despite the fact that you're speaking through a rhetorical mask. What's key here is to realize that an effective persona represents a version of yourself, not a completely new character, and you should support it in your writing with other elements that contribute to your trustworthiness as an author: unbiased language, reasoned claims, respect for alternate viewpoints, ethical use of sources, and supporting evidence for your points.

Choosing a Rhetorical Stance

To be persuasive, you must not only create a persona that responds appropriately to your specific rhetorical situation and engages both audience and text, but you must also convey a *position* that Wayne Booth, one of the most important revivalists of classical rhetoric, defined as the **rhetorical stance**. In essence, a writer's rhetorical stance refers to the position the author assumes in relation to subject, audience, and context; it is a careful and deliberate navigation of the rhetorical situation and appeals with an intent to persuade an audience. In this sense, we can understand rhetorical stance not just as the "stand" that you take in relation to an issue, but as a more dynamic position we assume to accommodate to our understanding of the rhetorical situation.

Booth argued that communication failed between people (or a text failed to persuade a reader) if the writer takes on a stance that ignored the balance of the rhetorical situation. We see examples of inappropriate rhetorical stances constantly: the TV evangelist who moves his congregation with a polished sermon that completely distracts them from flaws in his moral character; the used-car salesman who pads his sales pitch with offers of free gifts, rebate specials, and low percentage rates; the actor who uses her celebrity status to drive a product endorsement, rather than clearly articulating the merits of that product itself. In each case, the *rhetorical situation*—the relationship between author, audience, and text—is out of balance, and the argument itself, ultimately, is less persuasive.

In your own writing, therefore, you need to pay special attention not only to the *persona* you create but also to the *rhetorical stance* you assume in relation to your specific situation. Before you even begin writing, take some time to identify your stance and consider how explicitly you want to convey it to your audience. Are they likely to align themselves with your position? Resist it? What sort of tone, style, and approach should you adopt to most persuasively present your position to your readers? These choices will shape your reader's understanding of your argument.

AT A GLANCE

Three Poorly Constructed Rhetorical Stances

The famous rhetoric scholar Wayne Booth identified three ways in which communication can break down, resulting in a failure that indicates a lack of balance among author, audience, and text. Booth emphasized that a poorly constructed persona leads to this demise, so you should avoid these situations in your own writing:

- **The pedant or preacher:** the text is paramount and both the audience's needs and the speaker's character are ignored.
- **The advertiser:** the effect on the audience is valued above all, ignoring the quality of the text and the credibility of the speaker.
- **The entertainer:** the character of the speaker is elevated above the text and the audience.

3.5 How can I write a persuasive position paper?

CRAFTING A POSITION PAPER

One way to put into practice the canons of rhetoric—*invention*, *arrangement*, and *style*—and to explore constructing a persuasive persona and assuming an effective rhetorical stance—is to write a position paper. By definition, a **position paper** offers you the opportunity to write about your opinion on an issue. This can take many forms: a letter to the editor of a newspaper, an op-ed (opinion editorial), a brief short, oral position statement, or even a white paper in politics or a memory aid in law. In each case, the writer focuses in on an issue and presents opinion backed by evidence. Many times, a position paper contains a very strong tone, taking one side of a controversial issue, much as you would find in a debate, and actively arguing in direct opposition to alternative positions on the issue. A successful position paper incorporates the following elements:

An introduction that provides an overview of the topic, providing background and a sense of its relevance. The introduction also establishes the author's rhetorical stance and claim, usually culminating in a strong thesis statement.

A strong assertion of the author's position. The main force of the argument in a position paper lies in this section, where the author persuades the reader that his position on the issue is the stronger one, supporting his points through evidence and logical reasoning.

A fair treatment of counterarguments. For each counterclaim, the author objectively describes the position and then either refutes it, concedes the point, or qualifies the argument.

A conclusion that reemphasizes the author's claim and once again reasserts the larger relevance of the issue.

While all strong position papers contain these components, the arrangement of the different parts might vary depending on your style, rhetorical situation, and topic. As we saw in the Strategies of Arrangement table on page 108, you have many options available to you. You might choose a block structure where you separate your treatment of the opposition's claims from the section where you focus on your own position. Alternately, you might adopt a more point-by-point model, where you present a series of counterarguments, debunking each in turn before developing your own position. Sometimes, a position paper might be less adversarial, relying on the Rogerian technique of understanding the issue from another's point of view in order to communicate that material to a third party, such as found in policy statement papers delivered to the United Nations, or law briefs, or statements of original research. Because of such variance, when you write a position paper, you should select your strategy of arrangement as carefully as you craft your style for the essay. Moreover, both organization and style should relate to your purpose and audience, in support of the main point of invention.

Before we look at how style and arrangement come together in a full-length position paper, let's zoom in on three key features that help frame your audience's understanding of your argument in this sort of paper—and in other types of essays as well: title, introduction, and conclusion.

Composing a Title

Your reader's first encounter with your topic and position comes through your **title**; in this way, the title itself operates as a rhetorical act that provides a frame and sets up the argument. To better understand this, consider how headlines perform a similar function. On September 2, 2005, many newspapers featured the photograph shown in Figure 3.1 on their front pages—but accompanied by different headlines. Figures 3.15 and 3.16 offer two examples. Notice how each newspaper indicates its rhetorical stance through the combination of words and images contained on its front page.

How does the headline "Mayor Sends 'Desperate SOS'" (see Figure 3.15) suggest a different argument than "New Orleans Roiled by Chaos" paired with the same photo? The difference in tone, perspective, and rhetorical stance apparent from these contrasting examples underscores the role a headline—or title—plays in forming a reader's expectations for the argument that follows. In effect, a *title* is the first step in writing an interpretation or making an argument.

In writing your own essays, you should spend some time brainstorming your titles. Some writers find constructing a powerful title to be a useful *invention* activity to start their composition process; others construct the title only after completing the first draft of their paper, as a way of synthesizing the argument and bringing it into sharper focus. In either case, developing a strong title can help you both clarify your central claim and rhetorical stance and also set up clear expectations for your audience.

As you work with a title, think about its role in setting up your stance on your topic, indicating to your readers not only the scope of your analysis but also your angle on it. A strong title should accomplish at least two goals: first, it should clearly identify the essay's topic and (occasionally) the claim; second, it should capture the reader's attention. Keeping these goals in mind, experiment with the following strategies when writing titles for your essays:

■ *Link the title to your main point or claim.* Sometimes the most direct and transparent titles can be the most powerful. Example: "Why We Need to Re-think the Common Core Initiative."

FIGURE 3.15 Front page of the *Anchorage Daily News*.

FIGURE 3.16 Front page of the *Columbian*, a newspaper from Clark County, Washington.

■ *Pose a question raised by your argument.* A variation of the first strategy, this approach invites the reader to consider an issue rather than explicitly focusing on your stance. Example: "Should We Re-think the Common Core in Elementary and Secondary Education?"

■ *Play with language.* As an alternative, you may want to use techniques such as alliteration (using two or more words with the same initial sound) or a play on words to make a title more engaging. Examples: "The Trouble with Teens and Twitter" and "Great Expectorations: Behind the Culture of Chewing Tobacco."

■ *Connect to a key image, underlying metaphor, or guiding concept.* When composing an essay that relies on an extended metaphor or central idea, you can use the title as your first opportunity to introduce your readers to the concept that you will develop at length in your argument. Examples: "Rebuilding the Tower of Babel through Bilingual Education" and "Endlessly Propagating Networks without End … or Purpose; Reevaluating Social Media."

■ *Use a quote from one of your sources.* This strategy allows you to use a key quotation to establish *ethos* and set the stage for your argument. Example: "'Make It So'; Redesigning *Star Trek* for the Next Generation."

How you develop your title depends in part on your understanding of audience and your rhetorical situation. The title for a narrative essay might be more whimsical and creative, while the title for an expository essay might prioritize clearly articulating the essay topic. A title for an essay designed to be shared online might deliberately incorporate key words that would make it more searchable through Google or a database search. In academic essays and research papers, we often see authors using a two-part title, pairing a catchy initial title with a more descriptive subtitle after a colon. For instance, one student chose the following title and subtitle combination for her essay on the portrayal of women in videogames:

"Sexualized Sabotage: Representations of Female Protagonists in Video Games"

The two halves of the title work well together. The first part is catchy, implying the author's critical stance about the topic; however, on its own, it does not clearly convey the topic of the essay. The second half of the title much more directly communicates the focus of the essay, but it lacks flare and stops short of sharing the author's claim. Joined together, the two parts provide an engaging combination designed to pique the reader's interest while conveying relevant information.

Use some caution with two-part titles, however. While this style can be quite effective in certain situations, at times they also can seem overly complicated. Avoid sacrificing clarity for the sake of what some call "academese"—a style of writing intended to sound erudite, but which often instead obfuscates meaning or sounds pretentious due to relying on unnecessarily complex sentence structures, passive voice, or obscure vocabulary. As you devise your title, keep in mind your audience's knowledge, expectations, and the conventions of your disciplinary field and writing assignment. The style of a title for a lab report for a Biology class will differ from the style for a title for a paper you write for a Biomedical Ethics class. It's a matter of rhetoric: understanding the logistics of your rhetorical situation so as to determine how to create a title that most effectively engages your audience.

WRITER'S PRACTICE   MyWritingLab

Complete the steps below (many based on Richard Leahy's "Twenty Titles for the Writer") to experiment with creating different titles for an essay you've already written. Alternately, use the steps to develop alternate titles for the sample student essays in Chapter 1 or Chapter 2. The goal is not necessarily to develop a single perfect title but to explore a process of *invention.* As you work through this Writer's Practice, reflect on how the steps—individually or as a process—help you reflect more purposefully different strategies for composing an effective title. When you're done, discuss your alternate titles and your observations with a partner.

1. Combine key terms or concepts into a title.
2. Transform the drafted title from step 1 into one that clearly demonstrates your claim or rhetorical stance.
3. Select a phrase or sentence from your essay or from one of the sources you quote in your essay for your title (be sure to use quotation marks if it's a direct quote from a source!).
4. Use a gerund (an -ing verb) or the preposition "On" as the first word of your title.
5. Experiment with an alliterative title.
6. Develop a title that asks a question (one that starts either with Who/What/When/Where/How/Why or Do/Does/Is/Are/Will).
7. Create a one-word title, then a two-word title, then a three-word title, then a four-word title, and then, finally, a five-word title.
8. Develop a title that alludes to or makes a pun about a common phrase or the title of a movie, book, or song.
9. Write a two-part title; feel free to combine two of the titles you've created above.

Composing Your Introduction

Like your title, your introduction offers your readers insight into the persona and rhetorical stance that will characterize your essay as a whole. An introduction may be a single paragraph or a section composed of two or more paragraphs; in it, you establish your voice (informal? formal?), your tone (measured? firm? angry? cautious?), your persona, and your stance on your topic through careful attention to word choice, sentence structure, and strategies of development. Most introductions also provide some background information and the first articulation of your argument as well, moving from a general statement of topic to a more focused statement of your *thesis*.

However, perhaps just as importantly, the introduction is the place where you capture the attention of your reader, often through a stylistic device that we call a "hook." For instance, let's return to Ansel Adams's photo essay, *Born Free and Equal*. He hooks his audience through a combination of word and image from the very first pages of the book. On one page, he reproduces the Fourteenth Amendment to the U.S. Constitution, which states, "No state shall make or enforce any law which shall abridge the privileges or immunities of citizens of the United States ..."; he then juxtaposes that line with the smiling face of the "American School Girl" shown in Figure 3.17. Here *logos* and *pathos* work side by side to prompt readers to wonder about this apparent contradiction. This is the hook that gets readers interested—and compels them to keep reading.

In written texts, you can use your introduction to hook your readers through one of several methods. You might use one or a combination of the following techniques:

- Define your terms (especially if you're writing on a subject that may not be familiar to your audience).
- Include a significant quotation, thought-provoking question, or a startling statistic or fact.
- Present an overview of the issue you're discussing.
- Provide some background on the topic.
- Use an anecdote or narration.
- Incorporate a vivid example.
- Draw on a relevant analogy or metaphor.
- Use the second-person pronoun (*you*) to connect with your readers.
- Use the first-person pronoun (*I/we*) to demonstrate your personal investment in the topic.

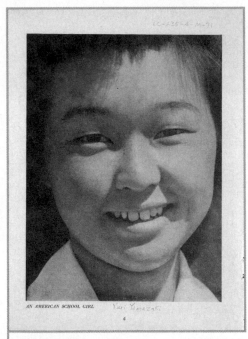

AN AMERICAN SCHOOL GIRL   Yuri Yamazaki
6

FIGURE 3.17

Your decision about how to craft your introduction will depend to a large extent on your broader stylistic choices about your essay and the way in which you want to develop your argument. For instance, for assignments that require a more formal, academic style, using "you" or "I" might not be an appropriate choice; alternately, that same sort of direct address might prove an extremely effective choice in an essay modeled after an op-ed or a call to action. The key to making the best stylistic choices lies in understanding the expectations of your assignment, your audience, and the genre that you're writing.

Let's look at how one student took style into consideration while composing her introduction to a position paper about the use of photo-retouching in teen fashion magazines:

I love my fashion magazines. I love flipping through the pages and seeing the cool fashions, the colorful ads, and all the beautiful celebs and models. But every time I read them, I can't help but feel a little worse about myself. Why can't I look like that? What do I have to do to be that beautiful, that perfect? (Interview)

This conflicted sentiment, expressed here by a 15 year old *Teen Vogue* reader, is not unusual. Even in this age of digital media, teen magazines such as *Teen Vogue* and *Seventeen* continue to have a strong following among teenage girls. However, these publications, which are meant to provide entertainment and "style inspiration" (Astley qtd. in Haughney), have a dark side effect: they promote an unhealthy culture of perfectionism that is detrimental to their readers. They do so not only by showcasing the Beautiful People of the fashion and entertainment industry, but also by making them even more beautiful through techniques like retouching, airbrushing, and photoshopping images. When considering that nearly 70% of middle school and high school aged girls report that their idea of the ideal body shape is influenced by magazines and, even more significantly, 50% say they want to lose weight because of it (Levin), the seriousness of this issue becomes clear. These unrealistic representations of beauty are putting teenage girls at risk, at best serving as sources for "thinspiration" and at worst inciting self-loathing in their readership. Teen fashion magazines need show a greater sense of responsibility to their readers; they need to listen to the many voices that are criticizing these photo altering practices and start making real changes to promote more realistic images of beauty in both the covers and contents of their magazines.

What hooks the reader first is the quotation that heads the introduction from a reader of teen fashion magazines. This quote announces the essay's topic at the same time that it provides a sharp contrast for the writing style of the main body of the introduction that follows. By comparison, the author's voice or writing style seems crisp, focused, and academic, establishing a *persona* that shows she is both informed on her subject and knowledgeable about the larger context. Note how she connects the hook to the rest of the introduction, fashioning her first sentence to serve as a bridge. From the rest of the introduction, we can tell that she will ground her argument in research and has developed a strong position on the topic. Notice the stylistic detail in the paragraph: the use of statistics to provide a *logos* appeal; judicious use of direct quotes, enough to provide *ethos*, but not enough to overwhelm her own voice; the strategic use of strong, specific words and phrases; the movement toward articulating her own stance and position on the topic. She ends the introduction with her thesis statement, pointing implicitly to how she will develop her argument (by discussing the strategies proposed by the "many voices" and advocating for change).

Writing Your Conclusion

If the introduction offers the writer the opportunity to hook the audience while providing a rhetorical stance on a subject, the **conclusion** is the final opportunity to reinforce an essay's argument while making a lasting impact on readers. For this reason, although a conclusion by its nature should include some gesture toward the materials covered in the essay and may synthesize the key points from the essay, it should also have a rhetorical power of its own. Let's look at how the author above concluded her essay:

> The collective momentum of the critiques and suggestions from these many anti-photoshop voices—from grassroots activists like Julia Bluhm, to media movements like "Keep it Real," and forward-thinking magazines like *Verily*— have promoted a climate that seems inclined toward change. In fact, to many, the cover of the April 2014 *Teen Vogue* seemed like a testament to how far the industry has come. Right on the cover, it featured an empowering quote from singer Lorde, announcing that "prescribed ideals of how girls should look are over" (Cover). However, even here a troubling ambiguity is still at work. The cover photo of Lorde that accompanies the quote, is, ironically, photoshopped, a fact that the artist herself pointed out, tweeting, "apart from the fact that i'm pretty sure this magazine gave me a new nose (:|), i really like this photo" (Lorde). When magazines continue to gesture toward compliance with a more natural standard of female beauty while simultaneously still reinforcing these negative ideals of female beauty, the conversation clearly is not over. If these magazines are finally to act responsibly toward their teenage readers, they need to not only talk the talk but also really *listen* and then make

substantive changes to their photoshopping policies. Only then will teen fashion magazines become what they should be: not a place that tears young women down, but instead a place that builds them up, helping them create a positive sense of self and affirm their own inherent strength and beauty.

While gesturing toward the different activist organizations she discussed in her position paper (the "anti-photoshop voices"), the author takes care to make her conclusion as stylistically sophisticated as her introduction. Notice her careful word choice ("forward-thinking," "conversation") that works in tandem with the idea of talking and listening that she integrated into her introduction. In addition, consider the effect of sharing a final concrete example that synthesizes her main takeaway. If we build on the metaphor of the "hook" as a way to draw readers into the introduction, then perhaps this element in the conclusion is the "sinker"—a compact, weighty element designed to make a final, lasting impression on the reader. Some writers save a representative statistic, quotation, or—as in this case—example to create this effect. The key is that is not to introduce a new point, but instead to use the "sinker" to draw together key elements discussed in the essay as a whole and to allow the author to rearticulate her argument one last time. Lastly, note how the author carefully structures her final sentence to end on an affirmative statement. Even though her position paper addresses a real problem and offers a pointed critique, it ends with a positive hope for the future.

In composing your own conclusion, you need to balance several priorities. First, you need to signal to your reader that you are moving to the end of your argument. Avoid relying exclusively on a phrase like "In conclusion" to signpost this for your reader; consider more elegant gestures—such as a more subtle transition or arranging your argument in a clear arc from beginning to middle to end. A second priority for your conclusion should be reiterating your main point or argument. This step is crucial for all types of argument, not just those that follow inductive reasoning; this is your last opportunity to make your case to your reader. Lastly, you should employ one or more of the following strategies to move your final section beyond simple summary toward a more robust, engaging, and well-designed close to your argument:

- Use a key quotation, example, or reference that either epitomizes or synthesizes your points (the "sinker").
- Return to an example, anecdote, allusion, or analogy from your introduction, offering a slightly different, perhaps more informed

perspective on it to connect to your opening paragraphs and provide a sense of a "frame" for your argument.

■ Use a chronological structure to move from the past to recent times, perhaps ending with a projection into the future.

■ Use your conclusion to suggest broader implications that could increase the reader's sense of the importance of the topic, whether it be its significance to you (the writer), to the reader, or to the larger community. As appropriate, consider including a call to action to motivate future change.

No matter which strategy you choose, remember to maximize the persuasive potential of your conclusion as a means of reaffirming the strength of your argument with your readers.

WRITER'S PRACTICE   MyWritingLab

Look back at either the student essay in Chapter 1 (p. 32) or the student essay in Chapter 2 (p. 79). Read the introduction of the essay aloud; then flip to the end and read the conclusion aloud. Note which strategies the author used to craft an effective opening and closing to her argument; use the bullet lists of strategies above to help you identify the author's rhetorical choices. Having done so, now experiment with rewriting either the introduction or the conclusion for that essay, relying on a different strategy or strategies that you feel would support or enhance the author's claim. Share your alternate version with a partner. Discuss:

• Why did you choose the strategies you used in revision?
• How did your revisions change the reader's experience with the essay or the way the claim was presented?
• To what extent did they produce a change in the author's persona or rhetorical stance?
• How would you need to change the other framing section (the conclusion, if you revised the introduction, or the introduction, if you revised the conclusion) to accommodate your revision?

Analyzing a Position Paper

Having carefully considered the components that contribute to framing a strong argument, let's look at how one published position paper puts into practice many of the strategies of invention, style, and arrangement that we've discussed above. In this opinion piece, Tufts Professor Bill Martel takes a strong stand on an issue we've already touched on earlier in this chapter: the right of the media at Dover Airforce Base to photograph the coffins of soldiers killed abroad. In the article, Martel is reacting to a change in policy that lifted the blanket ban on that practice, allowing the grieving families instead to make that decision about whether the caskets could be photographed. As you read through his article, consider the ways in which he uses invention, arrangement, and style to convey a strong position on this issue. In addition, notice how he carefully constructs a rhetorical stance that balances his own personal position with opposing viewpoints in order to craft a fully developed, persuasive argument.

BAN ON PHOTOGRAPHING MILITARY COFFINS PROTECTED GRIEVING FAMILIES FROM MEDIA
William C. Martel

The ban on photographing soldiers' coffins as they return to Dover Air Force Base in Delaware was not simply about images but also about shielding grief-stricken military families from a media maelstrom. It was not an issue of freedom of the press but one of respect and one of fairness.

Nevertheless, pressure built in Washington to change the old policy, which dated to 1991. On Jan. 7, 2009, Rep. Walter Jones, a Republican from North Carolina, introduced House Resolution 269, the "Fallen Hero Commemoration Act." This bill called for "the Department of Defense to grant access to accredited members of the media when the remains of members of the Armed Forces arrive at military installations in the United States."

President Obama and Secretary of Defense Robert Gates ordered a review of the issue, and an announcement of the Pentagon's conclusions came Thursday when Gates announced that media coverage would be allowed in cases where families give permission.

Critics of the ban argued that there are several benefits to be gained by allowing the media to photograph the coffins. For example, they argued that lifting the ban would affirm the public's right

While not overly catchy, the **title** clearly establishes Martel's **claim** that the article will later support.

Martel begins his essay with a statement of position in relation to the prior ban on photographing military coffins at Dover Air Force Base.

He then provides an overview of the issue, situating it in a particular historical moment (*kairos*) and introducing the context for the conversation about the ban.

Again, Martel invokes *kairos*, reminding his audience of the timeliness and relevance of this issue.

At this point, Martel shares the first **counterargument**. Notice his fair and balanced tone, building his own *ethos* as a writer.

In the next paragraph, Martel includes a second and then a third **counterargument** to his position. At this point, it is clear he is using a **block structure** for his argument and that he has decided to frontload the opposing arguments before moving on to his own position.

In this key paragraph, Martel **concedes** that the opposing arguments have some merit before indicating the turn in the essay toward arguing his own position.

Here he begins making a series of subclaims (smaller claims in support of his overriding position) supported by evidence and reasons.

He trades on the rhetoric surrounding the issue ("dignified transfer of remains") to make his point about the dangers of sensationalization.

Notice how he uses clear **signposting** (first, second, third) to help his reader clearly navigate the structure of his argument.

to know, a right that Americans deeply value. In addition, such photographs would show the American people the human cost of war.

Some also argued that it would prevent the Department of Defense from manipulating public opinion by suppressing images of the human cost of war. Finally, the ban was such a deeply polarizing and emotionally charged issue in American society that lifting it might start to heal the rift between those who legitimately differ over this policy.

These are all perfectly sensible arguments, made by reasonable people. But despite growing momentum that culminated in the lifting of the ban, there were several reasons to oppose such a reverse in policy.

First, the solemn act of bringing home our military dead will become sensationalized. We inevitably will see private family moments turned into public events.

The act of returning those who have died in war is known in U.S. military parlance as the "dignified transfer of remains." However, the very act of photographing the coffins of our fallen will be part and parcel of a classic public spectacle—featuring grieving military families who will be overwhelmed by media coverage.

Second, each family's right to privacy in this moment will be immediately and irrevocably sacrificed. We are obligated to honor those who have fallen in war in a way that preserves each military family's right to privacy. Otherwise, we risk exploiting their loss.

Military families deserve privacy, including the right to decide whether to allow the public to intrude, so including the family-permission clause helps some. Simply lifting the ban outright would have hurt families who are caught in the middle of searing pain and grief.

Furthermore, our obligation to put families first in protecting their privacy must trump the public's right to see the coffins of our war dead. Compassion for military families must outweigh well-intentioned arguments that defend the public's right to know.

The challenge for policymakers is to artfully balance what is in the best interests of democratic governance with compassion for those whose loved ones made the ultimate sacrifice in war. In such moments, we must err on the side of protecting those who bear the greatest burden.

Third, some argue that one reason for lifting the ban is to make political statements about the costs of war. The public's right to see photographs of soldiers' coffins—so that, as one reporter said to President Obama, they can "see the full human cost of war"—seems hollow in the face of private grief. If people want to understand the costs of war, they can visit Arlington National Cemetery, where 300,000 are buried—or read newspapers that routinely list names of the dead.

Images of grief-stricken military families will make powerful statements about war's human toll. Many were rightly offended when activists exploited military funerals for political purposes. Many members of the military have objected to having their images used for antiwar messages. How will this be any different?

What should the Pentagon have done? It is reasonable to give families the right to veto media coverage of the "dignified transfer of remains" at Dover Air Force Base. But what military family wants to make such a decision in its moment of grief?

Still, with this veto power, quite soon we will know how many military families are in favor of media coverage. My instinct is that fewer rather than more will want this private moment opened to cameras. According to polls of families who have lost a loved one in war, the vast majority oppose lifting the ban.

In the end, it is all the rage to talk about the sacrifices of military families. Many, in fact, have cited these sacrifices as reasons to withdraw U.S. troops from Iraq.

In fairness, by revoking the ban on media coverage of returning fallen heroes, allowing military families to be photographed when they are most vulnerable in their grief, we are not listening to military families or looking out for their best interests.

Put simply, lifting the ban on photographing coffins was not the right thing to do for military families who have lost loved ones in war.

He uses strong language like "must" to reinforce his position.

In his third subclaim, Martel once again shares an opposing viewpoint before refuting it. Notice the use of direct quotations that allows the reader to directly encounter the counter-argument before Martel rebuts it.

Martel draws on a parallel example here (photographing grieving families at military funerals) to support his point and then turns to rhetorical questions to prod at the additional complexity of this issue.

As he moves toward his final comments, he gestures toward the uncertainty of the public reaction to the lifting of the ban, pointing to both his "instinct" (personal opinion) and polls (more objective evidence) in speculating about the outcome.

He concludes by moving to a forceful articulation of his claim.

Bill Martel's article demonstrates interesting possibilities for developing your own persuasive writing. Sometimes when we write from our own point of view, we get so locked into our individual perspective that we fail to take into account diverse views on our topics. Such limited vision can weaken our persuasiveness; if we fail to consider or acknowledge alternative positions on our topics, we produce one-sided arguments that lack complexity or credibility with our readers. Recall our earlier discussion of photographs: each photograph suggests a different angle, a unique "version" of an event, and the perspective of a particular persona. When we bring these different sides to light, we find that suddenly an incident or issue that seems polarized—or "black and white"—is actually much more complex. The same holds true for the issues we confront every day as writers and rhetoricians: it is only through exploring multiple perspectives on an argument that we can engage it persuasively and effectively.

WRITER'S PRACTICE   MyWritingLab

Bill Martel originally published his piece in the opinion section of *US News & World Report* and so wrote it in a minimalist, journalistic style appropriate to his rhetorical situation. If you were writing a position paper on this topic for your class, how would you adjust the style and arrangement? Experiment by revising the title and either the introduction or the conclusion to be more appropriate for—and persuasive in—an academic context. Refer back to the criteria on titles, introductions, and conclusions above to aid you in your revision. In addition, feel free to draw some of his points or allusions from his main body into your expanded introduction or conclusion as needed.

THE WRITER'S PROCESS

In this chapter, you've learned to harness the canons of rhetoric—*invention*, *arrangement*, and *style*—to compose effective arguments of your own. You've developed strategies for crafting *titles*, *introductions*, and *conclusions*; you've explored the importance of *persona* and *rhetorical stance* in argument. You've learned the differences between three models of argumentation—classical, Toulmin, and Rogerian—and how they relate to your purpose and your audience. Now it's time to implement these skills. Practice inventing a position on an issue, arranging claims and evidence for your argument (including working with images as evidence for your points), developing a rhetorical stance, and working on persona through style by crafting your prose with care. Experiment with inventing diverse perspectives to achieve a thorough understanding of the complexity of the situation. Although you may be tempted to think of these various perspectives in oppositional terms—as the "pro" or "con" of an issue—such an approach closes off a richer understanding of the issue. In general, try to think of arguments not in terms of right or wrong but rather as a spectrum of differing perspectives. As you turn now to write your own position paper, recall the many options available to you and select the ones that best meet the needs of your rhetorical situation.

SPOTLIGHTED ANALYSIS: PHOTOGRAPHS   MyWritingLab

Select a photograph to analyze: you might select the work by a well-known photographer such as Ansel Adams, Dorothea Lange, Carrie Mae Weems, W. Eugene Smith, or Cindy Sherman; one from the Library of Congress "American Memory" archives online; or even a photograph from a newspaper, news magazine, or *Life* magazine's photographer Website. Sharpen your skills at analysis by writing out answers to the questions on the checklist below:

- **Content:** What does the photograph depict? Is it meant to represent reality, or is it deliberately abstract?
- **Argument:** What argument is the photographer conveying through the image? For instance, while the photo might show a group of people standing together, its argument might be about love, family unity across generations, or a promise for the future.
- **Photographer:** Who took this photograph? What is her or his reputation? What style of photography or famous photos is she or he known for?
- **Audience:** Who was the photographer's intended audience?
- **Context:** What was the historical and cultural context of the photograph? Where was it reproduced or displayed (an art gallery, the cover of a magazine, or the front page of a newspaper)?
- **Purpose:** What is the photograph's purpose or motive for capturing this image? Is it intended to be overtly argumentative and to move its audience to action? Or is the argument more subtle, even to the point of seeming objective or representational?
- **Rhetorical stance:** How does the composition of the photo convey a sense of the rhetorical stance of the photographer? Pay attention to issues of focus, cropping, color, setting, perspective, and editing or photo manipulation.
- **Word and image:** Does the photo have a caption or does it accompany written text? How does the image function in dialogue with this verbal text? As visual evidence? As a counterargument?

1. **Argument Analysis.** Read a news article or watch a recorded debate (such as on a news station) about a current controversial issue. Take notes on the elements of the argument. When does the speaker state her claim? her grounds or reasons? What are the unspoken assumptions or warrants that underlie her argument? To what extent does she take into account alternative positions? Does she rebut them, concede the point, or qualify her argument? What type of persona does she embody? What rhetorical stance does she assume in relation to her topic and her audience? Try to draft a persuasive, cohesive claim, referring back on the lessons from Chapter 1, about how the writer or speaker deliberately crafted her text to be persuasive.

2. **Draft Alternate Introductions.** Draft two alternate introductions for the analysis you brainstormed for Assignment #1. First review the section on introductions earlier in this chapter. Next identify your claim or thesis statement for your rhetorical analysis, using the techniques you practiced in Chapter 1. Then develop two possible introductions for the essay, utilizing different strategies for each one. As you craft the introductions, ask yourself:

   - Do you want to prioritize facts (*logos*), an emotional connection with the reader (*pathos*), or your own authority on the subject (*ethos*)?

   - Do you want to use comparison–contrast? Definition of terms? Process? Classification? Description? Narration? Definition? Cause–effect? Example?

   - Do you want to include a startling statistic? A relevant quotation or question? A vivid statement of the problem? An intriguing anecdote? A representative example or examples?

   - What type of persona will you construct? How will you use word choice, syntax, and tone to establish style?

   Keep in mind that you may employ several techniques or strategies in each introduction. Your goal is to imagine two alternate possibilities for how to introduce your topic and argument to your reader. When you have drafted the two introductions, share them with a partner in class and assess which offers the strongest foundation for your argument.

3. **Compose a Position Paper:** Develop the paragraph you wrote for the Writer's Practice on page 107 into a full position paper; alternately, write on a controversial topic about an issue that moves you and about which you can take a strong stance. Be sure to anticipate counterclaims and to address them through rebuttal, concession, or qualification. In addition, frame your essay with a powerful introduction and conclusion. When you complete your essay, preface it with a reflective memo in which you discuss your choices in relation to the arrangement and style of your argument.

4. **Consider Multiple Perspectives:** Identify different positions on an issue and then assign various members of your group each to write a position paper on one of those stances. You might, for instance, write about the conflict between your college campus and the surrounding town: one student could write a position paper that represents the staff perspective, another one on the administrator's perspective, another the city council's perspective, and a fourth person could represent the study body's perspective. Collaboratively write an introduction and conclusion for this series of papers that provide an overview of the topic and the conversation between the multiple perspectives.

My**WritingLab** Visit Ch. 3 Composing Arguments in MyWritingLab to complete the Writer's Practices, Spotlighted Analyses, and Writing Assignments, and to test your understanding of the chapter objectives.

Part II

PLANNING AND CONDUCTING RESEARCH

CHAPTER 4

Planning and Proposing Research Arguments

Chapter Preview Questions

4.1 How do I use questions to get started on finding a research topic?

4.2 How do I generate a productive topic?

4.3 What prewriting techniques can I use to narrow my topic?

4.4 What are the steps for developing a strong research plan?

4.5 How do I write a formal research proposal?

W hen we approach the task of research, it becomes clear that we can use many of the skills of analysis that we've practiced in previous chapters to help us interpret the meaning of texts and provide us with a starting point for our own line of inquiry. For instance, look at the poster shown in Figure 4.1. What you probably see first is a familiar image: the vintage 1943 Rosie the Riveter poster. With her hair tied up in a red kerchief, her direct, forceful gaze, and her bicep flexed as she rolls up her sleeve, she operates as a recognizable symbol for resilience, hard work, and motivation. However a closer look complicates this initial impression. How does realizing that Rosie's face has been redrawn in the fashion of a Guy Fawkes mask (a symbol used by the Anonymous movement) change your understanding of whom she represents? How do other alterations to the iconic image – a tattoo, a revision of her catch phrase, the reference to "99%" — sharpen your sense of the poster's context? As you begin to assess these different elements, you realize that the image has been repurposed into a call to action for the recent Occupy Movement. More specifically, by reading the additional information on the

FIGURE 4.1 How does this poster use visual elements and an iconic American image to motivate members of the Occupy Movement?

poster, you see that she has been appropriated to address longshoremen on the West Coast. Such careful observations will help you begin to develop an argument about the poster, but in order to back up or substantiate your claims, you need to do some research. That is, you need to place the rhetorical elements of the poster in their historical and critical contexts, including propaganda posters from the World War II era and the events related to the 2011–2012 Occupy Movement.

Research can be conducted in any number of ways, including interviews, fieldwork, and the exploration of sources both online and in print. However, the starting point of any research effort is to determine what questions to ask and what inquiries to pursue. In this chapter, you will learn how to become an active participant in a research community and begin to develop the skills for narrowing your research question and creating an effective research plan and a solid research proposal.

ASKING RESEARCH QUESTIONS

4.1 How do I use questions to get started on finding a research topic?

The discussion in this chapter focuses on the subset of persuasion—propaganda—because such texts make very powerful public statements and because, for many of us, we have to perform a certain amount of research in order to understand the motives and purpose behind them. Often this research involves seeking answers to questions we have formulated about the text. In fact, most research begins with the act of asking questions.

One way you can get started on your research is to pick a text that moves you and start brainstorming questions about it. Let's say that you came across the 1917 American enlistment poster shown in Figure 4.2 in an exhibit on campus or as part of a class discussion about World War I posters. Approaching it for the first time, you probably will start to analyze the visual rhetoric, much as we did in the earlier chapters of this book.

What are your eyes drawn to first, the words or the image? Maybe you look first at the simian figure in the middle, roaring menacingly at you, and then at the swooning, semi-naked woman in his arms. In contrast, maybe the person next to you is attracted first to the bold yellow text at the top and then to the bottom, where the words "U.S. Army" in black are superimposed on the imperative "Enlist." In synthesizing various responses to the text, you most likely would find yourself with more questions than answers—a good thing, for those questions can be the beginning of your research inquiry.

FIGURE 4.2 This World War I propaganda poster (originally published in 1917) offers a wealth of detail for historical analysis.

You might ask: Is that gorilla King Kong? Your research would allow you to confidently answer, No, since you would discover that the poster was made decades before the movie was released. That same research might lead you to discover several books that discuss the wartime practice of casting enemies as subhuman creatures, offering a possible explanation for why the enemy nation is portrayed as a threatening gorilla in this poster. Adding to that your observation that "culture" is spelled "Kultur" (on the club the gorilla is holding), you probably would realize that the enemy symbolized here is in fact Germany.

Then you might ask: What is the significance of that bloody club? Why is the woman unconscious and partly naked? More research might provide insight on how bestiality emerged as a wartime theme in World War I enlistment posters. If a nation's women were threatened with potential attack by such "monsters," these posters implied, then the men would surely step up to save and protect their wives, daughters, sisters, and mothers.

By asking questions about your text, you can move beyond an initial response and into the realm of intellectual discovery. In fact, your first questions about a text will lead you to ask more pointed questions about the context, political environment, key players, and social trends informing your text. For the propaganda poster in Figure 4.2, such questions might include:

- What conflict was America involved in at the time that this poster was made?
- What was the meaning of the word on the gorilla's hat, "Militarism," at that time?

- How would an appeal to enlist factor into that historical situation?
- Who was the poster's audience?
- Did other posters of the time use similar rhetorical strategies?

Many of these questions have fact-based answers that invite you to start to better understand the rhetorical situation of the text. By putting a rhetorical spin on traditional journalistic questions (who, what, where, when, how, why), you can sharpen your approach to the text and open up the possibility for it to serve as the foundation for a more rigorous line of inquiry:

- Who is the author?
- What is the claim?
- What strategies are used?
- Who is the audience?
- When was it made?
- What is the purpose and exigency of the argument?

Working with the poster from Figure 4.2, you might chart these questions in a way that both provides you with an enriched understanding of the text and also positions it as the starting point for additional research:

Who: Author	U.S. Army or the U.S. government
What: Claim	Americans (men) need to enlist in the Army to rescue Liberty from the grasp of German militarism.
How: Strategies	*Pathos* appeal: uses emotionally charged symbolism (Germany as the "mad brute"; Liberty as the female victim)
For Whom: Audience	The American public
When: Context	World War I (specifically 1917)
Why: Purpose and Exigency	With the United States joining the war in 1917, this poster seems a timely effort to persuade Americans to back the war effort, both ideologically (by identifying Germany as a threat) and practically (by enlisting).

Possible research topic: American enlistment posters and war propaganda in World War I

Using such questions to arrive at a possible research topic, you can then take the next step, moving from the individual text to consider it as part of a larger issue, event, or system of meaning. You could develop a line of questions that encourage you to make connections and explore the larger significance:

- To what extent did other World War I enlistment posters use similar imagery and rhetorical strategies? How did they differ in their strategies?
- How do the techniques used in early twentieth-century posters differ from those used during World War II?
- How are the rhetorical strategies used in this poster similar to or different from enlistment posters or advertisements you might encounter today?
- In what ways have enlistment propaganda changed over time?

Seeing Connections
Look at the invention questions in Chapter 3 for further ways to use questions to develop a topic.

Each of these questions could lead to a more focused *research topic* and, ultimately, a written essay that draws on and contributes to the arguments that others have made about such texts. Generating a range of interesting and productive **research questions** is the first step in any research project; they will guide your work and lead you to your final argument. You can generate these questions by responding to the rhetorical situation provided by a text and by considering what interests *you* most about either the text or the topic. This process of inquiry itself helps you to define a project and make it your own.

WRITER'S PRACTICE   MyWritingLab

I'm Proud... my husband
wants me to do my part
SEE YOUR U. S. EMPLOYMENT SERVICE
WAR MANPOWER COMMISSION

Using the poster in Figure 4.3 as a starting point, create your own analysis table like the one above, answering the questions:

- Who? (Author)
- What? (Claim)
- How? (Strategies)
- For whom? (Audience)
- When? (Context)
- Why? (Exigency and purpose)

Use this process of critical thinking and rhetorical analysis to lead you toward a topic that you might explore for a research topic.

FIGURE 4.3 This 1944 poster was produced by the Office of War Information and the War Manpower Commission.

GENERATING TOPICS

At the beginning of this chapter, we suggested that you might use an individual text as the starting point for developing a research topic. However, while sometimes you might find the inspiration for a research project in a text that you encounter inside or outside the classroom, other times you find yourself searching for other modes of inspiration to help you discover that perfect research topic.

If you think back to our discussion of *invention* in Chapter 3, you'll understand that one of the most crucial aspects of starting a research project is selecting a viable and engaging topic. The word *topic*, in fact, comes from the ancient Greek word *topos*, translated literally as "place." The earliest students of rhetoric used the physical space of the papyrus page—given to them by their teachers—to locate their topics for writing. Similarly, your teacher may suggest certain guidelines or parameters for you to follow when it comes to your topic; for instance, you may be given a specific topic (such as representations of race in Dr. Seuss cartoons) or you may be limited to a theme (the rhetoric of political advertisements on television, radio, and the Internet).

In some cases, you may not have any restrictions at all. Sometimes that might feel overwhelming, but consider ways to make the task of finding a topic more manageable. Review your class notes or readings to see what topics intrigued or even provoked you; do some additional background reading to spark ideas, talk with a friend about possible ideas, and consult with your instructor about topics that might match your interests.

As you consider possible research topics, keep this key principle in mind: successful topics need to interest you, inspire you, or even provoke you. Even with assigned topics, you should be able to find some aspect of the assignment that speaks to you. That is, there needs to be a *connection* between you and your topic to motivate you to follow through and transform it into a successful argument.

Regardless of the degree to which your topic has been mapped out for you, you still can—and should—make it your own. You do this partly by generating your own **research questions** about an issue, an event, a controversy, or—as we did above—a specific text. These questions can guide your work, help you identify a productive topic to explore, and lead you to your final argument. You can generate these questions by responding to the

AT A GLANCE

Looking for the "Perfect" Topic

1. *Look inward.* What issues, events, or ideas interest you? Are there any hot-button topics you find yourself drawn to again and again? What topic is compelling enough that you would watch a news program, television special, YouTube video, film, or relevant lecture on it?

2. *Look outward.* What are the central issues of student life on campus? Do you walk by a classroom and see the students inside busy writing on laptops or using interactive whiteboards? Topic: technology and education. Do you see a fraternity's poster about a "dry" party? Topic: alcohol on campus. Do you see workers outside the food service building on strike? Topic: labor relations at the college.

3. *Use creative visualization.* Imagine that you are chatting casually with a friend when you overhear someone talking. Suddenly, you feel so interested—or so angry—that you go over and participate in the conversation. What would move you so strongly?

4. *Use the materials of the moment.* Perhaps the *topos* might be closer to the classical Greek model; although not a roll of papyrus, your class reading list or a single issue of a newspaper can house many topics. Scan the front page and opinion section of your school or community newspaper to see what issues people are talking about. What issues are gripping the community at large?

rhetorical situation provided by your assignment and by considering what interests *you* most about the topic. Even if your whole class is writing on the same topic, each person will present a different argument or approach to the issue. Some will use a different stance or persona, some will rely on different sources, some will use different rhetorical appeals, and all will argue different positions about the topic.

In addition, while selecting your topic, you might consider the type of research you'll need to do to pursue it; in fact, you might select your topic based mostly on the sorts of research it allows you to do. For instance, a student writing on propaganda of the Prohibition era will draw extensively on paper sources, which might involve archival work with original letters, pamphlets, or government documents from that time period. A student writing on visual advertising for ethnic-theme dorms on campus will be more likely to complement paper sources with interviews with the university housing staff, student surveys, and first-person observations. A student writing on sexualized rhetoric in student campaign materials might take a poll, gather concrete examples, and research both print and online coverage of past and present elections. Think broadly and creatively about what kinds of research you might use and what types of research—archival work versus fieldwork involving interviews and survey taking—appeal most to you. Finally, consider whether you can actually get your hands on the source material you need to construct a persuasive argument.

WRITER'S PRACTICE   MyWritingLab

Select a preliminary topic for a research paper, whether from a list provided for you by your instructor or from your own interests. Put it to the test to assess its viability as the foundation for a successful project by answering the following questions:

1. **What is interesting about this topic?** We write best about ideas, events, and issues that we connect with through curiosity, passion, or intellectual interest.
2. **Can I make a claim or argue a position about this topic?** At this stage, you may not have developed a position on the topic, but you should see promise for advancing a new perspective or for taking a stand.
3. **Will I be able to find enough research material on this topic?** Brainstorm some possible sources you might use to write this paper.
4. **Does this sort of research appeal to me?** Since you will be working with this topic for an extended period, it is best to have a genuine interest in the type of research that it will require (for instance, doing archival work, reading scholarly sources, conducting original research, or engaging in fieldwork).

Constructing a Research Log

From the very beginning of your research process—as you move from asking questions about a text to identifying a productive topic, to gathering information and taking notes—keep track of your ideas in a *research log*. This log will help you organize your ideas, collect your materials, chart your progress, and assemble the different pieces of your research.

Your research log can take many forms, from a handwritten journal, to a series of word processing documents, a personal blog, a Google doc, or a collection of bookmarked Webpages. It can contain primarily written text, or it can include images, video, or audio files as well. The key lies not in what your research log looks like, but in the way you use it to help you develop an interesting and provocative research project that keeps careful track of the sources you encounter along the way.

In the early stages of a project, you can use your log to help you record and track your ideas; it provides you with an open, creative platform to begin your research journey. You might use your research log in a variety of ways:

- To list possible topic ideas
- To annotate excerpts from newspaper articles, magazine sources, blog posts, or even email or forum threads that offer interesting potential topics
- To respond to provocative images related to potential topics
- To write a reaction to ideas brought up during class discussion
- To list questions about your potential topics: What do you know? What do you need to find out? Note down answers as well.
- To track your preliminary Internet searches
- To explore some of the challenges of the topic and also note what excites you about it as well

This page from Oishi Banerjee's research log (Figure 4.4) shows how she used this space as a way to brainstorm ideas for a research paper on the suffrage movement. She moved from close analysis of a primary source—a variety of anti-suffragette postcards—to broader questions that help her situate the postcards in context, consider their cultural impact, and develop several powerful research questions that she could use as the foundation for her ongoing inquiry into this topic.

4.3 What prewriting techniques can I use to narrow my topic?

NARROWING YOUR TOPIC

Once you have selected a topic and generated some research questions, the next step in the research project involves *narrowing* your topic to make your research project feasible and focused. A productive way to do this is through **prewriting**, or writing that precedes the official drafting of the paper, but, practically speaking, can take many forms. Lists, scribbled notes, informal outlines, drawings—all different types of *prewriting* can help you move from a broad topic to a much more focused one.

Using Prewriting Techniques to Focus Your Topic

For many writers, **freewriting** is a very productive strategy to help focus and sharpen ideas. In its most pure form, freewriting involves writing without stopping for a set period of time; the idea is to simply keep writing out

Research Topic: Pro- and anti-suffrage propaganda in America, at the beginning of the 1900s

Primary Sources: Postcards from the Palczewski Suffrage Postcard Archive, at the University Northern Iowa (http://www.uni.edu/palczews/NEW postcard webpage/BSseries.html)

Anti-suffragette themes in the postcards:

- fear of a reversal of gender roles:
  - makes fun of men tending children
  - mockery of men attempting other domestic tasks (cooking and so on)
- vilification of suffragettes:
  - images of women using violence against men
  - wordplay with "suffragette" and men's "suffering"
  - images of crying children, implying suffragettes were bad mothers
  - misspelling "women" as "wimmen" on suffragettes' sashes (both implies that suffragettes were unfeminine and wanted to be men, and that suffragettes weren't well-educated)
  - reducing suffragettes to sex objects ("I'd rather kiss her than hear her talk")

Broader questions:

- Are there any other anti-suffragette themes in the postcards that I haven't yet noticed?
- How powerful were these postcards? To what extent could they influence political discourse in the early 1900s? Did they change public opinion, or simply reflect it?
- What made postcard propaganda different from propaganda in other media?
- Besides postcards, what other works so explicitly attacked suffragettes?
- Who made these postcards? Political groups? Commercial postcard businesses? Independent artists?
- Who bought these postcards? How were these postcards used? Were they kept as private mementos, or were they actually used and sent to other people?
- How do these anti-suffrage postcards compare to pro-suffrage postcards?

FIGURE 4.4 In her research log, Oishi recorded her analysis of her primary source as a first step to formulating broader questions.

your ideas, without worrying about grammar, punctuation, or even structure so that you can follow your thoughts fluidly and freely. The key is to not hesitate, edit, or even read the freewrite over before the time for writing is up. We've known some writers who even freewrite with their eyes closed or with their computer screen dimmed to prevent themselves from interrupting the flow of ideas.

Such stream-of-consciousness writing on a topic can yield useful insights into what interests you most, what questions you have, and how you might develop your ideas. In fact, many people see the act of writing itself as a way to make meaning and discover ideas. In that sense, freewriting doesn't just allow you to write out what you already know; it leads you to make new connections and create new knowledge.

When you're trying to narrow your topic, you might try a variation of this technique: **funneled freewriting**. Funneled freewriting asks you to do just what it suggests: progressively narrow your ideas into a more concentrated stream. You start by freewriting about your topic for a set amount of time, usually 5 or 10 minutes. When that's done, you stop and read over what you wrote, identifying one key idea or subtopic. Then you freewrite again for the same set amount of time, this time using that subtopic as your starting point. You continue this process for several iterations, each time reading what you've written, identifying a more focused key point, and using that for the next freewriting segment. At the end, you will arrive at a more narrowed topic, one that has been focused by your questions, interests, and ideas.

Occasionally, however, you'll have trouble anticipating when a research topic might be *too* narrow. An alternative prewriting method you might try is the **accordion prewrite**, a technique that asks you to slide between extremely broad and extremely narrow research questions as a way of finding one scaled most effectively for your particular assignment. Let's look at how one student used an accordion prewrite to brainstorm a possible topic about the use of propaganda related to same-sex marriage.

She began by drawing a horizontal line in her research log (Figure 4.5). On one end, she wrote a couple of overly broad questions (To what extent does advertising function as propaganda? How does propaganda affect civil rights?), on the other, she wrote an overly narrow question (Exactly how many Californians voted "Yes" on Proposition 8 because of Frank Schubert's ad campaign?). Having established the extremes, she then filled in a variety of different questions in the center of her "accordion," positioning them in relation to the broad or narrowed points as appropriate. When she was done, she had a spectrum of

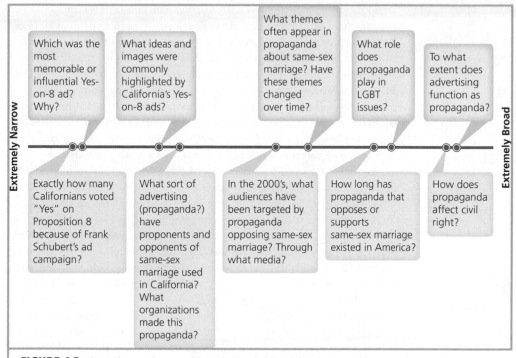

Extremely Narrow | Extremely Broad

Which was the most memorable or influential Yes-on-8 ad? Why?

What ideas and images were commonly highlighted by California's Yes-on-8 ads?

What themes often appear in propaganda about same-sex marriage? Have these themes changed over time?

What role does propaganda play in LGBT issues?

To what extent does advertising function as propaganda?

Exactly how many Californians voted "Yes" on Proposition 8 because of Frank Schubert's ad campaign?

What sort of advertising (propaganda?) have proponents and opponents of same-sex marriage used in California? What organizations made this propaganda?

In the 2000's, what audiences have been targeted by propaganda opposing same-sex marriage? Through what media?

How long has propaganda that opposes or supports same-sex marriage existed in America?

How does propaganda affect civil right?

FIGURE 4.5 This student used an accordion prewrite to help her define the scope of her research.

possibilities that helped her conceptualize how she might scale her topic to a manageable size. After brainstorming in this way, she chose to focus on the questions clustered to the left side—about California's "Yes on [Proposition] 8" campaign—allowing her to narrow her focus in a way that suited both her research interests and the requirements of her assignment.

One benefit of the accordion model is that it allows writers to experiment with more visual means of experimenting with the scope of a topic. The practice of **graphic brainstorming** offers another effective way to visualize different ways to narrow a topic. This technique transforms traditional **brainstorming**—jotting down a series of related words and phrases on a topic—into a more visible process. Also called *webbing*, *clustering*, or *mapping*, the goal of *graphic brainstorming* is to help you develop your topic by exploring relationships among ideas. Begin by writing a topic in a circle, and then come up with ideas and questions about that topic. Next, arrange them in groups around your main circle to indicate the relationships between them. As you answer each question and pose more developed ones in response, you begin to narrow your topic. You'll notice that Figure 4.6 shows how we might start to do this by writing questions that differentiate between various World War I posters and by grouping them by gender issues. In addition, in our brainstorm, we use various types of notations—including words, phrases, and questions—and insert lines and arrows to indicate the relationship between the concepts. We even use images and color to further emphasize these associations. These techniques help us develop the argument and eventually can lead to a more narrowed topic and perhaps even a preliminary thesis.

As we continue to brainstorm—whether for an hour or over several sessions—it becomes clear why some people call this technique **webbing** or **clustering**. As Figure 4.6 shows, our graphic turns into a web of ideas. By using this technique, we have done more than simply develop our topic; we have made it visually apparent that our topic is too broad for a standard research paper assignment. Our web now offers enough ideas for an entire book on the subject. But our diagram also provides us with clues about the direction in which to take our project. We can pick a subsection of ideas to focus on in our writing. If we zoomed in on one part of the diagram—the part, color-coded yellow, that asks key questions about the representations of women in military posters, for instance—we could set the foundation for a focused essay that examines the implications of the way women are depicted in these texts. We could explore how cross-dressing is used as a deliberate appeal to the audience, or how military posters evoke the image of wife and mother to mobilize troops.

A final mode you might use to narrow a topic is **heuristic questioning**. In this method, you begin with a general topic and then sharpen it with a series of increasingly focused questions. For instance, if you were to take the topic of gender roles in World War I, you might follow this heuristic process to distill key issues that might help make the topic more manageable:

1. Write down your topic.

   Topic formulation: gender roles in World War I.

2. Work with that topic by asking a pointed question based on close analysis of the text at hand.

   First question: Is there a sexual undertone to the posters?

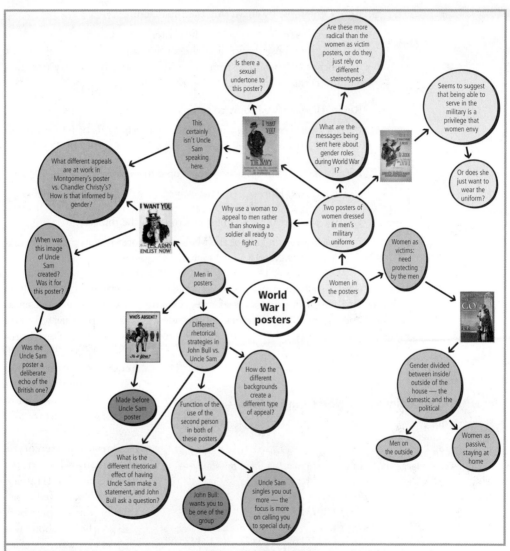

FIGURE 4.6 In this graphic brainstorm of the broad topic "World War I posters" (center white circle), the author identifies several more specific ways she might focus or narrow her research.

3. Refine the topic by answering that question.

   Topic narrowing: Yes, in one of the posters, the woman is standing in a provocative pose, looking at the audience in a sexual manner, but in another, the women seem more identified with family (mother, daughter) than with sexuality.

4. Revise the narrowed topic to be more specific.

   Revised topic formulation: the different constructions of femininity in World War I propaganda posters.

5. Identify significant aspects of that topic to explore.

   Second question: How so? In what way? What is the significance?

6. Use the answers to these questions to focus the topic.

   Final topic focus: the use of the Madonna–whore stereotype as a persuasive strategy in World War I recruitment posters.

By asking such questions—and we could come up with many others along different lines of inquiry (such as race, sexuality, international representations, and nationalism)—we begin to develop a *focused* topic that will offer us the opportunity for close analysis, rigorous research, and a sharp argumentative stance. That is, we can move from a topic loosely concerned with gender roles in World War I to one that focuses specifically on a subset of recruitment posters and how they deploy a particular sexist stereotype (the virgin–whore trope) as a persuasive strategy. With this narrowed topic, we'll be able to contribute a new opinion about war posters and write an essay that adds to the ongoing dialogue that we find in our research sources.

AT A GLANCE

Prewriting Techniques for Narrowing a Topic

- *Freewriting:* Write about your topic without stopping for a specific amount of time.
- *Funneled freewriting:* Complete a set of freewrites, each one focusing in a single specific question or idea generated in the previous freewrite.
- *Accordion prewrite:* Brainstorm research question on a scale from ridiculously broad to ridiculously narrow as a way of developing more appropriate questions in the middle.
- *Graphic brainstorm:* Use a clustering or webbing technique to explore questions, topics, and subtopics in a nonlinear fashion.
- *Heuristic questions:* Sharpen your topic through a series of progressively narrowed questions.

Working in a group or on your own, try out this practice of *narrowing a topic* with a selection of posters from the 2011 Occupy Movement. Look back at Figure 4.1 and consider it along with Figures 4.7 and 4.8 below; then use one of the methods described above (freewrite, funneled freewrite, graphic brainstorm, heuristic questions) to develop a feasible topic for a research paper. Be sure that you narrow your topic from "Occupy Posters" to a more focused one that you might pursue in a research paper. You might decide during your narrowing exercise to focus your topic by identifying which images you'd like to write about or by generating key questions to ask about particular texts: How do the words and images work together in these posters? How do they work against each other? How does symbolism operate in these posters? The more specific the questions you ask, the more focused your topic will be.

FIGURE 4.7

FIGURE 4.8

WRITING ABOUT YOUR RESEARCH PLANS

4.4 What are the steps for developing a strong research plan?

After you have narrowed your topic, you need to develop a plan for your research process. If you find yourself concerned that you don't have the knowledge necessary to write this essay or are worried that the gaps in your own knowledge will prevent you from answering those questions in a satisfactory way, then realize that you are in good company. All researchers and scholars fear the limitations of their knowledge. The key is to develop a concrete plan to guide you as you move forward with your project.

The Research Freewrite

One way to start planning your research process is complete a focused freewrite about your ideas in your research log—it's called a *focused* freewrite because while you still adhere to the principle of informal writing, you do so within the constraints of a concrete structure. In completing your research freewrite, follow a **three-paragraph model**: in the *first paragraph*, announce your topic and state a preliminary thesis so that you can begin the project with a critical and focused perspective; in the *second paragraph*, identify the sources you plan to use to investigate this topic; and in the *third paragraph*, speculate on obstacles or problems you might encounter in your research and how you might avoid or solve these problems. This freewrite will help you concretize your topic and assess your next steps in research.

Let's look at a freewrite from student Rafe Salinas, who shaped his research inquiry to explore the relationship between U.S. propaganda and the destabilization of Salvador Allende's government in Chile in the 1970s.

This first paragraph introduces the research topic and describes what Rafe thinks the main focus of his paper might be. At the end of the paragraph, he includes a preliminary research question to help him focus his interest and argument as he begins researching this topic.

Research Freewrite

The destruction of the government that Salvador Allende instituted in Chile in the early 1970s was as a result of several key factors, including direct and indirect intervention by the United States of America. I want to examine the extent to which the United States was responsible for the downfall of Allende's government by investigating the role of propaganda created and distributed by the U.S. government in Chile before and during Allende's term as president. I'm hoping to analyze specific examples of propaganda to get a closer look at the United States' rhetorical strategies, what the primary appeals and methods were, including how they used *ethos*, *pathos*, *kairos*, and *logos*. By analyzing sources that indicate the political atmosphere following the use of this propaganda, I hope to get a deeper understanding about the destabilization of his government as well. *Guiding research question:* How, why, and to what extent did the propaganda produced by the United States lead to Allende's downfall?

In terms of key sources, I hope to examine the U.S. propaganda itself to understand the persuasive strategies behind the various types of propaganda. This includes press, radio, films, pamphlets, posters, leaflets, direct mailings, paper streamers, street activities, wall painting, etc. By examining intelligence from the U.S. government—I'm thinking specifically of analyzing a congressional report examining the years 1963–1973 (*The Church Committee and Report and the Hinchey Report as Presented to the U.S. Congress*, 2008)—I will gain insight into how the U.S. intervened, and what the intentions behind intervention were. Finally, I'm sure it will be important to read secondary sources on intervention, particularly those with emphasis on U.S. propaganda and the resultant political climate. Currently, I plan to use *The Nixon Administration and the Death of Allende's Chile: A Case of Assisted Suicide* by Jonathan Haslam and *The Black Book of American Intervention in Chile* by Armando Uribe for this part of the research.

In the second paragraph, Rafe discusses the sources he intends to use. Notice the broad range of possibilities he considers: flyers, television commercials, radio broadcasts, and both American and international sources.

In the third paragraph Rafe anticipates the difficulties he might face and how he can solve them.

I have a feeling that I will encounter some difficulties in both the sources and the broadness of the topic (i.e., the reasons behind the destruction of Allende's government). Although I possess a working knowledge of Spanish, I know it's fairly limited, and given that propaganda targets a very specific audience in a very specific time period, I probably won't totally get the slang and popular references. I also realize that propaganda isn't the whole picture, and I will need to balance the analysis of the role of propaganda with an honest recognition of the impact of other elements (like military intervention) on Allende's downfall.

Drafting a Guiding Research Question and Research Hypothesis

In reading Rafe's freewrite, you might have noticed that as he developed this topic, he was simultaneously starting to experiment with how to formulate his own argument. That is, in his first paragraph, he moves from the open-ended language of a proposal ("I want to examine," "I'm hoping to analyze") to a restatement of his subject in terms of a guiding research question at the end of the paragraph. You might be tempted in your own freewrite to include a tentative thesis statement along with your research question. While an early hypothesis can be useful, be careful about forming your own argument about a topic too early. How can you responsibly make a claim about a topic that you have not yet researched completely? How can you know what to argue about an issue before you listen to what your sources have to say? These are often frustrating questions for many writers. If you decide on your claim too early, you may set in motion a research process that tempts you to cherry-pick your sources and dismiss

Seeing Connections
See Chapter 1 to review how to develop a strong preliminary thesis statement.

or ignore voices that do not concur with your hypothesis. For this reason, many scholars suggest that writers should focus on identifying a **guiding research question**, as Rafe does, at early stages of the research process, rather than formulating a tentative hypothesis.

There are many benefits to developing a question of this sort. A well-crafted research question can keep you focused as you delve into the research process. In addition, by posing your project as one grounded in inquiry, you can focus on finding sources that help you answer your question rather than prove your point, leading ultimately to a stronger, more persuasive argument. Your question may in fact undergo revision as you learn more about your topic; that is a natural step in the process of exploration and discovery that is at the heart of any research process. To begin, however, you can generate your guiding question by synthesizing some of the more pointed questions about your topic, similar to those we discussed at the beginning of this chapter. Alternately, you could use a prewriting activity like the accordion prewrite to help you identify a strong question to focus your research. In general, a strong research question:

- opens up a line of inquiry (rather than inviting a yes/no response)
- has a sharp focus, appropriate to the scope of the assignment (rather than being overly broad or overly narrow)
- avoids bias or preconceptions (rather than posing a "leading" question)
- offers a solid foundation for further research (rather than posing a question that you might not be able to answer, due to lack of sources or methods for exploring it)

Once you have your guiding research question and have begun to explore your topic, you can start to rework it into a hypothesis, or a working thesis that makes an argumentative claim that you'll attempt to prove. You may move to this step once you start researching, or you may wait until you begin drafting—or even revising—your research paper. Keep in mind that you will probably revise your hypothesis—and maybe your entire approach to the subject—several times over the course of your research. Indeed, this revision process is a natural part of what happens when you actually begin to read your sources, take notes in your research log, and read what your sources have to say about your topic.

4.5 How do I write a formal research proposal?

DRAFTING A RESEARCH PROPOSAL

In many academic contexts, you will be asked to formalize your research plan through composing a **research proposal**. This type of text—common in many disciplines and professions—is used by writers to develop agendas for research communities, secure funding for a study, publicize plans for inquiry and field research, and test the interest of potential audiences for a given project. In the writing classroom, the research proposal provides a similar formal structure for developing a project, but it also serves another purpose: it is a more structured means of organizing your thoughts to help you solidify your topic and move into the next stages of the research process. For these reasons, the *genre*, *organization*, and *content* of the research proposal differ in important ways from other kinds of popular and academic writing that you might do. To write your proposal, include the following elements:

- **Background:** What do I already know about my topic? What do I need to find out more about?
- **Methods:** How am I going to research this topic? What research questions are driving my inquiry?
- **Sources:** What specific texts will I analyze? What additional scholarly or popular sources can I research to help build my knowledge and my argument?
- **Timeline:** What are my goals for the different stages of research, and how can I schedule my work to most effectively meet these milestones?
- **Significance:** What do I hope to accomplish in my research? What are the broader issues or implications of my research? Why do these matter to me and to my readers?

As this list suggests, your proposal should explain your interest in your chosen subject and establish a set of questions to guide your inquiry. The proposal should delineate the timeline for your research and writing process—a crucial time management strategy.

Your proposal serves to clarify your research intentions, but it should also *persuade* an audience of the feasibility and significance of your project. In fact, perhaps the most important step in launching your research inquiry is to address the issue of your project's larger relevance or, as some writing instructors call it, the "So what?" part of the project. It is the

"So what?"—an awareness of the *significance* of the topic you're addressing and the questions you're asking—that moves the proposal from being a routine academic exercise to a powerful piece of persuasive writing. When addressing the "So what?" question, consider why anyone else would care enough to read a paper on your topic. Ask yourself:

- What is at stake in your topic?
- Why does it matter?
- What contribution will your project make to a wider community?

Let's look at an example: a research proposal Molly Fehr developed on Hitler's use of rhetoric.

Fehr 1

Molly Fehr
Dr. Alyssa O'Brien
PWR 2: Rhetoric and Global Leadership
Final Research Proposal
8 May 2016

Inspiring Nazi Germany:

How Hitler Rose to Power through the Use of Propaganda and Rousing Rhetoric

World War II involved all of the major world powers and was the deadliest conflict in human history. The men who led these powers into battle were extraordinary historical figures ranging from Winston Churchill to Franklin D. Roosevelt to Joseph Stalin. Perhaps the most infamous historical leader of all time, Adolf Hitler, was a major component of World War II. For this research project I will examine how Hitler used powerful rhetoric to inspire his followers. The speeches that Hitler gave to the German public were effective enough to convince an entire country to go to war to fight for his beliefs. His powerful

Molly's research proposal begins with a title that reflects her focused research question. In this way, she is sure to offer a more narrowed approach to her topic than the research freewrite.

The proposal opens with background, based on common knowledge.

In the last three sentences of the paragraph, Molly articulates her increasingly narrowed focus: from speeches to powerful rhetoric, to violent propaganda. This narrowed focus will help prevent her project from being too broad.

Fehr 2

rhetoric influenced a generation of German citizens to adopt his ideology and practice his principles. In addition to persuading countless people to embrace his ideas, he used a widespread and violent propaganda campaign to effectively silence his opposition.

As she generates specific research questions, Molly keeps her focus on "violence" as her main line of inquiry.

There are many different facets of World War II leadership and Hitler's power that one could explore. I will be focusing on Hitler specifically and how his use of violent rhetoric influenced both his supporters and his opposition. Some questions I will attempt to answer are: what part of his campaign was the most convincing? My focus will be on his overt use of violence and how that impacted his rise to power. So, what part did violence play in Hitler's rise to power? How did Hitler use fear as a rhetorical strategy? Is violent or emotional imagery the most powerful type of rhetoric? Then, more generally, how did Hitler's leadership affect Germany's role in the war? And finally, how does our understanding of his use of violence impact our view of Hitler as a leader?

Turning to research methods, Molly names and describes the texts she plans to analyze. This makes her proposal seem quite feasible and builds her *ethos* as a scholar.

Hitler's extremely lengthy and provocative speeches will be the cornerstone of my research as they are excellent examples of both *ethos* and *pathos*. I will examine several of Hitler's most famous speeches, focusing on those given each year on the anniversary of his rise to power. In each of these speeches he spoke of the superiority of the German race and his future plans for the great nation. My discussion of Hitler's leadership

Fehr 3

and rhetorical style will also include with an analysis of his book, *Mein Kampf,* which outlines his core beliefs. There have been several scholarly books and articles written about *Mein Kampf* that I will use as secondary sources in my analysis. One book in particular that I will devote time to is Felicity Rash's *The Language of Violence* in which she discusses how the linguistic style of *Mein Kampf* created powerful imagery and elicited strong emotions. Other secondary sources that I will explore include John Angus's article "Evil As the Allure of Protection," and Monika Zagar's *Knut Hamsun*. These sources and others investigate the violent imagery of Nazism and how its effects were far-reaching and dramatic. A possible field resource that I could interview might be a Stanford professor specializing in World War II. I could also interview one of the Stanford research librarians, specifically, either Nathalie Auerbach who specializes in German history or Patricia Harrington who is a general reference librarian.

This project has significant implications for the manner in which historical and contemporary leaders inspire their followers into controversial actions. Understanding how Adolf Hitler employed violent rhetoric to convince people that genocide was not only acceptable but desirable is crucial to unraveling the power of other infamous leaders. Additionally, it is interesting to explore why Hitler was so successful. If certain types of

> She refers to several books that have made important contributions to her topic.

> She also includes field research as part of her plan, identifying scholars she might interview to learn more about the field.

Molly ends the formal writing of the proposal with a strong statement of significance. Suggesting the "So what?" will help her focus on the importance of her work as a writer and researcher. This section on implications is often the most crucial to readers who evaluate proposals for merit and funding.

Fehr 4

rhetoric such as emotional imagery or evocation of pride are so profoundly effective, how can they be used for good? This brings me to my final point: practical application. There are relatively few historical examples of people who succeeded in amassing so many followers to support a cause that is inherently wrong.

A closer look at how Hitler managed to propagandize and affect a nation could reveal important lessons about how contemporary leaders can mobilize their supporters. Conversely, it could give important wisdom about how to prevent or combat such an influential leader in the future.

In her timeline, Molly lists not only deadlines assigned by her instructor but also key steps in the research process: finding books, evaluating sources, reading and taking notes, constructing a thesis, peer review, a second round of research, drafting, and revising.

Fehr 5

Timeline

1/20: Research Proposal due

1/21–1/23: In-depth research of speeches; write up notes

1/22–1/27: Read secondary sources and write up notes; search for more articles using online databases

1/27–2/1: Review notes and write a preliminary thesis; talk with peers and instructors for advice on thesis as well as for guidance on argument. Evaluate sources in research log and continue to read sources.

Fehr 6

2/2–2/7: Outline due: decide on major argument. Use subheads to indicate sections of the essay.

2/8–2/10: Conduct field research interviews, using my argument and questions.

2/12–2/17: Write first draft of argument. Compose topic sentences for each section. Include evidence for my claims in drafting the argument.

2/18–2/21: Peer review feedback and instructor conference (get feedback).

2/22–3/2: Additional research and revision, as necessary.

3/5: Submit second full draft for feedback.

3/8–3/12: Final revisions, proofreading, works cited list, format paper, include images where appropriate.

3/15: Submit final revision. Done!

With this detailed time-line, Molly shows her careful time manage-ment and builds her *ethos* by demonstrating her understanding of the research process.

Fehr 7

Preliminary Bibliography

Auerbach, Nathalie [Bibliographer for Germanic collections, Stanford Library]. Personal Interview. Feb. 2013 [to be scheduled].

Campbell, John Angus. "Evil as the Allure of Protection." *Rhetoric & Public Affairs* 6.3 (2003): 523–30. *Academic Search Premier*. Web. 22 Jan. 2013.

Fehr 8

Harrington, Patricia R. [Coordinator of Content Delivery, General
Reference, Stanford Library]. Personal Interview. Feb. 2013
[to be scheduled].

Hitler, Adolf, and Ralph Manheim. *Mein Kampf*. Boston:
Houghton, 1943. Print.

Hitler, Adolf. "Germany's Declaration of War against the United
States. Reichstag Speech of December 11, 1941." *Institute
for Historical Review*. N.d. Web. 19 Jan. 2013. http://www.
ihr.org/jhr/v08/v08p389_Hitler.html

——. "Speech before the Reichstag." 30 Jan. 1937. *World Future
Fund*. N.d. Web. 17 Jan. 2013.

——. "Speech at the Berlin Sportspalast." 30 Jan. 1940. *World
Future Fund*. N.d. Web. 17 Jan. 2013.

——. "Speech at the Berlin Sportspalast." 30 Jan. 1942. *World
Future Fund*. N.d. Web. 18 Jan. 2013.

Jowett, Garth S., Victoria O'Donnell, and Garth Jowett. *Readings
in Propaganda and Persuasion: New and Classic Essays*. Thousand Oaks: SAGE, 2006. Print.

Maser, Werner. *Hitler's Mein Kampf: An Analysis*. London: Faber,
1970. Print.

Rash, Felicity J. *The Language of Violence: Adolf Hitler's Mein
Kampf*. New York: Peter Lang, 2006. Print.

Žagar, Monika. *Knut Hamsun: The Dark Side of Literary
Brilliance*. Seattle: U of Washington P, 2009.
Print.

THE WRITER'S PROCESS

Now that you've learned about the process of generating research questions, narrowing your topic, developing a hypothesis, and then writing up your plans for research in a three-paragraph freewrite or a formal proposal, what might you argue about the first poster of this chapter (Figure 4.1) if you were asked to use it as a starting point for a research project?

In answering this question, you might start to work through the writing activities related to the research process that we've discussed. You might develop a research focus that begins with questions and ends with a "So what?" or statement of significance. You might speculate about which sources that you could use to answer your questions and on opportunities and obstacles you might encounter when pursuing this project. You might try to develop a proposal that concludes with a clear statement of your future authority on this topic as a researcher. Along the way, you might use a research log to keep track of your ideas and work in progress, setting a strong foundation for the next steps of research—gathering and evaluating sources—that we'll be exploring in the next chapter. Now it's time to get started on the research process for writing a persuasive argument about an issue that matters to you.

SPOTLIGHTED ANALYSIS: PROPAGANDA POSTERS   MyWritingLab

Use the following prewriting prompts to follow the example from the beginning of the chapter and analyze the propaganda poster of your choice (for instance, from the Library of Congress online archive):

- What is the poster's underlying message?
- What rhetorical situation informs this text? Who produced the poster? Who was its intended audience? How was it distributed or shared?
- What is its historical context? What was the contemporary social and political situation of the country that produced it?
- What types of rhetorical appeals (*logos*, *pathos*, *ethos*, *kairos*, or *doxa*) does the poster feature and how do they operate in the poster?
- Recalling Chapter 2's discussion of exaggerated use of appeals, does the poster rely on any logical fallacies? Any exaggerated use of *pathos*? Any fallacies of authority? If so, how do these work to persuade the audience?

- How do design elements such as color, font, layout, image selection, and the relationship between word and image operate as persuasive elements?
- How does the poster use stereotypes or symbols to convey its message? What is their cultural significance?
- What research questions can you develop about this poster?

WRITING ASSIGNMENTS   MyWritingLab

1. **Brainstorming Topics:** Early in this chapter, we used propaganda posters as a starting point for generating research topic ideas. Choose a written text—an essay you read for class, a newspaper article, a government report, a transcript of a speech—and create an analysis table such as the one on page 139 for it in which you answer questions about its author, claim, strategies, audience, context, and purpose. For added challenge, fill out the table on your own, but then circulate a blank version—accompanied by your text—among a small group of classmates. Have them answer the questions about your text in the table, each one filling in one or more of the columns and adding a potential research topic at the bottom. When they have done, compare the collaboratively authored table to the one you filled out yourself to get a deeper understanding of the text and how it might lend itself to additional research.

2. **Narrowing Topics:** Follow the instructions for the Writer's Practice on page 151, but instead of focusing on the Occupy posters, use your own research topic as the foundation for the narrowing exercises. Record your prewriting in your research log.

3. **Research Freewrite:** Develop your ideas for your research project by composing a three-paragraph freewrite. In the first paragraph, introduce your research paper topic and describe what you think the main focus of the paper might be. Include a guiding research question or a preliminary thesis in this paragraph. In the second paragraph, discuss the sources that you intend to use. In the third paragraph, speculate about what obstacles you foresee in this project and/or what you anticipate to be the most difficult part of the assignment. If appropriate, use an image to complement your written text. Share your three-paragraph freewrite to your instructor or your peers for feedback.

4. **Research Proposal:** Write a detailed research proposal that discusses your topic, planned method, and purpose in depth. Be sure to cover your topic, your hypothesis, your potential sources and problems, your method, timeline, and, most importantly, the significance of the proposed project. When you are done, present your proposal at a roundtable of research with other members of your class. Answer questions from your classmates to help you fine-tune your topic and troubleshoot your future research.

5. **Peer Review:** Collaboratively peer review your research proposals with a small group of classmates. Assume that you are on the review board granting approval and funding to the best two proposals of your group. Read through each proposal, and then draft proposal review letters for the members of your group that evaluates each proposal's strengths, weaknesses, and your assessment of whether it deserves funding. When you are done, discuss your letters with your group and what changes you can recommend to strengthen the proposal. Then revise your proposals to make them stronger, better written, and more persuasive. See Chapter 6 for more discussion of effective peer feedback sessions.

MyWritingLab Visit Ch. 4 Planning and Proposing Research Arguments in MyWritingLab to complete the Writer's Practices, Spotlighted Analyses, and Writing Assignments, and to test your understanding of the chapter objectives.

CHAPTER 5

Finding and Evaluating Research Sources

Chapter Preview Questions

5.1 What does the research process look like?

5.2 How do I develop effective search terms for my research?

5.3 What is the difference between a primary and a secondary source?

5.4 How do I critically evaluate both print and online sources?

5.5 How do I pursue field research for my project?

5.6 How can I understand the conversation my sources are having about my topic?

5.7 What is an annotated bibliography, and how can it help me develop my argument?

FIGURE 5.1 Cover of *Science*, March 24, 2006.

As you move from planning to conducting research, you'll need to investigate resources and evaluate them for your project. You can use your analytical skills to make important distinctions when locating, evaluating, and using research sources for your research project. Look, for instance, at the covers in Figures 5.1 and 5.2. Although they focus on the same topic—climate change—the visual rhetoric suggests that the content of each journal will be quite different. The audience for *Science* magazine differs from that of *The Economist*, and, consequently, the writing styles within the articles will be different as well. The cover of each magazine previews the content inside. As a researcher, studying the covers could help you understand the different ways that climate change has been understood over time. In this way, you are finding and evaluating research sources for your project.

Specifically, the cover of *Science* in Figure 5.1 conveys how the editors chose to represent global warming to their audience in 2006. It features a photograph of an ice-covered lake that appears to have been taken with a "fish-eye" lens, bringing several ice fragments into prominence in the foreground. Ask yourself: What is the argument conveyed by the visual rhetoric of the cover? What is the significance of the choice to use the lake as the "main character" in the image? How is color used strategically? What kind of stance toward the dangers of global warming does the cover suggest?

In contrast, *The Economist* cover from a few years later (see Figure 5.2) provides a very different perspective on the topic. While the *Science* cover focuses on the environmental effects of climate change, *The Economist* cover draws the reader in with its comic re-rendering of Grant Wood's famous *American Gothic* painting. It

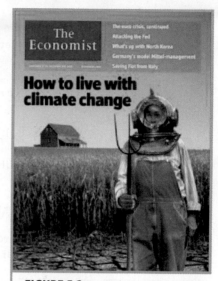

FIGURE 5.2 Cover of *The Economist*, 2010.

shows the impact of global warming not just on the landscape (dried up crops and cracked earth) but also on the individual (the farmer, his startled face hidden behind a diver's helmet). Consider the way that this rhetorical move humanizes the issue of global warning, framing it in a way that is designed specifically to resonate with readers of *The Economist*: the central figure is not just a person, but a farmer, a symbol of American agriculture; the setting is not just a natural landscape, but a farm, representative of U.S. agriculture more broadly. Notice that the language also suggests the magazine's stance. "How to live with climate change" is not a call to action, but a statement about the inevitability of a fact of life.

Clearly, in each case, the editors deliberately located, evaluated, and used materials for the covers that would reflect their magazine's contents. As a researcher, you can use your skills in rhetorical analysis to help you evaluate sources for your own research project, looking to the different elements of a text—from the cover design, to the table of contents, the index, and the writing itself—to better understand the text's perspective on your topic and its usefulness for your project.

Your task as a researcher is quite similar to that of the editors of *Science* and *The Economist*. As you begin gathering and evaluating sources for your own research argument, keep in mind that you will need to shape the argument into a paper addressed to a particular audience: your writing class, a group of scientists, a lobbying organization, an advertising firm, or browsers on the Web. To take part in any of these conversations, a researcher needs to learn:

■ what is being talked about (the *topic*)
■ how it is being discussed (the *conversation*)
■ what the different positions are (*research context*).

5.1 What does the research process look like?

VISUALIZING RESEARCH

To grasp the specifics of the topic, the conversation, and the research context, it is helpful to take a moment to visualize the research process.

When you think of the act of research, what comes to mind? Surfing the Web? Looking through a library? Interviewing experts in the field? All these images represent different research scenarios. The material you gather in each situation will compose the foundation for your research; it will inform your essay, but not all of it will find its way into your final paper. Nevertheless, you need to research widely and thoroughly to be fully informed about your topic and write a compelling research-based argument. One helpful way of visualizing the relationship between the *process* and the *product* of research is through the metaphor of the iceberg of research (see Figure 5.3). In essence, your final argument will be a synthesis of your research; beneath the surface lie the many different sources you will explore: books, journal articles, websites, field surveys, historical materials, interviews, multimedia, and more. All these constitute the research material. Your task as a researcher is to move beyond a surface knowledge of your topic; you need to gather, assess, keep, throw out, and ultimately use a variety of sources.

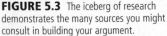

FIGURE 5.3 The iceberg of research demonstrates the many sources you might consult in building your argument.

By exploring such a wide range of material, you will encounter a rich array of scholarly and popular perspectives on your topic. In many ways, your research argument will be, in fact, a discussion with those research sources themselves. You add your voice to theirs. But your final paper may appear as only the tip of the iceberg or a result of your careful study of the work of others.

Sometimes, this process of building on others can be intimidating; we fear that we will have nothing new to add to the conversation. Yet if we think of research sources as texts written by people who were once, like us, struggling to figure out what they were trying to say, then we can see the process of gathering and assessing sources as a very social one, a process in which you *respect* and *acknowledge* the ideas of others and then seek to add your own voice to an ongoing conversation. One way to begin that conversation is to discover what others before you have said, thought, written, and published—and to keep track of that process in your research log, as explained in Chapter 4.

In this chapter, we'll use the metaphor of the *conversation* to accentuate the point that the research process is an act of composing a response to an ongoing dialogue about a topic. By gathering, synthesizing, and sorting the perspectives of others, you begin to shape your own stance on a research topic. By adding your voice as a writer, you are responding to others. Research is a *relationship* that you develop with the source material and the writers you encounter along the way.

DEVELOPING SEARCH TERMS

5.2 How do I develop effective search terms for my research?

The first step in the research process lies in locating relevant and interesting sources to draw into your conversation. This involves finding the best **search terms**—usually a noun or short phrase—to use when looking for sources on your topic. While online search engines like Google and Bing often can complete complex searches based on a colloquial phrase (i.e., "how eating broccoli prevents cancer"), most rigorous research projects rely on more academic search mechanisms, such as scholarly databases, online library catalogues, or reference materials (like encyclopedias or bibliographies). To use these tools effectively, you need to learn to speak their language; instead of using everyday terminology, you need to use **keywords** and **strategic search syntax** to set the parameters for your search.

A good starting point for developing your search terms is to look carefully at your research topic. If you write out your topic or your research question, what key concepts or words can you identify? For instance, if your preliminary topic is "the effect of fracking on groundwater," logical keywords might be "fracking" and "groundwater." To expand your search, you might consider ways to multiply your terms, through first identifying *synonyms* (e.g., drinking water, hydraulic fracturing, drilling), then *related concepts* (e.g., natural gas extraction, contamination), and then *specific examples or stakeholders* (e.g., Pennsylvania water contamination, Chevron). Adding these keywords and phrases to your initial search terminology will help diversify your search results so you can start to explore the different aspects of your topic.

While developing **search** terms is an important starting point for research, using specialized **syntax strategies** can help you conduct more productive searches in academic databases. Boolean searches combine keywords such as AND, NOT, and OR to help you refine your searches; similarly, techniques of truncation and quotation can likewise help you tailor your search results. Let's see how these techniques sharpen a search for a research project on the relationship between vaccines and autism.

AND: When you connect two keywords with "AND," you'll receive all results that include both terms, helping you narrow your search results.

Example: A search for vaccines AND autism *will find articles, books, and other texts that include both terms.* (Note: In Google searches and many database searches, the "AND" is automatically implied, so many search engines automatically would understand a search for *vaccines autism* as *vaccines* AND *autism*.)

OR: When you connect two keywords with "OR," you'll receive all results that contain either of those keywords, helping you expand your search results.

Example: A search for vaccines OR autism *will return a long list of texts that might be just tagged with the keyword* vaccine, *just tagged with the keyword* autism, *or is tagged with both words.*

NOT: When you connect two keywords with "NOT" or "EXCEPT" you'll receive all the results for the first keyword that do not also contain the second keyword, helping you better focus your search results.

Example: A search for vaccines NOT autism *will return texts about vaccines that do not mention autism.*

QUOTATION MARKS: When you enclose a keyword phrase in quotation marks, most search engines search for that specific phrase, helping you get more specific search results.

WRITER'S PRACTICE   MyWritingLab

Develop search terms for your research project by filling in this chart in your research log. Focus on expanding your search by moving from keywords to *synonyms* (that allow you to explore similar ideas) to *related concepts* (that allow you to broaden your scope) to *specific examples* (that show you ways to narrow your search).

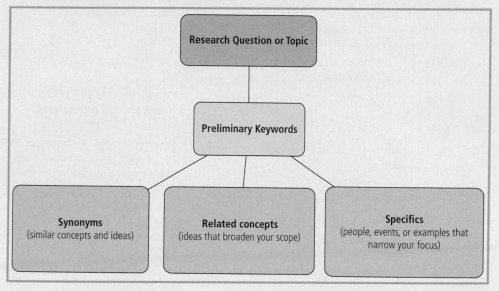

Example: If you searched "autism spectrum disorder," *you would get only results that include that exact phrase.*

TRUNCATION*: In some databases, you can search for different versions of a word by shortening it and appending an * to the end.

Example: Searching autis* *would produce results that include the terms autism or autistic.*

COMBINE TERMS: When you combine terms, you can customize your search even more powerfully.

Example: Searching (vaccines AND autism) NOT "Jenny McCarthy" *will yield results on autism and vaccines that don't mention actress Jenny McCarthy.*

Let's look at how one student adapted her search strategies to accommodate the different types of resources she was using on her project on the recent California drought (see Figure 5.4). Like many students, Ellie started

FINAL RESEARCH PROJECT
Topic: California drought and global warming
Preliminary search term chart and thoughts ...

What I searched and when	Search terms	Results	Notes
Google (4/2/15)	California drought caused by global warming	472,000(!!!)	Mostly news articles (see email for links to top hits)
Google (4/2/15)	California drought caused by climate change	976,000 (!!!)	A lot of repeats from the first search – too broad.
Library catalog (4/2/15)	Climate change	13,760	Too many! Next time try subject header "Climactic Changes > Environmental Aspects > United States"
Library catalog (4/2/15)	California drought	170	Not much useful here – one book from 2008 about a drought that occurred then might provide a historical comparison (see email!)
Library catalog (4/2/15)	California drought global warming	11	Really nothing helpful except one reference book – *Encyclopedia of Global Warming and Climate Change.* ***Go to reference section at library to look at it ***
EBSCO database (4/4/15)	"California drought" AND "global warming"	2	*Nature* article (1/2014) really the only one worth looking at– see email
EBSCO database (4/4/15)	"California drought" AND "climate change"	21	Great articles! See email – esp. look at Tsiang et al (2014 – full text!!) and Mann (2015)

***For next time:**
- Try limiting searches to "video" in the library to see if there's a documentary in one of the searches – might be interesting to watch if recent enough
- Try subject searches in EBSCO database – "CLIMATIC changes"; "droughts"; "RAIN & rainfall"; "California"; "Global warming – Environmental aspects"; "Global environmental change"
- Look up some of the studies mentioned in the news articles (i.e. Diffenbaugh, 2015) to get to the studies themselves (articles are good, but studies themselves would be great!)
- Climate change seems a better term for databases than global warming for this topic!
- Need to find a way to narrow my searches more. Read some articles – find more names of people, places, researchers etc. that I can use in my next searches
- Librarian suggested looking at some other databases: Web of Knowledge; Web of Science; BioOne; LexisNexis (only if you need more articles!); Environment index; GreenFile

FIGURE 5.4 This page from a student's research log shows how she tracked her initial searches.

with an Internet search based on her research question, What's the relationship between the California drought and climate change? Her phrasing—"California drought caused by global warming"—mirrored her everyday language and was designed to target the controversy surrounding this issue. As you might expect, her initial Google search yielded more results than she could use, leaving her to speculate about ways to include more specific keywords in future searches. Moving to her library catalog, she shifted from vernacular phrasing to keywords: "Climate change" and "California drought." The first provided too many results, leading her to identify a subject heading she found listed in one of the source records ("climatic change > environmental aspects > United States") that she could use in the future to narrow her search. Her second library search offered a more manageable range of materials; however, she recognized they would primarily serve as background material and reference sources for her topic. In her quest for more timely sources, she moved to the academic database, EBSCO. Here she used the Boolean operator "AND" to connect her key terms. Through trial and error, she determined that the phrase "climate change" yielded much better results than "global warming," and she was able to find over 20 current and relevant articles about her topic.

As you can see from Ellie's example, often the list of potential sources returned to you by your initial searches will be much larger than you can efficiently process. Your main task, then, will be to find ways to narrow your

AT A GLANCE

Tips for Choosing Search Terms

- *Colloquial terminology and phrases:* Use popular or colloquial terminology and phrases in your Internet searches because search engines pick up actual terms from the webpages they index.

- *Keywords and strategic syntax:* Use keywords for library catalogues and database searches. Since databases can house a wide range of materials, from academic publications to popular articles, experiment with different search terms to find the ones that work best for each database. In addition, use strategic search syntax (AND, OR, NOT, quotation marks, truncation) for more powerful Boolean searches.

- *Subject headings or tags:* Many times, the individual article or book citations that you find in your library catalog or scholarly database will include subject tags or headings that librarians use to catalog information and cross-reference related materials; most are based on the Library of Congress Subject Headings (LCSHs). Use these tags to expand your search. You can find the official LCSH terms online through the Library of Congress website. Subject tags also usually appear under the summary in a source record in your library catalog.

search and to adapt your strategies and terminology based on your search engine. Experimenting with a range of terms—particularly more limited ones—can help you with this task by finding materials specific to your topic; keeping track of your search terms, perhaps in a research log, can also be an invaluable way to organize your ideas and develop best practices for search protocols on your topic.

5.3 What is the difference between a primary and a secondary source?

UNDERSTANDING PRIMARY AND SECONDARY SOURCES

Your initial searches will yield a range of sources—from magazine articles to books, video recordings, and perhaps even manuscripts or a photograph collection. Each of these sources can play a vital role in your research. Scholars divide research into primary and secondary research, and sources, likewise, into **primary sources** (original texts you analyze in your research) and **secondary sources** (sources that provide commentary on your primary material or on your topic in general).

Consider, for instance, Molly Fehr's project, examined in Chapter 4. Hitler's speeches and his book, *Mein Kampf*, were her *primary sources*, and the articles, books, and transcribed interviews providing analysis of Hitler's propaganda were her *secondary sources*. Her own essay, when completed, became *another* secondary source, one that contributes to an ongoing intellectual discussion about the power of Nazi propaganda.

As you search for your research materials, keep in mind that no sources are *inherently* primary or secondary; those terms refer to *how you use them* in your paper. For instance, if you were working with the topic of Internet advertising, you might use actual Facebook ads and Flash animations as your primary sources, as well as press releases and advertising websites. For secondary sources you might turn to articles that discuss innovations in social media marketing, a Website on the history of digital advertising, and perhaps even a book by a famous economist about the impact of technology on corporate marketing strategies. However, imagine that you shift your topic slightly, making your new focus the economist's theories about the corruption of traditional advertising by multimedia technology. Now, that same book you looked at before as a *secondary* source becomes a *primary* source for this new topic.

As you can see, your inquiry will determine which sources will be primary and which will be secondary for your argument. In most cases, you will need to use a combination of primary and secondary materials to make a persuasive argument. The primary sources allow you to perform your own analysis, whereas the secondary sources offer you critical viewpoints that you need to take into account in your analysis and integrate into your argument to build up your *ethos*. How you respond to and combine your primary and secondary sources is a matter of choice, careful design, and rhetorical strategy.

Finding Primary Sources

The term *primary source* refers to any material that you will analyze for your paper, including speech scripts, advertisements, photographs, historical documents, film, artwork, audio files, and writing on Websites. Primary sources also can include testimonies by people with firsthand knowledge, direct quotations from a text, or, in some cases, interviews. Whatever is under the lens of your own analysis constitutes a *primary source*.

Searching for **primary sources**—original texts you analyze in your research paper—can be challenging, but they can be found in many places: in your library (whether in the general stacks, archives, or multimedia collections); at community centers such as library exhibits, museums, and city hall; or even in online digital archives such as the one maintained by the Library of Congress. These materials can be some of the most exciting sources to work within your research process and might include:

- original documents (examples: a handwritten letter by Mahatma Gandhi or Charles Lindbergh's journals)
- rare books and manuscripts (examples: a first edition of a Charlotte Brontë novel or Roger Manvell's manuscripts on the history of the Third Reich)
- portfolios of photographs (examples: photos of Japanese American internment camps or of Black Panther demonstrations from the 1960s)
- government documents (examples: U.S. censuses and surveys, reports from the Department of Agriculture or congressional papers)

■ other one-of-a-kind texts (examples: AIDS prevention posters from South Africa, a noted artist's sketchbook, or a series of leaflets produced by the U.S. Psychological Warfare Department)

In many cases, you can work directly with these materials so you can perform your own firsthand analysis of that piece of cultural history.

Consider the sources that student Cam Russell used in her project on the history of computer programming. As she started her research, she came upon information about ENIAC, a World War II Army–run project involving the first programmable, electronic computer. Intrigued by the idea of a 1940s computer, she decided to look at some primary sources—photographs taken by the U.S. Army of the project. While searching the archives, she noticed something surprising: the programmers featured in the images were mostly women (see Figure 5.5). Intrigued by this discovery, Cam decided to narrow her research topic to focus on early women programmers. Image searches of online and university archives led her to another discovery—a cover of *Radio & Television News* featuring a woman working at a sprawling computer console, confirming the fact that as late as 1957, women occupied a public presence as computer programmers.

Seeing the *Radio & Television News* cover online prompted Cam to form questions about the magazine itself. Were female programmers just "cover girls" for this issue or were they discussed in the article itself? How did the magazine in general represent gender and its relation to technology? She also found herself thinking more expansively about how much the stereotype had changed over the past several decades. In this way, through her initial analysis of these primary sources, Cam was able to refine her research question to ask, If some of the earliest computer programmers were women, what caused the shift toward the "bro-grammer" stereotype that dominates today's Silicon Valley culture? This question provided a strong foundation for her further research that involved using secondary sources to provide key background information and critical perspectives on her topic.

FIGURE 5.5 One of Cam's first discoveries was this U.S. army photograph of Ester Gerston and Gloria Ruth Gorden programming the ENIAC computer.

Searching for Secondary Sources

As Cam's example suggests, while primary materials play an important role in your research, just as important are your **secondary sources**—texts that analyze or provide a perspective on a primary source. These include scholarly articles, popular commentaries, background materials (in print, video, or interview format), and survey data reinforcing your analysis. Whatever sources you can use as a lens to look at or understand the subject of your analysis constitutes a *secondary source*. The writers of such texts offer the voices with which you will engage in scholarly conversation as you develop the substance of your argument.

Although your instinct may send you directly to the Internet, your first stop in your search for secondary sources should actually be your library's reference area, the home of reference librarians—people trained to help you find what you need—as well as a treasure trove of encyclopedias, bibliographies, and other resource materials. These storehouses of information can be invaluable in providing you with the *foundational sources* for your project, including basic definitions, historical background, and bibliographies. Yet, while such "background" materials are necessary to help you construct a framework for your research argument, they represent only one part of your iceberg of research. For more rigorous analysis, you should turn to books and articles that provide critical analysis and arguments about your specific research subject.

AT A GLANCE

Finding Secondary Sources

- *Dictionaries, guides, and encyclopedias* provide helpful background information for your topic.
- *Library catalogs* allow you to search the library holdings for relevant books, newspapers, journals, documentaries, or other materials.
- *CD-ROM indexes and bibliographies* contain vast amounts of bibliographic information.
- *Academic databases and indexes* provide access to full-text versions of articles from a range of sources. Most are available by subscription only; many universities subscribe to multiple databases for student research.
- *Electronic journals and ebooks* offer access to the full digital versions of books and academic journals from a wide range of disciplines.
- *Google scholar and Google books* can be helpful resources, especially when used in conjunction with academic databases and library catalogs.

To locate these more specific secondary sources, you might search your library catalog for relevant books and films and other published materials.

You can also consult databases and indexes, indispensable research guides that will provide you with bibliographic citations for academic articles on your topic. Databases can come in many forms: collections of electronic journals, searchable Internet resources, or even CD-ROMs. Although some databases provide bibliographic citations that you can use to locate the source in your library catalog, many include a detailed abstract summarizing a source's argument, and others link you to full-text electronic copies of articles. Consider using a citation management program such as Zotero or RefWorks to help collect your citations or carefully record your search results in your research log; organizing your citations now will streamline both your research and writing processes moving forward.

Finally, although databases, catalogs, and search engines provide indispensable tools for conducting your research, remember also that your classmates can serve as secondary sources you might consult or even interview. Ask others who are working on similar topics to share resources, and help each other along the route of your research. This is particularly true for the stage in your research when you produce a **preliminary bibliography**—a working list of the sources for your iceberg of research.

AT A GLANCE

Recording Searches in Your Research Log

Use your research log to keep careful track of the dates, details, and key terms of your searches and to organize your sources and your notes:

- Date each entry in your log to keep track of your progress and show the evolution of your ideas.
- Track keywords, search terms, and the search engines and academic databases you've used.
- Keep a running list of your sources by call number, author, and title.
- Write down complete identifying information for any source you consult, including online images or articles, print copies of journals or magazines from the library, articles from library databases, and book chapters. Be sure to keep track of URLs for online sources and download them if possible.
- Double-check transcribed quotations for accuracy while you still have the source before you, and include page numbers (or paragraph numbers for Website articles). Be sure to include quotation marks around each direct quote you transcribe, even in your research log.
- Include printouts (or digital copies, if your log is electronic) of relevant articles or database entries, and especially of online articles, images, or Websites that might disappear when their site is updated.
- Annotate the entry by including an evaluation of the source and an indication of how you might use it as part of your final paper.

EVALUATING YOUR SOURCES

Implementing these research strategies will provide you with access to many interesting sources, but how do you discriminate among them to find those that are credible, reliable, and authoritative? How do you know which ones will be the most useful for your argument? The key rests in understanding the argumentative perspective, or *rhetorical stance*, of each source. At times, the source's stance may be self-evident: you may automatically gravitate toward experts in the field, well known for their opinions and affiliations. It is just as likely, however, that you may not be familiar with the names or ideas of your sources. Therefore, it is essential to develop a method for evaluating the sources you encounter.

5.4 How do I critically evaluate both print and online sources?

Seeing Connections
See Chapter 3 for a more complete discussion of rhetorical stance.

Questions for Evaluating Sources

As you begin to work with your sources, you'll need to repurpose the skills of critical thinking and rhetorical analysis that we discussed in earlier chapters to work through the following questions:

Authorship. Who is the author? Is he or she an expert on the topic? What institution or organization is he or she affiliated with? What else has he or she written on this subject? Have other sources that you've read referenced him or her, or his or her work? To answer this question, you might look the author up online or in a bibliography index to assess his or her *ethos*.

Publication information. Who published the source? Is it a university press or online academic journal (suggesting peer-reviewed scholarship) or a trade press or commercial website (suggesting a commercial venture)? Is it published by a foundation or organization (suggesting a political agenda) or self-published (suggesting the author's struggle to have his or her views accepted for publication)? If it's an online source, does the site include a gesture of accountability for the information it publishes, such as a "contact us" link?

■ *Tip: For online sources, look at the URL to see if it's a ".gov" (government-affiliated site), ".com" (commercial site), ".org" (an organization's site), ".mil" (a military website), or ".edu" (educational or university site). Caution: If a site contains a tilde (~), that indicates it's a personal website rather than one sponsored by the organization or institution.*

Publication date. When was it published? Is it a recent contribution or an older study? If it's an electronic source, does it have a "last updated" notation? If not, do embedded links still work?

■ *Tip: Don't dismiss older materials too quickly; sometimes an older source can provide historical context or provide a foundational perspective on your issue. However, usually you should use the more recent sources to engage the most timely perspectives on your topic.*

Purpose, occasion, and exigency. What was the occasion for the source? Was it written in reaction to a specific text or event or in response to a particular research question? Was it designed to inform? To instruct? To provide a call to action?

■ *Tip: Sometimes the purpose or occasion might be explicit; other times it is less obvious. A quick online search (of author or the name of a key event or cited publication) can help you understand cultural or historical context if it not readily apparent; understanding the purpose behind the source can help you better assess the source's argument and motives.*

Audience. Who is its intended audience? Scholars? Experts in the field? A popular audience? A particular demographic, such as college students, parents, teens, or senior citizens? How is the argument and language shaped to address this audience? Does the author use rhetorical strategies—such as definition or community-specific terms (like jargon) to speak to his or her audience? Are you a member of the intended audience? If not, how does that affect the persuasiveness of the argument?

■ *Tip: Keep in mind that there sometimes is a difference between the audience that an author intended to address and the audience who actually reads the argument. Is the argument flexible enough to speak to both types of readers?*

Argument. What is the source's argument? Does the author have a clear argument? Are there any implicit or unstated assumptions underlying the argument? Check the opening paragraphs, preface, or introduction to the text: does the author lay out his or her theoretical framework or a roadmap of how he or she will structure his argument?

■ *Tip: As you work with a source, always write a paraphrase of its main claim in your research log for easy reference. To see others's critical assessments of a source's argument, consider looking at book reviews or literature reviews that discuss the text; for more popular reactions to electronic texts, check the "comments" section, if available, beneath blog posts or online articles.*

Evidence. What types of evidence does the author use to support his claim? Does he use primary research, such as analysis of primary texts or his own surveys or interviews? Does he use secondary sources as evidence? Does he use a combination of the two? Does he include a variety of sources or perspectives, or does he seem to cherry-pick his examples? Does he address counterarguments? Does he treat them respectfully? Does he cite his sources ethically and appropriately? Does he provide a works cited or list of references at the end? If it's an online source, does the author provide links to any Internet sources he cites?

■ *Tip: Use your source's citations as the starting point for further research; if you find a cited quotation or piece of evidence from your source's argument particularly striking, use the associated link or the citation in the works cited to track down that additional source and read it to see how it might contribute to your own project.*

Tone. What is the tone of the source? Does it use objective language? Is its tone comic? Serious? Scholarly? Casual? Does it seem to represent a particular political, cultural, or ideological position or world view (i.e., feminist, conservative, fundamentalist, American)?

■ *Tip: Just because a source is associated with a particular ideological position doesn't mean that you need to disqualify it from your research; however, you'll need to take into account how any bias might influence the strength of its argument and the evidence it provides for your research.*

As this evaluation criteria suggest, you probably won't use every source that you discover through your research. Sometimes you might need to set aside sources even though they have extremely strong *ethos* or arguments because they are outdated or represent a focus or stance that is not useful for your purposes. Be sure to keep a record of such sources, however, in your research log in case you have cause to return to them later in your research.

Let's look at how you might put this evaluation method into practice with the different types of sources that Cam discovered as she moved forward with her research project on women and computer programming. Consider, for instance, the online article "Researcher reveals how 'Computer Geeks' replaced 'Computer Girls,'" one of Cam's top hits on her Google search for "women and computer programming." Cam began the process of evaluating the source by looking at the URL: http://gender.stanford.edu/news/2011/researcher-reveals-how-computer-geeks-replaced-computergirls. In this case, she noted that the address of the host site (gender.stanford.edu) ends with .edu, indicating that this website is affiliated with an accredited educational institution and is not a commercial (.com), government (.gov), or personal site. She confirmed this affiliation by looking at the homepage itself, which features "Stanford University" and "The Clayman Institute for Gender Research" prominently in its header, granting it a strong *ethos* appeal. Cam identified other aspects of the page that enhanced its credibility: a clean and engaging design; a clearly identified author, Brenda Frink, who (Cam discovered through a quick Google search) is a social and cultural historian with a PhD from Stanford; a recent publication date; and a prominent "About" button in the top left and the "Contact Us" link at the bottom that speak to the site's accountability for the material it puts online.

Yet, evaluating a website involves more than simply assessing the *ethos* of its design. Cam recognized that she needed to look at the content of the article itself to assess its viability as a source for her project. As she began to read the article, she found it confirmed her initial impression from reading the title, namely that the subject matter spoke directly to her research question about how and why male computer culture displaced female programmers. However, she took her analysis further and looked carefully at other elements as she assessed the text:

- **Structure:** Cam noted that the article has a clear structure, scaffolded with subheads, and concludes with a paragraph that reasserts the author's main point.
- **Tone:** Cam was impressed by Frink's even, unbiased tone, which avoided jargon and used inclusive pronouns like "us" and "we" to connect with her readers.
- **Audience:** Cam found evidence that the author was making certain assumptions about her audience with lines like "It may be surprising

to learn ..." and "The world described in the Cosmopolitan article seems foreign to us today." In assessing these choices, Cam recognized that Frink is speaking specifically to an early twenty-first-century audience, one who is familiar with the contemporary male computer nerd stereotype.

- **Argument and evidence:** As Cam moved further through the text, she confirmed that Frink made a clear and solid argument, supporting her points with direct quotations and evidence (historical and statistical) from historian Nathan Ensmenger's work.
- **Scholarly conversation.** Lastly, Cam saw further evidence that the author situated her argument in terms of a larger, ongoing conversation on this issue by the way that Frink populates her paragraphs with links designed to point the reader toward reference sources, additional articles, and even secondary websites.

After evaluating the online article in this way, Cam found it to be persuasive, relevant, and credible—a solid source for her project. However, the open comment section underneath the article gave her pause. While the reader comments provided some interesting perspectives on the topic, Cam noted that the website had tagged each commenter with the label "unverified." In some rare contexts, online comments—whether on a blog, discussion forum, or online article—can be useful sources. However, unless the comments are moderated or approved by the website, they should be approached – as in this case—as "unverified," both in terms of the credibility of the author and the accuracy of the information. In most instances, the problematic nature of online comments is self-evident; you only have to look at the inflammatory comments posted under most YouTube videos to see how often biased and empty claims dominate these spaces. However, even more even-handed comments should be approached with care unless there is a way to verify either the identity of the writer or the validity of the information. Many researchers warn against using comments at all, and this is probably the best practice in most cases. Cam, for instance, decided against using the reader comments as part of her research, opting instead to focus on more credible online sources, scholarly books, and peer-reviewed articles.

Let's look now at another of her sources—a scholarly article by Jennifer S. Light, "When Computers Were Women." Cam found this source by searching "women AND Eniac" in an academic database, encountering it first as

◂ Result List | Refine Search ◂ 5 of 14 ▸

When Computers Were Women.

Authors: Light, Jennifer S.

Source: Technology & Culture. Jul99, Vol. 40 Issue 3, p455. 29p. 2 Black and White Photographs.

Document Type: Article

Subject Terms: *COMPUTERS
*COMPUTER technicians
***WOMEN** in computer science

NAICS/Industry Codes: 334111 Electronic Computer Manufacturing
443144 Computer and software stores
443142 Electronics Stores
334110 Computer and peripheral equipment manufacturing
417310 Computer, computer peripheral and pre-packaged software merchant wholesalers
423430 Computer and Computer Peripheral Equipment and Software Merchant Wholesalers

Abstract: Relates the history of Electronic Numerical Integrator and Calculator (**ENIAC**), the first electronic computer in the United States. Invention of **ENIAC**; Female technicians whom existing computer histories have rendered invisible; How the job of programmer originated as feminized clerical labor; **Women** in wartime; **Women's** entry into computing; Female computers and **ENIAC** girls.

ISSN: 0040-165X

FIGURE 5.6 One of Cam's search results for her search for "women AND Eniac" through a scholarly database.

a search result that she needed to assess to determine if she should read the source (Figure 5.6). Although brief, the record offered her much information:

- Clicking on the **author** link took her to a page listing many of Jennifer Light's other articles, helping her assess her *ethos* and expertise on the topic.
- Clicking on the **publication** link (*Technology & Culture*) brought her to a description of the journal, which confirmed that it was an academic, peer-reviewed journal.
- Looking at the **date** of the article, Cam realized that it was over 15 years old but decided the content might still be relevant given it was detailing a historical phenomenon.
- Scanning the page, she noticed the helpful linked **subject terms**, which she recorded in her research log for her future searches.
- Reading the abstract provided her with a brief summary of the **argument**, confirming the article's usefulness for her research.

Seeing Connections
See Chapter 8 for a full discussion of academic abstracts.

In this case, Cam conducted what we might call a **"cover" evaluation**—an initial evaluation process that helps a researcher determine whether a text might be a useful source. With popular magazines, we might look at the actual cover for such a preliminary assessment, as we did with Figures 5.1 and 5.2 at the beginning of the chapter. Web materials provide much of this information as part of their design, integrating the *cover evaluation* with the process of reading the text. We might be most familiar with this process for books—a savvy researcher flips between the title page, the table of contents, and the index to assess authorship, publication information, Library of Congress subject headers (back of title page), argument, and relevance to topic. However, academic journal articles require a different approach; many times, we don't see the cover of an academic journal at all because we use library copies that have been rebound for permanent shelving or we access issues online. In that case, search records such as the one in Figure 5.6 provide us with a virtual "cover" to assess.

To responsibly evaluate a text, however, we need to move past the cover to look at the argument itself. Let's look, as Cam did, at the first section of Light's article (Figure 5.7) and consider which characteristics suggest its suitability as a source for her project.

As you skim the first page of the article, notice the following elements:

- Light utilizes an objective, academic style of writing that suggests that this source will provide an authoritative and unbiased perspective on the topic.
- Her attention to style (for instance, the deliberate repetition of "While ..." phrases at the top of the second page) shows she deliberately crafted her piece to engage her readers.
- She carefully documents her sources through footnotes, demonstrating her ethics as a researcher and the fact that her argument is founded in a knowledge of the scholarship on the topic.
- Even further, she clearly indicates her unique contribution to the conversation and the methodology she will use.
- Finally, the author's biography at the bottom of the first page further contributes to her *ethos*, both by providing her institutional credentials and showing that the article derived from peer review—not just at the level of the publication but also in the drafting stages through feedback from her colleagues.

Such deeper evaluation makes clear that this is a useful source that you could trust for a research project on shifting gender stereotypes related to computer programming. As you can see, it is not enough simply to locate your sources: you need to use your skills of analysis to assess their viability for your individual project.

When Computers Were Women

JENNIFER S. LIGHT

J. Presper Eckert and John W. Mauchly, household names in the history of computing, developed America's first electronic computer, ENIAC, to automate ballistics computations during World War II. These two talented engineers dominate the story as it is usually told, but they hardly worked alone. Nearly two hundred young women, both civilian and military, worked on the project as human "computers," performing ballistics computations during the war. Six of them were selected to program a machine that, ironically, would take their name and replace them, a machine whose technical expertise would become vastly more celebrated than their own.[1]

The omission of women from the history of computer science perpetuates misconceptions of women as uninterested or incapable in the field. This article retells the history of ENIAC's "invention" with special focus on the female technicians whom existing computer histories have rendered invisible. In particular, it examines how the job of programmer, perceived in recent years as masculine work, originated as feminized clerical labor. The story presents an apparent paradox. It suggests that women were somehow hidden during this stage of computer history while the wartime popular press trumpeted just the opposite—that women were breaking into traditionally male occupations within science, technology, and engineering.

Dr. Light recently completed her Ph.D. in the history of science at Harvard University; beginning in the fall of 1999 she will be assistant professor of communication studies at Northwestern University. She thanks Peter Buck, Herman Goldstine, Rachel Prentice, Sherry Turkle, John Staudenmaier, and four anonymous reviewers for their contributions to this article. An early version of the article was presented at "Gender, 'Race,' and Science," a conference at Queen's University, Kingston, Ontario, 12–15 October, 1995.

1. History has valued hardware over programming to such an extent that even the *IEEE Annals of the History of Computing* issue devoted to ENIAC's fiftieth anniversary barely mentioned these women's roles. See *IEEE Annals of the History of Computing* 18, no. 1 (1996). Instead, they were featured two issues later in a special issue on women in computing.

TECHNOLOGY AND CULTURE

JULY

1999

VOL. 40

A closer look at this literature explicates the paradox by revealing widespread ambivalence about women's work. While celebrating women's presence, wartime writing minimized the complexities of their actual work. While describing the difficulty of their tasks, it classified their occupations as subprofessional. While showcasing them in formerly male occupations, it celebrated their work for its femininity. Despite the complexities—and often pathbreaking aspects—of the work women performed, they rarely received credit for innovation or invention.

The story of ENIAC's female computers supports Ruth Milkman's thesis of an "idiom of sex-typing" during World War II—that the rationale explaining why women performed certain jobs contradicted the actual sexual division of labor.[2] Following her lead, I will compare the actual contributions of these women with their media image. Prewar labor patterns in scientific and clerical occupations significantly influenced the way women with mathematical training were assigned to jobs, what kinds of work they did, and how contemporary media regarded (or failed to regard) this work. This article suggests why previous accounts of computer history did not portray women as significant and argues for a reappraisal of their contributions.[3]

2. Ruth Milkman, *Gender at Work: The Dynamics of Job Segregation by Sex During World War II* (Chicago, 1987).

3. Two books currently offer some information on the participation of women in computer history: see Autumn Stanley, *Mothers and Daughters of Invention: Notes for a Revised History of Technology* (Metuchen, N.J., 1993), and Herman Goldstine, *The Computer from Pascal to Von Neumann* (Princeton, 1972). For recollections from women who worked on the ENIAC, see W. Barkley Fritz, "The Women of ENIAC," *IEEE Annals of the History of Computing* 18, no. 3 (1996): 13–28. Other histories tend to make passing references to the women and to show photographs of them without identifying them by name.

FIGURE 5.7

USING FIELD RESEARCH

5.5 How do I pursue field research for my project?

In addition to the primary and secondary sources you will consult as you develop your research project, you may also have the chance to go out across campus, into the community, or into the virtual world to engage with people's opinions and use that information in your essay. That is, your project might provide you with the opportunity to enrich your argument by carrying out your own **field research**—conducting *interviews*, developing *surveys*, and engaging in *fieldwork*. Consider the possibilities: for an essay on YouTube mash-ups and copyright infringement, you could interview a faculty member who has written extensively on the Digital Millennium Copyright Act; for a project investigating cyberbullying, you could use your own survey of 50 college students to bring the voices of cyberbullying victims—and perhaps even bullies—into your paper; for an essay about urban murals, you could visit several local murals, take photographs, and even talk with local artists. In each case, you would be using *field research* to complement your text-based research and to strengthen your research-based claim.

Conducting Interviews

One of the most common forms of *field research*, an interview provides you with the opportunity to receive in-depth information from an expert on your topic. The information you gather from these interviews can supplement the material you've found in published sources, providing you with the opportunity to make an original research claim or unique contribution to the scholarly conversation on your topic. Keep in mind, however, that conducting interviews involves much more than simply having a chat with someone; it involves a careful process of planning and preparation before the meeting even takes place. If you decide to conduct an interview as part of your field research, you might incorporate these steps into your research process:

1. *Identify your purpose*: Even before setting up an interview, you need to clarify your research goals. What information would an interview provide that other types of research would not? What do you hope to get out of the interview?

2. *Decide on your interview subject*: Who would provide you with the most insight into your topic? Is the best source for your field research a professor at your college who is an expert in this area? A professional from the community? Peers in your class, dorm, athletic team, or town?

3. *Determine your preferred interview format*: Interviews can be conducted in many ways: face to face, over the phone, through videochat or text-chat, or by email. You'll need to choose the method that best suits your needs and your interviewee's preferred mode of communication.

4. *Prepare*: Know your interviewee: read an online biography or browse an online résumé or curriculum vita; familiarize yourself with what he or she has written and read any articles related to your topic; and understand your interviewee's position on your research issue. This information will

help you both construct useful questions and also cultivate your own *ethos* during the interview by showing you've taken the time to prepare.

5. *Develop questions*: Your questions will provide the framework for your discussion, so craft them with care. A successful range of questions can yield not only a wealth of in-depth information about a subject but also some useful "quotable moments" that can be featured as direct quotations and evidence in your essay. In designing your questions, therefore, keep these strategies in mind:

- ■ **Use specific language, be concise and clear:** If your interview subject has a hard time following your question, it's likely that he or she'll have trouble giving you a helpful answer. Be focused and eliminate wordiness.

- ■ **Avoid Yes/No questions:** Questions that lend themselves to yes or no answers can limit explanation and elaboration. Opt for open-ended questions instead. So, instead of asking, "Do you agree with the recent Faculty Senate vote?," you might ask, "What is your opinion on the recent Faculty Senate vote?"

- ■ **Watch out for leading questions:** Even if you have developed a tentative claim, you should avoid influencing your interview subject's answer. In other words, if you ask, "Don't you agree that there need to be more female faculty members in the Computer Science Department?", you are sending signals about your own opinions that might affect how your interviewee answers. Try to use neutral terms and to design unbiased questions.

- ■ **Frame your questions:** While drafting your questions, also take some time to develop ways to contextualize them in reference to your knowledge about your subject and your interviewee's areas of expertise. By showing that you've done some preliminary research, you enhance your own *ethos* and lay the groundwork for a richer conversation.

6. *Make contact*: In contacting your potential interviewee, clearly explain who you are, the topic of your research, and your goal for the field research. If you are planning a face-to-face interview or a video or text-based chat, suggest two or three possible times for the session; for all types of interviews, include your timeline in your request. In addition, provide a summary of the types of questions you might ask so that your interviewee can think them through before meeting

with you. Follow up unanswered requests with polite emails or phone calls. Don't hesitate to persist, but do so respectfully. Once you've set up the interview, be sure to confirm time and place the day before for a face-to-face interview or chat session.

7. *Maintain your ethos*: Your *persona* as an interviewer can be key to a successful session. Dress nicely, maintain a professional tone throughout the meeting, and have your materials organized before you start. Respect your interviewee's time: arrive on time for the interview, and keep it within the agreed on time span. Use your interview questions as a guide, but don't follow them too rigidly; listen to your interviewee's answers and follow up on key points even if it means asking a question that's not on your list. Conversely, be careful not to digress. Keep the conversation focused on the research topic.

8. *Record and document*: In your notes, be sure to write down the full name of the person, his or her title, and the time, date, and location of the interview; you will need this information to properly cite the interview in your essay. While you'll want to take some notes during the interview, recording the session can help you resist the impulse to transcribe the conversation word for word. However, be sure to ask your interviewee's permission before recording the meeting. At the end of the interview, get written permission from your interview subject to use direct quotations from the conversation in your essay. It is possible that she or he might ask be quoted anonymously, in which case you'll need to respect that request when incorporating material from the interview into your paper.

Seeing Connections
See Chapter 7 for instructions on how to cite an interview in a research paper.

9. *Analyze the conversation*: If you record an interview, create a transcript as soon as possible after the meeting. Take some time to process the information you received, highlighting key quotes or ideas in your notes or on the transcript, listing ideas or readings for further research, and reflecting on connections to your other sources. If you conducted a face-to-face or videochat interview, analyze the conversation or transcript shortly after it happens, while your impressions are still fresh.

10. *Follow-up*: Send a thank-you note to the person you interviewed and offer a copy of your completed paper.

Developing a Survey

In your research, you may come across published surveys that can provide important statistical data for your project, whether in scientific journals, newsmagazines like *Time*, or research organizations such as the Pew Research Center. Alternately, you might consider developing your own survey in order to retrieve information tailored to your particular research question or line of inquiry. The benefit of a survey is that it enables you to accumulate data from a broad range of participants; it works particularly well for gathering quantitative data but can also yield deeper insightful perspectives on your topic through short answer questions.

As you compose your survey, remember that it is like any other writing project in that it benefits a careful drafting process, one that takes into account the rhetorical situation and purpose of your project. The following steps can help you develop an effective survey:

1. *Identify your purpose*: The first step in developing any survey is clarify your goals. What research question are you trying to answer? What type of results would be most useful to your research? Do you want to gather statistical data? Do you want to solicit reflective or detailed responses that can use for qualitative analysis? The answers to these questions will help determine the shape of your survey.

2. *Determine your survey population*: In order to receive useful answers, you need to carefully target your survey population. You might select your survey subjects by age (i.e., teenagers, college students, parents, senior citizens); by occupation (i.e., students, instructors, administrators, athletes, artists); by location (i.e., residents of your town, your college campus); or by other characteristics, such as gender, political or religious affiliation, or even nationality.

3. *Aim for a representative sample*: To insure the most reliable results, don't skew your sample out of convenience (for instance, only distributing your survey to your fraternity brothers when the research question requires both a male and female perspective). In addition, consider how sample size influences the viability of your results: the results from a survey of ten students are less likely to yield persuasive findings than a survey of 40 students.

4. *Develop your questions*: In many ways, your purpose will determine the format of your survey. You have many options available to you:

   ■ Close-ended questions tend to generate quantitative data and offer no little or no opportunity for elaboration. Two typical formats for these questions include multiple choice (where the subject chooses one or more of a variety of options) and ranked questions (where the subject ranks a series of items according to a clear scale).

■ Open-ended questions invite reflection and nuanced responses, whether they be as short as a single sentence or as long as a paragraph.

In general, it is best to design surveys that balance short, multiple choice questions, which yield primarily statistical data, with short answer questions that will produce more complex responses. Keep your survey short; the longer your form, the fewer completed surveys will probably be returned to you.

5. *Draft your survey*: As with any rhetorical text, you should craft your survey carefully:

■ Assess the best delivery method for your survey given your target population: Paper survey? Email? Electronic form? Your choice of medium might influence your survey design.

■ Consider the canon of arrangement. Put your questions in a logical order, use subcategories to help organize information, consider giving your survey subjects a sense of the scope of the survey (i.e., including an introduction that states, "This survey contains 10 questions …") or markers that indicate their progress through it (e.g., if your survey is divided into pages, include a header with a notation such as "Page 3 of 4").

■ Focus on style. Use clear, concise language, and avoid creating Yes–No questions ("Was your freshman orientation session effective?") when you want to generate more nuanced responses ("Please comment on the most effective and least effective aspects of your freshman orientation session"). Avoid biased language or leading questions.

■ Construct an expository frame for the survey: a very brief introduction of a sentence or two that indicates the purpose and relevance of the survey; a concluding sentence that appears after the last question, thanking the participant for completing the survey.

6. *Test and revise your drafted survey*: As with any rhetorical text, it is important to take into account *audience* as you construct your argument. Test your draft by having a friend complete your survey and give you feedback on its clarity, organization, length, and the relevance of its questions to your purpose. Use that feedback to revise.

7. *Distribute your survey*: State your deadline clearly, and make sure the respondents know where and how to return the form.

8. *Analyze the results*: As you read through the completed surveys, look for patterns or trends in the responses and categorize them in a table or "code" the survey responses using a highlighter or jotting key terms in the margin; start to think about how to best organize and showcase data (through percentages? charts? graphs?); highlight key comments in the open responses to include as direct quotations in your research paper. Most of all, *listen* to your respondents, even if the data do not necessarily confirm your hypothesis: your developing research claim should be informed by your research findings.

Seeing Connections
See Chapter 7 for instructions on how to cite a survey in your research paper.

9. *Follow-up*: Consider sharing your findings with survey participants, if possible, through an article in a local newspaper or college publication.

WRITER'S PRACTICE   MyWritingLab

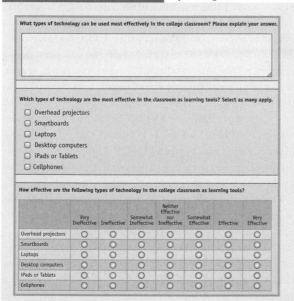

For a research project on the use of technology in the college classroom, one writer decided to construct a survey to collect student perspectives on this issue. During the drafting process, she experimented with different variations of the same question to consider how format influenced the answers she might receive. Look over each variation carefully.

What is the implied purpose behind each question? Is it the same for each one? How might the questions elicit different responses? What would the author need to do to make sure she received useful responses from this survey? What revisions might you suggest?

Other Models of Fieldwork

While interviews and surveys represent two modes of fieldwork available to you, you might take your research even more actively into the field. Let's look at a more ambitious approach to this type of research. Student Vincent Chen used field research quite prominently in his research project about the rhetoric of climate change. As part of his research, Vincent attended the Copenhagen Conference on Climate Change in December of 2009. Included in this conference was a special session on the "15th Conference of the Parties to the UNFCCC (United Nations Framework Convention on Climate Change)," commonly known as "COP15." At the COP15, Vincent conducted extensive field research, such as talking to conference participants, taking photographs of people milling through the halls, attending talks, and listening to speakers present position statements about the environment. One of the most powerful products of Vincent's field research was a photo he took, showing the crowds of attendees stopping mid-motion to hear the speech of Mohamed Nasheed, then-president of the Republic of Maldives. The photo became central to making his argument that President Nasheed strongly differentiated himself from other climate leaders at the conference through his inflammatory rhetoric about the danger of rising seas as well as the *logos* argument of his country's small size and limited economic power. To argue this position, Vincent used his photo as visual evidence documenting the conference-stopping power of President Nasheed's speech (see Figure 5.9). He also supported his argument through additional field research in the form of interviews with other students who attended at the conference and an interview with Professor Stephen Schneider of the Interdisciplinary Environmental Studies Program at his university.

This field research added depth and power to Vincent's argument by allowing him to include his own evidence as strategic argumentative support for his argument. With regard to the photo in Figure 5.8, rather than just asserting his claim to be true, Vincent could allow his readers to *see* the evidence that would support his point that President Nasheed, out of all leaders at the climate conference, made people stop and listen to an argument for action.

Of course, not all fieldwork involves trips around the world. Sometimes you can gather your own evidence for your research project by using resources available within your local community. Consider these scenarios: if you were studying the impact of a new park in your community, you might meet with a city planner or the landscape architect responsible for the project and look at blueprints or concept art for the project; if you were writing about a city water reservoir, you might visit the site, take photographs, and meet with the site manager; and, if you were writing on the marketing strategies of a local baseball team, you might even write a letter to that team's marketing coordinator to set up an interview or gather information. Fieldwork such as this allows you to take your research to the next level and make a truly original contribution of your own.

FIGURE 5.8 Vincent Chen's field research includes this photo of Mohamed Nasheed, president of the Republic of Maldives, making a powerful speech to a riveted audience at the 2009 Copenhagen Climate Conference. © Vincent Chen 2009.

Evaluating Field Research Sources

When you conduct interviews and surveys, you are looking for materials to use in your paper as secondary sources. But keep in mind the need to evaluate your field research sources as carefully as you assess your other sources. If you interview a professor, a marketing executive, a witness, or a roommate, consider the rhetorical stance of that person. What kind of bias does the person have concerning the topic of your project? If you conduct a survey of your peers in your dorm, assess the value and credibility of your results as rigorously as you would evaluate the data of a published study. Don't fall into the trap of misusing statistics when making claims if you haven't taken into account the need for **statistical significance**, or to paraphrase the social psychologist Philip Zimbardo, the measure by which a number obtains meaning in scientific fields. To reach this number, you need to design the survey carefully, conduct what's called a *random sample*, interview a *large enough* number of people, and ask a *range of different people*. These are complex parameters to follow, but you will need to learn about them to conduct survey research that has reliable and credible results.

As Professor Zimbardo points out, statistics—though we often think of them as Truth—actually function rhetorically. Like words and images, numbers are a mode of persuasion that can mislead readers. You need to be

"Statistics are the backbone of research. They are used to understand observations and to determine whether findings are, in fact, correct and significant ...But statistics can also be used poorly or deceptively, misleading those who do not understand them."

—*Philip Zimbardo* (595)

especially vigilant when using a survey or statistics as a supposedly "objective" part of your iceberg of research, particularly if you plan to depend on such materials in your argument.

Take as much care with how you convey information visually as you do with how you convey it in writing. Consider Ryan O'Rourke's project about the student perceptions of the political environment on his college campus. Having uncovered some general statistics about politics on campus from secondary sources, Ryan decided to sharpen his argument—and make his own unique contribution to the conversation—by measuring student sentiment on this issue at his own university. Consequently, he designed and distributed a survey on the topic, which was filled out by over 71 students. In addition to including the data in the body of his essay, he created a series of bar graphs (see examples in Figure 5.9) to represent his findings. His argument was more powerful not just because of his impressive research but also because of how he represented it visually through responsible use of

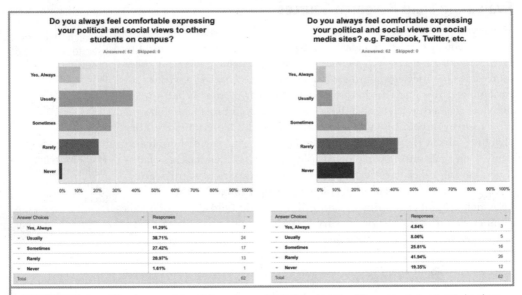

FIGURE 5.9 Ryan O'Rourke created these information graphics to help show the difference in students' attitudes about sharing their political views in person versus on social media.

statistics. The ability to create such powerful visualizations of information is within reach of many researchers these days as numerous software programs (from PowerPoint, to Excel, to Qualtrics) contain built-in shortcuts to help you display your original data as pie charts, bar graphs, and scatterplots.

Evaluating Sources by Use

The terms *primary source*, *secondary source*, and *field work* that we've been using so far in this chapter are familiar to most researchers and form a typical understanding of how texts operate in relation to the research process. However, scholar Joseph Bizzup has formulated an alternative way to conceptualize source materials—through how the materials are *used* rather than what they *are* (i.e., primary or secondary sources). Bizzup calls this approach "BEAM," and we find it useful specifically in how it asks writers to evaluate texts. BEAM stands for Background, Exhibit, Argument, and Methods and can be understood as follows:

- A **background** source provides foundational or general information for the topic.
- An **exhibit** source operates as an example or case study that the writer analyzes.
- An **argument** source is one that contributes an analytic perspective.
- A **method** source offers either a theoretical framework, overarching concept, or methodology that the writer incorporates into his or her own writing.

For many writers, the first three classifications are relatively easy to understand: exhibits often are what we might consider primary sources, texts to be analyzed; background and argument texts often fall under the category of secondary sources, texts that feature another author's analysis. Understanding the method source can be more challenging, for many researchers might not be in the practice of distinguishing between whether a source provides an argumentative perspective or contributes a critical framework. To help understand how this works, let's return to Jennifer Light's excerpt, which we considered above. In that case, the sources she refers to in footnotes 1 and 3 provide *background*; the media images that she says she'll analyze on the second page will function as *exhibits* in her article; Ruth Milkman's article serves as both an *argument* text (with its "idiom of sex-typing" thesis) and *method* (providing Light with a theoretical/methodological approach that she will "follow" in her own work).

By adjusting focus in this way from what a source *is* to how it can be *used*, you can approach the task of composing a research essay from a more rhetorical perspective, considering your collection of sources as another strategy designed to help you make best use of the available means of persuasion. The BEAM approach shifts your understanding so that your research-based writing becomes less a collection of source texts that support your argument and more a set of resources that you deploy meaningfully and deliberately to persuade your audience.

For this reason, as you evaluate your sources, you should ask one final set of questions:

> How might you use this source in your own research? Does the approach (popular, scientific, scholarly, informational) seem appropriate to your project's focus and goals? Does it offer a counterargument or a different disciplinary perspective? What will it contribute to your argument? Background? Exhibit material? Another person's analytic perspective? A guiding methodology, concept, or theory?

5.6 How can I understand the conversation my sources are having about my topic?

CREATING A DIALOGUE WITH YOUR SOURCES

Throughout this chapter, we have emphasized that research is social, a conversation with the people whose ideas and writing came before yours. As you gather, assess, and use sources, you are contributing to this conversation, building on the work of others, and adding a new perspective. Indeed, this notion of writing as communal is the reason why you need to use the author's name when citing a quotation or an idea; remember that all your sources are authored sources; each source mentioned in this chapter was composed by a person or a group of people. If you think of these texts as written *by people like you*, you will have an easier time remembering to acknowledge their ideas and integrate their quotations into your essay. In the process, you will go a long way toward avoiding unintentional plagiarism. You can begin this process through an exercise we call a **dialogue of** sources—a fictional conversation among the primary and secondary sources of your research paper designed to help you identify each one's central argument and main idea.

For instance, to prepare for her research paper on the dangers of America's dietary dependence on sugar, Kim Felser wrote a dialogue between several sources she had found: John Yudkin, author of *Pure, White and Deadly*, a book on the dangers of sugar; Dr. Robert Lustig, professor of pediatrics at University of California, San Francisco, and author of *Fat Chance: The Bitter Truth about Sugar*; Nicole M. Avena, Pedro Rada, and Bartley G. Hoebel, co-authors of the scholarly article, "Evidence for sugar addiction"; and, Michael Moss, a *NY Times* award-winning journalist and author of *Salt, Sugar, Fat. Smoking?*. She read each text first, taking notes and analyzing their stance, and then put them in dialogue so as to better assess the nuances of her topic and distinguish between the sources' differing perspectives.

Seeing Connections
See Chapter 7 for a more complete discussion of plagiarism and intellectual property.

AT A GLANCE

Creating a Dialogue of Sources

- *Identify the key players* from your research log and your notes. Which ones have the most influential or important arguments?

- *Create a cast of characters list* with a short bio for each speaker, perhaps even including yourself. Describe each person's credentials and rhetorical stance—his or her *ethos* and argument. (You may even want to create identifying icons or pictures to give "faces" to the participants.)

- *Draft the script.* Write the key questions you want to ask your sources about your topic. Use quotes from your sources to respond where possible, and include page numbers or footnotes.

- *Consider what your sources would say to each other.* Write their fictional conversation by using quotes from your sources.

- *Create a "moderator" to guide and catalyze the conversation.* This can be either a character based on yourself or on one of the sources. Don't let the moderator be neutral; allow the moderator to develop a stance, respond to the sources, and use this process to develop an argument about the topic.

- *Conclude with a synthesis statement.* Use the closing paragraph to tie together the various views presented in your "dialogue of sources" and then indicate how you will build on that collection of knowledge. In this way, you offer both a summary and a synthesis, by bringing together and then adding to the conversation of research.

Kim's complete dialogue began with a list of speakers and their bios. Then she introduced the topic of her research project. She reproduced the argument of each source through paraphrase.

By allowing debate to evolve, Kim begins to see how she might use information from these sources in her paper.

Dialogue of Sources [excerpt]

John Yudkin: Sugar is poisoning our society. It's addictive, it's everywhere. It's inescapable. In short, it's sweet and dangerous. I'll make it easy on you: you've *got* to read my book, *Pure, White, and Deadly*. It's got some pretty revelatory information packed in those pages, if I do say so myself. And I was a trailblazer! *P,W&D* came out way back in the 1970s.

Robert Lustig: John, you're on the right track, though I'm not sure I'd brag about publishing a work that long ago. My recent research suggests that *fructose* is the incredibly toxic one, not just "sugar." A calorie isn't just a calorie, as I like to say; a bottle of high-fructose corn syrup and a jar of brown rice syrup are digested entirely differently in the body. Your poor liver takes a beating with HFCS. My lecture at UCSF back in 2013, "Sugar: The Bitter Truth" does a neat job of explaining the scientific processes. You can find it on YouTube; I recommend taking a look.

John: Maybe you have a point. But the real issue is that we can't just pick and choose sugars for the ultimate health. We need to remove all of them. We need some grade-A restriction on every type of sweetener.

Avena, Rada, Hoebel: Look, guys, maybe we should examine the mind-body factors, too. You seem to be neglecting the brain entirely, and that plays a key role in the sugar-dependency epidemic. We've been researching how rats respond to consuming sugar-water solutions, from both behavioral and neuroscientific perspectives, and, honestly, the evidence that sugar might be a substance of abuse is compelling.

Avena, Rada, Hoebel (continued): And, John, you said it yourself: sugar is addictive. It releases endorphins and we become hooked. That's where the real danger lies; the impact on the body is secondary when we examine the causal effects.

Michael Moss: Whoa, whoa, whoa—calm down there. I think you're forgetting a key element. If you're trying to understand why we're so addicted to the stuff, I think you need to look more closely at the way our food system is structured. Hello capitalism! CEOs for Coca-Cola and other big industries will stop at nothing to reshape our taste buds and drive us back to the convenience stores again and again—all for profit! Addiction is certainly a part of it, but maybe we need to look at why and how we got into this mess in the first place.

Robert: Michael, I can't tell you how right you are. As I began scouring the shelves of grocery stores in my quest to better understand the causes of childhood obesity, I realized that an astounding 80% of all food products in the typical American supermarket have been loaded with added sugar. *Eighty percent*! That's over two-thirds of the food products available to us as a nation!

Most importantly, through the dialogue she begins to understand the conversation between the sources so she can start formulating her own stance and contribution to this discussion.

Notice how Kim's work allowed her to write out the process of research *as a conversation*. This process helps her gain a more sophisticated understanding of her sources and topic, allowing her to evaluate their strengths, and encouraging her to move past a simple pro-con approach to the issue to better appreciate the different approaches (scientific, cultural, economic) that researchers have taken on the topic. In addition, by giving her sources *voices*, she is more likely to remember to attribute the ideas to her sources while writing her research paper, avoiding unintentional plagiarism. Moreover, she can conclude the dialogue with a summation of the arguments she has uncovered through her research and predict how she will build on them as she develops her thesis for her own research-based argument.

WRITER'S PRACTICE   MyWritingLab

Put your own sources in dialogue by composing a social media version of the Dialogue of Sources activity. Select at least four sources, and identify each one's argument and rhetorical stance. Do a quick Google search on the author to understand his or her background and credentials. Then create a fake Twitter username for each one; be creative—even funny—but try to capture the *ethos* of the author in the Twitter handle. Make sure to create a Twitter identity for yourself as well. Next, imagine you were discussing your research topic with these authors on Twitter. What sort of conversation would you have? How would your sources communicate their positions? How would they react to each other? Write out the Twitter thread, creating hashtags as appropriate to underscore points and provide additional commentary on the conversation. Be sure to keep to the 140 character limit in creating each faux Tweet. At the end, take 5 minutes to free write about your Twitter Dialogue in your research log. What did you learn about the conversation about your topic from your dialogue? How do you better understand the relationship between your sources?

5.7 What is an annotated bibliography, and how can it help me develop my argument?

WRITING AN ANNOTATED BIBLIOGRAPHY

As you move further into your research, you might want to use your notes to create what researchers call an **annotated bibliography**—a list of research sources that provides informational notes about each source and how you might use it as you turn to drafting your paper. An annotated bibliography can work in conjunction with your research log and active note taking to encourage you to think critically, helping you to understand the larger research conversation on your topic and start to develop your own persuasive claim.

The format of an annotated bibliography follows a fairly standard pattern. For each source, you compose an entry containing:

- the **bibliographic citation**, correctly formatted to follow a particular citation form (such as MLA, APA, or Chicago Style)
- a **brief annotation** that concisely summarizes the content of the source and indicates its relevance to your project.

Seeing Connections
For a discussion of MLA style and guidelines, see Chapter 7.

Some researchers distinguish between two different types of annotation: the *descriptive annotation* and the *analytic annotation*. In writing the first type of annotation, you essentially create your own brief academic abstract for the source, providing an overview of its features and argument and suggesting its relevance to the larger conversation. In doing so, you would refer many of the elements we discussed above in relation to evaluating sources: author, place of publication, date of publication, purpose, audience, argument, evidence, tone, and relevance. For instance, consider this example of a *descriptive annotation* from a research project on teenagers and online privacy.

Ivester, Matt. *lol ... OMG! What Every Student Needs to Know About Online Reputation Management, Digital Citizenship, and Cyberbullying*. NV: Serra Knight Publishing, 2011. Print.

In *lol ... OMG!*, Matt Ivester provides an overview of the changing nature of digital citizenship; Ivester argues that in today's world we need to be conscious creators and curators of our online identities. A Duke University and Stanford Business School alumnus, Ivester was also creator of the infamous gossip website, JuicyCampus, providing him with an informed perspective on the more problematic elements of online culture. The book analyzes several powerful examples from the media of the dangers of digital citizenship, including the Duke Sexlist Powerpoint scandal, Alexandra Wallace's YouTube Rant, and the Tyler Clementi cyber-bullying tragedy. Of particular interest is Chapter 7, "Active Reputation Management," which provides seven steps readers can take to check their own online reputation. Aimed at a college audience and written in a direct and no-nonsense style, this book provides both valuable insight into the changing definitions of digital citizenship for the millennial generation and a concrete course of action that people can take to protect themselves online.

Notice that the annotation provides specific details about the source, including a summary of the argument; however, while the final sentence suggests the source's relevance, it refrains from critiquing the argument, producing an annotation that focuses more on summary than analysis. Some instructors also may request that you include at the end a note about which search engine or academic database you used and which keywords returned this result. This additional step would allow you to reflect on your own research methodology and what have been the most successful strategies that you've employed.

An *analytic annotation* follows the same model as the descriptive version, with one addition: it moves past simple summary to critique. For this reason, you'll find the *analytic annotation* an even more useful tool in your research process. Let's look at an example of this type of annotation for a research project on social activism and video games.

McGonigal, Jane. *Gaming Can Make a Better World*. TED Talks. Feb 2010. Web. 23 April 2013.

In this TED talk, video game designer Jane McGonigal passionately argues that we can use video games to solve larger cultural problems, such as the energy crisis and world hunger. Using examples from massive online games such as *World of Warcraft*, McGonigal insists that we embody the best qualities of ourselves when we play computer games: that we collaborate more readily, think more creatively, and have more self-confidence. In a provocative moment at the beginning of the talk, she suggests that we need to play video games more, not less—but that we need to play games designed to harness these qualities toward positive social good. While she offers some interesting examples of such games drawn from her work at the Institute of the Future (such as *World without Oil*), she discusses them only in the last four minutes of her 20-minute talk, so that key component of her argument (implementation) remains under-defined and under-developed. Overall, despite her compelling personality and her "exuberant" enthusiasm (11.43), her argument lacks in *logos* and evidentiary support; she provides some intriguing ideas for a future that unites gaming with social activism but does not convince her audience that it is actually possible.

This annotation has much in common with the *descriptive annotation* we looked at above: it addresses the credentials of the author, summarizes the argument, includes specific relevant detail, describes tone, and suggests its relevance. However, note the way the annotation's author integrates her own critique of McGonigal's claim throughout paragraph; she looks at this source through a critical lens, indicating that she will bring a similar approach to her treatment of this source material in her research paper. In some cases, you might even expand on the analytic model by including a final sentence that specifically indicates how you will use this source in relation to your

WRITER'S PRACTICE   MyWritingLab

Choose two sources from your preliminary research. Using the Questions for Evaluating Sources that start on p. 179 as a guide, evaluate the sources. Now write a *descriptive annotation* for one source and an *analytic annotation* for the other, drawing on the information from your evaluation. Be concrete and descriptive but also concise, writing no more than 150 words for each paragraph. Reflect on the two annotations when you have finished. How did each help you better understand your source material and how each text relates to your overall project and the development of your own thesis claim on the topic?

AT A GLANCE

Composing an Annotated Bibliography

1. Put your sources into alphabetical order; you can also categorize them by primary and secondary sources.
2. Provide complete identifying information for each source, including author's name, title, publication, date, page numbers, and database information for online sources.
3. Compose a concise annotation for each source:
   - Summarize the main argument or point of the source; use concrete language. Include quotations if you wish.
   - Take into account the writer's ethos and stance. How credible or biased is this source?
   - Consider the usefulness of this source to the conversation on this topic. Does the source provide background information? Does it offer a contrasting perspective to other sources you have found? Does it provide evidence that might back up your claims?

own research, perhaps even categorizing it according to Joseph Bizzup's BEAM taxonomy. In this way, you would provide your readers with more than a critical review of the text; you would offer them an understanding of how that source contributed to the way you were developing your own claim.

As the examples above demonstrate, writing an annotated bibliography involves more than merely recording information: it is a way for you to identify arguments and add your response to what the source has to say about your research topic.

THE WRITER'S PROCESS

As you begin to articulate your contribution to the research conversation about your topic, use the strategies that you've learned in this chapter. These include visualizing research as a conversation that you are joining and understanding the process of researching your argument as a movement from surface to depth. As you learn to search and locate your sources, you can engage in critical evaluation of these texts in your research log. You can also conduct innovative fieldwork of your own to generate original resource material to use in your argument. In writing your own annotated bibliography, remember that effective annotations and note-taking practices can help you develop the strategies of an academic writer and that these practices will move you toward finalizing your own argument about the topic.

AT A GLANCE

Note-Taking Strategies

As you read through your sources, take notes on materials that you could use in your paper:

- particularly memorable quotations
- background information
- a well-written passage providing context or a perspective useful to your argument

Be sure to double-check your notes for accuracy, use quotation marks for direct quotes, and include complete source details and page numbers.

Along the way, be sure to take careful notes. This is a crucial step in your writer's process. Many students make sense of the rich and diverse perspectives they encounter during their research through careful note taking. You can use the dialogue of sources method as a note-taking strategy while you work through your research sources. Or, you can take notes using a software program such as Endnote or Citelighter, bookmark pages and PDFs on your computer, or use the time-tested method of a spiral notebook or paper note cards. Whatever your method, be vigilant in your practice now so you won't have to retrace your steps and relocate your sources or quotations later. By putting into practice the techniques and lessons of this chapter, you will start to see connections among various research sources and begin to articulate your own research-based argument.

SPOTLIGHTED ANALYSIS: COVERS   MyWritingLab

Use the following prewriting prompts to follow the example from the beginning of the chapter and analyze the "cover" of your choice focused on a specific social, political, or cultural issue, whether that be a popular magazine cover (such as from *Time*, *The Economist*, or *Scientific American*) or a Website homepage (which serves as the "cover" for the larger site). Practice the techniques of rhetorical analysis that we used in relation to Figures 5.1 and 5.2, and brainstorm how the cover reflects its stance on the issue in question. Use the checklist below to guide your analysis:

- What images are featured on the cover? Are they photographs, hand-drawn sketches, cartoons, polished artwork? Are the images zoomed in (close-ups), portraits, or panoramic? What is the rhetorical effect of the style of the images?

- Does the cover feature people? Places? Symbols or abstract concepts? What do the cover images suggest about the contents of the larger text? How do they suggest a specific rhetorical stance or point of view?

- How do the words on the cover work in conjunction with the image suggest the entire text's rhetorical stance?

- To what extent does the cover appeal to the audience make an appeal based on facts, reason, or logic? Through emotion? Through an appeal to authority? To what extent does the cover trade on *kairos* in making its argument?

- Does the cover rely on any specific strategies of development to make its argument about its contents? Does it use narration? Comparison/contrast? Definition? Analogy? Example? Categorization? Process? How does its use of strategies make an argument about its contents?

- How does the layout function rhetorically? Does the cover use juxtaposition? Symmetry or asymmetry? To what extent does it draw the audience's eye through a pre-determined and strategic path?

WRITING ASSIGNMENTS MyWritingLab

1. **Research Log Entries:** Keep a running commentary/assessment of potential research sources for your project. Realize that careful research notes are a crucial part of the process and will help you avoid unintentional plagiarism of material. Include a combination of notes, scanned articles, emails, sources from databases, scanned images, and other means of processing all the information you encounter. Be sure also to record your search terms and research methods so you can evaluate and fine-tune their effectiveness as you move forward.

2. **Source Analysis:** Using the criteria on page 179 as a starting point, write up a one- to two-page analysis of a source for your research project. Be sure to consider authorship, publication information, date, occasion, purpose, audience, and tone. Also evaluate its argument and how it uses evidence to support its points. Finally, identify how you might use it in your essay, drawing on BEAM terminology.

3. **Dialogue of Sources:** Using the instructions in the At a Glance box on page 200, create a *dialogue of sources* to showcase the conversation around your topic. Be sure to select sources that represent diverse views or perspectives to provide a well-rounded approach to your issue. Use your central research question as the starting point for the conversation and be sure to include your own voice in the dialogue.

4. **Annotated Bibliography and Reflection:** Expand on the Writer's Practice on page 207 and compose an analytic annotated bibliography to showcase the primary and secondary sources you intend to employ in your essay. After each citation, categorize it according to the BEAM taxonomy (background, exhibit, argument, method) and, if you wish, as a primary source, secondary source, or as field research. When you are done, review the bibliography as a whole and assess what types of additional sources you need to locate to construct a powerful argument. Write a reflection in your research log on this process, including a "wish list" at the end of the types of sources you still want to find.

5. **Collaborative Peer Review:** Present your annotated bibliographies to one another in groups. Pull the "greatest hits" from your research log, and tell the class about how your research is going. In other words, *present a discussion of your work in progress.* Identify obstacles and successes so far. You'll get feedback from the class about your developing research project.

6. **Analytic Note Taking:** Choose one of your research sources to focus on. Before you begin taking notes, divide your document into two columns, whether by folding your notebook sheet in half or applying a dual-column layout to your word-processing document. Use the left column to take summary notes on your source; be sure to enclose any direct quotations in quotation marks. For each note, also record the page number to indicate where you got it (if your source is not paginated, consider using paragraph numbers instead). Then read back through your summary comments. Use the right column to record your analysis of the text: What questions do you have? What connections can you make? How do you evaluate the source's claims? What responses do you have? Use the same technique for your other sources so that you can bring an analytic perspective to your research as a way of helping you move toward your own research claim.

MyWritingLab Visit Ch. 5 Finding and Evaluating Research Sources in MyWritingLab to complete the Writer's Practices, Spotlighted Analyses, and Writing Assignments, and to test your understanding of the chapter objectives.

Part III

DRAFTING AND DESIGNING ARGUMENTS

CHAPTER 6

Organizing and Writing Research Arguments

Chapter Preview Questions

6.1 What strategies of organization will work for my essay?

6.2 What strategies can I use to create an outline for my argument?

6.3 What are the best ways to get started writing a full draft and integrating research sources responsibly and rhetorically?

6.4 How do I analyze a draft of a research-based essay?

6.5 What strategies can I use to revise my draft?

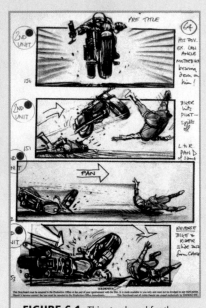

FIGURE 6.1 This storyboard for the James Bond film *Golden Eye* shows an initial draft for one of the film's action scenes.

Constructing a research argument is a complex and ongoing process. From selecting a topic to locating and evaluating sources and taking notes, it involves a series of interrelated steps. This is true of the drafting stage as well. In fact, organizing, drafting, and revising information is a prominent part of the process of creating any text—an academic essay, a research proposal, a podcast, a television commercial, or even a film.

Figure 6.1, for instance, lets us glimpse the drafting process behind the James Bond film *Golden Eye* (1995). This action scene from early in the film finds Bond fleeing from a Soviet chemical plant after the capture and execution of one of his colleagues. What you see in Figure 6.1 are a brief set of storyboards for part of this scene—an artist's draft that lays out the action in chronological increments, mapping out not only the movement of the characters but also the camera angles and thus the audience's experience of the events depicted. Notice how the storyboard shapes the narrative as it shifts between different angles on the chase: the first panel shows a close-up of the Soviet henchman who is pursuing Bond, establishing the threat; the second panel captures a sense of motion as the cyclist falls from his bike; the third panel gives camera direction ("pan") and follows the momentum of the biker's fall; the final panel zooms in further to focus on the fallen rider and the skidding bike – a bike that James Bond will then commandeer as the scene proceeds. Storyboards like this clearly operate as visual outlines, an organizational strategy that underlies almost all films. The polished final version seen in the theater is actually made possible by drafting steps like this one.

You probably recognize some implicit similarities between producing a research argument and producing a film:

- Both entail many small steps that support a grounding vision or main idea.
- Both have a carefully planned structure.
- Both involve rigorous editing.

Since they share such rich similarities, we can use the medium of film as a metaphor to help us understand the process of writing a research paper: from constructing a visual map and formal outline to integrating sources, key quotations, and evidence. We'll talk about incorporating sources responsibly in a way that sustains the conversation you began in the previous chapter, and we'll walk through the drafting and revision process. Just as filmmakers leave many scenes on the cutting room floor, you too will write, edit, cut, and rearrange much of the first draft of your research paper before it reaches its final form. You'll find that the process of completing your research argument is as collaborative as film production. Additionally, both film and writing require you to consider issues of length, cost, and time as you work to produce the best possible text. So let's get started moving from notes to writing the complete paper.

ORGANIZING YOUR DRAFT IN VISUAL FORM

6.1 What strategies of organization will work for my essay?

It can be quite challenging to turn on the computer and try to generate a complete draft of an essay without first taking the time to arrange your materials and ideas into some kind of order. Storyboards like those shown in

Figure 6.1 are just one example of the type of innovative, visual, or nonlinear technique you could use as part of your prewriting process. These methods of *invention*, similar to those that we discussed in Chapters 3 and 4, allow you to experiment with organizing your research notes and argumentative points in order to sort, arrange, and make connections between ideas.

You probably already instinctively organize your materials as you get ready to write. Perhaps you stack your research books, notes, and source printouts, either in the order you plan to use them or in groups by subject or relevance to your argument. Alternately, you might arrange and rearrange your notes on your desk or your computer, again spatially organizing them in a way that connects with how you plan to use them in your writing. If you've used notecards for taking notes, you probably shuffle and regroup them as you prepare to write. All these organizational strategies offer concrete ways to categorize the resources you have and figure out, visually, how they relate to one another.

Taking the practice of storyboarding as an inspiration, consider some additional strategies you might use to channel the canon of invention as part of your prewriting strategy.

- **Bubble web.** In Chapter 4, we explored using webbing or clustering as a technique for narrowing your topic. It can also provide a useful technique for experimenting with how to arrange your ideas by allowing you to explore relationships between them in a nonlinear fashion.
- **Graphic flowchart.** While a bubble web tends to focus on showing multiple connections between elements, a graphic flowchart foregrounds the more linear and hierarchical relationships between elements. In creating your flowchart, you list one idea and then draw an arrow to suggest connections between subsidiary points. Figure 6.2, for example, shows Thomas Zhao's preliminary flowchart for analysis of the changes in the process of adapting Japanese video games for U.S. audiences.
- **Idea roadmap.** You can push this technique further by "mapping" your argument on a large whiteboard space. Simply write out your thesis at one end of the board, and your conclusion (or your "destination") at the other, and then fill in the "sights" (ideas, arguments, evidence) that you'll see along the way. Visualizing your essay as a journey helps you keep your audience in mind and creates an underlying arc to your argument.
- **Post-it diagram.** Post-it notes offer you a very versatile medium for storyboarding. By writing your main ideas on post-its and

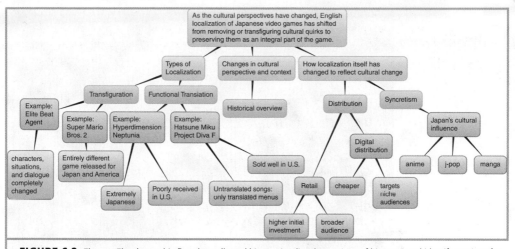

FIGURE 6.2 Thomas Zhao's graphic flowchart allowed him to visualize the sections of his essay and identify portions for which he needed to do additional research.

then arranging and rearranging them on a table or wall, you can easily experiment with different configurations for your argument. Figure 6.3 shows an example of how one writer used post-its to explore how she might organize her argument, using blue post-its for her main points, orange post-its for her supporting points, and smaller yellow post-its to indicate sources and notes.

Each of these strategies relies on some of the same principles that make storyboarding so powerful for filmmakers: they provide a flexible and dynamic mode of organizing the "story" of your essay; they allow you to zoom in on specific details, while also encouraging you to step back and assess the shape of the argument as a whole. When engaging in your own visualizations of your argument, be sure to use this prewriting process as an opportunity to ask yourself some key questions:

■ Is each of my points developed thoroughly? What else do I need to make the points persuasive? *This will give you insight into whether you need to do more research or if you need to reformulate your argument or strengthen how you support your points.*

■ Do I have a balance among the sections of my argument? *By answering this question, you will consider the relationship between the parts of your*

FIGURE 6.3 This student writer created her post-it note "outline" on a white board, so she could better experiment with arrangement and show connections between ideas through notes and arrows.

argument, identifying whether you've developed one section more than the others.

■ Does the argument as a whole seem coherent? Are there outlier elements? *This big-picture question will help you discern whether your argument moves forward purposefully and clearly, or whether you stray into digressions along the way.*

WRITER'S PRACTICE   MyWritingLab

Explore different ways to organize an essay you're writing by experimenting with a post-it note diagram, such as the one in Figure 6.3.

- Write out your central claim on a post-it note. Place it on a flat blank space, such as a wall or table.
- Jot down some of your main ideas on other post-it notes, using one post-it for each idea.
- Arrange them next to your claim, positioning them according to their relationship to the claim and to each other.
- Write additional ideas on other post-its, grouping them near your first post-its according to how they support, develop, or even challenge those points. You might include here specific

examples or evidence, facts, counter arguments, unspoken assumptions (or warrants) that influence your argument, definitions, or background information.

- Select different color post-its and use them for notes about your sources, positioning these source notes adjacent to post-its representing points they'll support in your argument.
- Arrange and rearrange your post-its to consider the best flow possible between your ideas and to experiment with different structures of arrangement, referring to Chapter 3 for some ideas. For example, arrange them first in a block or thematic organization; then re-arrange them in a problem–solution or cause–effect structure; finally, experiment with a narrative or chronological structure. Which mode of arrangement best supports your argument?

When you've completed your diagram, write a 10-minute reflection on the process. What did you learn about the best ways to organize your argument? What challenges did you encounter? What insights do you have about further research you need to do or the best ways to support your claim?

LEARNING OUTLINING STRATEGIES

6.2 What strategies can I use to create an outline for my argument?

The visual organization strategies we discussed above can help you sort out your materials and prepare you for the next step: the detailed, written **outline**. For a longer, more complex paper, such as a research-based argument, an *outline* is an extremely useful method of arranging ideas and expediting the drafting process. Outlines offer a plan for your paper and should show the relationships among the various sections in your argument. If your outline simply consists of a list of topics, you won't be able to see the argument of the whole paper, nor will you be able to check for a strong progression between your individual points. In other words, the secret to producing a successful outline—and by extension a successful paper—is to pay special attention to the flow or development of ideas.

It's often hard to know for certain the best way to put together points in an outline: faced with so much information and so many ideas, even if you've created an effective visual brainstorm, you might have difficulty aligning your points sequentially so they effectively support your claim. Let's return to our focus on films to reflect on how an outline can work to draw different points together into a cohesive argument.

Looking at cinematic trailers can be instructive for thinking about organization. Although they generally are created after-the-fact (once the movie is through production), what trailers present to the audience is essentially a brief outline of the film, the elements arranged in a way designed to make a certain argument about the movie. In fact, many films have not one but several trailers, each one slightly different, designed with a particular context or audience in mind. For instance, one of the earliest trailers for the 2009 film *Avatar* organized its clips from the film to focus on the experience of taking on an alternate identity. By propelling the audience through a set of images—the wheelchair-bound protagonist, his first encounter with his avatar floating in a tank, the process of his coming to inhabit that body, and a series of rapid fire impressions of the adventure, war, and love that he experienced in that alternate form—the trailer argues that the film will be about a fantasy of identity and escape.

However, the official theatrical trailer arranged its film clips differently, promulgating a more provocative message. Although, like the previous version, it uses a narrative structure as its underlying strategy of arrangement, this longer trailer privileges plot over character. The images in Figure 6.4 illustrate this movement, taking the viewer from an introduction of the human characters in the corporate research facility, to scenes showing the protagonist's encounters with the native people (the Na'vi) and his gradual integration into their world, to scenes of the final explosive conflict between the soldiers and the indigenous inhabitants. In doing so, the trailer reproduces two of the central themes of *Avatar*: the dangers of imperialism and the clash between a spiritual worldview and one filtered through corporate greed.

In essence, then, the power of the trailer as an organizational tool or outline is that it allows filmmakers to experiment with order and, ultimately, meaning. Similarly, in your outline, you are deciding on the "story" you want to tell your readers about your research and your argument. The way you arrange the elements will influence how they understand the claims you make and how persuaded they will be by your argument.

Developing a Formal Outline

Like storyboards or movie trailers, a **formal outline** presents you with the opportunity to work step by step through the process of arguing your position. It asks you to organize your ideas hierarchically, arranging them in a detailed list that uses numbers and letters to indicate the main points of your argument and then the supporting points beneath.

FIGURE 6.4 These still shots from one of several trailers for the film *Avatar* transition the viewer from the human perspective into the world of Pandora, and then into the climactic conflict between the worlds.

While each finished outline differs, the basic template for a formal outline follows this logical pattern:

I. Main point for the first section
   A. First supporting point for section I.
      1. First supporting point, evidence, or detail for A.
      2. Second supporting point, evidence, or detail for A.
      3. Third supporting point, evidence, or detail for A.
   B. Second supporting point for section I.
      1. First supporting point, evidence, or detail for B.
      2. Second supporting point, evidence, or detail for B.
        a. First supporting point, evidence, or detail for 2.
        b. Second supporting point, evidence, or detail for 2.
II. Main point for the second section
   A. First supporting point for section II.
      1. First supporting point, evidence, or detail for A.
      2. Second supporting point, evidence, or detail for A.
      3. Third supporting point, evidence, or detail for A.
   B. Second supporting point for section II.
      1. First supporting point, evidence, or detail for B.
      2. Second supporting point, evidence, or detail for B.
        a. First supporting point, evidence, or detail for 2.
        b. Second supporting point, evidence, or detail for 2.
III. Main point for section III. [etc.]

Your outline's shape should be like an accordion—the different sections will expand or contract depending on your material, research, and argument. In general, it's useful to think of the main sections (I, II, III, etc.) as just that—sections—not necessarily as paragraphs. If you start limiting the way you think about your argument to concrete units (paragraphs, number of pages, or amount of sources), you risk losing touch with the most important aspect of writing an essay: the conceptual development of your argument.

As you move toward outlining, approach it as a useful stage of your pre-writing and drafting process. A strong, well-developed outline can help you in a number of ways. First and foremost, it allows you to work with the rhetorical canon of **arrangement**, experimenting with different organizational structures, such as those we discussed in Chapter 3: chronological, process, narrative, cause–effect, problem–solution, block structure, thematic or topical,

Seeing Connections
See Chapter 3 for more on the canon of arrangement.

or inductive. As you can see from the At a Glance box, it's useful to consider which mode of organization best suits the type of argument you intend to make and how you want to lead your reader through your information.

Furthermore, an outline—like the visual techniques we discussed above—provides you with a more panoramic perspective on your argument so that you better assess if you need to do supplement research or which areas of your argument are particularly troublesome or conceptually underdeveloped. In fact, if you write your outline with full sentences and include source notations, you can begin the process of generating content and language that you can draw on as you move toward your full written draft. At the same time, keep in mind that an outline is not a formal contract; it is a starting point. As you begin to write your essay, you may very well find it necessary to alter and reorganize your points, the same way you might have rearranged the post-its on the wall in the Writer's Practice above. However, a strong initial outline gives you a solid foundation to build from in constructing a well-conceived and well-developed argument.

Let's look at an outline generated by a student for a research project on the environmental impacts of vegetarianism. As you read through the outline, think about how the author used the formal outline form to organize her ideas in a way that developed her points and created a logical progression of ideas.

AT A GLANCE

Useful Organization Strategies for Writing

- *Chronological:* Works best with arguments tied to a progression of temporal events, so well-suited for historical discussions
- *Process:* Effective for leading readers from beginning to end through a series of steps
- *Narrative:* Employs personal experience or a story arc to move the reader through the argument
- *Cause-effect:* Works well for arguments that focus on consequences
- *Problem-solution:* Useful for papers where the writer proposes a particular solution for a problem, such as social issue papers
- *Block structure:* Effective structure for when you're working through a series of case studies or extended examples
- *Comparison-contrast:* Often arranged as a variant of block structure, this mode is most effective when you're discussing one element in relation to another
- *Thematic or topical:* Helpful for arguments that center on different conceptual categories or themes
- *Inductive reasoning:* Appropriate for essays where you want to move from general evidence to your specific conclusion

Notice how Ada includes a notation about her hook, right in the outline, showing how she prioritizes reaching her audience even in the early stages of writing her essay.

She includes a draft of her thesis claim, showing how she is using it to anchor how she develops and organizes her ideas.

She ends her outline of the introduction with questions designed to engage the reader and point to the larger "So what" of her topic.

For each section, she identifies the strategy of argumentation that would best support her subclaims, here choosing cause-effect as her mode of arrangement.

Ada Throckmorton

Research Paper—Outline

I.   Introduction: Vegetarianism is Growing and Should Continue to Grow

    A. Hook: A brief anecdote about the fact that October is International Vegetarian Awareness Month and the fact that vegetarians are growing in number.

    B. Thesis: When it comes to many environmental concerns, skipping meat is an effective way to reduce our personal ecological footprints.

    C. Implications: How does vegetarianism compare to other ways that individuals can preserve the environment? In what way does eating meat harm the environment and contribute to climate change?

II.   Direct Impact on Climate Change

    A. Cause: Energy input overall is greater to produce animal protein than plant protein due to the many steps required.

    B. Effect (and impact): Emissions of certain greenhouse gases are extremely high (Source: Kathy Freston's "Vegetarian Is the New Prius" in the Huffington Post on January 18, 2007).

        i.   9% of U.S. CO_2

        ii.   37% of U.S. methane (23 times more powerful than CO_2)

        iii.   67% of U.S. nitrous oxide emissions (296 times more powerful than CO_2)

III. Other Environmental Impacts

   A. Meat production requires huge inputs of water.

      i. Context: 100× more water per gram of animal protein than plant protein (Source: David and Marcia Pimentel's "Sustainability of Meat-Based and Plant-Based Diets" from American Journal of Clinical Nutrition in January 2003).

      ii. Context: Comparison of meat's water usage to showering, drinking shows it is a much larger water user (Source: Mike Sage's "Meat is the Huge Water Waster" in the Sierra Club April 2014).

      iii. Suggested solution: Even skipping one hamburger can help as much as not showering for six months (Source: Lynn Hasselberger's "Veganism and the Environment: By the Numbers" in Elephant Journal on February 23, 2013).

   B. Meat production pollutes water.

      i. Context: Livestock waste (130× that of humans) is not treated and runs off into local water sources (Source: Worldwatch Institute's "Is Meat Sustainable?" in January 2013).

      ii. Context: Nitrogen fertilizers and pesticides used to grow vast amounts of feed for livestock runs off into rivers (Source: Roddy Scheer and Doug Moss's "How Does Meat in the Diet Take an Environmental Toll?" in the Scientific American on December 28, 2011).

      iii. Impact: Water pollution affects ecosystems but also hurts human health.

Note that she includes her sources right in her outline so she'll be sure to weave them into her essay.

In this early part of her outline, which is designed to present the environmental impact of meat-consumption, she uses a context-impact structure, first providing facts and then interpreting them for the reader.

C. Land dedicated to producing meat is large and displaces other activities.

    i.   Context: 30% of ice-free land on earth is dedicated to feed-growing and grazing land for livestock (Source: Bryan Walsh's "The Triple Whopper Environmental Impact of Global Meat Production" in TIME Magazine on December 16, 2013).

    ii.   Impact: This land is often cleared forests, which act as carbon sinks (removing CO_2 from atmosphere).

    iii.   Impact: Land use can cause habitat fragmentation that harms biodiversity.

IV.   Approaching a Solution

A. Argument: Dietary choices are something that we all have personal control over so it has a greater impact.

    i.   Supporting Claim: comparison to voting as civic duty

    ii.   Supporting Claim: linear contributions make a difference

B. Argument: Polarized political climate necessitates that we act on our own.

C. Conclusion: We all can make a difference in whatever level we choose to cut our meat consumption.

    i.   Context: Although vegetarianism is increasing as a percentage of the population, total meat consumption is increasing faster (Source: Kathy Freston's "Vegetarian Is the New Prius" in the Huffington Post on January 18, 2007).

As she moves to the solution portion of her essay, she identifies two claims that she will use as part of her argument. Even though she is still working on developing these ideas, she includes them as placeholders here.

Note how clearly Ada conceives of her conclusion as a place to clearly restate her claims, backed by clear evidence from sources. She resists simply summarizing and instead uses her closing section to reinforce her argument and implicitly call the reader to action.

    ii.   Supporting Claim: This makes it more important to cut meat now, and it means we can make more of a difference not less.

    iii.   Supporting Claim: If every American cut one serving of chicken, it would be equivalent to taking 500,000 cars off the road (Source: Lynn Hasselberger's "Veganism and the Environment: By the Numbers" in Elephant Journal on February 23, 2013).

    iv.   Final claim: Individual action is effective because it improves the situation regardless of what happens in any other sphere of action.

AT A GLANCE

Assessing Outlines

- **Thesis:** Is it complex, arguable, and interesting?
- **Argument:** Is there a logical and fluid progression of ideas? Does each one relate back to the thesis? Is there extraneous information that you can cut?
- **Arrangement:** Does your outline follow a consistent and clear model of arrangement?
- **Development:** Do any points need to more development? Do you see any areas that need further research? For instance, is there an "A" without a "B"? Is there one section that is much less developed than the others?
- **Sources:** Do you identify any primary sources that you'll analyze in the paper? Do you list your secondary sources at relevant points to provide support and authority for the argument? Are there sufficient sources listed for each point?
- **Format:** Is there a clear hierarchy of information, with main points associated with supporting points? Are the headings in corresponding sections (like the I, II, III headings or A, B, C headings) parallel in structure (i.e., all gerunds, all noun phrases, all questions)? Do they move the argument of the essay along?

As you can see from Ada's example, you can use your outline as an opportunity to combine argument and arrangement—developing your claims, starting to work through how to support those claims with evidence from your sources, and constructing an organizational framework (in her case, a problem-solution mode of arrangement) that can support a persuasive line of reasoning.

WRITER'S PRACTICE   MyWritingLab

Evaluate the logical structure of an outline by disassembling and reassembling it. Print out a copy of the outline for your essay. Take scissors and cut up the outline so that each section is on a separate slip of paper, being sure to remove the Roman numeral or letter that labels each section. Then shuffle the different pieces of paper so that they are no longer in order. Having done so, reassemble your outline, trying to sequence them in a logical order to develop your argument. Alternately, have a partner try to reassemble your outline for you. When you are done, compare your new creation with the original version of your outline. How did the process help you reflect on the choices you made for organizing your argument?

6.3 What are the best ways to get started writing a full draft and integrating research sources responsibly and rhetorically?

DRAFTING YOUR RESEARCH ARGUMENT

As you continue to forge ahead with your research argument, turning it from an outline to a full draft, remember that there are many strategies for getting it done. The key is to start writing—and then just keep going. As the many methods in the At a Glance box indicate, there is no single right way to draft an essay; what's most important is to find the one that best supports your writing style. Whichever method you choose, you'll want to address several questions as you begin to flesh out your argument: how to retain a strong structure, facilitate clear connections between your ideas, spotlight your argument, integrate source material, and, most importantly, how to keep writing.

Structuring Your Argument with Subheads

One way to retain a clear structure while drafting is to borrow a practice from outlining and incorporate subheadings into your essay. You can use these as a temporary organizational aid in your draft (like the scaffolding surrounding a building under construction that eventually is dismantled and taken away) or you could incorporate them as permanent headings for your essay's sections (like the signposts that mark city streets and landmarks). In either case, such subheads help you transition from your outline to an essay while still allowing you to clearly map the progression of your argument. Subheads work particularly well for longer, research-based essays, especially ones that ask the reader to make sense of a complex argument.

Some disciplines, such as the social sciences, require subheadings like "Introduction," "Methods," "Results," and "Discussion," while others—such as those in the humanities—might even discourage the use of subheadings in academic essays. You'll need to assess your rhetorical situation and the parameters of your assignment to determine what part they might play in your essay. However, whether you use them as scaffolding (temporary) or signposts (permanent), consider the power of designing *rhetorical subheads* to help you sharpen your argument. A rhetorical subhead reinforces not just structure, but your claim; that is, rather than simply announcing a structural unit ("Case Study #1"), it situates the section in relation to the argument ("Case Study #1: Low Income and Low Status at an Elite University"). In addition, each subhead offers a mini-preview of the points to come in the section and can help keep your overall argument on track, for both your readers and for you as a writer.

AT A GLANCE

Strategies for Drafting

- *Following the linear path:* Start at the beginning, write the introduction, and then move sequentially through each point of argument.
- *Fleshing out the outline:* Gradually transform the outline into a full draft, moving from a keyword outline to a prose outline by systematically expanding each of the sections; as you add more detail, the keywords fall away, leaving behind drafted paragraphs.
- *Writing from the middle:* Start writing from a point of greatest strength or start with a section you can complete easily and then write around it and fill out sections as you go.
- *Freewrite and then reverse outline:* First, freewrite a few pages, then compose a **reverse outline** in which you record the point of each paragraph to assess the argument's flow and structure, and finally reorder and rewrite the paper until it begins to take the proper form for the argument.

When designing rhetorical subheads, you might link them thematically or use a single metaphor to add a rich layer of vivid words to your essay. This technique can provide consistency in language that can enhance the overall cohesiveness of the essay and make it more engaging to read. For instance, let's look at the subheads that one student, Ali Batouli, used in his essay on how the Internet enables online dissent in countries under authoritarian rule. Ali chose to thread a David-and-Goliath metaphor throughout his essay to heighten his analysis of the individual Internet user's confrontation with the authoritarian behemoth. Look at the way his subheads (listed below) help develop his argument:

- David's Slingshot of Freedom (*In this section, the first in the main body of his essay, Ali defined how individuals were using the Internet to circumvent censorship and oppression in their countries.*)
- Goliath's Defense (*In this section, he analyzed the government's response to such online dissent.*)
- Goliath's Intimidation (*In this section, he delved further into the government response, looking at the more aggressive actions.*)
- David's Size Disadvantage (*In this section, Ali assessed the reasons that the individual Internet user seemed unequal to the task of defeating government censorship.*)
- Goliath's Own Slingshot (*In this section, he examined some of the "weapons" that the authoritarian government used to squelch online dissent.*)
- Goliath's Unique Weapon: The Economy (*In this section, he focused his analysis more narrowly on how national economies contributed to these conflicts.*)
- A Revision: Goliath's Victory (*In this concluding section, Ali used the subhead to suggest his surprising claim: that in this version of David-and-Goliath, the giant wins.*)

These carefully developed subheads guide the reader through the argument much more powerfully than would more generic ones such as "Dissent Online" or "Government Response." While such creative subheads might not be appropriate for all contexts, the principle behind them—that subheads can be designed to reinforce the argument as much as to signpost structure—is worth considering no matter what writing situation.

Connecting Your Ideas with Transitions

Whether or not you use subheads, you can attend to the flow and development of your argument by careful attention to transitions. In fact, one myth associated with using subheads is that they obviate the need for transitions between paragraphs. This is not the case. With all the essays you write—especially longer, research-based arguments—you need to take care to provide clear connections and transitions between paragraphs and sections to help ensure that your arguments are both *coherent* (clear and easy to follow) and *cohesive* (unified).

In their simplest form, a transition gestures back at ideas you've already presented and then gestures forward to ideas you're about to present, providing a seamless, smooth connection between the two. In many cases, transitions might take the shape of a single word or phrase that provides links between paragraphs or sections in your essay. For instance, you might incorporate terms like that imply *addition* (e.g., furthermore, in addition, additionally), *sequential arrangement* (e.g., next, first, second, third, finally), *similarity* (e.g., likewise, similarly, in the same way), *contrast* (e.g., yet, however, conversely, on the one hand/on the other hand), *cause–effect* (e.g., therefore, consequently, as a result), or *elaboration* (e.g., for example, for instance, in other words). In each case, the word or phrase suggests a relationship between two elements: what you've already said and what you're about to say.

As our taxonomy of transitional words and phrases indicates, at their core, transitions represent relationships or connections between *ideas*. For this reason, you might decide to use more overtly *conceptual transitions* to streamline your writing. This sort of transition produces cohesion by using key terms from your argument or crafting more complex transitional sentences to connect your points. Consider, for instance, these three transitions from an essay critiquing the increased popularity of gluten-free diets:

> Version 1: Next, it is crucial to consider the role of the media in propagating an ill-informed, pseudo-scientific position that vilifies gluten-based foods.
>
> Version 2: Even more importantly, it is crucial to consider the role of the media in propagating an ill-informed, pseudo-scientific position that vilifies gluten-based foods.

Version 3: Although such attention to contradictions in food label-ing is important, it is even more crucial to consider the role of the media in propagating an ill-informed, pseudo-scientific position that vilifies gluten-based foods.

The first version provides a sequential transition. As a reader, you under-stand that you are reading the *next* in a series of points; however, there is no sense that this point is any more or less important than the others. The second version gives you a greater understanding of how this point relates to the one before it, suggesting that this section of the argument relies on an underlying structure of escalating importance. The final example takes the time to remind the reader of what he or she has just read (a discus-sion of contradictions in food labeling) before indicating the move to the next—and more important—topic (the role of the media). In many ways, it provides the most nuanced and clear transition between ideas, one that reinforces the essay's structure while facilitating the argument's forward momentum.

Whether you choose to rely primarily on transitional words/terms or to augment them with more expansive conceptual transitions, you'll need to go through the same process: in each case, think about how you can sig-nal the next idea, build on the previous idea, or reiterate the key terms as you advance your argument. Many students like to think of the game of dominoes when composing transitions: each domino can only touch another domino with a matching number; two connects with two, three with three. Using this notion of progressive, connecting terms and ideas, you can incor-porate transitions within sections of your outline to give it overall structure and flow.

Integrating Research Sources into Your Draft

A key moment in drafting your essay involves working with the sources you've uncovered in your research. However, before you begin this process, you must gain clarity about your own voice and rhetorical stance on the topic. The most important feature of your essay is in fact *your argument*, and—to continue our film metaphor—you need to decide how you will **spotlight your argument** so that it doesn't get lost in amid the many per-spectives that inform your paper.

AT A GLANCE

Working with Sources Appropriately and Effectively

- **Read.** Read the source actively and carefully, underlining passages that suggest moments of deep meaning or that might contribute to your argument. If you are working with online texts, cut and paste the citation into a document and note the paragraph number (for websites) or page number. Always note the page number if you transcribe quotations as you read.

  You'll need this part in order to provide the citation in your own writing.

- **Record.** Keep a notebook or an annotated file of citations in which you record your reactions to a particular passage you've read. Does this passage strike you as important? Does it reveal the theme of the text, the climax of a scene, the point of the argument, the purpose of the passage?

  You'll need this part in order to provide your interpretation of the citation.

- **Relate.** While drafting, integrate the source material and your interpretation in an appropriate place in your essay. Think about where in the essay, and in which particular paragraph, the information should appear. Think about the context—what comes before and after the summary, paraphrase, or quotation? How does it related to the text around it?

  You'll need this part in order to integrate your source material effectively.

There is no single correct way to strike a balance between your position and your sources. At certain points in your essay, you might want to put your sources center stage and direct from behind the scenes, and sometimes you might want to step out of the shadows and articulate your argument more explicitly to the audience. The key is to choose the role that will produce the most effective argument on your topic, one that fits the needs of your rhetorical situation. After you decide on your approach to working with sources—as a strong explicit narrator or as the strategic synthesizer of information—you can turn to the task of evaluating how to most effectively utilize your source material to support your argument.

This is no simple task: you'll need to introduce and weave the voices of your sources into your written prose, integrating your sources appropriately (to avoid plagiarism), rhetorically (to decide on how much of a presence you will have in the paper), and also strategically (to provide a range of quotations and supporting evidence for your paper). This complex process of **integrating sources** occurs in three basic ways:

- **Summary:** synthesizing a great deal of information from a source
- **Paraphrase:** putting a source quotation into your own words
- **Direct quotation:** excerpting a specific passage from a source, enclosing it in quotation marks

You'll want to alternate among these methods while incorporating your sources for stylistic variety and to accommodate the different ways you'll be using your research as evidence for your argument. This means knowing your options as a writer and selecting the best method for each rhetorical situation within your research essay. Realize that you have many choices for how to integrate research sources and your decisions should be determined by the specific need of each part of your argument as well as the value of the research to build your *ethos*, provide background, offer an alternative perspective, or convey foundational knowledge.

Seeing Connections
For an example of summary paragraph in an annotated bibliography, see Chapter 5, pages 204–205.

Selecting Summary   A **summary** is a brief version—in your own words—of the content of a text. You might want to summarize the plot of a film or a book in a review, or you might want to summarize the basic argument presented by one of your sources in order to respond to it. Summaries are not analyses; you are not exploring your own ideas when you summarize but merely laying out the ideas explored by another writer in another text. In general, summaries do not use first person since it is the source material and not your interpretation of it that is most relevant. You need to make sure that you tell your readers exactly what you are summarizing and provide complete bibliographical information at the end of your paper. For example, a research paper about the Italian films produced after World War II might include a summary that begins:

> In their influential study *Italian Neorealism and Global Cinema*, cultural critics Laura Ruberto and Kristi Wilson provide a concise history of film innovations at the turn of the twentieth century and argue that Italian documentaries allowed international conflicts to seem real to viewers...

Your summary would follow, and your list of works cited at the end of your paper would include the following reference:

> Ruberto, Laura E. and Wilson, Kristi M. *Italian Neorealism and Global Cinema*. Detroit: Wayne State UP, 2007. Print.

If you wanted to include a brief quote within the body of your summary, then you would use quotation marks and a page number, as follows:

> In their influential study *Italian Neorealism and Global Cinema*, cultural critics Laura Ruberto and Kristi Wilson provide a concise history of film innovations

at the turn of the twentieth century and argue that Italian documentaries "had a way of making the global seem local" (2).

Note that in this case, you are still writing a summary, but you include a direct quotation because it is rhetorically concise and powerful (with *pathos*-laden language) but also because citing the text gives you more *ethos* or authority as a writer.

Picking Paraphrase   Unlike a summary, a **paraphrase** focuses in and restates one part of a text. While a summary is often shorter than the text it summarizes, a paraphrase may be longer or shorter than the text it paraphrases. You might want to paraphrase a text to help your readers understand it, particularly if the original text is dense or difficult. Or you might simply want to paraphrase to make sure that you understand the source yourself—to offer yourself an opportunity to think clearly about the words you are reading. For instance, you might select the following lines to paraphrase:

> "Film had a way of making the global seem local, and the effect of movement, and, later, sound created an immediacy that still photos and written narratives could not approach" (Ruberto and Wilson 2).

Your paraphrase might read as follows:

> Italian film brought world events home to viewers, especially through moving images and audio (Ruberto and Wilson 2).

Note that you replace all the words, not just some of them, for a paraphrase. You need to be careful that you are using your own words to create a new text, not simply cutting and pasting the words of your source together in a different order. For instance, the following sentence represents a failed and problematic paraphrasing:

> Film made the global seem local, and the effect of motion and audio tracks constructed a connection to the audience that photographs and books could not (Ruberto and Wilson 2).

Notice the strong echo of the original text: if you follow both the structure and the language of the source closely, substituting only an occasional synonym to avoid directly quoting, then you are actually plagiarizing—even if you do so accidentally and even if you provide an appropriate citation. You are plagiarizing because you are not informing your reader that the structure, ideas, and much of the language used in your paper were created by someone else.

Seeing Connections
See Chapter 7 for a more detailed discussion of plagiarism and intellectual property.

How to avoid this problem? As you paraphrase, try not to look at the original sentence; move beyond its specific wording to try to get at its meaning. Double-check after you've written your paraphrase to be sure that you don't too strongly replicate the original in phrasing or structure. In addition, be sure to provide your reader with the appropriate bibliographical information about your source by offering a lead-in phrase ("As Ruberto and Wilson argue in their book *Italian Neorealism and Global Cinema* ...") and then list the complete reference for this source at the end of your paper. Or you can provide a parenthetical citation after the summary or paraphrase including the author's name and, for a paraphrase, the page number where the passage you are paraphrasing appears in the original text. When in doubt, consider using a direct quotation instead of a paraphrase to bring your source's voice directly into your essay.

Using Direct Quotations   Quoting directly from a source may seem much simpler than paraphrasing or summarizing, but quotations should be included to accomplish a specific rhetorical purpose, and they must be integrated responsibly so that you give the original writer credit. Consider how you might feel if someone took your writing and recycled it without acknowledging that it was your work. More importantly, realize that naming the author and background of a great passage can build your authority and *ethos* as a writer, so it is a wise move to name your sources in your paper. However, be careful not to swing to the opposite extreme and overfill your paper with quotations from others. If a quotation does not fit into any of the categories listed in the At a Glance box, consider paraphrasing or summarizing it.

What you want to avoid is a paper dominated by unnecessary quotations; in such a case, your argument—what readers expect most in your paper—gets buried. It's similar to what happens in film when the filmmaker splices together too many different scenes; the audience becomes lost in the montage and can no longer follow the narrative.

AT A GLANCE

Reasons to Use Direct Quotations

- *Evidence:* the quotation provides tangible evidence for part of your argument.
- *Ethos:* the original author is a primary source or an expert on the subject, and including a direct quotation would increase the *ethos* of your argument.
- *Language:* the original author used memorable phrasing or has a particular voice that would be lost in paraphrase.

Working with Quotations in Your Writing   But how, practically, do you go about *integrating* direct quotations appropriately and effectively? The key is to think carefully about how you are using the source material first and then choose an appropriate structure. Your temptation might be simply to "drop" a quote in between two of your sentences, as in the example below:

> More recently, *Hunger Games* protagonist Katniss has challenged the anti-feminist stereotype prominent in today's young adult fiction. "She's Jo March as coal miner's daughter in hunting boots, the opposite of Bella, the famously drippy, love-obsessed heroine of the *Twilight* books—and unlike clever and self-possessed Hermione of the *Harry Potter* series, she's the lead, not the sidekick" (Pollitt 10). Translated to the big screen in a blockbuster film, Katniss solidifies this image, providing a much-needed positive model for today's young women.

While Pollitt's sentence merits being quoted directly because of its language, the danger in this method is that you are using the quotation not as evidence, but as a substitute for your own writing. The original writer (Katha Pollitt) is given little credit for her work besides the parenthetical citation, making her more a ghostwriter than a source for your argument.

Rather than using a drop quote, integrate direct quotations strategically into your writing so as to leverage them more effectively as you develop your claim. One typical practice is to use a **signal phrase** to indicate the context of the quotation and to orient it in terms of your argument. A signal phrase can be located in many different positions in relation to the quotation, but most often it appears as an introductory phrase or clause that refers to the original author or title of the source, heightening the *ethos* of the source.

> In her 2012 article, Kate Pollitt argues, "She's Jo March as coal miner's daughter in hunting boots, the opposite of Bella, the famously drippy, love-obsessed heroine of the *Twilight* books—and unlike clever and self-possessed Hermione of the *Harry Potter* series, she's the lead, not the sidekick" (10).

An alternate method would be to limit the amount of text quoted and **integrate small sections into your own sentence**. This strategy works particularly well when you are trying to capture a unique turn of phrase or concept from the original text and tends to maintain the strength of your own voice as a writer. For example, consider how in this example, the author integrates a few words of direct quotation into her sentence so as to spotlight Pollitt's memorable characterization of Bella Swan's character:

> Pollitt argues that, unlike the "famously drippy, love-obsessed" Bella from the *Twilight* series, Katniss offers a smart, positive role model for today's young women (10).

In another variation, the author includes a slightly longer section of the original text that works in conjunction with paraphrase:

> Kate Pollitt offered a persuasive intertextual interpretation of Katniss's character when she suggested that Katniss is "Jo March as coal miner's daughter in hunting boots," directly opposing the model of femininity embodied by *Twilight*'s Bella (10).

This model can also be adapted to allow the writer to follow up the quotation with an end comment that advances the argument.

A third integration strategy involves **appending the quotation to one of your own sentences with a colon.** The syntactical function of the colon implies that what follows it (the quote) is directly related to what precedes the colon (your own observation). For this reason, this structure works well to suggest that the direct quotation operates as an elaboration of your point or as evidence.

> Pollitt argues that Katniss represents a new-and-improved model of female heroine: "She's Jo March as coal miner's daughter in hunting boots, the opposite of Bella, the famously drippy, love-obsessed heroine of the *Twilight* books—and unlike clever and self-possessed Hermione of the *Harry Potter* series, she's the lead, not the sidekick" (10).

At times, you may even decide to include a lengthier quotation in your essay, perhaps because of the strength of the author's argument or because you intend to analyze the passage. For direct quotations of four lines or longer, set the passage off from the rest of the text as a **block quote.** Here's an example using Pollitt once again.

> In discussing Katniss's role in revitalizing the female pop culture protagonist, Pollitt argues,
>
> > She's Jo March as coal miner's daughter in hunting boots, the opposite of Bella, the famously drippy, love-obsessed heroine of the *Twilight* books—and unlike clever and self-possessed Hermione of the *Harry Potter* series, she's the lead, not the sidekick. We're worlds away from the vicious-little-rich-girls of *Gossip Girl* and its knockoffs, where everything revolves around looks, clothes, consumerism, social status, and sexual competition (10).
>
> As Pollitt suggests, some of Katniss's appeal lies in how she embodies the intelligence and fortitude of previous female protagonists, qualities that have been increasingly obscured beneath superficiality and sentimentality in more recent years.

It's worth noting some technical details here: the quotation as a whole is indented one inch from the left margin; quotation marks are omitted in block quotes because the formatting itself marks it as a direct quotation; the final period precedes the parenthetical citation for a block quote; the author's analysis ("As Pollitt notes...") resumes flush with the left margin, indicating it is part of the same paragraph and same line of argument.

While including blocks of text might be tempting, especially when dealing with a particularly rich source, be judicious in your use of lengthy quotes. Including too many of them can fragment your argument, interrupt the flow of your essay, and drown out your own voice. Always follow up a block quote with analysis to clarify to your reader how it contributes to your argument and to return the spotlight onto your own research and claim.

As you work with direct quotations in your own writing, you might find these additional strategies helpful:

- To quote a source within a source, use (qtd. in ——) to indicate where *you* found the quotation, for instance:

  > Film critic Millicent Marcus argues that "neorealism is first and foremost a moral statement" (qtd. in Ruberto and Wilson 7).

  If you don't include the author's name in the signal phrase, insert in the parenthesis:

  > A different perspective might argue that "neorealism is first and foremost a moral statement" (Marcus qtd. in Ruberto and Wilson 7).

- To edit part of a quote, use square brackets, such as [ ]. This abridgement allows you to get concisely to the heart of the issue in your chosen quotation. For instance, you might edit the Pollitt quote above:

  > Kathy Pollitt argues in her 2012 article from *The Nation*, Katniss is "the opposite of Bella [...] and unlike clever and self-possessed Hermione [...], she's the lead, not the sidekick" (10).

Experiment with these strategies in your own writing to determine which best serves your rhetorical purpose. One key to remember is to avoid overusing any one type of integration strategy; in that case, your writing style might become

AT A GLANCE

Check for Integrating Sources

- Did you **introduce** the quotations that you used in various ways?
- Did you **link** the source material to your argument to show the relevance?
- Did you **comment** on them afterward to advance your argument?
- Did you **cite** them properly using the appropriate documentation style for your subject area?

monotonous, like a film that relies too heavily on the same types of shots. For instance, if you want to draw attention to the *author* of a quotation to add *ethos* to your argument, you might opt to provide attribution through an introductory clause; however, if you want to emphasize *information* rather than authorship, an incorporated structure might be more effective. Remember that the purpose of integrating sources is to demonstrate your work as a researcher and to show that you are building your argument on the work of others. Therefore, choose what types of integration strategies work best for each source and for each part of your paper.

Documentation During Integration

When integrating sources into your draft, be sure to include citations for each quotation or paraphrase. This would also be a good time to begin drafting your preliminary bibliography or Works Cited list, in order to save time later. The purpose of documentation is not only to provide a "list of credits" for your references but also to supply interested readers with the resources to continue learning about your topic. Just as you undoubtedly found certain articles inspiring while investigating your topic and used them as springboards for more focused research, so too might your paper serve as a means of leading your readers to intriguing ideas and articles. You can go back over the correct format for citations in your final edit, following the guidelines in Chapter 7 for documentation to do so.

WRITER'S PRACTICE MyWritingLab

In your efforts to integrate sources effectively, keep in mind that source material should *support* your argument, not supplant it. If you're worried that you have integrated too many sources (and lost your own voice), spend some time reviewing the draft and ask yourself:

- Am I still the moderator of this conversation?
- Is my voice clear, compelling, and original?
- Do I allow my own argument to emerge as foremost in this piece?

Keeping Your Passion to Keep Writing

As you move deeper into the writing process, working on the flow of your argument and integrating quotations, don't lose sight of your enthusiasm for your subject. Re-read your earliest freewrites and your entries in your research log. What goals prompted you to begin the project? What aspects of your topic excited you, angered you, or inspired you? What contribution did you imagine yourself making to this discussion? Remember, your audience will be reading your paper to learn *your* particular point of view on the subject.

Also realize that to write is to struggle with the process, as noted by Stanford University psychologist David Rasch: "Almost all writers are familiar with the experience of feeling stuck, blocked, overwhelmed, or behind schedule in their writing." What can help? Staying motivated and relying on others. A conversation with a classmate, your instructor, or even a writing tutor can help give you the inspiration and impetus to keep writing.

To keep yourself energized, you should also allow yourself well-needed breaks. Brief periods away from the writing process can often recharge and reinvigorate your approach to the paper and help you think through difficult points in the argument. Ironically, a pause in drafting can also help you avoid writer's block by allowing you to remember what interested you about this project in the first place.

Finally, if you are having trouble getting through the draft process, allow yourself to write what Anne Lamott, author of *Bird by Bird,* famously calls the "shitty first draft." In the words of Lamott, "All good writers write them. This is how they end up with good second drafts and terrific third drafts." That is, you should realize that the first version by no means has to be perfect or even close to what the final paper will look like. It is instead simply your first attempt at getting your ideas on paper. Freeing yourself to write something—anything—can help you escape from the weight of perfectionism or the fear of failure that often paralyzes writers. Allow yourself to experiment, play, arrange, rearrange, leave temporary placeholders, and jot notes to yourself. You will have plenty of opportunities to rework the material, show your draft to others, and move forward with the writing process. The key is to stop procrastinating, to get writing, and keep writing.

ANALYZING A STUDENT'S DRAFT OF A RESEARCH-BASED ESSAY

6.4 How do I analyze a draft of a research-based essay?

Let's examine now the draft of Stanford student Wanjin Park, who developed a research project comparing Gore's film *An Inconvenient Truth* (2006) to Gore's more recent PowerPoint slide show from his TED talk. Wanjin conducted a range of academic and field research, wrote a detailed outline, and then composed his draft. After feedback from his course instructor and his classroom peers, he revised his first partial draft and outline substantially, as demonstrated later in this chapter. But throughout, Wanjin kept his passion for his project and his respect for Gore as a leader trying to use rhetoric to persuade people of the importance of attending to climate change. We can study his first draft and conduct a rhetorical analysis of his writing strategies to see how you, too, can approach writing your research argument.

You'll see that the excerpt from Wanjin's draft integrates research sources in a variety of ways, begins to showcase Wanjin's own voice as a writer, and effectively relies on the outline as a prewriting tool.

Park 1

Wanjin Park
Working Draft + Outline

Environmental Leadership:
How Al Gore Illuminated an Overlooked Crisis

Rising levels of carbon dioxide emissions do not contribute to global warming. It has become silly and naïve to argue thus even before a group of middle school students. The awareness of the dangers of our carbon addicted lifestyle, however, would not be as widespread as it is today had it not been for the one man spearheading the global movement against climate change: Al Gore. Gore's rise to environmental influence is in large part due to Davis Guggenheim's documentary *An Inconvenient Truth*, which was then followed by a revised presentation at the TED Conference in March 2008. What strikes the audience, however, is not the revision of data and graphics in the slides, but rather, it is the change in Gore's rhetoric. In *An Inconvenient Truth*, Gore focuses on drawing in the audience and persuading them to join the environmental movement through the depiction of himself as a warm, dedicated, but lonely leader in the face of a global crisis; by contrast, at the TED presentation, Gore has garnered huge

Wanjin's working title is strong and raises an interesting issue—but in the revision, he will introduce his argument more forcefully.

His organizational strategy is to open with a counterargument, acknowledging that, today, even middle-schoolers know about global warming.

Then he introduces the film fully as well as his second primary source: Gore's 2008 TED talk.

Park 2

support, but senses a lack of change in the United States, and thus focuses on pushing the public toward increased initiative through his urgent and passionate rhetoric.

Gripping the Flames: Gore Leading the Environmental Movement

At the forefront of the global environmental movement against climate change is Al Gore. In fact, the Nielsen Company, a leading global marketing and advertising research company, conducted a survey in conjunction with Oxford University which serves as a testament to Gore's environmental prominence. In a survey of 26,486 people across 47 countries, Gore has been voted as "the most influential spokesperson to champion the global warming debate," even "ahead of former United Nations" Secretary General Kofi Annan (Nielsen).

Gore has been active with the environmental movement since the beginning of his political career; however, his lasting, and perhaps most influential contribution did not come until the release of Davis Guggenheim's *An Inconvenient Truth* in May 2006. Although based on lectures "that Gore has been presenting in one form or another for nearly three decades," *An Inconvenient Truth* has achieved levels of popularity and influence unrivalled by those of any other medium employed in the environmental movement (Rosteck and Frentz). Earning over $49 million, it currently ranks as the fifth highest grossing documentary in the history of the United States. Further indicative of the documentary's influence are the results of another survey conducted by the

---

Even in his draft, Wanjin has strongly developed his thesis—this work will sustain him through the rest of the paper. He can use the key terms of the thesis to structure the remaining sections of the essay.

Wanjin's subheads show his gift for creative language; he uses *pathos* but also indicates this new part of his argument with the subhead.

Already bringing in research, Wanjin starts with facts and statistics (*logos*) from survey and field research.

Next, he provides background and cites an article from his research (Rosteck and Frentz).

Park 3

Nielsen Company in April 2007. Of the viewers who have seen *An Inconvenient Truth*, eighty-nine percent reported to have become "more aware of the problem"; sixty-six percent "changed their mind about global warming"; and most importantly, seventy-four percent changed their habits as a result (Nielsen).

Considering the fact that *An Inconvenient Truth* is Gore's most influential rhetorical medium, an analysis of the documentary will thus illuminate the key characteristics that define the success of Gore's environmental leadership.

Contrasting Images: The Beautiful and the Doomed

An Inconvenient Truth begins with a beautiful depiction of nature. The camera focuses close-up on a branch full of small green tree leaves. The green hue is accentuated by the bright sunlight that is reflected off of the leaf blades. After a few seconds, the camera shifts to the right to reveal a sparkling river. The soft piano music in the background adds to the calm and peaceful mood. Al Gore then narrates in the background, purposefully emphasizing the sibilants as if to imitate the sounds of the river and the rustling leaves:

> You look at that river gently flowing by. You notice the leaves rustling with the wind. You hear the birds. You hear the tree frogs. In the distance, you hear a cow. You feel the grass. The mud gives a little bit on the riverbank. It's quiet; it's peaceful. (Inconvenient)

The first thirty seconds of the film is beautiful. However, Gore interjects and introduces human neglect of nature by

At this point, Wanjin offers a road map for the rest of his essay, referring back to his title and his thesis in a way that offers powerful coherence for the essay.

As Wanjin gets into the body of his essay, he takes his evidence one piece at a time, first providing a strong rhetorical analysis of the visual and audio elements of the film, then quoting directly from Gore's voice-over.

Park 4

stating, "all of a sudden, it's a gearshift inside you and it's like taking a deep breath and going 'Oh yeah, I forgot about this'" (Inconvenient). By using the word "gearshift," Gore metaphorically compares the audience to machines that are equipped with a gear; in essence, Gore argues that we have become the products of our industrial production, and have thus become so separate from our nature that we have completely forgot about it.

The consequences of our neglect are horrifying. After the establishment of our neglect, Gore's presentation shows images of the damages we made to nature. We see images of factories emitting thick black smog that obscures the sun. In one of the images, the hue of the sky is grayish purple; considering how the corpses of formerly sick bodies usually show this hue, this image is suggestive of the damage we have done to nature. Furthermore, as a demonstration of how global warming has aggravated natural disasters, we see footages of the aftermath of Hurricane Katrina. We see footage of crying babies without shelter and caretakers, a bloated dead body lying face down in the water, and a man stroking the forehead of his dead wife. Although Hurricane Katrina has been an American natural disaster, these scenes shock even the most foreign audience.

The presentation of these images after Gore's argument that we have forgotten about our nature compels the audience to feel guilt and responsibility. In effect, Gore induces the audience to

---

With the word, "However," Wanjin lets us know his view, introducing his argument.

The careful analysis of specific words such as "gearshift" makes this rhetorical argument persuasive.

Just as he analyzed the words in the film, Wanjin carefully analyzes the images, building his argument. His own voice as a writer here becomes adamant and urgent, evoking the mood of the film but also forcing us to take his argument seriously.

This section ends with a mini summary and strong statement of Wanjin's argument. In this way, he creates an effective organization for his larger paper, and from here can go about completing it one section at a time.

personalize the issue of climate change, thereby making us more receptive to Gore's message of change.

The Dedicated Leader

- after fear, Gore portrays himself as a dedicated leader
- autobiographical threads in the documentary
- vulnerable moments in Gore's personal history
- Source: these stories "strengthen[ed] the hero's resolve"
- Secondary source: Kathryn Olson, Director of the Rhetorical Leadership Graduate Certificate Program at University of Wisconsin-Milwaukee, claims the autobiographical threads "persuasively documents Gore's single-mindedness in pursuing his public cause, often at his own expense, through a lifetime of disappointments and sacrificing a comfortable retirement to carry the message globally."
- Gore in a Beijing taxi on way to Tsing Hua University.

Lonely Leader

- personal footage depicts Gore as "emotional suffering"
- Senator James Inhofe attacks Gore's ideas
- Secondary source: Gore "inviting impression that encourages auditors to join him or her in social action" (Olson).

TED Presentation

- more passionate; more religious; his sense of urgency is raised
- his tone of voice, joking, moral issue

The next sections of the draft show in outline form the content Wanjin plans to cover, including his main arguments, his section of evidence, and his secondary source citations.

He provides an *ethos*-building introduction for his secondary source.

By working with more than two sources in this section—Inhofe and Olson—Wanjin shows potential to move from merely quoting sources (as we saw in Chapter 3) to synthesizing them in conversation with one another. He can then build on their combined ideas as he advances his own argument.

Park 6

- Quote: "The only two countries that didn't ratify—and now there's only one. Australia had an election. And there was a campaign in Australia that involved television and Internet and radio commercials to lift the **sense of urgency** for the people there. And we trained 250 people to give the slide show in every town and village and city in Australia."

- There has been progress: Gore contributed to the change through his environment

- "The cities supporting Kyoto in the US are up to 780"

- Returning to religious rhetoric, passion, urgency

- Evidence: He does not begin his presentation about how far we have come since 2006, when the documentary film *An Inconvenient Film* was released. Instead, he begins by quoting Karen Armstrong (I believe she is someone prominent in religious studies) who said "religion really properly understood is not about belief, but about behavior."

- In arguing this, he essentially says that what we lack with our response to climate change is a change in behavior.

- "But, as important as it is to change the light bulbs, it is more important to change the laws. And when we change our behavior in our daily lives, we sometimes leave out the citizenship part and the democracy part."

By selecting and arranging quotes in his draft, Wanjin can approach the writing with a keen sense of his argument and overall plan for persuading the reader. He has chosen his evidence and uses the draft to sort through it effectively.

Once more considering multiple sources, here Wanjin demonstrates careful *source evaluation*, a process that will in turn help him write a stronger argument. For more on evaluating sources, see Chapter 5.

As shown by Wanjin's paper, a working draft should have a strong and well-developed thesis. This will drive the entire argument. Then, you can begin to work through the sections of an outline, providing specific evidence and secondary source support in what in Chapter 5 we called "a conversation with your sources." As you continue, fill in parts of your draft and rely on your peers for support and feedback.

6.5 What strategies can I use to revise my draft?

REVISING YOUR DRAFT

As many professional writers can attest—and Wanjin would agree with this based on his drafting experience—a text goes through numerous drafts on its way to becoming a polished final product. Even filmmakers produce multiple drafts of their movies before they release their film, experimenting with different sequencing, camera shots, and pacing to create what they consider to be the fulfillment of their artistic vision. We've all seen the results of this process: deleted scenes or *outtakes* from popular films or television programs. What these segments represent are moments of work (writing, producing, and shooting) that, after review and editing, were removed to streamline the film.

As you might imagine, often it's difficult or even painful to reshape your work during revision; it's hard to leave some of your writing behind on the cutting room floor. However, as your project develops, its focus may change: sources or ideas that seemed important to you during the early stages of research may become less relevant, even tangential; a promising strategy of argumentation may turn out to be less suitable to your project; a key transition may no longer be necessary once you reorganize the argument. As you turn to your draft with a critical eye, what you should find is that in order to transform your paper into the best possible written product, you'll need to move beyond proofreading or editing and into the realm of macro changes, or **revision**.

Troubleshooting

Proofreading remains a critical part of the revision process. Careless grammatical and punctuation errors and spelling mistakes can damage your *ethos* as an author, and they need to be corrected. It is very probable that you've been doing such micro-revision throughout the drafting process—editing for style, grammar, punctuation, and spelling. However, sometimes it's difficult to do broader revisions until you have a substantial part of your paper written. It is only once your argument starts coming together that you can recognize the most productive ways to modify it in order to optimize its effectiveness. This is the key to successful revision: you have to be open to *both* micro-editing and large-scale, multiple revisions. Think of this process as **re-vision**, or seeing it again with new eyes, seeing it in a new light.

Let's look at decisions some students made during the revision process:

- **Content Overload.** Reading over her draft about the propagandistic elements in World War II films, Jennifer realized that she had gotten so caught up in presenting background information that her paper was top-heavy, with pages of background in the begnning and her own analysis and argument deferred too long to be effective.

  Revision: Jennifer sharpened her focus and adjusted her treatment of background information, eliminating some of the more extraneous material and also redistributing key foundation information throughout her essay so as to reprioritize developing her own argument.

- **Patchwork Paragraphs.** Similarly, in his essay about presidential rhetoric in the Health Care Debate, Ben let his sources take over. He focused so exclusively on including quotations from his primary and secondary sources that his paragraphs began to read like a patchwork quilt of other people's voices without sufficient analysis or exposition to situate them in terms of Ben's own argument.

  Revision: Ben reevaluated which direct quotations were necessary to his argument, eliminating some and transforming others into summary or paraphrase. In addition, he spent more time contextualizing and analyzing the source material, spotlighting his own argument first, and then using the source material as evidence.

- **Lack of Reliance on Sources.** Miranda had the opposite problem; in her draft she made a compelling argument about the literary status of graphic novels but did not really quote from or mention any of her sources, so she wasn't showcasing her work as a researcher.

> **Revision:** She more prominently integrated her source material into her argument, both by referring to specific authors and articles she had read and by using additional direct quotations. In doing so, she greatly increased her *ethos* and the persuasiveness of her argument.

- **Overly Broad Thesis.** After drafting her paper on hip-hop and gender identity, Sharita realized that her thesis was too broad and that in trying to cover both male and female imagery, she wasn't able to be specific enough to craft a really persuasive argument.

  > **Revision:** Realizing that her interest really lay in exploring the conflicted stereotype of powerful, sexualized women in hip-hop videos, Sharita cut large sections of her paper revolving around the male imagery. The result was a provocative argument based on concrete, persuasive examples.

- **Inconsistent Argument.** In reading over his drafted essay on the benefits of windfarms as an alternate energy source, Kyle discovered that in the process of writing the essay, he had actually changed his claim, so that the thesis statement in his introduction differed from what he actually argued in his essay and stated in his conclusion.

  > **Revision:** Recognizing that his newer claim probably reflected the stronger argument, Kyle adjusted his thesis statement and the early sections of his draft to produce a strong, cohesive argument throughout the essay.

- **Tunnel-vision Argument.** The first version of Max's essay on the aesthetics of design in the Apple product line was visually stunning, detailed, and eloquently written. But it was so one-sided that it read more like a marketing brochure than an academic argument.

  > **Revision:** Max's task in revision was to provide a more balanced perspective on the Apple computer phenomenon. After further research, he incorporated a greater diversity of perspectives in his paper and softened some of his language to be less biased in favor of Apple products.

As these examples indicate, you need to enter into the research process looking not just for mistakes to "fix" but also for larger issues that might relate to your structure, your thesis, your scope, or the development of your ideas.

AT A GLANCE

Revision Strategies

1. ***Read your essay out loud or have someone read it to you.*** This process will help you hear mistakes and inconsistencies that you unknowingly skipped over when reading silently.

2. ***Gain critical distance.*** Put your essay away for a few hours, or even a few days, and then come back to it fresh.

3. ***Don't be chained to your computer.*** For a change of pace, print out your draft, making revisions by hand. We conceptualize information differently on paper versus on a screen.

4. ***Look at your writing in different ways.*** Take a paragraph and divide it into distinct sentences, which you line up one under another. Look for patterns (for instance, is the repetition deliberate or accidental?), style issues (is sentence structure varied?), and fluidity of transitions between sentences.

5. ***Reevaluate your organization.*** Create a reverse outline for your essay by looking at your draft and listing out, in order, the main point of each paragraph in formal outline form. Looking at these points, assess whether their order is logical and clear, whether they refer back to the thesis, and whether there are any redundancies or omissions in the trajectory of development.

6. ***Answer peer review questions for your essay.*** Use materials provided by your instructor to guide your feedback on your classmates' work as a set of questions you can apply to your own revision process.

7. ***Share your draft with others.*** Whether you talk to your instructor, a classmate, or a writing tutor, consider getting some reader response to guide your revisions. Take their feedback into account, even if it initially doesn't seem significant. You might not decide to act on the advice, but at least consider it before dismissing it.

8. ***Revise out of order or in sections.*** Choose paragraphs at random and look at them individually, or begin at the end. Sometimes our conclusions are the weakest simply because we always get to them last, when we're tired; start revision by looking at your conclusion first.

9. ***Look at the revision as a whole.*** As you correct mistakes or prose problems, consider the impact that the revision makes on the rest of the essay. Sometimes it is possible just to add a missing comma or substitute a more precise verb, but often you need to revise more than just the isolated problem so that the sentence, paragraph, or essay as a whole continues to "fit" and flow together.

Collaboration Through Peer Feedback

In addition to your own assessment of your writing, you should take into account **peer evaluations** of your drafts; you might consider your peer feedback sessions to be "advance screenings" with your audience. In the film industry, such test screenings are standard practice, and through this process the audience becomes a collaborator with the director, producer, screenwriters, film editors, and actors in determining the final form of a film. Many films have been altered after audience feedback during test screenings, from their titles (*Licence to Kill*) to their narrative structures (*Blade Runner*), length (*Titanic*), and, most typically, their endings (*Pretty Woman, Fatal Attraction, 28 Days Later, World War Z*). In each case, test audience feedback shaped the final edit and made evident the rhetorical relationship between audience, writer, and text. Similarly, writing needs to take into consideration the audience's expectations; we write to show our audience our thoughts, our research, and our claim, so we need to respond to audience needs when we write and revise our texts.

Peer feedback sessions provide you with an opportunity for a test screening of your argument. While a casual conversation about your draft with a peer can provide useful insights, taking a more structured approach can provide you with a stronger foundation for revision. To facilitate a productive peer review session:

- Write a cover memo that points your readers to specific questions you have about your draft. Your peer reviewers can customize their responses to address the particular issues that concern you as a writer.
- Write down peer feedback; don't rely exclusively on oral comments. You can take notes during your peer review session, or each of your partners could bring written comments to the meeting. This will give you more tangible feedback to work with as you revise.
- Model good peer review behavior for your partners in how you work with their drafts: come prepared to the session, having read their essays and prepared written comments; praise the strengths of their work; offer constructive feedback in an even tone, pointing to specific points in the draft that need revision; balance attention to micro-editing (stylistics, punctuation, grammar, usage) with discussion of higher order thinking (argument, structure, use of evidence).

AT A GLANCE

Questions for Peer Review on the Draft

- **Argument consistency:** Do the introduction and conclusion argue the same points, or has the argument shifted by the end?
- **Organization and progression:** Does the paper flow logically, developing one idea seamlessly into the next? Does the author provide important theoretical foundations, definitions, or background at the beginning of the paper to guide the audience through the rest of the argument?
- **The author's voice in relation to the sources:** Does the essay foreground the author's argument, or does it focus primarily on the sources' arguments, locating the author's point of view primarily in the conclusion?
- **Information:** Are there any holes in the research? Does the author need to supplement his or her evidence with additional research, interviews, surveys, or other source materials?
- **Opposition and concession:** Does the author adequately address counterarguments? Does he or she integrate alternate perspectives into the argument (i.e., deal with them as they arise), or does he or she address them in a single paragraph?

■ Listen to the feedback you receive. Don't become defensive about your writing. Take the suggestions in the spirit of collaboration, and ask questions to be sure that you understand your readers' comments.

Sometimes you'll find that your peer reviewers vocalize ideas that echo your own concerns about your draft; other times you may be surprised by their reactions. Keep in mind that their comments are informed *suggestions,* not mandates; your task, as the writer, is to assess the feedback you receive and implement those changes that seem to best address the needs of both your argument and your audience as you move forward with your revision process.

Analyzing a Student's Revision of a Research-Based Essay

Let's return now to Wanjin's draft paper and see how he used his own self-assessment and peer review suggestions to revise his paper and strengthen his argument.

Park 1

Wanjin Park
Research-Based Argument—Final
15 March, 2010

Wanjin's revised title actually conveys part of his argument—he has traded the general claim "Illuminates" to offer several new terms: soft, passionate, and dynamic rhetoric.

His introduction has a new sense of urgency, shown in short and long sentence variety, strong diction, and sign-posting (the two-part rhetoric).

Moreover, Wanjin spends a great deal of time advancing a more developed thesis, naming Gore as lonely leader with soft rhetoric and then as passionate leader with dynamic rhetoric. With this thesis, the paper will offer a more forceful argument.

Most importantly, Wanjin ends the opening with a "So what?" significance statement.

Balancing the Soft and the Passionate Rhetorician:

Gore's Dynamic Rhetoric in His Environmental Leadership

At the forefront of the global environmental movement is one man with the power to blur national boundaries, urge political leaders to adopt reforms, and motivate hundreds of thousands. That man is Al Gore. Gore has been a pivotal leader, attracting unprecedented levels of support for the once overlooked issue, especially through Davis Guggenheim's *An Inconvenient Truth*. The success of the documentary can be attributed to Gore's two-part rhetoric. He first induces fear and guilt in us, the audience, making us more receptive to his message. He then portrays himself as a warm, dedicated, but lonely leader, thereby arousing our desire to join him in social action. Despite the success of his soft rhetoric, Gore set it aside two years later at the TED2008 Conference and adopted a heightened sense of passion and urgency. The shift in rhetoric mirrors a change in Gore's agenda, and it is this dynamic rhetoric which Gore molds to fit specific goals that defines the success of his leadership. An understanding of Gore's rhetoric offers us invaluable insight on how to use dynamic rhetoric to bring overlooked social issues into the light.

Park 2

Before showing us a change in his rhetoric, Gore uses soft rhetoric in *An Inconvenient Truth*. Soft rhetoric, a newly coined term, refers to a rhetorical tool that draws in a guarded audience, not through impassioned words, but through the appeal to the audience's sense of guilt and the establishment of a warm and inviting *ethos*. Because the public was still guarded toward the issue of climate change before the release of the documentary, Gore shies away from passionate speech that is meant to inspire, and instead focuses on convincing his audience to join him through soft rhetoric.

Contrasting Images: The Beautiful and the Doomed

Gore begins his soft rhetoric by inducing fear and guilt in us, the audience, through the juxtaposition of beauty and doom. He first offers us a beautiful depiction of nature. The camera focuses close-up on a branch full of green tree leaves. Bright sunlight reflects off of the leaf blades, accentuating the green hue. After a few seconds, the camera turns to the right to reveal a glistening river. The river is a mix of green and blue, both defining colors of nature. The soft piano music in the background adds to the calm and peaceful mood. Gore then narrates in the background, purposely emphasizing the sibilants as if to imitate the sounds of the river and the rustling leaves:

> You look at that river gently flowing by. You notice the leaves rustling with the wind. You hear the birds. You hear the tree frogs. In the distance, you hear a cow. You feel the grass. The mud gives a little bit on the riverbank. It's quiet; it's peaceful. (*An Inconvenient Truth*)

He introduces his own term—one he made up.

Wanjin did not want to use "I" so he speaks in third person, but he clearly establishes his own argument in this revision.

His microedits to style and descriptive language make his writing even more vivid and memorable.

In the revision, Wanjin begins with a topic sentence that conveys his argument, rather than just launching into the rhetorical analysis of the film's details.

Since Wanjin quotes more than four lines in this passage, he formats the citation as a **block quote**.

Park 3

He has also incorporated more research, so he is not over-relying on only one source.

The sequence of images and narration encapsulates the beauty of nature so well that Professors Thomas Rosteck and Thomas Frentz write in "Myth and Multiple Readings in Environmental Rhetoric: The Case of *An Inconvenient Truth*" that "we experience, visually and through Gore's voiceover, the awe, sublime beauty, and wonder of Earth" (5).

Gore suddenly interrupts the experience and interjects that we have forgotten about nature in spite of its beauty: "all of a sudden, it's a gearshift inside you and it's like taking a deep breath and going 'Oh yeah, I forgot about this'" (*An Inconvenient Truth*). Through the use of the word "gearshift," Gore metaphorically compares us, the audience, to machines that are equipped with a gear; in essence, he argues that we have become so addicted to the industrial age that we have transformed into its products, becoming separate from and oblivious to our nature.

Here, Wanjin cites the article analyzed earlier in this chapter. He picks a strong quotation, sets it up by building the *ethos* of the source, and then, most importantly, comments on it in the next paragraph, emphasizing "frightening" and the building on Schulte's reading to develop his point about guilt.

* * *

The images arouse such horror that Bret Schulte, Assistant Professor of Journalism at University of Arkansas, writes that Gore shows us "the frightening future promised by global warming—an apocalyptic world of deadly hurricanes, rising oceans, disease, drought, and famine" (Schulte).

Notice here, he offers a strong conversation with many of his sources: Rosteck and Frentz, Olson, and looking back to Schulte.

By deliberately introducing the "frightening" images only after his "gearshift" metaphor, Gore compels us to feel not only frightened, but also responsible and guilty for the

Park 4

damages done to nature (Schulte; *An Inconvenient Truth*). The arousal of guilt is crucial in shaping *An Inconvenient Truth* into an effective environmental medium, as it "sets up the rhetorical tension with which Gore will leverage his message" (Rosteck and Frentz). Kathryn Olson, the author of "Rhetorical Leadership and Transferable Lessons for Successful Social Advocacy in *An Inconvenient Truth*," agrees and elaborates on what Gore's message is: "he asks [us] . . . to share the guilt of insufficient action with him and to redeem [our]selves . . . now that [we] grasp the gravity . . . of climate change" (11). The arousal of guilt, the first part of Gore's soft rhetoric, thus draws in a once guarded and reluctant public into the environmental movement.

Most powerfully, he ends with his own point, making sure the spotlight is on his argument.

Dedication Molded by Frustration and Failure

After rendering us more receptive through the appeal to our sense of fear and guilt, Gore portrays himself as a warm, vulnerable, and dedicated leader. Rosteck and Frentz also explore the second part of Gore's soft rhetoric and argue that Gore establishes such *ethos* through "personal images of frustration and failure" that are interspersed throughout the documentary (9). In fact, Gore expresses his frustration right from the beginning of *An Inconvenient Truth*, confessing that "I've been trying to tell this story for a long time, and I feel as if I've failed to get the message across" (*An Inconvenient Truth*). We then meet a naively optimistic Gore who fails to change the world through the first Congressional hearings on global warming; he

The revised subheads show his advanced thinking and reflect the suggestions of his classmates from peer review.

almost loses his son to a car accident; he loses the presidential election in 2000; and his family, a group of tobacco farmers, loses Gore's sister, Nancy, to lung cancer (*An Inconvenient Truth*).

He has fleshed out the points from his working draft and outline. He strategically cites the words from his research sources (Rosteck and Frentz) to show how he views the text through the lens of those sources.

What these stories of failure and pain have in common are that they "strengthen[ed]" Gore's "resolve" and dedication to the environmental movement (Rosteck and Frentz 7). His son's near-death accident taught him how anything taken for granted, even our beautiful environment, can easily vanish. His sister's death taught him the importance of connecting the dots, of connecting our actions to future consequences. His presidential election campaign "brought into clear focus the mission that [he] had been pursuing all these years," convincing him to "[start] giving the slideshow again" (*An Inconvenient Truth*).

Here, Wanjin demonstrates writing as synthesis, in that he puts the many sources in conversation with one another and adds his own voice to that dialogue.

Because these stories "persuasively [document] Gore's single-mindedness in pursuing his public cause, often at his own expense, through a lifetime of disappointments," Olson also agrees with Rosteck and Frentz that the stories of personal failure and frustration are essential to Gore's portrayal as a human, vulnerable, but dedicated leader (Olson 99). This portrayal places us "in a position to hear demand for action in a more sympathetic light," and when coupled with our sense of guilt, it renders Gore's message irresistible (Rosteck and Frentz 10). And Gore's message is clear. He "shows his evolution from interested observer to committed activist" with the goal of "invit[ing] our own journey of transformation" through the environmental movement (5).

Park 6

Rosteck, Frentz, and Olson's arguments have merit. Gore's transformation into a dedicated leader as a result of his frustrations and failures does create an "inviting impression that encourages [us] to join him . . . in social action" (Olson 102). However, they leave unexplored a crucial aspect of Gore's rhetoric. What is more responsible for creating the warm and inviting *ethos* is the portrayal of Gore as a lonely leader.

* * *

No Longer the Soft Leader

Despite the success of his soft rhetoric as a lonely leader in *An Inconvenient Truth*, Gore sets it aside and instead adopts a heightened level of passion and sense of urgency two years later in his follow-up presentation at the TED 2008 Conference. The change reflects a shift in Gore's primary agenda. Gore's primary goal is no longer attracting support for the environmental movement, as he has already achieved that goal. Gore even acknowledges in his TED presentation the extent of his success. He claims that "68 percent of Americans now believe that human activity is responsible for global warming, [and] 69 percent believe that the Earth is heating up in a significant way" (Gore 9.21). Furthermore . . .

* * *

Even his body language is imbued with the increased level of passion. As he delivers the line, "we need a worldwide, global mobilization for renewable energy, conservation, efficiency, and a global transition to a low carbon economy," he not only

At this point, Wanjin will credit the research that has come before him and then build on it.

Through effective synthesis, he acknowledges the opposing positions before him, but then adds to them, as if adding another brick on a foundation. His original contribution as a writer is to focus on the concept of *ethos*.

After a significant amount of evidence (not represented here in this abridged version of his essay), Wanjin moves to the next point in his argument. His heading refers to terms in his title, using diction to offer coherence and force in the writing.

He sets up the argument about Gore's 2008 TED talk through citing Gore's own words and leading the reader through the *logos* from his rough draft.

In this revision, Wanjin took the suggestion of his peers: he analyzes not only the images and words but also the embodied rhetoric or body language of Gore's persona.

stresses each word, but also moves his hands up and down as he speaks, visually emphasizing each word (Gore, 4.39). He also twists his upper body from left to right, with his arms extended, as he says, "the political will has to be mobilized," visually enacting the word "mobilized" (Gore, 4.57).

The heightened passion in Gore's rhetoric becomes fully manifested near the end of the presentation when Gore appeals to honor and heroism, both qualities we have treasured throughout history, as he stresses the need for a hero generation:

> What we need is another hero generation. We have to . . . understand that history has presented us with a choice. And we have to find a way to create, in the generation of those alive today, a sense of generational mission. (Gore, 17.39)

Gore then alludes to the "hero generation that brought democracy to the planet . . . another that ended slavery . . . and that gave women the right to vote" in order to illustrate the level of passion and dedication that we need to emulate as we fight the climate crisis (Gore, 18.44). The climate crisis is no longer just a global issue, but is now the "opportunity to rise to a challenge that is worthy of our best efforts" (Gore, 20.12). In his last efforts to move the audience toward increased sense of urgency and initiative, Gore closes with the line:

Introducing new concepts such as "honor" and "heroism," Wanjin increases the power of his words and the significance of his argument. He chooses then to use a direct quote as evidence.

Park 8

We are the generation about which, a thousand years from now, philharmonic orchestras and poets and singers will celebrate by saying, they were the ones that found it within themselves to solve this crisis and lay the basis for a bright and optimistic human future. (Gore, 20.47)

The appeal to *pathos,* the appeal to honor, heroism, and love for our children and the ensuing desire to promise them a better future illustrates how Gore sets aside his soft rhetoric and transforms into an impassioned leader, urging his audience to become heroes of our generation.

He carefully chooses his lines and concludes with a strong interpretation of their meaning.

Seesaw: Balancing the Soft and the Passionate Rhetorician

Gore adopts different styles of rhetoric in *An Inconvenient Truth* and in his follow-up presentation for the TED2008 Conference. Gore uses a two-part soft rhetoric in *An Inconvenient Truth* in order to draw in a guarded audience. He first compels us to feel fear and guilt through the juxtaposition of images of the beautiful and the doomed, making us more receptive to his environmental message. He then builds his *ethos* as a warm, dedicated, but still lonely leader, creating the inviting impression that draws us in and encourages us to join him in social action. When Gore delivers his TED presentation, his primary goal changes to motivating increased initiative and political will; he thus sets aside his soft rhetoric and adopts a heightened level of passion and sense of urgency.

Moving to his conclusion, Wanjin explains the final term in his paper: dynamic rhetoric.

He also brings in contemporary events, appealing to *kairos* to make the reader receptive to his argument.

The impassioned tone in Wanjin's own writing suggests that he is moving toward the end of his paper, and indeed he closes with a compelling call to action.

Park 9

This dynamic rhetoric, which Gore molds to fit his specific agenda, is the key to Gore's successful environmental leadership. He can be the warm, authentic, and soft leader when he wants to disarm a guarded audience. He can be the energized leader when he needs to inspire increased initiative in those that look up to him. In light of the recent sufferings caused by earthquakes in Haiti and Chile, the understanding of Gore's rhetoric offers us invaluable insight. In order to bring the countless pertinent but overlooked issues into the light à la Gore, we need to learn how to mold our rhetoric and master the art of balancing the soft and the passionate rhetorician in us.

The Works Cited, on a separate page, provides proper MLA citation for all the research Wanjin quoted, paraphrased, or summarized in the paper.

MLA suggests that writers include URLs in their Works Cited only when absolutely necessary to find the original source, but this student's professor required that they be included as part of the assignment.

Wanjin shows a well-balanced "iceberg of research"—including scholarly journals, popular articles, videos, and surveys.

Park 10

Works Cited

An Inconvenient Truth. Dir. Davis Guggenheim. Perf. Al Gore. Paramount Classics, 2006. DVD.

Gore, Al. "Al Gore's New Thinking on the Climate Crisis." Lecture. *TED: Ideas Worth Spreading*. TED.com, Apr. 2008. Web. 15 Jan. 2010. <http://www.ted.com/talks/lang/eng/al_gore.html.>

---. "Al Gore on Averting Climate Crisis." Lecture. *TED: Ideas Worth Spreading*. TED.com, Feb. 2006. Web. 20 Jan. 2010. <http://www.ted.com/talks/lang/eng/al_gore.html.>

Nielsen Company. "Global Consumers Vote Al Gore, Oprah Winfreyand Kofi Annan Most Influential to Champion Global

Warming Cause: Nielsen Survey." *Nielsen: Trends & Insights*.

2 July 2007. Web. 18 Jan. 2010. <http://nz.nielsen.com.>

Olson, Kathryn M. "Rhetorical Leadership and Transferable

Lessons for Successful Social Advocacy in Al Gore's *An

Inconvenient Truth.*" *Argumentation & Advocacy* 44.2 (2007):

90-109. *Communication & Mass Media Complete*. EBSCO.

Web. 24 Feb. 2010.

Rosteck, Thomas, and Thomas S. Frentz. "Myth and Multiple Read-

ings in Environmental Rhetoric: The Case of *An Inconvenient

Truth.*" *Quarterly Journal of Speech* 95.1 (2009): 1-19.

Communication & Mass Media Complete. EBSCO. Web. 24

Feb. 2010.

Schulte, Bret. "Saying It in Cinema." *U.S. News*. 28 Mar. 2006.

Web. 17 Jan. 2010. <http://www.usnews.com/usnews/

news/5warming.b.htm.>

The strong ending of Wanjin's paper shows how careful revision can help you develop a compelling argument and use the last lines to leave your reader with your own memorable rhetoric. Consider, too, how the ending of Wanjin's essay expanded to encompass a broader frame and then addressed the reader directly, using "you." Finally, you might notice that his revised essay analyzed rhetoric in all the ways we have learned to understand it through the chapters in this book: that is, rhetoric as texts that are spoken, written, visual, multimedia, as well as embodied. As you turn to craft your own research-based argument, keep in mind the many approaches to rhetoric explored here, and offer your own original insights by building on the work of writers and scholars who have come before you.

WRITER'S PRACTICE   MyWritingLab

To assess the writing you have done on your research-based argument, exchange your essay with a peer in class. Then, create annotations using the comment feature of your word-processing program and indicate what strategies are at work in each section of the essay. You might compare the draft to the final revision in those comments.

Alternatively, you could comment on your own essay, adding marginal notes about what improvements you made from the draft to the final revision. Then, you can summarize your revisions in a concluding reflective paragraph. That will inform both you and your instructor about your progress as a writer, researcher, and rhetorician.

THE WRITER'S PROCESS

In this chapter, you have learned strategies for visual mapping, organizing, outlining, drafting, and revising your research paper. You have explored ways of casting your argument and acquired concrete methods for integrating both written sources and visual texts as evidence for your argument. Chances are you have written the first full draft of your paper. But don't forget revision. Revision shows us the way that all *writing is rewriting*.

Sometimes, when writing, we may continue to revise our papers even after we have "finished." While you may be satisfied with your final essay when you turn it in, it is possible that you have set the groundwork for a longer research project that you may return to later in your college career. Or you may decide to seek publication for your essay in a school newspaper, magazine, or a national journal. In such cases, you may need to modify or expand on your argument for this new rhetorical situation; you may produce your own "director's cut"—a paper identical in topic to the original but developed in a significantly different fashion. Keep in mind that revision is indeed "re-vision."

SPOTLIGHTED ANALYSIS: FILM TRAILERS   MyWritingLab

Put your strategies of rhetorical analysis into practice and analyze a film trailer. Use the prewriting checklist below to help guide your analysis.

- How does the genre of the film (comedy? horror? drama? documentary?) affect the audience's response to its content? Does the trailer combine elements of different genres? What is the rhetorical effect of this combination?

- What is the "plot" of the trailer? Alternately, what argument is it making about the longer film? What does it suggest the film is about?
- What is its organizational structure? Chronological? Thematic? Chronological? Reverse chronological? What is the rhetorical significance of arrangement?
- What types of shots does the filmmaker use in the trailer (e.g., zoom-ins, cuts between scenes, fade in/fade out, montage)? What is the rhetorical effect of these choices?
- Is there a narrator? Voice-over? What is the effect on the audience?
- Is there any framing—a way of setting the beginning and end in context?
- How are *pathos, ethos,* and *logos* produced by the different cinematic techniques? For instance, is *pathos* created through close-ups of characters? Is *ethos* created through allusions to famous films or filmmaking techniques? Is *logos* constructed through the insertion of a narrator's viewpoint?
- What is the audience's point of identification in the trailer? Is the audience supposed to identify with a single narrator or protagonist? Does the film negotiate or manipulate the audience's reaction in any specific ways? How?
- How is setting used to construct a specific mood that affects the impact of the message of the trailer?

WRITING ASSIGNMENTS

MyWritingLab

1. **Visual Outline:** Create a visual representation of your research argument: a bubble web, graphic flowchart, idea roadmap, or a post-it diagram. Write an annotation for each part of your drawing, model, or storyboard to help you move from mass of material to coherent research-based essay. Start by writing down your thesis statement, and then jot down the main points you want to make in your essay. Next, beneath each of them, include supporting material, asking yourself, "What details should I include? What evidence or material from my sources supports this point? What subclaim do I want to make? What order would make the most sense for my reader?" Continue expanding on your visual outline until you have developed your points, started integrating your sources, and have arrived at a structure that seems both logical and persuasive.

2. **Detailed Written Outline:** Working with your research materials and notes, or building from your work in Writing Assignment 1, create a written outline of your ideas, including your thesis statement and using numbers and letters to indicate subsections of your argument. As appropriate, layer into your outline definitions, examples, counterarguments, and additional details. For added challenge, experiment with crafting rhetorical subheadings for the different sections. After you've completed your outline, go back and insert your primary and secondary sources where you'll use them to inform your argument. Insert actual quotations (with page numbers) from your research where possible, and also don't forget to cite your sources for both paraphrase and summary. When you're done, use your outline to check the balance of sources, the progression of ideas, and the complexity of your argument.

3. **Research-Based Argument:** Write a 12- to 15-page argumentative research paper on a topic of your choice. Use the types of sources that best speak to your research topic: these may include articles, books, interviews, field research, surveys (either published or that you conduct yourself), documentaries, Internet texts, and other primary and secondary sources, including visuals. Be sure to balance primary and secondary materials as you construct your argument. Ultimately, your goal should be proving a thesis statement with apt evidence, using appropriate rhetorical and argumentative strategies.

4. **Reflection Essay:** After you have completed your essay, compose a one-page reflection letter that serves as a self-evaluation. Think back on the development of your argument through research and revision. Include comments on the strengths of the essay, the types of revisions you made throughout your writing process, and how the collaborative process of peer review improved your essay. Conclude by explaining how you might continue to write about this issue in future academic or professional situations.

MyWritingLab Visit Ch. 6 Organizing and Writing Research Arguments in MyWritingLab to complete the Writer's Practices, Spotlighted Analyses, and Writing Assignments, and to test your understanding of the chapter objectives.

CHAPTER 7

Documenting Sources and Avoiding Plagiarism

Chapter Preview Questions

7.1 What do the terms "intellectual property" and "plagiarism" mean?

7.2 What are the conventions of documentation style?

7.3 How do I produce a Works Cited list in MLA style?

"Creativity always builds on the past." For many writers, the debt to those who have written before them is carefully acknowledged—whether through direct references, parenthetical citations, or a list of sources. Even visual artists and multimedia writers name their sources explicitly to show that they belong to a larger community of writers and that they respect the work of others.

But Justin Cone, a designer and animator based in Austin, Texas, makes this point more emphatically through the multimedia montage shown in Figure 7.1, from a short film called *Building on the Past*, which recycles and modifies public-domain film footage to make an argument about the relationship between creativity and legislation. The visuals are accompanied by a musical score and a voice-over that repeats the same sentence intermittently throughout the film: "Creativity always builds on the past." In the scene shown here, which opens the film, Cone re-edits the public-domain footage to run

FIGURE 7.1 Justin Cone's film, *Building on the Past*, remixed visuals and sound to emphasize how all our ideas rely on the works of those before us.

in reverse, showing the children running backward uphill instead of forward downhill, offering a powerful argument about how we rely on others for our own creativity. Cone expresses that idea visually through his strategy of organization, word choice, and design.

Your research project, too, will undoubtedly draw its strength from previous work on the subject. It should be a merger of your argument and the already existing dialogue on the topic. So even as you re-edit it to suit the purpose of your paper—by selecting passages to quote, paraphrase, summarize, or even argue against—it is crucial that you let your readers know where the ideas originated by providing what we call complete and ethical **source attribution**, or the acknowledgment and identification of your sources.

In this chapter, you'll learn how the rhetorical art of imitation—the process by which we all learn to write, compose, speak, and produce texts—differs from the theft of others' ideas, which is called **plagiarism**. We'll discuss why it is important to respect the work of others—which in legal terms is now called *intellectual property*—and you'll acquire strategies for avoiding unintentional plagiarism. Finally, we'll provide a means of understanding the process of constructing in-text and end-of-paper citations, and we'll explain the logic of MLA, APA, CSE, and Chicago documentation styles. You'll discover that there is actually logic governing the arrangement of elements in documentation practices, much as there is logic shaping mathematical or chemical formulas, and that the specific order of a style addresses the values of a particular audience. Moreover, you'll find that correct source attribution actually builds your *ethos* as a writer and researcher by confirming your membership in that scholarly community.

7.1 What do the terms "intellectual property" and "plagiarism" mean?

UNDERSTANDING INTELLECTUAL PROPERTY AND PLAGIARISM

In ancient times, **rhetorical imitation**, or the practice of taking after others, was a celebrated form of instruction. Students carefully would copy a speech out word by word, studying the word choice, organization, rhythm, and art of the work. That is, students would compose a rhetorical analysis (as you have done in earlier chapters) to understand the speech's strategies of argumentation, use of rhetorical appeals, and organization. Finally, students would rearrange and reuse elements of the speeches they studied, including content (words) and form (arrangement), to create their own speeches. Through this process of imitation and reediting, the earliest students learned to become great rhetors.

This ancient process is actually very similar to your task as a modern writer. After analyzing articles and studying argumentative strategies from samples of student writing, at some point you need to move on to create your own text, inspired by what you learned and perhaps reediting parts, since "creativity builds on the past." But importantly, today, we don't just borrow and recycle the ideas of others without acknowledgement. We need to be aware that ideas, not just actual words but also the concepts developed by others, must be considered in terms of **intellectual property**, that is, words and ideas often legally belong to someone else as a form of property. In this increasingly litigious society, you need to understand when to stop imitation and when to start acknowledging your sources so that you preserve the rights of others and protect yourself as a developing writer.

Plagiarism—using another person's idea as your own—was not a crime in classical times, according to scholars Peter Morgan and Glenn Reynolds. But with the invention of printing technology, copyright law, and a cultural emphasis on the profitability of intellectual concepts came a concern about taking someone else's ideas—and therefore their earning potential—whether intentionally or unintentionally. Consequently, in colleges and universities today, plagiarism can lead to suspension or even expulsion because the perpetrator is charged with literally stealing someone else's *intellectual property*. In professional circles, charges of plagiarism can ruin a career and destroy the credibility of the writer.

But there is another reason for acknowledging sources and avoiding plagiarism: as we discussed in Chapter 5, research is always a conversation with those who came before. This reason is an ethical, not legal one. As you work with sources, realize that the claims you are able to make are in fact based on the foundation provided by others. Identifying your sources thus becomes an ethical writing strategy that you practice out of respect for those who have come before you. By acknowledging their names, ideas, and words, you contribute to a body of knowledge, graciously extending thanks to those who have paved the way. Therefore, while there are legal issues related to intellectual property, copyright law, and "fair use" that you need to know about, if you keep a principle of *respect* in mind, you will rarely fall into the trap of inadvertently "stealing" someone's work.

AT A GLANCE

When to Cite Sources

Remember that you must provide citations for your sources when you:

- Quote a source word for word
- Summarize or paraphrase information or ideas from another source in your own words
- Incorporate statistics, tables, figures, charts, graphs, or other visuals into your work from another source

You do not need to provide citations for the following:

- Your own observations, ideas, and opinions
- Factual information that is widely available in a number of sources ("common knowledge")
- Proverbs, sayings, or familiar quotations

Avoiding Unintentional Plagiarism

When you're working with many sources, it can be all too easy to fall into habits that lead you to assimilate the information you've read and then begin to think the ideas are your own. Indeed, unintentional plagiarism can happen for many reasons: fatigue, oversaturation of information, poor memory, or sloppy note taking. However, as we have discussed, plagiarism is a serious offense, even if it occurs unintentionally. To avoid accidentally taking someone else's ideas or words as your own, you might follow two practices:

■ First, develop effective ways of taking notes while reading through your sources. If you come across a particularly relevant or striking quotation, don't just underline it or highlight it. Copy it directly into your notes or your research log and encase it in quotation marks; alternately, paraphrase it immediately, being careful to paraphrase in a way that distinguishes it clearly from the original phrasing. As you work with the material, jot down ideas how you might use the quotation, your own analysis, or how it connects to the topic you're exploring. Most importantly, write down the page number and source attribution right next to the quotation or paraphrase so that there's no confusion about where it came from.

■ Second, review the guidelines for citation practices in the At a Glance box so that you make sure that you give attribution as needed when using direct quotations or specific ideas from your sources.

These practices might seem to add extra steps to your research process, but they help support you in developing a more persuasive—and ethical—argument. Keep in mind that, regardless of the circumstances, many colleges and universities have plagiarism policies that do not distinguish between intentional and unintentional plagiarism; the act will bring consequences ranging from a failure in the course to expulsion.

Working with Images and Multimedia as Sources

When you choose to include visuals or multimedia in your writing, keep in mind that it is not enough to include just the source and provide the citation for it. You also need to spend a few moments thinking about issues of **copyright** and **permissions**. Since oral culture gave way to print culture, copyright—or the *right* to *copy*—has been a pressing legal issue. However, with the advent of digital technologies, the problem has been exacerbated; with the prevalence of photo scanners, digital copy and paste tools, cell phone cameras, seemingly omniscient search engines, and the ever-expanding reach of the Internet, the possibilities for copying, sharing, and distributing materials are in more people's reach than ever before. As a writer yourself, it is important that you respect copyright restrictions and ethically attribute all your sources that you use in your own writing—including visual texts.

When you browse through catalogs of images, you need to record the source of each image you decide to use. If you have found a visual (such as a photograph, chart, ad) from a print source and scanned it into a computer, you need to list the print source in full as well as information about the original image (the name of the photographer, the image title, and the date). If you have copied an image from the Internet, you need to note as much of the full source information as you can find: the website's author, the title, the sponsoring organization, and the date. Listing Google as your source is not sufficient; be sure to find the original source and list it in full. Keep careful track as you locate images, give appropriate credit when you use them. If you plan to publish your work online or submit it to a campus publication, use public domain images (such as from the Library of Congress), select from images licensed appropriately through Creative Commons, or write the image's owner, asking for permission to use it.

UNDERSTANDING DOCUMENTATION STYLE

7.2 What are the conventions of documentation style?

So far in this chapter, we've emphasized the importance of *source attribution* as a means of avoiding plagiarism. But it might interest you to know that the method you use to provide information about your source corresponds to the values of a particular academic community. This is where **documentation** comes in—the responsible and correct acknowledgment of your sources and influences according to a specific *style*. Today, with software programs that can format your source attributions for you, it may seem confusing or even frustrating to worry about which documentation style to use. But realize that the guidelines for each style have a rhetorical purpose corresponding to the way that knowledge is constructed for that community (see the table below). Taking a moment to understand the logic behind the styles will help you practice proper citation without having to look up every instance of how to do it. In this chapter, we will focus on MLA style, but by familiarizing yourself with the rationale between the different citation styles, you can identify which ones might be most appropriate to your chosen discipline or your major and so build your *ethos* as a writer by showing that you understand how to speak the language of a particular academic community.

DOCUMENTATION STYLE	COMMUNITY OF WRITERS	DEFINING FEATURES	PURPOSE OF FEATURES	EXAMPLE
MLA	Modern Language Association (language, literature, writing, philosophy, and humanities scholars and teachers)	Citation begins with author's name (last name first, full first name), then publication information, date, medium of publication (then, if a Website, date you accessed it).	Knowledge advances based on individual author's contributions; thus, names are prioritized over dates; place of publication matters for building *ethos*.	McCloud, Scott. *Understanding Comics.* New York: Harper Perennial, 1994. Print.
APA	American Psychological Association (psychologists and social scientists)	Publication date immediately follows designation of author, multiple authors may be listed (last name and initials), titles are in sentence style (first word capitalized, rest lowercase).	Since knowledge advances based on dated contributions to the field, dates are prioritized; most writing is collaborative, so up to six authors are listed; titles, typically long and technical, are in lowercase.	Bruce, V., & Green, P. (1990). *Visual perception: Physiology, psychology, and ecology* (2nd ed.). London, England: Erlbaum.
CSE	Council of Science Editors (such as biology and physics)	References include last name and date; often superscript numbers are used.	Like APA style, emphasis is on knowledge advancing through studies and scientific research; a heavily cited style of writing.	[1]Goble, JL. Visual disorders in the handicapped child. New York (NY): M. Dekker; 1984. p. 265.
Chicago	University of Chicago (business writers, professional writers, and those in fine arts)	Sources are listed as footnotes or endnotes and include page numbers.	Knowledge is incremental, and readers like to check facts as they go along.	[2]Scott McCloud, *Understanding Comics* (New York: Harper Perennial, 1994), 33.

In-Text Citations: Documentation as Cross-Referencing

In addition to responsible source attribution, documentation also functions as a *road map* for your audience to locate the source—both in your bibliography and in the library or online. Accordingly, for sources appearing as **in-text citations**—or quoted right in the essay itself—the purpose of proper documentation is to point readers clearly to the list of sources at the end of the paper. The way this works is through **cross-referencing**, such that the reference in the text of the essay should correspond to the first word of the source listed in the bibliography.

Let's take a look at an *in-text citation* from Grady Thompson's paper on online activism and social media. As you can see, he follows typical MLA style that always places such references inside parentheses to set them off from the rest of the writing. Notice that the last name and page number in parentheses point the reader directly to the author's name in the "Works Cited" list.

> . . . over 94% of contributors to the Facebook "Save Darfur Cause" donated only once, meaning that most of the financial contributions came from a very small number of "hyperactivists" (Lewis, Gray, and Meierhenrich 2).
>
> * * *
>
> ### Works Cited
>
> Ayers, Michael. "Comparing Feminist Identity in Online and Offline Feminist Activists." *Cyberactivism: Online Theory and Practice.* Ed. Martha McCaughey. New York: Routledge, 2003. 145-64. Print.
>
> Lewis, Kevin, Kurt Gray and Jens Meierhenrich. "The Structure of Online Activism." *Sociological Science 1* (2014): 1-9. *Academic Search Premier.* Web. 2 Feb. 2015.
>
> Yang, Guobin. "Online Activism." *Journal of Democracy* 20.3 (2009): 33-36. *Project Muse.* Web. 2 Feb. 2015.

In his Works Cited (excerpted here), Grady has alphabetized the list by authors' last names, which corresponds to MLA documentation style and the logic of the humanities as an academic community. Readers need only scan down the page to look for the last name of the source cited earlier. This makes it very easy, and once you understand that this *cross-referencing logic* governs all MLA documentation, then you can begin to understand how to document sources—even new multimedia sources.

If there is no author to put in your parenthetical citation, begin with the first word of the source entry on the Works Cited page. Here is an example from Jamie Kesner's paper on the politics behind the World Cup, where she quotes an article from *The Economist.* Many of the articles in this magazine are collectively written, so no authors are named. In this case, Jamie uses the first words of the title. See how the cross-referencing logic of MLA style helps readers find the source in the Works Cited list:

Notice also that Jamie does not list a page number since her online source does not include them. However, the attribution is still clear. Using this system, you can easily direct your readers to the correct source.

But there are two additional cases that can be tricky. First, occasionally you might come across a phrase or sentence that is one of your sources has quoted and decide that you, too, want to include that direct quotation in your own essay. Here's an example: when reading danah boyd's book, *It's*

Complicated: The Social Life of Networked Teens, you come across a line she quotes from cultural critic John Perry Barlow where he describes the Internet as a place that allowed for "identities [that] have no bodies." Given time, the best practice would be to flip to boyd's Works Cited, find the Barlow source citation, go online or to the library and find the Barlow text, and read it yourself to better understand his argument. However, in some cases, you might not have access to Barlow's original source and so decide to simply incorporate his quote into your own essay. To do that, you need to cite the quotation in a way that makes it clear that these are *Barlow's* words, not boyd's. Here are two options:

As John Perry Barlow has suggested, the internet is a place that allows for "identities [that] have no bodies" (qtd. in boyd 37).

The internet provides a space for people to fashion and re-fashion themselves; it is, in effect, inherently a home for "identities [that] have no bodies" (Barlow, qtd. in boyd 37).

Your Works Cited in each case would be identical, directing the reader toward boyd's text:

---

boyd, danah. *It's Complicated: The Social Life of Networked Teens*.
New Haven: Yale P, 2014.

Both versions of the in-text citation make it clear that you found the direct quotation in boyd's book but that Barlow is the quote's author.

Here's a second complicated citation issue: how would you handle creating an in-text citation for an author when you will be listing multiple sources by that author in your Works Cited? For instance, as we can see in this case, putting only the last name in parentheses would not suffice since the reader does not know which source by Clive Thompson the quotation is from.

. . . a screenshot is "photography for life on the screen" (Thompson).

Works Cited

Thompson, Clive. *Smarter Than You Think: How Technology Is Changing Our Minds for the Better*. New York: Penguin, 2014. Print.

---. "The Invention of the Snapshot Changed the Way We Viewed the World." *Smithsonian*. Sept., 2014. Web. 12 June 2015.

---. "The Most Important Thing on the Internet is the Screenshot." *Wired,* 24 Mar. 2015. Web. 11 June 2015.

To resolve this issue, you need to list *both* the author's name and the first major keyword of the correct title in your in-text citation; following this practice, our example above becomes more clear:

. . . a screenshot is "photography for life on the screen" (Thompson, "The Most Important").

Let's look at how Stephanie Parker mastered this situation. Here are two examples from her essay—an excerpt from which appears later in this chapter—where Stephanie cites from different works by Daniel Shim. Notice how the keyword following the author's last name functions as the *cross-reference* to the correct source:

Example 1: Here, since Stephanie mentioned the author in the sentence, she needs only include the keywords and the page number if there was one, but since this is an online text, there is no page number to cite.

> Daniel Shim relates his own experience: "I was born in Canada in white communities & I grew up to be like them. Soompi has given me knowledge about Asian culture that I would not get from my school or family" (Online interview).

Example 2: In this next case, Stephanie has not mentioned the author by name in the sentence, so she includes the author's last name as well as the first keyword of the source title in her MLA in-text citation. Moreover, since she is citing an article title, she includes the quotation marks; for a book title, she would italicize the keyword:

> . . . his YouTube videoblog, in which he comments on events in his daily life and makes fun of Asian stereotypes, has almost 30,000 subscribers and is the 4th most popular comedy blog in all of Canada (Shim, "Shimmycocopuffsss's").

Now let's look at the Works Cited list to locate those two sources. Note the color coding to see how the *cross-reference* system operates.

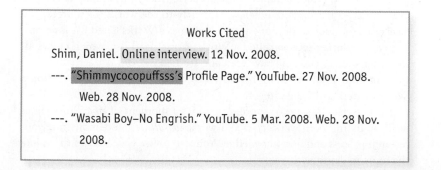

Works Cited

Shim, Daniel. Online interview. 12 Nov. 2008.

---. "Shimmycocopuffsss's Profile Page." YouTube. 27 Nov. 2008. Web. 28 Nov. 2008.

---. "Wasabi Boy–No Engrish." YouTube. 5 Mar. 2008. Web. 28 Nov. 2008.

Using Footnotes and Endnotes

Although MLA style relies primarily on in-text citations and a final bibliography—unlike Chicago style, which uses primarily footnotes or endnotes—there are two specific cases when you will want to include a note. First, if you want to include extra explanatory information (definitions of key terms, background material, alternative perspectives, or historical data) but don't want to break the flow of your argument, you can provide that information in a **content note**, whether as an endnote, which appears at the end of your paper, before the bibliography, or as a footnote, which appears at the bottom or *foot* of the page. Each would be anchored to your main argument through use of a superscript numeral that links the note to that particular point in your essay.

A second use of notes offers you the chance to point readers to additional information without the need for an explanatory narrative. In this case, you would create a **bibliographic note**, simply listing additional sources in that note that relate to a specific point. This strategy not only directs your reader to supporting materials but also builds your *ethos* as a writer and researcher who is situating her work in terms of the larger conversation about your topic.

7.3 How do I produce a Works Cited list in MLA style?

PRODUCING A WORKS CITED LIST IN MLA STYLE

You've seen how documentation works as a cross-referencing system, in which the in-text citation within parentheses points the reader directly to the source in the bibliography. In MLA style, the bibliography is called a **Works Cited** list because it refers explicitly to the works (or sources) you have cited (or quoted) in your paper. Sometimes a Works Cited list is accompanied by another section called a **Works Consulted** list, which names all the other sources you may have read and studied but did not actually quote from in your final revision. You can also combine the two by creating a **Works Cited and Consulted List**.

Realize that this list of sources provides a moment of *ethos* building as well: by listing both works *cited* and works *consulted*, you demonstrate your research process and new knowledge. You also invite your readers to explore the topic in depth with you.

LOGIC OF MLA STYLE

AUTHOR'S NAME	TITLE	PUBLICATION INFORMATION
List the author's name first, by last name. If there are multiple authors, include them all, following the order listed in the publication. If there is no author, use the publishing organization (if available) or just move on to the title.	The title comes next. For books and films, italicize the title. For shorter pieces (such as articles, TV shows, songs, etc.), put the title in quotation marks, with the larger publication (the collection of essays, TV series, or album) italicized.	Last comes publication information: place, publisher or company, date, and medium of publication. For shorter pieces, include the complete range of page numbers, followed by a period. For online articles, list the medium of publication (Web) followed by a period and conclude with a date of access.

PRINT EXAMPLE:

Satrapi, Marjane. *Persepolis: The Story of a Childhood*. New York: Pantheon, 2004. Print.

ONLINE EXAMPLE

Yagoda, Ben. "You Need to Read This: How Need to Vanquished Have to, Must, and Should." *Slate*. Washington Post Newsweek Interactive, 17 July 2006. Web. 20 July 2006.

Documentation for Print and Online Text-Based Sources

Below, you'll find example citations for print and online text-based sources that apply the logic of MLA style. Use them as a reference to guide your own citation practices:

- Single-Author Book
- Multiple-Author Book
- Electronic Books (e-books)
- Anthology or Edited Collection of Essays
- Introduction, Preface, Foreword, or Afterword in a Book

- Two or More Books by the Same Author
- Article in a Collection of Essays
- Article from a Print Journal
- Article from a Journal Published Only Online
- Article from a Popular Magazine Published Monthly (print and online)

- Article from a Newspaper or News Website
- Article Found through a Database (including Google Books)
- Website (entire)
- Page from a Website
- Definition
- Letter to the Editor
- News Op-Ed
- Letter or Memo

- Dissertation (unpublished)
- Government Publication
- Interview
- Survey
- Email
- Blog Post
- Facebook Post
- Tweet
- Reddit Post
- Text Message, Chat Room Discussion, or Real-Time Communication

Single-Author Book

Satrapi, Marjane. *Persepolis: The Story of a Childhood*. New York: Pantheon, 2004. Print.

Multiple-Author Book

Heath, Joseph, and Andrew Potter. *Nation of Rebels: Why Counterculture Became Consumer Culture*. New York: Harper, 2004. Print.

Booth, Wayne C., Gregory G. Colomb, and Joseph M. Williams. *The Craft of Research*. 3rd ed. Chicago: U of Chicago P, 2008. Print.

Electronic Books (e-books)

For an e-book, list the type of medium at the end of the citation (e.g., Nook file, Kindle file, iBooks file, Google Books file). When in doubt, use the term "Digital file" at the end instead.

Brooks, Max. *World War Z: An Oral History of the Zombie War*. N.p.: Crown, 2006. iBook file.

Davis, Mike. *City of Quartz*. N.p.: Verso, 2006. Nook file.

Anthology or Edited Collection of Essays

Waggoner, Zach, ed. *Terms of Play: Essays on Words That Matter in Videogame Theory*. Jefferson: McFarland, 2013. Print.

Andrews, Maggie, and Mary M. Talbot, eds. *All the World and Her Husband: Women in Twentieth-Century Consumer Culture*. London: Cassell, 2000. Print.

Introduction, Preface, Foreword, or Afterword in a Book

Gerbner, George. Foreword. *Cultural Diversity and the U.S. Media*. Ed. Yahya R. Kamalipour and Theresa Carillia. New York: State U of New York P, 1998. xv-xvi. Print.

Cohen, Mitchell, and Dennis Hale. Introduction. *The New Student Left*.

    Ed. Cohen and Hale. Boston: Beacon Press, 1967. xvii-xxxiii. Print.

Two or More Books by the Same Author

Palmer, William J. *Dickens and New Historicism*. New York: St. Martin's,

    1997. Print.

---. *The Films of the Eighties: A Social History*. Carbondale: Southern

    Illinois UP, 1993. Print.

When you have two or more texts by the same author in your works cited, use dashes in the place of the author's last name for the second book. Alphabetize by the title of the book or article.

Article in a Collection of Essays

Boichel, Bill. "Batman: Commodity as Myth." *The Many Lives of the*

    Batman. Ed. Roberta Pearson and William Uricchio. New York: BFI,

    1991. 4-17. Print.

Article from a Print Journal

Roberts, Garyn G. "Understanding the Sequential Art of Comic Strips

    and Comic Books and Their Descendants in the Early Years of the New

    Millennium." *Journal of American Culture* 27.2 (2004): 210-17. Print.

Article from a Journal Published Only Online

Martin, Paul. "The Pastoral and the Sublime in *Elder Scrolls IV: Oblivion*."

    Game Studies 11.3 (2011): n. pag. Web. 8 Nov. 2012.

Parish, Rachel. "Sappho and Socrates: The Nature of Rhetoric." *Kairos*

    17.1 (2012): n. pag. Web. 12 Dec. 2012.

Note that for online sources, the most the most recent MLA Handbook states, "You should include a URL as supplementary information only when the reader probably cannot locate the source without it or when your instructor requires it" (182).

Article from a Popular Magazine Published Monthly (print and online)

Maney, Kevin. "The New Face of IBM." *Wired* July 2005. Web. 18 Aug. 2005.

Sontag, Susan. "Looking at War." *New Yorker* 9 Dec. 2002: 43-48. Print.

Article from a Newspaper or News Website

Haughney, Christine. "Women Unafraid of Condo Commitment."

    New York Times 10 Dec. 2006, sec. 11: 1. Print.

Cowell, Alan. "Book Buried in Irish Bog Is Called a Major Find." *New York Times*. New York Times, 27 July 2006. Web. 31 July 2006.

Quade, Alex. "Elite Team Rescues Troops Behind Enemy Lines." CNN.com. Cable News Network, 19 Mar. 2007. Web. 19 Mar. 2007.

Article Found through a Database (including Google Books)

If you use a database (such as ProQuest, LexisNexis, or EBSCO) to locate an article, you include that information in your citation. The MLA Handbook includes Google Books under this category.

Chun, Alex. "Comic Strip's Plight Isn't Funny." *Los Angeles Times* 27 Apr. 2006, Home ed.: E6. *LexisNexis*. Web. 4 May 2006.

Gottesman, Jane. *Game Face: What Does a Female Athlete Look Like?* New York: Random, 2001. *Google Book Search*. Web. 15 July 2004.

Rosette, Ashleigh Shelby and Robert W. Livingston. "Failure is Not an Option for Black Women: Effects of Organizational Performance on Leaders with Single versus Dual-Subordinate Identities." *Journal of Experimental Psychology* 48.5 (2012): 1162-1167. *Academic Search Premier*. Web. 5 Jan. 2013.

Website (entire)

Wounded Warrior Project. N.p. 2015. Web. 12 Feb. 2015.

Library of Congress. N.p. N.d. Web. 1 Jan. 2014.

Page from a Website

"Marie Curie—Facts." *NobelPrize.org*. N.d. Web. 14 June 2015.

"Calamity Jane—Rowdy Woman of the West." *Legends of America*. N.d. Web. 3 Feb. 2013.

Definition

"Diversity." *American Heritage Dictionary of the English Language*. 4th ed. Houghton, 2000. Print.

"Greek Mythology." *Wikipedia*. Wikimedia Foundation, 16 Apr. 2010. Web. 5 May, 2010.

Letter to the Editor

Tucker, Rich Thompson. "High Cost of Cheap Coal." Letter. *National Geographic* July 2006: 6-7. Print.

News Op-Ed

Woodlief, Wayne. "Time Heals Biden's Self-Inflicted Wound." *Boston Herald* 26 Jan. 2007: 19. Print.

Letter or Memo

Greer, Michael. Letter to the authors. 30 July 2006. Print.

Dissertation (unpublished)

Li, Zhan. "The Potential of America's Army: The Video Game as Civilian-Military Public Sphere." Diss. Massachusetts Institute of Technology, 2004. Print.

Government Publication

United States. Census Bureau. Housing and Household Economics Statistics Division. *Poverty Thresholds 2005*. US Census Bureau, 1 Feb. 2006. Web. 20 May 2006.

Interview

Tullman, Geoffrey. Personal interview. 21 May 2006.

Cho, Ana. Telephone interview. 4 June 2005.

When writing a citation for an interview, include the mode of interview (e.g., telephone interview, Skype interview).

Survey

Meyer-Teurel, Fiona. "Hacking and Modding in Video Games." Survey. 23 May 2013.

For a survey you conduct yourself, list yourself as the author, then the name of the survey (or the word survey), and the date you conducted it.

Email

Tisbury, Martha. "Re: Information Overload." Message to Max Anderson. 27 Mar. 2008. Email.

Blog Post

Gardner, Traci (Tengrrl). "Oh Internet, You Pandora's Box!" *Pedablogical*. Pedablogical, 13 Apr. 2009. Web. 14 June 2013.

When citing an online posting (from a blog, Twitter, Reddit, etc.), use the author's real name if you know it, followed by the username in parenthesis. If the real name is unknown, simply list the username.

Facebook Post

Pond, Amelia. "Time travel is possible . . ." Facebook.com. 24 Apr. 2010.
Web. 25 Apr. 2010.

The White House. "Spurring Innovation, Creating Jobs." Facebook.com.
5 Aug. 2009. Web. 13 Feb. 2010.

When writing a citation for a Tweet, include the entire tweet as the title.

Tweet

Booker, Cory (CoryBooker). "I'd rather have my ship sunk at sea than rot
in the harbor. To exceed our limits we must test them; to fly we must
risk falling." 11 June 2013, 6:51 a.m. Tweet.

Reddit Post

Examples of Good. "My Mom Made Me Lunch." Reddit.com. Fri. 23 Apr. 2013.

Text Message, Chat Room Discussion, or Real-Time Communication

Zhang, Zhihao. "Revision Suggestions." *Cross-Cultural Rhetoric Chat
Room*. Stanford U. 25 May 2006. Web. 5 June 2008.

Documentation for Visual, Audio, and Multimedia Sources

MLA documentation style was devised principally with text-based images in mind. However, since some of the materials for your research project might be visual or multimodal texts, you need to consider ways to adapt the principles of MLA citation style to these different forms.

This may seem daunting at first, but if you remember the logic of MLA style, you'll find you can apply the basic principles of this format to any medium. In a humorous but informative YouTube video, "How to Cite a Cereal Box in MLA 2009," Martine Courant Rife makes exactly this point by taking her viewer through the steps for citing a cereal box (because, as she says, "if you can cite a cereal box, you can cite anything"). The key is to examine and evaluate your source closely—for a cereal box, looking at each side of the box, even inside—and then consider how the information provided there helps you fill out the categories of *author*, *title*, and various *publication* information that we discussed above.

FIGURE 7.2 Examining the front of the cereal box provides us with the title for our citation.

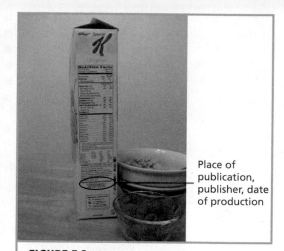

Place of publication, publisher, date of production

FIGURE 7.3 Close analysis of the side shows us the place of publication, publisher, and the date of production.

Consider how we might cite this Special K box. As Figure 7.2 shows, while there is no clear author, we can identify the title as "Kellogg's Special K: Original." Publication data can be found on the side: as seen in Figure 7.3, we can find place of publication (Battle Creek, MI), publisher or corporate sponsor (Kellogg Sales Co.), and date of production or publication (2013) in the fine print. The medium itself is clear: It's a cereal box. Our citation, then, following the model of a citation for a print text, might look something like this:

"Kellogg's Special K: Original." Battle Creek: Kellogg, 2013.

Cereal Box.

While there may be no official way to confirm the accuracy of this particular citation, the principles we used to create it follow the rationale of MLA form. Below, you'll find example citations for many types of media texts you might use in your research paper. However, if the type of source you are using does not appear in the list below, simply follow the logical steps for citing print and online sources (as we did with Special K).

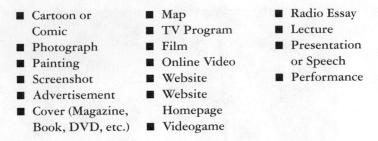

- Cartoon or Comic
- Photograph
- Painting
- Screenshot
- Advertisement
- Cover (Magazine, Book, DVD, etc.)
- Map
- TV Program
- Film
- Online Video
- Website
- Website Homepage
- Videogame
- Radio Essay
- Lecture
- Presentation or Speech
- Performance

Editorial Cartoon or Comic Strip

Grondal, Cal. "Reasonable Search." Cartoon. *Cagle.com* 11 June 2013.

    Web. 12 June 2013.

Pastis, Stephen. "Pearls before Swine." Comic strip. *Comics.com* 18 Apr.

    2006. Web. 16 May 2006.

Wilkinson, Signe. Cartoon. *San Francisco Chronicle* 1 June 2010: A13.

    Print.

Photograph

When writing a citation for a photograph you took yourself, list yourself as the photographer, then the title or location of the photo, the year you took it, and then the file type.

Alfano, Christine. "Golden Gate Bridge, San Francisco." 2004. JPEG file.

Goldin, Nan. *Jimmy Paulette & Misty in a Taxi, NYC.* 1991. Photograph.

    San Francisco Museum of Modern Art, San Francisco.

Liss, Steve. "Trailer-Park Picnic in Utah, 1997." *Great Images of the*

    20th Century. Ed. Kelly Knauer. New York: Time Books, 1999. 41–42.

    Print.

Sherman, Cindy. *Untitled Film Still.* 1978. Museum of Modern Art. *The*

    Complete Untitled Film Stills of Cindy Sherman. Web. 7 July 2006.

Painting

Warhol, Andy. *Self Portrait.* 1986. Andy Warhol Museum, Pittsburgh.

    The Warhol: Collections. Web. 3 Aug. 2006.

Screenshot

Fielding, Geri. "Happy Doggie." *Instagram,* 24 Feb. 2010. Web. 26 Feb.

    2010.

"Star Wars Galaxies." Sony Online Entertainment, n.d. Web. 5 Feb. 2005.

Advertisement

Diet Coke. Advertisement. *Wired* Oct. 2012: 78. Print.

Doritos. Advertisement. ESPN. 7 June 2013. Television.

Nike. "We Are All Witnesses." Advertisement. *Nikebasketball*. 3 Jan.
   2006. Web. 15 June 2006.

Palmolive Soap. "Would Your Husband Marry You Again?" *Harper's
   Bazaar*. 1921. *Ad*Access*. Web. 25 Feb. 2013.

Cover (Magazine, Book, DVD, etc.)

Adams, Neil. "Deadman." *Comics* VF.com. Comics VF, 1978. Web. 23 Oct.
   2005.

Cover. *Gameinformer*. May 2013. Print.

Map

Hong Kong Disneyland Guide. Map. Disney, 2006. Print.

"Providence, Rhode Island." Map. *Google Maps*. Google, 11 Mar. 2012.
   Web. 1 Mar. 2012.

TV Program

"The Diet Wars." *Frontline*. PBS, 2004. Web. 16 Aug. 2006.

"Farmer Guy." Prod. Seth McFarlane, et al. *Family Guy*. Fox, 12 May
   2013. *hulu*. Web. 15 May 2013.

Film

Beyond Killing Us Softly: The Impact of Media Images on Women and Girls.
   Dir. Margaret Lazarus and Renner Wunderlich. Prod. Cambridge
   Documentary Films, 2000. Film.

"A Brief History of America." *Bowling for Columbine*. Dir. Michael Moore.
   United Artists, 2002. *Bowling for Columbine*, n.d. Web. 13 June
   2006.

Online Video

Ingham, Ben. "An African Race." Vimeo. 7 June 2013. Web. 13 June
2013.

Wesch, Michael. "A Vision of Students Today." YouTube. 12 Oct. 2007.
Web. 31 Mar. 2010.

Website

Cartoonists Index. MSNBC, n.d. Web. 4 Nov. 2005.

Website Homepage

Corrigan, Edna. Home page. *Ednarules*. N.p., n.d. Web. 24 Oct. 2005.

Videogame

Infinity Ward. *Modern Warfare 2*. Activision. 2009. Playstation 3.

Rovio Entertainment. *Angry Birds Space*. Apple App Store. 2012. iPhone.

Second Life. Your World. Linden Labs, n.d. Web. 7 May 2006.

Radio Essay

Ydstie, John. "Book Marketing Goes to the Movies." *Morning Edition*.
Natl. Public Radio. 18 July 2006. Radio.

Lecture

Connors, Fiona. "Visual Literacy in Perspective." English 210B. Boston
U. 24 Oct. 2004. Lecture.

Delagrange, Susan, and Ben McCorkle. "What Is a Public Service
Announcement (PSA)?" Writing II: Rhetorical Composing. Coursera.
May 2013. Lecture.

Presentation or Speech

Bu, Lisa. "How Books Can Open Your Mind." TED Conference Feb. 2013.
Lecture. *TED: Ideas Worth Spreading*. TED, May 2013. Web. 23 May 2013.

Jobs, Steve. Commencement Address. Stanford U., Palo Alto, 12 June
2005. *iTunes U*. Apple. Web. 27 July 2006.

Reagan, Ronald. "The Space Shuttle *Challenger* Tragedy Address."

28 Jan. 1986. *American Rhetoric*. Web. 5 Mar. 2006.

Rheingold, Howard. "Technologies of Cooperation." Annenberg Center

for Communication. U of Southern California, Los Angeles. 3 Apr.

2006. Speech.

Performance

Phedre. By Jean Racine. Dir. Ileana Drinovan. Pigott Theater, Memorial

Hall, Stanford, 10-13 May 2006. Performance.

Student Paper in MLA Style

To see how texts you might encounter in your research process today will range across varied formats and media, let's consult a student paper by Stephanie Parker, who focused on how digital communities, such as Soompi (a Korean pop culture Website), have transformed ideas of racial identity. Stephanie incorporated an impressive array of both print and electronic sources in her project, including books, book chapters, and journal articles; e-books, online newspaper articles, and telephone and online interviews; YouTube videos, Websites, screenshots, blog posts, and more.

Parker 1

Stephanie Parker
Dr. Christine Alfano
PWR 2 Cultural Interfaces
7 December 2008

Soompi and the "Honorary Asian": Shifting Identities
in the Digital Age

Every morning at 7:00 am, Norwegian James Algaard turns on his computer and joins Soompi IRC: a chatroom for members of a Korean Pop Culture discussion forum. James' daily entrance into the chatroom is enthusiastically greeted by online acquaintances who know him as <SeungHo>, a connoisseur of Korean

Stephanie heads her paper in proper MLA form, with her name, her instructor's name, the class title, and the date, all flush to the left margin.

Parker 2

Hip Hop and a collector of limited edition sneakers. Seungho Lee was born in South Korea, but was adopted by a Norwegian family; websites like Soompi are his only connection to Korean culture. Thousands of miles away in Los Angeles, it is 10:00 pm when I, an American with a strong interest in Asia, join the same chatroom to spend time with Seungho and thirty other "Soompiers," people from around the world who have come together to form a strong and tight-knit online community. The chatroom itself […] is visually mundane—a window that gradually fills with text as different users type, but Soompi IRC is an organic and multicultural part of cyberspace where people communicate in English, Korean, Mandarin, Cantonese, Spanish, Norwegian, Swedish, Vietnamese, Japanese, Tagalog, and French about every topic imaginable, 24 hours a day.

We Soompiers are representatives of "Generation I"—we have grown up with the Internet and are using it to define ourselves in a more globalized society (Gates 98). A decade ago, cultural identity for people like Seungho and me was limited by factors like geography, language, and ethnicity; with the emergence of new technology and online communities, we have access to an ever-growing variety of choices for personal expression. Soompi and other cyber communities are at the forefront of a larger movement towards redefining how we culturally relate to one another. This movement will extend past the reach of the Internet and act as a catalyst for cross-cultural interaction and understanding on a level never seen before.

* * *

Stephanie lists both the author and page number in her citation. Notice that she is citing this source even though she is only paraphrasing his ideas.

Stephanie closes her introduction with a two-sentence thesis that outlines the claim that she will support through her textual and cultural analysis in the rest of the paper.

Parker 9

"This Site is My Life": Soompi Addicts and the Asian Fix

For the past decade, most academic research on cyber culture has focused on the type of social interaction that takes place within the digital medium. Scholars Howard Rheingold, Elisabeth Reid, Amy Jo Kim, and Lisa Nakamura have all helped to build the foundations for the study of online group behavior. But there is also another important part of Internet life that is only beginning to develop with the current generation of web users—how membership in an online group affects a person's self-perception in relation to others in real life. Nessim Watson is a Professor of Communication at Westfield State College, and has devoted years to the study of American mass media and cultural representations. After spending two years participating in and studying an online fan club, he concluded that, "those youth formed a community which created not only individual benefits for participants but also a group strength" (102). It is those "individual benefits" that should provide the next source of material for research. The strong allegiance to a web-based group is not something that an Internet user logs in and out of—they take this allegiance with them and it influences their decisions and behavior in the real world: their mode of personal expression, their opinions about other groups, and especially their cultural identity.

Soompi is one of the best venues to observe the brand new phenomenon of people gaining a real sense of culture from an online source. According to Quantcast, a free internet ratings site, Soompi.com has 26 million page views per month, with a full 66% accomplished by "Addicts," or users who log on more than once every day ("Traffic Stats"). For them, Soompi is the most convenient place to get their fix of Asian culture. This makes sense, and is in line with a report published in 2001 by the Pew Internet & American Life Project, "Asian-Americans and the Internet: The Young and Connected." According to the study, English-speaking Asian-Americans "are the Net's most active users...and have made the Internet an integral part of their daily lives" (Spooner 2). For hundreds of thousands of people in this demographic, Soompi has definitely become an important force in their personal lives and decisions, and in some cases, is the only website visited besides

---

Stephanie's page numbers skip to 9 here since we've abridged her paper.

In this section, midway through her paper, Stephanie synthesizes a variety of different types of sources to make her point.

Stephanie cites the page number for the print source from which she took this direct quote. Notice that because she used the author's name earlier in the sentence, she does not need to include it again in her parenthetical citation.

She cites the source for the statistics she uses. Since her source had no author, she refers to it here with an abbreviation of its title, which she places in quotation marks since it is the title of the article. In the Works Cited, she lists this source by its title as well, so it is easy for the reader to cross-reference.

Even though Stephanie reads this as an electronic file, Spooner's study was in PDF form and therefore has page numbers that she could refer to in her citations.

This source is a discussion thread from the Website that Stephanie is discussing, but for the purposes of citation, she refers to it by its title, just as she would for an article that had no author listed.

Since Stephanie is working with two different texts written by Nakamura, here she specifies which she is referring to by including the title as well as the author and page number in the citation.

The second time that Stephanie references Nakamura's book, she does not need to include the author or title in the citation since they are exactly the same as in the previous citation.

Since this quotation is from an interview, there is no page number to cite. However, since Stephanie lists more than one source from Shim in her Works Cited, here she includes a citation that makes it clear that this quote was taken from her online interview with him.

Parker 10

social utilities like Facebook ("What Would You"). They can use Soompi to build their knowledge of Asian culture, and to form new connections with other people they can relate to around the world. In September of 2008, a discussion topic was posted on the Forums: "What Would You Do Without Soompi?" Certain self-proclaimed "addicts" left replies such as, "I probably wouldn't be so into Asian stuff," and "I would be a lot less knowledgeable about the world" ("What Would You"). For thousands of Soompiers, the Forums are where they learn Asian-specific modes of fashion, style, speech patterns, and other cultural behaviors of expression.

This part of personal development is extremely important in the case of Asian-Americans living in predominantly non-Asian areas, without an "Asian group" of friends to participate in cultural activities with. Prominent scholars in Asian-American studies constantly emphasize the unique relationship between the Asian-American community and New Media, and its power to change traditional ideas about identity, culture, and the potential fluidity of both (Nakamura, *Digitizing Race* 184). Lisa Nakamura recognizes in *Digitizing Race: Visual Cultures of the Internet* that "[i]nteractive media like the Web can question identity while building discursive community in ways that other static media cannot" (184). It allows anyone who wishes to contribute to the evolution of Asian-American culture to effectively "log in" and express their approval, resistance, or creativity in the largest Forum on the planet, all while strengthening the bonds of a real community. Daniel Shim relates his own experience: "I was born in Canada in white communities & I grew up to be like them. Soompi has given me knowledge about Asian culture that I would not get from my school or family" (Online interview). To follow that point further, in her book, Nakamura argues that the Internet provides a Forum for "questioning a rigid and essentialized notion of Asian American 'authenticity'" (185). This is extremely important—the idea of culture being inextricably linked to ethnicity, language, and geographic location becomes irrelevant in the face of rising online communities, the organic and global nature of which forces the issue of what makes a person "Asian," or "American."

Parker 11

Since Daniel joined Soompi and began to use the Internet as a tool for personal expression, his popularity online has grown enormously: his YouTube videoblog, in which he comments on events in his daily life and makes fun of Asian stereotypes, has almost 30,000 subscribers and is the 4th most popular comedy blog in all of Canada (Shim, "Shimmycocopuffsss's"). Without having grown up around many Asian young people, Daniel has been extremely successful in navigating the cultural landscape with the help of his online community, even producing his own ideas about Asian-American identity as a New Media celebrity (see Figure 6). For young people like Daniel in Toronto and Seungho in Norway, Susan Kang says that "online is pretty much the only place they feel like they can connect to other Asians." Soompi makes it not only possible, but easy for Asians who live in a non-Asian place to immerse themselves in Asian culture and comment on it—an unprecedented step in the separation of culture and a static location.

FIGURE 6 Daniel Shim's parody video, "Wasabi Boy–NoEngrish" confronts Asian stereotypes with comedy and has been viewed almost 200,000 times. Author screenshot.

Stephanie once again takes a direct quote from an interview she conducted and so does not cite a page number or author here. The curious reader would look up "Kang" on the Works Cited and discover that the quote came from a personal interview.

This Works Cited represents an abridged version of the much longer Works Cited that Stephanie included with her full paper.

All the sources in the Works Cited listed in alphabetical order by author's last name, or, in the cases where there is no identified author, by title.

Stephanie lists a variety of sources here, from academic journal articles, to books, newspaper articles, advertisements, and even online sources such as Webpages, YouTube videos, and discussion list postings.

Notice the formatting of the entries: the first line of each entry is flush left, with a hanging indent in the wrapped lines so readers can skim the Works Cited easily.

When there is no author, the title is listed first.

Parker 20

Works Cited

Bell, David. *An Introduction to Cybercultures*. London: Routledge, 2001. Print.

Chen, Louie Haoru. Online interview. 16 Nov. 2008.

"Crazy Sale for Korean Fashion." Advertisement. *Yesstyle*. 10 Nov. 2008. Web. 10 Nov. 2008.

Dator, Jim, and Yongseok Seo. "Korea as the Wave of a Future: The Emerging Dream Society of Icons and Aesthetic Experience." *Journal of Futures Studies* 9:1 (2004): 31-44. Print.

Gates, Bill. "Enter 'Generation I.'" *Instructor* Mar. 2000: 98. Print.

Gulia, Milena, and Barry Wellman. "Virtual Communities as Communities: Net Surfers Don't Ride Alone." *Communities in Cyberspace*. Ed. Mark A. Smith and Peter Kollock. New York: Routledge, 1999. 167-194. Print.

Herring, Susan C. "Questioning the Generational Divide: Technological Exoticism and Adult Constructions of Online Youth Identity." *Youth, Identity, and Digital Media*. Ed. David Buckingham. Cambridge: MIT Press, 2000. 72-95. Print.

Jones, Steven G. *Virtual Culture: Identity and Communication in Cybersociety*. London: Sage, 1997. Print.

Kang, Susan. Online interview. 25 Oct. 2008.

Kim, Amy Jo. *Community Building on the Web*. Peachpit Press, 6 Apr. 2000. Web. 24 Oct. 2008.

Ko, Shu-ling. "GIO Looking to Take Foreign Soap Operas off Prime Time TV." *Taipei Times* 11 Jan. 2006. *AsiaMedia*. 11 Jan. 2006. Web. 20 Nov. 2008.

"Korea Wave Hits Middle East." *Dae Jang Geum* 13 Dec. 2005. Web. 1 Nov. 2008.

Lee, Hyuk Min. Telephone interview. 15 Oct. 2008.

Nakamura, Lisa. *Cybertypes*. New York: Routledge, 2002. Print.

---. *Digitizing Race: Visual Cultures of the Internet*. Minneapolis: U of Minnesota P, 2008. Print.

Parker 21

Reid, Elisabeth. "Electropolis: Communications and Community on Internet Relay Chat." Honors Thesis. U of Melbourne, 1991. Print.

Rheingold, Howard. *The Virtual Community: Homesteading on the Electronic Frontier*. Addison-Wesley, 1993. Print.

Shim, Daniel. Online interview. 12 Nov. 2008.

---. "Shimmycocopuffsss's Profile Page" YouTube. 27 Nov. 2008. Web. 28 Nov. 2008.

---. "Wasabi Boy–No Engrish." YouTube. 5 Mar. 2008. Web. 28 Nov. 2008.

Spooner, Tom. "Asian-Americans and the Internet: The Young and Connected." *Pew Internet and American Life Project*. 12 Dec. 2001. PDF file.

"Traffic Stats for soompi.com." Quantcast.com. 1 Nov. 2008. Web. 1 Nov. 2008.

"Wannabe Asians/Wasians" 1721 Posts. *Soompi*. Started 28 July 2006. Web. 1 Oct. 2008.

Watson, Nessim. "Why We Argue about Virtual Community: A Case Study of the Phish.net Fan Community." Jones 102-110. Print.

"What Would You Do without Soompi? How Would Your Life Be Different?" 95 posts. *Soompi*. Started 1 Sept. 2008. Web. 1 Oct. 2008.

Yang, Jeff. "On Top of YouTube: Happy Slip, Choi, KevJumba." *San Francisco Chronicle* 6 June 2008. Web. 20 Oct. 2008.

When an author's name appears more than once, three hyphens (—) stand in for the name in the second and subsequent entries, and the entries by the same author are alphabetized by title.

Notice here how in the Watson entry, Stephanie cross-references with the Jones citation above so as not to be redundant.

THE WRITER'S PROCESS

In this chapter you've learned about the importance of source attribution, the concept of intellectual property, the dangers of plagiarism—whether accidental or not—the rhetorical purpose for documentation styles, the cross-referencing system of in-text citations, and the logic behind constructing entries for your MLA Works Cited and Consulted list. Now it's time for you to implement these practices in your own writing.

Take a look at your own research sources as they appear in your written draft. Have you acknowledged all your sources in full? Are the names of authors "hidden" in parentheses or in notes listing a range of sources? Should you instead name the authors in the prose of your essay and include just the page numbers in parentheses? In that way, you make your conversation with these authors move overt, and your source attribution of their work is more respectful.

Now take a look at all your online, visual, and multimedia sources. Did you include proper and concise parenthetical attributions for each one in the paper? Does your Works Cited list provide an alphabetized account of all your research, even the materials that may be so new that we haven't invented ways to cite them yet? Realize that you, as an emerging writer, can use the lessons from this chapter in order to think through the logic of documentation, include the newest sources in your essay, and develop your contribution to an ongoing research conversation.

WRITING ASSIGNMENTS   MyWritingLab

1. **Documentation Log:** Develop your own system of note taking and ethical citation of sources to avoid unintentional plagiarism. Create citations for your works cited using MLA form. Follow the order in the checklist below in formatting your citation; keep in mind, depending your source, not all of these categories may apply:

❑ Author or authors

❑ Title of book or article

❑ If an article, title of journal or book within which it was published

❑ Place of publication

❑ Publisher

❑ Date of publication

❑ If a printed or PDF article, page span

❑ If online article from a database, the database or search engine

❑ Medium of publication

❑ The URL for a Website, inserted in brackets, if your instructor requires it or if the site would be difficult to find without it

2. **Citations Peer Review:** Share your draft paper with your peers and have them check to see which sources need citation. Does your paper contain knowledge you must have obtained from a source? If so, you need to acknowledge the source of that knowledge. Do certain passages seem to be common knowledge? If so, you don't need to cite them. What paragraphs could go into notes? What aspects of your paper need more explanation and could use a note?

3. **Writing with Technology:** You might find it helpful to turn to one of the scholarly tools for producing a Work Cited list. These include *Easybib*, *Ref Works*, *End Note*, *Citelighter*, and *Zotero*. Many researchers and scholars depend on these tools, keeping notes right in the program, inserting all identifying information for a source, and then selecting the documentation format needed for their papers. The technology then produces a list in the chosen documentation style. However, you will definitely need to double-check the list for accuracy, using what you learned in this chapter.

MyWritingLab Visit Ch. 7 Documenting Sources and Avoiding Plagiarism in MyWritingLab to complete the Writer's Practices, Spotlighted Analyses, and Writing Assignments, and to test your understanding of the chapter objectives.

CHAPTER 8

Designing Arguments

Chapter Preview Questions

8.1 What is decorum and how does this rhetorical principle govern document design?

8.2 What are the conventions for academic writing?

8.3 What techniques can I learn to integrate images effectively into my writing?

8.4 How can I compose an abstract about my essay, a "bio" about myself as a writer, or a writing portfolio?

8.5 How do audience and purpose affect my document design?

8.6 How can I create multimodal arguments, such as op-ads, photo essays, and Websites?

FIGURE 8.1 This opinion advertisement by DCVote.org relies on a carefully designed visual argument.

We've used the word "writing" so far in *Envision* to refer predominantly to written text, printed letters and words. However, as you probably know from your own experience, today's definition of "writing" incorporates many different forms of communication, and, as we've seen through the numerous examples that we've examined in the last seven chapters, the idea of argument itself is not bound to just words on page: it can assume any one of a number of forms, from a traditional academic article, to a political cartoon, advertisement, photo essay, propaganda poster, website, film trailer, or even a mash-up of different texts. This is the reason rhetoric itself is such a powerful lens through which to understand how to be persuasive communicators: it is flexible and adaptive, focusing on *strategies of persuasion* rather than a particular type of text. Rhetoric allows us to be versatile communicators, choosing the type of argument best suited to our audience, purpose, occasion, and context.

The protean nature of modern argument is evident all around us. Consider, for instance, the way the advocacy group DC Vote mobilized its message about the need to give the District of Columbia local budget control and equitable representation in Congress through a variety of platforms: press releases, a website, YouTube videos, and even an op-ad campaign featuring posters such as the one seen in Figure 8.1. Notice the way in which that visual argument enacts many of the same strategies as you might find in a written argument: it structures itself conceptually and visually as a comparison/contrast argument; it relies on *logos*, or a logical line of reasoning, to argue its position; it uses strategic arrangement of elements (the mirrored figures, the hierarchical structure of information, from broad claim to increased detail); it employs culturally resonant language ("taxation without representation") to connect with its audience. As an argument, it is as carefully designed as a written text – but is perhaps better suited than that form to an audience who might be riding the Metro or waiting for a bus or train. DC Vote recognized that they needed to adapt their arguments to suit different rhetorical situations, a strategy essential for effective communicators in today's society.

In this chapter, you'll learn how to deliver your own arguments in a variety of modes. As you read the pages that follow, we invite you to consider how you can communicate your ideas, research, and writing in various formats—including the conventional academic paper but also expanding out to include creative cover pages, multimedia representations in word and image, and even texts that combine voice, moving images, and animation. But whether your project is conventional or creative, you need to learn the principles of **document design**—the guidelines that determine the best medium and method of communicating your idea in a specific format. We'll provide specific guidelines for academic essays, including line-spacing, margin size, page numbering, and other considerations. You'll learn how to write an academic abstract to provide an overview of your argument, a short biography to build your credibility as the author, and a portfolio of your work, as well as how to insert images correctly into your written essay. Then, in the second half of the chapter, we'll examine ways you can compose effective arguments in less traditionally "academic formats," such as op-ads, photo essays, newsletters, brochures, Websites, online videos, and other multimodal projects. In doing so, you'll receive an overview of the many modes of persuasion available to you as a twenty-first century writer.

8.1 What is decorum, and how does this rhetorical principle govern document design?

UNDERSTANDING DOCUMENT DESIGN AND DECORUM

First, in order to grasp the concept of document design more fully, let's return to Alex, our hypothetical student from Chapter 1. For one of her classes, she has completed a research paper on "greenwashing," that is, the corporate practice of promoting a "green" public image in order to deflect attention from environmentally questionable business practices. She now needs to format her paper to submit it to her teacher, and she also is considering submitting it for publication in her college's undergraduate research journal. Moreover, her teacher wants her to convert her paper into a visual argument to appear in a class exhibit. She therefore has an important task in front of her: to learn appropriate design strategies for both academic essays and visual arguments. In each case, she has four key decisions to make: Alex must identify her *argument* (her main point); her *audience* (whom she intends to reach); her *medium* (printed article, abstract, advertisement, photo essay, or multimedia montage); and the specific *form* (the layout and design aspects) for her composition. What governs her choices is a matter of document design strategy, or the choices writers make in formatting their work.

To use terms from classical rhetoric, the decisions you face for document design have to do with **decorum**—a word defined as "appropriateness." In everyday language, someone who exhibits decorum in speaking knows the right kinds of words and content to use given the circumstances and audience. For example, you might swear or shout with joy at a baseball game, but not at a job interview when talking about how your team won the game. But decorum as a rhetorical principle extends beyond choosing the right words and phrases for the occasion.

Seeing Connections
Chapter 3 offers additional discussion of style in relation to argumentative writing.

In the Roman rhetorical tradition, Cicero separated decorum into three levels of style that he assigned to different argumentative purposes. Cicero defined the *grand style* as the most formal mode of discourse, employing sophisticated language, imagery, and rhetorical devices; its goal is often to move the audience. He considered *middle style* less formal than grand style but not completely colloquial; although it uses some verbal ornamentation, it develops its argument more slowly in an attempt to persuade the audience by pleasing them. The final level, *plain style,* mimics conversation in its speech and rhythms, aiming to instruct or inform the audience in a clear and straightforward way. By adding decorum to our rhetorical toolkit, we can make decisions about how to design documents. As demonstrated in the Levels of Decorum table, we can attend to argument, audience, medium, and form by understanding the *level of style* for a particular occasion. Like our classical counterparts, we must understand our rhetorical situation and use a style that best suits the circumstance.

LEVELS OF DECORUM

LEVEL	CHARACTERISTICS	EXAMPLE: WRITTEN ARGUMENT	EXAMPLE: VISUAL ARGUMENT
Grand or high style	Ornate language, formal structures, many rhetorical devices	Academic paper to be published in a scholarly journal	An information graphic in a scholarly journal
Middle style	Some ornamentation, less formal language, argument is developed at a leisurely pace	Feature article or editorial column	A photo essay for a school exhibit
Plain or low style	The least formal style; closest to spoken language; emphasis on clarity, simplicity, and directness	A blog post or contribution to an online forum	A series of Tumblr posts, showcasing personal perspective or experience

For the rest of this chapter, we'll look at various models for document design, examining the way in which we need to adjust our choice of style according to the formal and rhetorical demands of each situation.

UNDERSTANDING ACADEMIC WRITING CONVENTIONS

8.2 What are the conventions for academic writing?

The format of a page matters to an audience: from the paragraph indents to the margins and double-spaced lines, to the rhetorical placement of images—all these design decisions are ways of conveying your level of decorum and your purpose to your specific audience. When we say "first impressions," we often mean how well a writer meets the conventions anticipated by the audience. From the perspective of *decorum*, the conventional academic essay falls under either grand or middle style, depending on the preferences of your audience. Characteristics of academic writing include:

- Using language more sophisticated than ordinary speech
- Using formal structures to organize your paper, including the following elements:
  - ❏ An informative and catchy title that comes under your identifying information
  - ❏ A complete introduction containing your *thesis statement*
  - ❏ Clear subsections for each part of your argument, often using rhetorical subheads
  - ❏ A substantial conclusion in its own paragraph
- Accurately and ethically acknowledging your sources and providing a Works Cited list

Seeing Connections
See Chapter 6 for guidance on writing rhetorical subheads.

Adhering to these characteristics in the document design of your writing signals your membership in a scholarly community, since you demonstrate knowledge of the format conventions for academic papers. It's similar to using table manners in a particular community or waiting in line to pay at a store; the conventions reflect consensus concerning shared expectations or practices that in turn to promote unity, consistency, and familiarity.

AT A GLANCE

Key Elements of Academic Document Design

- Double-space all pages.
- Provide 1-inch margins on all sides.
- Use a professional but easily readable font, such as Times New Roman or Arial.
- Number pages at the top right; include your last name before the page number.
- Use subheads to separate sections.
- Use citations to acknowledge research sources.
- Use endnotes or footnotes for additional information.
- Include a list of references at the end, preferably a Works Cited and Consulted List.
- Staple, clip, or bind the paper together.

These guidelines are very pragmatic in nature, driven by a deeper purpose than simply following rules. Most have to do with the rhetorical relationship between yourself, your text, and your readers. By double-spacing your document and providing 1-inch margins on all sides, you leave ample room for reviewers to comment on lines or paragraphs. You include page numbers and your name on the corner of your essay to enable readers to keep track of whose paper they are reading and to easily refer to your writing by page number when commenting on a specific point. By using subheads, you help structure what might be a complicated argument to make it more accessible to your audience. Finally, when you include citations, footnotes, and references, you demonstrate your *ethos* as a writer and researcher by giving credit to your sources.

It might seem like an overstatement to argue that a detail as basic as the spacing and alignment of words on a title page can contribute to your *ethos*. However, consider the different rhetorical force of the three cover pages reproduced in Figures 8.2, 8.3, and 8.4. The first contains all the relevant information: the title, the author's name, the date, and the class for which the essay was written, yet it makes a less powerful impression than the other examples. Why is that? In Figure 8.3, Alex took into account very simple design principles when formatting the page. She changed to a more accessible font, to increase *readability*. She used *contrast* to differentiate the title, with its large, bold font, from the rest of the words on the page. She experimented with *proximity*, grouping related items together to help her reader conceptualize levels of importance. In Figure 8.4, she took the process one step further. She used the principle of *alignment,* moving elements into visual connection with one another on the page so as to give a sense of rhetorical purposefulness behind the layout; finally, she decided to reformat

Seeing Connections
See Chapter 3 for a discussion of crafting a rhetorically effective title.

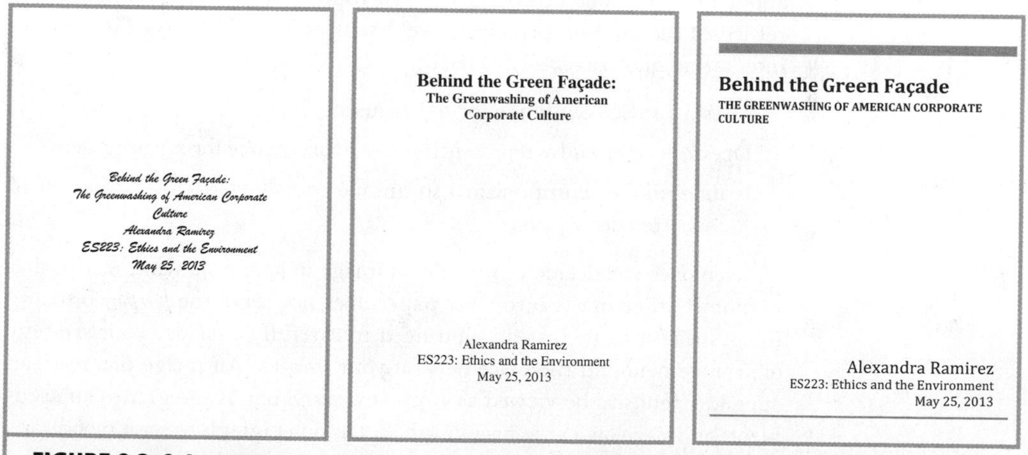

Behind the Green Façade:
The Greenwashing of American Corporate
Culture
Alexandra Ramirez
ES223: Ethics and the Environment
May 25, 2013

Behind the Green Façade:
The Greenwashing of American
Corporate Culture

Alexandra Ramirez
ES223: Ethics and the Environment
May 25, 2013

Behind the Green Façade
THE GREENWASHING OF AMERICAN CORPORATE
CULTURE

Alexandra Ramirez
ES223: Ethics and the Environment
May 25, 2013

FIGURE 8.2–8.4 Alex experimented with several different formats in designing her cover page for her research project.

her subtitle in small capitals, a technique she would use for her subheads in the rest of the essay, to give the entire document a sense of coherence through strategic *repetition*. She could even have integrated a relevant cover image or quotation to set the mood for her essay.

As these examples indicate, format is not something simply imposed on you and your writing. It involves a set of *rhetorical acts* that influence the way that your readers encounter, experience, and are persuaded by your argument.

8.3 What techniques can I learn to integrate images effectively into my writing?

INTEGRATING IMAGES IN ACADEMIC WRITING

Just as there are proper academic conventions for designing the writing and layout of your essay, there exist specific guidelines for how best to integrate images into your writing. But first, consider the rhetorical purpose of your images. If they are just for decoration, then they are not essential to your argument. By contrast, if your essay focuses on a visual topic, such as the analysis of ads or films, then you probably want to include images or screen shots as *primary sources* or *exhibits* to analyze in the essay itself. Moreover, if your argument relies on images—such as political campaigns from billboards or Websites—as supporting *evidence* for your thesis, then you also want to allow your readers to consult that material alongside your prose about the text. When considering how to include an image in your essay, return to the guiding principles we discussed in Chapter 6 in relation to integrating quotations; ask yourself:

Does it provide **evidence** for my argument?

Does it lend *ethos* by representing a primary source for my argument?

Is its design or **composition** so unique that elements would be lost in written description?

Even once you decide to include an image in your argument, realize that randomly inserting it into your paper does not serve the *purpose* of using images rhetorically. Instead, you need to carefully consider your strategy of arrangement and the placement of your images. An image placed in an appendix tends to be viewed as supplementary, not as integral to an argument; an image on a title page might act as an epigraph to set a mood for a paper, but it is less effective as a specific visual example. If you want to use your images as *argumentative evidence*, you need to show them to your readers as you analyze them; therefore, what would be most successful would be inserting them next to the part of your argument that they support. Each decision is both a stylistic and rhetorical choice.

Once you have determined the placement that best serves your rhetorical purpose, you need to insert the image in a way that maximizes its

AT A GLANCE

Including Visuals in a Paper

- Decide whether it's appropriate to include an image based on assessing its function in terms of evidence, *ethos*, and composition.
- Position it strategically and describe its relevance in your main text so that your readers don't skim over it.
- Include a figure number and caption or brief description that explains how the image contributes to your argument.
- Refer to the figure number or image title when writing the prose of your essay (e.g., "See Figure 1").
- List the complete image source information in your bibliography.

impact on your argument. Like a quotation, an image cannot be dropped into a text without comment; it needs to be **signposted**, or connected to your argument through deliberate textual markers. You can accomplish this by making explicit **textual references** to the image—for example, "shown in the image at the right" or "(see Figure 3)"—and by taking the time to explain the rhetoric of the image for readers. In addition, just like words quoted from a book or an interview that you might use as evidence, visual material needs *your interpretation* for readers to view it the way you do. Your analysis of its meaning will advance your argument by persuading readers to see the image as you do, and in the process, readers will pause to consider the evidence rather than skip over it.

It is also crucial to draft a **caption** for the image that reiterates the relationship between the point you are making in the paper and the visual evidence you include. This dialogue between image and ideas will help remind you to use your images rhetorically and analytically, as evidence, rather than just as decoration. Remember, however, that what is most important is the analysis of the image you include in the body of your paper; don't hide the meaning of the image in the caption. Captions should be concise; they should not do the work of the written argument.

Design of Academic Papers

A page from student Kim Felser's essay on the addictive properties of sugar provides an example of both effective academic writing conventions and the strategic placement and captioning of visuals (see Figure 8.5). In Chapter 5,

Sugar addiction, of course, satisfies all of these categories, just as fully as do more widely recognized drugs of abuse like cocaine, hydrocodone, and alcohol.

Consuming the highly concentrated sugars that abound in our current food market not only triggers the feelings of pleasure associated with agreeable flavors, as is suggested by our evolutionary development, but also releases opiate chemicals – substances just a few bonds away from heroin and morphine.[1] Consumption of such substances is quickly followed by a the priming of endorphins and dopamine in the region of the brain known as the nucleus accumbens, often called the "hedonic hot spot" by researchers in the field (see Figure 3 to the right).[2] The impact is immediate: the opiates moderately anesthetize pain,[3] while the abundance of endorphins and dopamine encourages a sugar "high" of chemically synthesized happiness.[4] Alcohol, too, acts upon the same chemical pathways in the brain by priming the release of dopamine in the

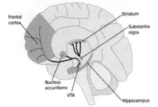

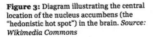

Figure 3: Diagram illustrating the central location of the nucleus accumbens (the "hedonistic hot spot") in the brain. *Source: Wikimedia Commons*

nucleus accumbens, and encouraging a similar state of artificial bliss.[5] These "euphoric neural effects"[6] of both sugar and alcohol, as Dr. Jeffery L. Fortuna puts it, prove highly addicting, for in both cases a severe inability to inhibit additional consumption of the substance follows.[7] Despite the fact that the high is not as intense as that of cocaine or alcohol, users still find themselves returning to the drugs again and again in an unconscious endeavor to recreate such a pleasurable mental state, especially as "highs" grow less intense with further use – just as with other drugs of dependence. In short, willpower proves ineffectual, and repeated use of the drug only serves to worsen the addiction as tolerance to the substance at hand increases.

FIGURE 8.5 This excerpt from Kim's essay, "Sugar: The Hidden Drug," provides an example of polished academic design.

we looked at an excerpt from Kim's Dialogue of Sources on this topic; here we can see how in this final draft, she has spotlighted her argument and integrated her source materials to support her points. In addition, we can see her strategic use of visual evidence to help her reader visualize the different areas of the brain affected by sugar consumption. Rather than relegate this image to an appendix, Kim positioned it in the paper with the text wrapped around it, making the visuals an integral part of her argument that resonated with the surrounding text. She then emphasized the importance of the image by giving it a meaningful, rhetorical caption that paraphrased his central point.

Kim's careful attention to academic conventions—from her last name and page number at the top, to the readable typeface, clear structure, and purposeful integration of an image as evidence for her central claim—adds *ethos* to an already articulate and well-researched argument.

TOOLS OF DESIGN FOR ACADEMIC AUDIENCES

8.4 How can I compose an abstract about my essay, a "bio" about myself as a writer, or a writing portfolio?

In addition to attending to the format of the research paper itself and integrating visuals as evidence correctly, you may also need to write supplemental materials that provide readers with a preview of your argument and information about yourself as the author. The materials are commonly known as the academic abstract and author bio. In some cases, you also may be asked to collect a sample of your writing into a writing *portfolio*, prefaced by a reflective cover memo. These are all standard components of conventional academic writing; by learning their formal design properties, you can confidently add them to your toolkit of writing strategies.

Writing an Abstract

The **research abstract** is a professional academic genre designed to present the research topic and to lay out the argument. Abstracts differ depending on the disciplinary audience and the purpose of the writing. When applying to academic conferences in the humanities, for example, scholars often must write abstracts that predict the paper's argument, research contribution, and significance, while writers in the sciences or social sciences typically write abstracts *after* the paper has been completed to serve as a short summary of the article. You will encounter abstracts when you begin searching for research articles; they often precede a published paper or accompany

Seeing Connections
Chapter 5 discusses
how you might evaluate
published abstracts
during your research.

bibliographic citations in online databases. Abstracts can range from a few sentences to a page in length, but they are usually no longer than two paragraphs. The key in writing an abstract is to explain your argument in one brief, coherent unit. While some characterize an abstract as simply a summary, others suggest it can have a more complex structure. In their seminal work, *The Craft of Research*, Wayne Booth, Gregory Colomb, and Joseph Williams propose the following model for abstracts: Context + Problem + Main Point or Launching Point. According to their interpretation, an abstract clarifies not only the topic, but a tension in that topic and the way that the written piece addresses that tension. As you read the abstract below, consider the ways in which the author adheres to this structure.

In the first sentence, the authors establish the context for their research.

The second and third sentences convey the tension or problem that their particular project addresses.

In the final sentences of the abstract, the authors suggest both their main point and some of their methodology, providing the reader with a clear overview of what to expect when reading the whole paper and their contribution to the conversation on this topic.

Serious games have received much positive attention; correspondingly, many researchers have taken up the challenge of establishing how to best design them. However, the current literature often focuses on best practice design strategies and frameworks. Fine-grained details, contextual descriptions, and organisational factors that are invaluable in helping us to learn from and reflect on project experiences are often overlooked. In this paper, we present five distinct and sometimes competing perspectives that are critical in understanding factors that influence serious game projects: *project organisation, technology, domain knowledge, user research*, and *game design*. We explain these perspectives by providing insights from the design and development process of an EU-funded serious game about conflict resolution developed by an interdisciplinary consortium of researchers and industry-based developers. We also point out a set of underlying forces that become evident from viewing the process from different perspectives, to underscore that problems exist in serious game projects and that we should open the conversation about them.

AT A GLANCE

Design for Composing an Abstract

- What level of decorum do you wish to use?
- How will the style predict the tone of your essay and establish your persona as a researcher?
- If you use "I" in the prose, can it be *ethos*-based in terms of your research or experience?
- How much specificity should you include from the essay?
  - Do you want to identify key examples you analyze in your writing?
  - Do you want to give an overview of your argument?
  - Should you name any important sources you use in making your argument?
  - What is your major research contribution?
  - What is the larger significance of your essay?

In composing your abstract, you will need to make several rhetorical decisions, outlined in the questions in the "At a Glance" box.

Constructing Your Bio

While the abstract offers a concise statement of the argument, the **bio**, short for biography, is a brief paragraph that conveys aspects of the author's experiences or credentials to the intended audience. In this way, the bio functions as a short written account of your *persona*. Its purpose is to persuade readers of your depth of knowledge about or research into your topic. Moreover, a successful bio usually connects aspects of the research topic to the writer's experiences, interests, and motivations for engaging in research work. Eric Wiebacher's bio for his essay, "India's National Solar Program: A Case Study in Developing Clean Energy Infrastructures," follows this model, resembling the polished "About the Author" paragraph that you might find at the back of a book or in the headnote of an academic article:

Eric Wiebacher is a junior pursuing a double major in Public Policy and Environmental studies. He has taken several environmental policy courses focused on natural resource policy, climate change and alternate energy, and international policy and management. While spending a semester abroad in India,

Eric names specific qualifications and experiences he has had that make him an authority in this area.

he had the opportunity to visit the village of Dharnai, the first village in India to be powered exclusively by solar energy. He has used this research project to help him deepen his understanding of India's microgrid project and to formulate ways to share his ideas with a broader audience. For his major capstone project, he plans to build on this research by expanding to consider the intersection between policy and implementation of alternate energy programs in other countries as well, such as China, Kenya, and Turkey.

He ends the bio with his future plans in this area of research that suggest his pursuit of a "research line" or academic path of scholarly inquiry.

When formatting your own bio, you might decide to include a photograph of yourself. Select your picture carefully, with attention to its rhetorical impact in conveying your *persona*. Many students who choose to write a traditional bio like Eric's opt for a formal school portrait; other students might choose a more humorous picture to complement the tone of their bios. One student, when writing about online gaming communities, even used Photoshop to create a portrait of herself standing next to her onscreen avatar identity to represent the two perspectives she was bringing to her research. As you can tell, the picture works with the bio not only to construct a *persona* for the writer but also to suggest that writer's rhetorical stance.

Creating a Portfolio

In some cases, you might need to take a step back from focusing in individual essays and assignments and create a *writer's portfolio*, a collection or sampling of your work. You might be asked to produce a portfolio for one of any number of contexts: as the culmination of your work in a writing class, as a representation of your work in your major, as a requirement for graduation, or even as part of an application for graduate school or a job. Each of these situations implies a slightly different purpose and audience, both of which will influence the shape of your portfolio.

The first step in assembling an effective portfolio is to determine its goals. In general terms, a portfolio can serve one of two functions:

- to showcase excellence
- to demonstrate improvement or development over time

The first instance might be the most intuitive: you would select those pieces of writing (or other types of work, depending on the portfolio requirements) that best represent your proficiency and, more to the point, your mastery of a form, convention, discipline, or practice.

However, you might find the second scenario more challenging. Your goal would be to include process-related documents, some of which might not always show off your work to its best advantage. In this case, however, remember that your portfolio is operating as a *narrative*; you are essentially telling the story of your growth as an author (or researcher, or disciplinary specialist, etc.) to your readers. For this reason, the steps along the way are an integral part of that journey. In such a portfolio, you might choose to include the following:

- draft and revised versions of the same paper
- process-related materials, such as freewrites, graphic brainstorms, or outlines
- peer review comments on your drafts
- feedback from your instructor that guided your revision
- reflective letters or cover memos related to the different pieces of writing

In both cases, the key is to be *selective* in the materials you choose to include. As with any argument, it's more important to be focused and specific rather than to be expansive and dilute the force of your message. Likewise, you'll also need to attend to organization and the canon of arrangement in creating your portfolio. Think about the best order for your materials, the one that puts them in dialogue with one another in a productive way. This might be most straightforward for the "development" portfolio; its change-over-time approach lends itself directly to a predominantly chronological mode of arrangement. For the "excellence" portfolio, however, you might need to be more mindful about how to use arrangement persuasively. You will need to identify key characteristics of the different samples (do they exemplify a particular strategy? a particular disciplinary approach? a different genre?) and order them in a way that allows them to dialogue productively with one another and make a cogent argument about you and your work.

However, perhaps equal in importance to the material that comprises your portfolio is the text that pulls it all together: the reflective statement or cover memo. This letter offers you the opportunity for meta-commentary, so you can direct the reader's understanding of your portfolio and present an argument about the significance of the work you included. The criteria and content for your reflective letter will vary depending on your assignment and the type of portfolio you're creating, but the chart below provides an overview of some common goals.

"Excellence" portfolio reflection	"Development" portfolio reflection
• Identify and define the qualities of excellence (related to your writing, your research, or your work in your discipline) that you've designed your portfolio to present	• Identify the goal (as a writer, as a researcher, as a member of your discipline) that you're trying to achieve
• Describe the reason you selected the materials: how do they represent excellence?	• Describe the reason you selected the materials: how do they contribute to understanding your development?
• Clarify the rationale behind the way you arranged the texts; suggest the "arc" of your materials	• Clarify the rationale behind the way you arranged the texts; suggest the "arc" of your materials (often, for this type of portfolio, you might arrange materials chronologically)
• Explain how each text demonstrates one or more of the qualities of excellence, providing context and dialogue between the different examples	• Explain your writing process, the rhetorical choices you made as a writer, the changes you made during revision, and any particular challenges you faced
• Reflect on your achievement—and the process it took to accomplish it—rather than just summarizing the examples	• Assess your final written products and how close they come to fulfilling your objective, what you have learned, and what you'd still like to accomplish
• Share any additional information that might be relevant to your reader's understanding of how the texts demonstrate excellence	• Reflect on your overall development as a writer
	• Share any additional information that might be relevant to your reader's understanding of how the texts demonstrate your development

In general, you should approach your reflection letter as you would any other argumentative text: make sure you have a thesis or central claim (what is the main point you want your reader to understand about your portfolio based on reading the letter?) and point to specific examples from your materials to support your claims, prioritizing critical thinking and analysis over summary. Additionally, keep in mind the importance of the letter as a rhetorical text; since it provides the framework through which your reader understands your portfolio, take care to develop an effective persona through attention to style and your own rhetorical choices.

WRITER'S PRACTICE   MyWritingLab

To prepare for writing a reflective letter about your own portfolio, freewrite answers to the following questions:

- What is the rhetorical situation of your portfolio? Consider purpose, audience, genre, and exigence.
- What's the story you want your portfolio to tell to your reader? What argument would you like to make about your persona as a writer/scholar? What supporting materials would you point to in order to support that claim?
- How do these materials reflect your writing process and your growth as a writer/scholar? Alternately, how do these materials reflect your strengths as a writer/scholar?
- What work have you done that you're most proud of and/or what work shows your greatest development as a writer?
- Which do you consider the weakest piece in your portfolio? Why? How could it have been improved?
- How do the materials interconnect with one another? How does the arrangement of materials reinforce this?
- What else would you want your reader to know about you or your writing that's not necessarily reflected in the materials you included?
- What opportunities or constraints were presented by the medium of your portfolio (binder; online folder; website)?

FORMATTING WRITING FOR AUDIENCE AND PURPOSE

8.5 How do audience and purpose affect my document design?

The types of texts we've discussed so far in this chapter – the essay, the abstract, bio, and even portfolio reflection – all tend to follow the format of academic writing, aligning with the reader's expectations of traditional written discourse. When your argumentative purpose and your audience allow you to move an exclusive focus on written text, you have the opportunity to produce a **multimodal composition**—literally a composition that operates in more than one mode, such as visual, aural, or written. A feature article for a magazine, a newsletter aimed at a community audience, or an online

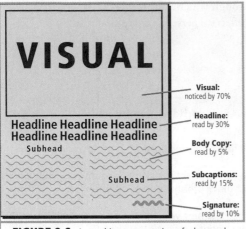

Visual:
noticed by 70%

Headline:
read by 30%

Body Copy:
read by 5%

Subcaptions:
read by 15%

Signature:
read by 10%

FIGURE 8.6 A graphic representation of what readers notice most on a page: visuals grab attention most.

article for diverse readers: each of these texts has the potential to operate through multimodality. An important factor to keep in mind in designing such texts is that research conducted by Adbusters, an organization devoted to cultural criticism and analysis, has shown that readers notice the *visual part* of any page significantly more than any text on the same page (see Figure 8.6). Adbusters uses this finding to provide advice for creating ads, but we can apply the insight to all rhetorical compositions—whether academic or popular—that combine multiple elements.

Let's look at how this attention to design informs a style of writing that is increasingly common in today's society: the online article.

In the following reading, originally published online, the author employs many conventional elements of document design, including a title, subheads, references, and a list of sources at the end. But notice how it adapts some of these elements to meet the viewing needs of online readers. The author also includes hyperlinks, ALL CAPS for some titles, and sections of varying lengths. Finally, is not just the format that sets this article apart from traditional academic discourse: the writing style itself has been changed to meet the expectations of the online writing audience.

The title is in plain style and all capital letters, with the subtitle in lowercase. This font decision makes it appealing to online readers.

WHAT'S WRONG WITH THE BODY SHOP?
—a criticism of 'green' consumerism—

REFERENCED VERSION—all the facts and opinions in THE London Greenpeace A5 'Body Shop' leaflet validated. Note: most references are given just by way of example.

The Body Shop have successfully manufactured an image of being a caring company that is helping to protect the environment

[1] and indigenous peoples [2], and preventing the suffering of animals [3]—whilst selling 'natural' products [4]. But behind the green and cuddly image lies the reality—the Body Shop's operations, like those of all multinationals, have a detrimental effect on the environment [5] and the world's poor [6]. They do not help the plight of animals [7] or indigenous peoples [8] (and may be having a harmful effect), and their products are far from what they're cracked up to be [9]. They have put themselves on a pedestal in order to exploit people's idealism [10]—so this leaflet has been written as a necessary response.

Companies like the Body Shop continually hype their products through advertising and marketing, often creating a demand for something where a real need for it does not exist [11]. The message pushed is that the route to happiness is through buying more and more of their products. The increasing domination of multinationals and their standardised products is leading to global cultural conformity [12]. The world's problems will only be tackled by curbing such consumerism—one of the fundamental causes of world poverty, environmental destruction and social alienation [13].

FUELLING CONSUMPTION AT THE EARTH'S EXPENSE

The Body Shop have over 1,500 stores in 47 countries [14], and aggressive expansion plans [15]. Their main purpose (like all multinationals) is making lots of money for their rich shareholders [16]. In other words, they are driven by power and greed. But the Body Shop try to conceal this reality by continually pushing the message that by shopping at their stores, rather than elsewhere, people will help solve some of the world's problems [17]. The truth is that nobody can make the world a better place by shopping.

20% of the world's population consume 80% of its resources [18]. A high standard of living for some people means gross social inequalities and poverty around the world [19]. Also, the mass production, packaging and transportation of huge quantities of goods is using up the world's resources faster than they can be

The numbers correspond to notes and sources at the end. These notes are hyperlinked, so readers can jump there easily while reading on the web.

Here, the writing itself verges on *low style* with the contraction and the slang work "cracked"— this serves to entice online audiences to keep reading.

The article employs British spelling for many words, such as standardised, colours, criticised, and organise, since the authors are located in Britain. Moreover, as this line indicates, the article against the Body Shop is one in a series of pieces that critique multinational corporate practices.

The article uses argumentative subheads, as might an academic paper. They convey points of argument being made in the article. Moreover, they keep readers interested.

renewed and filling the land, sea and air with dangerous pollution and waste [20]. Those who advocate an ever-increasing level of consumption, and equate such consumption with personal well-being, economic progress and social fulfillment, are creating a recipe for ecological disaster [21].

Rejecting consumerism does not mean also rejecting our basic needs, our stylishness, our real choices or our quality of life. It is about creating a just, stable and sustainable world, where resources are under the control of local communities and are distributed equally and sparingly—it's about improving everyone's quality of life. Consuming ever more things is an unsatisfying and harmful way to try to be happy and fulfilled. Human happiness is not related to what people buy, but to who we are and how we relate to each other. LET'S CONSUME LESS AND LIVE MORE!

Notice how the article uses all CAPS to draw the online reader's attention and even begins a new section with a two-word question.

MISLEADING THE PUBLIC

Natural products? The Body Shop give the impression that their products are made from mostly natural ingredients [22]. In fact like all big cosmetic companies they make wide use of non-renewable petrochemicals, synthetic colours, fragrances and preservatives [23], and in many of their products they use only tiny amounts of botanical-based ingredients [24]. Some experts have warned about the potential adverse effects on the skin of some of the synthetic ingredients [25]. The Body Shop also regularly irradiate certain products to try to kill microbes—radiation is generated from dangerous non-renewable uranium which cannot be disposed of safely [26].

CENSORSHIP

Some sections are very short, a common feature in online writing, where information is "chunked" into accessible segments.

As the Body Shop rely so heavily on their 'green', 'caring' image, they have threatened or brought legal action against some of those who have criticised them, trying to stifle legitimate public discussion [46]. It's vital to stand up to intimidation and to defend free speech.

WHAT YOU CAN DO

Together we can fight back against the institutions and the people in power who dominate our lives and our planet. Workers can and do organise together to fight for their rights and dignity. People are increasingly aware of the need to think seriously about the products we use, and to consume less. People in poor countries are organising themselves to stand up to multinationals and banks which dominate the world's economy. Environmental and animal rights protests and campaigns are growing everywhere. Why not join in the struggle for a better world? London Greenpeace calls on people to create an anarchist society—a society without oppression, exploitation and hierarchy, based on strong and free communities, the sharing of precious resources and respect for all life. Talk to friends and family, neighbours and workmates about these issues. Please copy and circulate this leaflet as widely as you can.

> The article uses direct address, the pronoun you, to engage readers. This design strategy again indicates the use of the plain style.

> The conclusion's turn to ask a rhetorical question and then end with a strong call to action also reflect a writing style more common to online writing than to conventional essays, which are often more subdued in tone.

REFERENCES

1. See "Fuelling Consumption" paragraphs in the leaflet and associated references.

2. See "Exploiting Indigenous Peoples" paragraphs in the leaflet and associated references.

3. See "Helping Animals?" paragraph in the leaflet and associated references.

4. See "Natural products?" paragraph in the leaflet and associated references.

[…]

10. [Numerous publications, statements, advertisements, etc. by the Body Shop.] For example, the company's Mission Statement (1998) says that they are dedicating their business "to the pursuit of social and environmental change" and are trying to ensure that their business "is ecologically sustainable, meeting the needs of the present without compromising the

> Since these notes are positioned far down on the page, they can go into more detail because they assume that only very interested readers will be accessing this part of the composition.

future.""For us, animal protection, human rights, fair trade and environmentalism, are not just fads or marketing gimmicks but fundamental components in our holistic approach to life of which work and business are a part" [Gordon Roddick (Chairman) quoted in 1996 *Body Shop* publication "Our Agenda".] "I'd rather promote human rights, environmental concerns, indigenous rights, whatever, than promote a bubble bath" said Anita Roddick (the *Body Shop* founder and Chief Executive) [speech at 'Academy of Management', Vancouver (Aug 95).]

Back to 'Beyond McDonald's—Retail' Section

London Greenpeace Press Release

WWW Body Shop FAQ

London Greenpeace reply to Body Shop statement

A5 Version of 'What's Wrong with the Body Shop'

From a design perspective, the final series of links for future reading signifies one of the great benefits of writing in a digital environment.

As you can tell from this article, the same strategies of design that shape academic research papers also apply to other modes: what is most important in each is a consideration of *purpose, audience,* and *argument.* Think about how readers will interact with your writing—whether as a print copy handed in for comments (in which case you double-space and follow academic guidelines); as a newsletter (in which case you might open with a powerful image, lay out the writing in columns or boxes, and use an interesting page size); or as a piece to be read on the web (in which case you include hyperlinks, single-space, create shorter chunks, and use font strategically).

In your own writing, you likewise will have the opportunity to present your arguments in multiple modes. In the pages that follow, we'll walk through some of the most common forms you might encounter and consider how to apply the design strategies we have discussed so far to a diverse range of texts.

DESIGNING ARGUMENTS IN POPULAR FORMATS

While it is important to understand the conventions of academic writing, increasingly teachers are inviting students to experiment with alternative forms of making arguments, often modeled on popular or nonacademic texts. Many of these—such as op-ads, photo essays, Websites, or short films—are visual or multimodal in nature, yet still rely on the same foundations of rhetoric that govern persuasion as a whole. When you construct an argument in a more popular format, you should still apply strategies for inventing, arranging, and producing the design, just as you would for a conventional essay. The goal is the same: to design a powerful text to persuade your audience to agree with your message.

Keep in mind, however, that each medium structures information in a distinct way. A photo essay is set up differently than a Webpage, just as a Webpage is set up differently than an online video. Therefore, part of creating a powerful multimodal argument lies in identifying your chosen medium's conventions of structure and style and adjusting the form of your argument—its layout, design, style, and organization of information—to be the most appropriate choice for your project.

In order to transform your research into a more popular format, you should follow a process of *selection, organization,* and *translation.* First, **select** the subset of research you intend to share with your audience. To facilitate this process, ask yourself:

- What matters most about this project?
- What is my purpose in sharing my argument?
- What do I want my audience to walk away thinking when I'm done?

You may find invention strategies such as we discussed in Chapter 3 and Chapter 4 useful for refocusing your argument in this way.

Once you've decided upon the material you wish to include, you now face the task of **organization**. Approach it like you would the task of organizing information for a written argument, using outlining strategies (from post-its, to storyboards, graphic flowcharts, to formal outlines) such as those discussed in Chapter 6. You might ask yourself the following questions:

- How can I hook my audience?
- How will I convey my thesis claim?

8.6 How can I create multimodal arguments, such as op-ads, photo essays, and Websites?

■ What strategies and structures can I use to organize my content?

■ What opportunities and constraints of the mode I'm using?

The final step in developing your multimodal argument is to **translate** your argument into more popular discourse. Some modes rely predominantly on the visual to convey information; others represent a collaboration between both verbal and visual rhetoric. Assess the balance you need to achieve between these elements and the level of decorum most appropriate to your mode, audience, and purpose.

In the pages that follow, we explore more specific guidelines for developing many of the different multimodal genres that you might consider while designing your argument.

Crafting an Op-Ad

The **op-ad**, or **opinion advertisement**, is one of the most concise forms of visual argument and one favored by many nonprofit organizations, special interest groups, and political parties as a way of reaching their target audiences. Like all ads, the op-ad is a compact persuasive text, one that uses rhetorical appeals to convey its message. However, what makes it different from traditional ads is that what it advertises is not a commercial product, but an opinion or strong stand on an issue.

The op-ad in Figure 8.7, for instance, makes a strong argument in favor of a national ban on assault weapons. The organization, Moms Demand Action, crafted a striking argument that communicates its message through a collaboration between visual and verbal elements. The centerpiece and primary focal point is the pair of young girls – a clear *pathos* appeal – that sets up an implicit comparison/contrast strategy: we notice that one girl holds a copy of *Little Red Riding Hood* and the other an assault rifle, an odd juxtaposition for a setting that looks like an elementary school library. The book, the backdrop, and the American flag in the corner put us in mind of school shootings, making the weapon seem even more out of place and alarming. Our eye next moves to the header above the girls' heads: "One child is holding something that's been banner in America to protect them. Guess which one." Based on our initial interpretation of the photo, this riddle seems like an easy one to solve.

However, our final move – to the fine print – confounds our understanding of what the image means. By revealing that it is *Red Riding* Hood that is banned, not the assault rifle, the op-ad invites us to reexamine our own assumptions. It is through such strategic rhetorical crafting of the op-ad –

Seeing Connections
See Chapter 2 for strategies for analyzing op-ads rhetorically.

creating an incongruity of the messaging and the image as well as a seemingly flawed logical circuit between question and answer — that Moms Demand Action succeeds in delivering its powerful message. In this way, the op-ad makes its audience think twice about its assumptions about gun control and what's banned – and what's not banned – to "protect" children in America.

To understand how to compose your own op-ad, let's look at the process by which one student, Angie Sorentino, constructed her visual argument. After writing an effective research paper that presented the dangers of texting while driving, Angie decided to reformulate her argument as an op-ad to reach a larger audience. Her initial considerations were her visual format and her headline—two elements of her ad that underwent some revision. In her project reflection letter, she explained:

FIGURE 8.7   This powerful op-ad draws attention to logical incongruities in how we "protect" American children.

> I originally thought I wanted to lay it out as a text message, using text lingo (LOL, OMG, and the like) because I thought it would appeal to my audience, who I assumed would be teenagers. However, then I realized that I wanted to use a different appeal instead. I wanted the people who looked at my op-ad to have a really powerful emotional reaction to the argument. Also, I started to think that maybe my idea of my audience was too narrow. So, while I tried to avoid blood and graphic imagery (I thought that might be too much like a scare tactic fallacy), I wanted to shock them. I decided on the shattered phone and car wreck because they seemed like symbols that could convey the seriousness of the issue.

As shown in her completed op-ad (see Figure 8.8), Angie paired those powerful images with strong language ("It's not worth it") and a striking statistic. It's in the collaboration between word and image that we find the main work of argumentation in

FIGURE 8.8   Angie Sorentino's op-ad uses foreground and background images in combination with a powerful statistic to make its argument against texting while driving.

AT A GLANCE

Guidelines for Designing an Op-Ad

- Decide on your purpose (to inform, to persuade, to move to action).
- Identify your audience.
- Know your argument.
- Determine which appeals to use (*pathos, logos, ethos*).
- Select key images for your ad.
- Write your print text; decide how it will function in relation to your image(s).
- Draft a gripping headline to complement your image.
- Experiment with layout—arrangement, image size, organization of text—to arrive at the most effective design.

her op-ad. She used the visual to grab the attention and hook her audience, but then amplified the effect with a strong headline, statistic, and the implicit direct address to her audience ("Don't become a statistic"). It's also worth noting that she chose public domain images and cited the source for her statistic, both in the op-ad itself and separately in a works cited. Through such careful (and ethical) practices, she created a powerful rhetorical argument designed to speak to a teen audience.

Creating a Photo Essay

Although an op-ad offers a concise, forceful argument, you may wish to develop your points more thoroughly than one page allows or use visual space to show the range of material with which you've been working. If so, consider the **photo essay**—a text in which photographs, rather than print text, convey the central argument. In a word-based essay, the verbal text takes priority, and images often appear as isolated points of evidence. In a photo essay, by contrast, the visual either collaborates with the verbal or becomes the *primary mode* of argumentation and persuasion.

As a genre, the photo essay first emerged in 1936 with the launching of *Life* magazine, whose mission statement was "to see life; to see the world." Over the 63 years it remained in print, *Life* hosted many of America's most famous photo essays, covering a range of topics from the space race to the Vietnam War, the civil rights movement, and rock and roll. But the photo essay can assume many different forms and use diverse media: it could be a series of documentary photographs and articles about southern sharecroppers published together in book form, such as Walker Evans's and James Agee's *Let Us Now Praise Famous Men* (1941); it could be a book-length photo essay that juxtaposes images with first-person narratives, such as Lauren Greenfield's *Girl Culture* (2002); it could be a striking 27-page color spread in a magazine, such as William Albert Allard's "Solace at Surprise Creek" in the June 2006 issue of *National Geographic*; or it could even be an online arrangement of captioned photos, such as *A Rescue Worker's Chronicle*, created by paramedic Matthew Levy. In each case, the photographs and written text work together, or the images themselves carry the primary weight of the argument.

Today electronic photo essays are essential conveyers of important events, a result of Internet news sources like CNN.com, Time.com, and MSNBC.com, which routinely publish photo essays as "picture stories" on their Websites. Such texts are composed of a series of images and words that work together to convey an argument about a person, event, or story. Each electronic photo essay typically contains (1) a photo, (2) an accompanying caption, (3) an audio option, and (4) a table of contents toolbar that allows readers to navigate through the images. The result is an electronic text that maintains many structural similarities to print text: it offers readers a clear sense of progression from beginning to end while investing its argument with the rhetorical force of multiple media (word, image, sound).

Let's now consider how Conor Henriksen created a photo essay to fulfill an assignment about outdoor art on campus. Figures 8.9 and 8.10 represent two different pages from the longer piece, in which the author complemented photographs he took himself of sculpture and fountains around campus with brief captions, descriptions, and relevant quotations from secondary sources. The photographs themselves clearly appeal to the reader most directly through their vibrant color, strategic arrangement, and visual composition. Despite the surface similarities in layout, we can see that there are different strategies at work: in Figure 8.9, Conor paired a wide shot of the sculpture with a close-up of one figure to give a dual perspective on the installation; in Figure 8.10, he provides a variety of vantages on the fountain, each designed to focus on a different way of understanding it in context. The text he includes works in conjunction with the images it accompanies, but does not dominate. While it provides a

FIGURE 8.9 Through this photo essay, the author makes a visual argument about art on campus.

FOUNTAINS: *The Claw* (1964)

"When you hear the splash of the water drops that fall in the stone bowl, You will feel that all the dust of your mind is washed away"

- Zen Tea Master (qtd in Herda 94)

FIGURE 8.10 A second page from Conor's photo essay.

AT A GLANCE

Guidelines for Designing a Photo Essay

1. Decide on the argument for your project.
2. Arrange your images so they support this argument.
3. Draft written text to accompany or preview each image or set of images.
4. Determine your layout by experimenting with ways of formatting the words and images.

conceptual frame, the photographs themselves provide the most forceful argument about the beauty and significance of outdoor art on campus.

The photo essay works best if you have a topic that can be effectively argued through an accumulation of visual evidence presented as a sequence of images. Keep in mind that designing a photo essay is like drafting a research paper: you may take pages of notes, but the task of crafting the argument involves sifting through information, deciding between relevant and irrelevant materials, and arranging the most powerful evidence in your finished product. In addition, while images have priority in a photo essay, keep in mind the importance of strategically selected and deployed text to accompany your visual argument. Overall, remember to shape your photo essay around your argument through carefully made rhetorical choices about purpose, audience, and medium.

Composing in Newsletter or Magazine Format

Another familiar multimodal format is the newsletter or magazine article. Even with the explosion of online texts, publishers have gone to great lengths to devise ways for articles to retain this popular format even when they appear on the screens of Nooks, Kindles, and iPads. The advice from Adbusters is particularly resonant when we consider the design principles of this form of writing. As Figure 8.6 suggests, a much higher percentage of readers notice visuals than any other component, with the headline being second in significance. We can see the truth in this assertion every time we open an issue of *Time, Wired,* or *Vogue.* An engaging image captures our eye; a provocative headline draws us in; only then do we settle in to dive into the main body of the article.

Taking this into account, consider the importance of visuals as you approach designing your own articles of this sort. Choose images with rhetorical impact to hook your reader and position supporting images strategically in the main body to complement your main points. As for your headline, follow a suggestion from Adbusters: "The most important thing to remember here is that your headline must be short, snappy, and must touch the people that read it. Your headline must affect the readers emotionally, either by making them laugh, making them angry, making them curious, or making them think." Clearly, headlines work through rhetorical appeals: you need to think carefully about which appeal—*pathos, ethos,* or *logos*—would provide the most effective way to engage your audience.

Let's look at the design decisions Miranda Smith made in formatting her writing project on the topic of famine relief in Africa. The assignment invited her to experiment with a popular publication format, so Miranda decided to create her own feature article from a news magazine, taking *Time Magazine* as her model. In designing her text, she not only took into account her argument but also, as Figure 8.11 makes clear, deliberately designed

FIGURE 8.11 Miranda Smith's research project on famine relief in Africa, presented in the form of a feature article.

AT A GLANCE

Guidelines for Designing a Newsletter or Magazine Article

1. Decide on the thesis for your project.
2. Categorize your images, arranging them within thematic groups.
3. Organize them into different configurations: by chronology, concept, and subject.
4. Draft written text in the form of headings, captions, and paragraphs.
5. Determine your layout by experimenting with formatting the words and images.

the layout, placement of images, font size, color, and overall look of the piece with painstaking care. Her rhetorical choices establish a hierarchy of information: she strategically uses a header and subheader; she pulls out a key quote on her second page to accentuate an important point; she uses the *logos* of statistics to frame and define the information in the second half of the article; and finally, she selects several images to complement her written argument. Her article ends powerfully with a *pathos*-based appeal, namely, a small child looking directly at the reader as if inviting her to "get involved," a visual echo of the call to action positioned above his head. We can see here how the visual and verbal operate in tandem as powerful persuasive tools for this multimodal composition.

Composing a Website

If you decide to move your project online and produce a Website, your readers will then encounter your visual argument as a series of interlinked pages (or *hypertext*). Web authors construct a framework for an argument through the **homepage** (the site's introduction), the **navigation scheme** (the site's organizational structure), and the contents of individual pages, offering both internal and external links designed to guide readers through the various levels of argument and evidence. In effect, a *hypertext argument* is produced by the interactive collaboration between the author's direction and the readers' participation, so that the audience plays an active role in the construction of meaning.

This dynamic determines the argumentative structure for Causes.com's homepage (see Figure 8.12). The site's target audience is one that is probably already predisposed to participate in social activism or community service, therefore much of the page is designed to provide readers with examples of opportunities and prompt them to action. The site's primary level of decorum is plain style: through simple language, clean, uncluttered design, and engaging visuals, the Website seeks to persuade viewers that they too can make a difference in the world.

Part of the power of this multimodal argument lies in its engaging opening hook—similar to the hook you would find in the introductory paragraph of an academic essay—which centers the audience's attention on an example of a person who took action for social good. The *homepage* cycles through a series of such examples, such as Paul who protected the rainforests, Kellie who is protecting pets, Jo who speaks out against animal cruelty, and Eric who fought cancer (see Figure 8.12). Looking closely at Eric in Figure 8.12, we can see the effective design decisions at work: the header is punchy and succinct, putting us on a first-name basis with the character and clearly identifying his accomplishment; the realistic cartoon, with Eric dressed in business casual attire, making eye contact with the audience, relies on *pathos*; the more detailed explanation below the header creates *ethos* by mentioning Eric's full name and also draws the readers even deeper into the site with the lure, "read the whole story." Taken together, these elements effectively personalize the Causes.org experience to appeal to its audience.

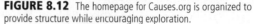

FIGURE 8.12 The homepage for Causes.org is organized to provide structure while encouraging exploration.

Even more significant than the example itself is the way it operates in tandem with the Website frame. Text above and below the central example deliberately encourages audience participation. The top menu offers the principal navigational menu for the site, organized thematically around particular issues. The intent is not linearity, but that exploration of the site will be guided by the visitor's interests; the prominence of the search field in the upper left attests to this as well. Similarly, in the upper right, the audience is prompted to "Start a Campaign," a call to action that is articulated even more forcefully beneath the image. In the footer beneath Eric, in large font, the visitor is asked to put himself in Eric's (or Jo's, or Kellie's, or Paul's) shoes: "How will you use Causes to make a difference?" The shift to second person, coupled with the green "Get Started" imperative that follows, makes clear the argument of this site: its entire design is geared toward providing

Seeing Connections
See Chapter 3 for instructions and advice on writing a hook for the introduction of your essay.

visitors with possibilities and inspiration that will prompt them to start their own activist campaign.

Clearly, while the Causes.org Website on the surface seems simplistic and minimalist, its design was informed by strategic rhetorical decisions that took into account audience and purpose. Based on this example, the process of authoring your own Website may seem daunting at first. However, in many ways drafting text for the web resembles drafting the complex argument of a long research paper: in both cases, you need to identify the necessary elements of your composition, and then you need to follow a process of careful planning and organization.

In designing your Website, you will need to account for three levels of information: a *homepage* at the **primary level** (which will serve as the introduction to your site and draws your audience further into your site); a *series of topic pages* at the **secondary level** (which will contain both content and, sometimes, links to further, more specialized subtopic pages); and the *subtopic pages* at the **deep level** (which will contain content and perhaps even more links). There is no limit on the number of topic and content pages you can include; you should determine the scope of your project and number of pages based on your assessment of how to make your argument most effectively.

WRITER'S PRACTICE   MyWritingLab

In terms of design, composing a Website resembles the process of outlining a research paper. Yet there are important differences between digital writing and writing for print readers. For a Website:

- *Chunk* your information—or divide it into manageable parts.
- *Strive for consistency* of theme, font, and/or color throughout your site; avoid visual clutter and ineffectual use of images.
- *Consider creating a template,* or visual precedent, that establishes the key elements for the rest of the site, much as an introduction in a written paper often sets the style and conventions for the rest of the argument to follow.
- *Use subheads* to structure your argument and help readers navigate your text.

Let's now look at a student's web project on the visual rhetoric surrounding the 1963 March on Washington. In designing the site, Hailey Larkin intended to encourage readers to engage with the primary texts within the framework of a researched argument.

The march was an "editorial in movement" whose "eloquence could not be the same in only frozen word or stilled picture."
- Jack Gould, New York Times (qtd. in Thomas)

When people think of the March on Washington that took place on August 28, 1963, they usually think of Dr. Martin Luther King Jr., who delivered his powerful "I have a dream speech" there. However, what tends to get overshadowed in history classes is the fact that this was an event far larger than Dr. King, that involved between 200,000 and 300,000 people, all demonstrating for "jobs and freedom" ("March").

The press was watching, though. There were more cameras there than there had been to cover the presidential inauguration ("Media").

In this project, I examine the visual rhetoric of the March on Washington by looking at the pictures taken of it. Although Jack Gould argued that its "eloquence could not be the same" in photographs, I will show that the media's perspective was in fact powerful and did shape how we understood, and continue to understand, this historic event.

FIGURE 8.13 This project on the 1963 March on Washington uses a carefully designed Website as its medium.

The homepage for this site (see Figure 8.13) models the composition of the entire project. The most striking element is the photograph, used here to underscore the author's argument. Notice the way the homepage:

- pairs image with text
- uses a quote (in blue) as an epigraph
- explicitly states its argument in bold
- meticulously cites its sources (with parenthetical, hyperlinked references to the Sources page)
- shows careful attention to copyright issues by using public domain images

On the subpages, Hailey supports her researched argument through reference to secondary sources and analysis of the primary texts. For

AT A GLANCE

Guidelines for Designing a Website

- Decide on your audience and purpose.
- Draft a header; include an image in it.
- Map a logical organization for your site to help readers find information easily and understand your purpose and argument.
- Be consistent in imagery and font; avoid jarring color combinations or visual clutter.
- Be strategic in your use and placement of images; be clear in your word choice.
- Link to subpages and external sites.
- Provide a feedback link for comments, and include a "last updated" notice.
- Test your site for usability—both in terms of its general user friendliness and its accessibility to users with disabilities.

instance, on the "Celebrities" page, she analyzes photographs of Joan Baez, Bob Dylan, Harry Belafonte, Sammy Davis, Jr., and Charlton Heston. The homepage also demonstrates the site's attention to organization. The tabbed menu at the top is duplicated by the visual menu below, where each subpage is assigned a representative image. Color is used strategically in both instances (white font; yellow border) to help the viewers locate themselves in relation to the larger structure of the argument.

As you compose your own Website as a visual argument, be sure to consider **usability**—how user friendly your hypertext is and how accessible to users with disabilities. Even a site with professional design and a state-of-the-art graphic interface is ultimately ineffective if the audience cannot navigate it. Learning to write with attention to diverse readers will make you a more rhetorically savvy and effective communicator.

Creating a Podcast

If given the opportunity to choose a popular format for your argument, you might consider the podcast—a short audio essay such as those broadcast as part of WNYC's *Radiolab* or NPR's *This American Life*. While a podcast can be comprised of a scripted argument or essay read by a narrator, it is very well-suited to research projects that rely on interviews as a primary sources. By integrating interviews into your script, you have the unique opportunity to bring your sources' voices literally into your argument. In this way, your project comes closer to the model of *conversation* that we explored in Chapter 5 as a way of understanding the process of research.

While in many places in *Envision* we've talked about using visual rhetoric as a strategy of persuasion, with podcasts you can explore the potential for *sound* to function as a persuasive tool. Podcasts can use sound in many ways as a strategy of development:

- To tie the audio essay together by using the same musical tracks to accompany the introduction and conclusion, and sometimes even the transitions between segments
- To set the tone through voice intonation, music, and style
- To signal transitions between segments or parts of your argument
- To accent or enrich points through integrating sounds that suggest setting, background, or an ambient awareness of context
- To give added power to direct ("live") quotations from sources

AT A GLANCE

Guidelines for Creating a Podcast

- Decide on the format you want to use (completely scripted, interview based, combination model).
- Use colloquial language in plain or middle style.
- Lead with a two- to three-sentence introduction that previews the topic and focus of the podcast.
- Include a "hook" in the first segment of your podcast to engage your audience.
- Develop your ideas in additional segments.
- Include a conclusion that sums up the main point and argument.
- Use music to tie the podcast together, especially the introduction and conclusion.

As with any persuasive text, however, be sure to start by analyzing your rhetorical situation when creating a podcast. What is your argument? Who is your audience? What is the purpose of your podcast? What is your rhetorical stance? What persona do you want to project? Finally, consider how this medium affects the delivery of your argument: How does the audio format influence the way in which you'll craft your argument? What extra opportunities does the rhetoric of sound afford you? What limitations will you face as you move from printed to spoken word?

WRITER'S PRACTICE   MyWritingLab

Listen to two different podcasts, one from *RadioLab* and one from *This American Life*. Pay particular attention to the following:

- What is the purpose of the podcast? The audience? How do you know?
- How is music used rhetorically in the podcast? How are other sounds used rhetorically?
- What level of decorum does the narrator use? How does she or he establish that style? How does she or he establish tone, mood, and persona?
- How are sources integrated?
- What is the structure of the podcast? Where is the argument most clearly articulated?

Use these questions as the foundation for brainstorming your own list of best practices for creating an audio essay or podcast as a way of sharing a research-based argument.

Producing an Online Video

Another popular format you might consider is one that you encounter everyday on the channels of Vimeo, YouTube, and the like: the online video. Whether you watch weekly videoblogs, technology product reviews, make-up or fashion tips, celebrity gossip reports, or even gaming walk-throughs, chances are you are quite familiar with one of the genres of homegrown video currently available on the Internet. And with camera hardware and editing software coming hardwired with increased frequency on smartphones, laptops, and tablets these days, more and more people find themselves with the opportunity to be their own cameraman, director, producer, and film star.

Consider the Internet sensation *danisnotonfire*. British-born Dan Howell rose quickly to fame in 2010–2011 for his vlog and, as of November 2015, his YouTube channel boasted over five million subscribers. His video blogs often center on personal narrative; in typical YouTube style, he directly addresses the audience, looking into the camera as if to make eye contact; his pieces incorporate occasional cuts between takes to enhance continuity, create a story structure, and emphasize certain ideas. He also at times superimposes text onto the screen to accentuate a point. While clearly gravitating toward a plain or low style, he creates an engaging text defined by his own persona and through a perspective that keeps his viewers coming back for more.

You may notice similar strategies enacted on other Internet celebrity's channels. PewDiePie; Tyler Oakley; Jenna Marbles; Joey Graceffa: all these vloggers trade on similar rhetorical principles for success: they rely on plain style; they use camera techniques to simulate direct interaction and conversation with their followers; they develop engaging personas through the visual and verbal style of their videos; and they assume an effective (if not amusing) rhetorical stance in relation to their audience and topic.

Seeing Connections
See Chapter 3 for a discussion of persona and rhetorical stance

If creating a video, take into account how best to use the particular features of this genre to connect with or persuade your audience. While you might narrate or appear in the video, you might also use footage of events, interviews, locales, or even animation to drive your argument. Consider the ways some students have utilized the short video format to convey a powerful message:

- For a collaborative project on the impact of the Nintendo 64, one group of students constructed its video around a series of interviews they conducted, creating an argumentative structure in which they presented the interview question in type on the screen, following each with "answers" in the form of footage from the interviews. The *ethos* of the interviewees and the careful selection of sound bytes drove home their argument.

■ Another student designed a short video argument about current war protests, showing an escalating sequence of images—news photographs of the war-torn landscape, of protest demonstrations, and politicians speaking about the military campaign—set against the soundtrack of the song "Wake Me Up" by Evanescence. The rapid succession of images paired with stirring music provoked an emotional reaction in the audience, without the need for verbal commentary. Since this project included copyrighted materials, the students did not publish it online but instead simply showed it at a class exhibit.

■ Yet another group, designing a video argument on *locavorism* (the movement to eat foods grown locally rather than those shipped from around the world), filmed footage inside two markets: the local Albertsons (a big chain supermarket) and their nearby Whole Foods (a natural food market). Using a news reporting style, they examined fruits and vegetable in the produce section in both locales, comparing price, availability, and quality so as to make their argument about the feasibility of adhering to a locavore diet.

In your own film project, use *invention*—perhaps drafting your ideas on a storyboard, as discussed in Chapter 6. Consider levels of style—plain, middle, or grand—and how to best convey these through tone, choice of images, types of camera shots, and persona or voice. Work with the canon of arrangement, as discussed in Chapter 3, to consider how edits, order of scenes, and transitions can contribute to the persuasiveness of your argument.

AT A GLANCE

Guidelines for Producing an Online Video

1. Decide on how you might approach video as a medium to best engage your audience.
2. Use storyboarding to brainstorm or *invent* your ideas.
3. Create a script and build on your storyboard to develop a visual outline.
4. Practice your drafted scenes; if you film the drafts, do a self-assessment or peer review to help you revise.
5. Film your revised scenes, labeling each "draft" as a take for future analysis.
6. Use the strategies you learned in Chapter 6 for revision as you edit your film.
7. When you feel the text is complete, prescreen it with a test audience and receive feedback.
8. Finally, submit it to your audience and then write up a reflection on your work.

Designing a Poster

In some cases, you might be asked to provide a summary of your research in the form of a research poster. This presentation style is used most frequently in the sciences, where **poster sessions** are common at conferences and large conventions. Visitors walk through exhibit halls where hundreds of posters are on display, stopping to read those that interest them and often requesting copies of the complete research paper. If you plan on pursuing a science major, you might want to ask your instructor if a poster presentation would be an acceptable form to use for reporting your research findings.

One of the challenges of creating a poster lies in deciding what information to include. The argument presented by a poster is limited by both space (the physical dimensions of a poster constrain the amount of information that realistically can be included) and time (most readers rarely spend more than 5 minutes perusing a poster). For this reason, it's important to be *selective* in the material you use, *clear* in the way you convey it, and *strategic* in your persuasive design. A poster is a glimpse or summary of your work; a longer research essay or article would be the place to more fully represent your findings and argument.

Another consideration is the logistics of the *delivery* of the information. At times, researchers create "stand-alone" posters, which are designed to be self-contained and present the information without any accompanying oral component. That is, the researcher does not physically stay with the poster to explain it; it "stands alone" in presenting the research. In an alternative model, however, authors stand with their posters in the exhibition hall, symposium, or poster session, using the poster as a way to direct or focus a discussion of their research (see Figure 8.14). Therefore, in determining what information to include, you likewise should consider whether you're developing a stand-alone poster or one that will serve as a visual/

FIGURE 8.14 Poster session.

verbal complement to your oral presentation of research. That decision will influence how much information you include and how you communicate it.

Once you determine what type of poster is most appropriate, you can turn to questions of design. Effective poster design balances two priorities: audience engagement and clear organization. Your design must both draw the audience in—through effective display of visual information and concise and clear writing—and lead them clearly through your information.

Many posters facilitate this process by relying on a column-based mode of organization, where information is distributed in almost a newspaper column format, so that readers are encouraged to follow the flow of information from top left, through columns, until they arrive at the bottom right. Alternately, sometimes more innovative poster designs use a key, central image as an anchor and then organize the information so it radiates out from there. What's most important is that your viewer can follow the progression of your ideas and that you adhere to the requirements of your poster session. Both types of posters can benefit from implementing strategic tactics to signpost for their viewers information and its degree of relevance: clear headers to guide readers, often linked to recognizable components of the research process (i.e., Methods, Results, Discussion); visual hierarchies, so the most important words and images are larger than the less important; and strategic repetition in design to help pull the poster as a whole together.

Let's look at how these elements work together in an award-winning poster from an undergraduate research symposium (Figure 8.15). The poster demonstrates certain key features:

- A hybrid form that organizes information in columns, but around a central image
- Bold headings that are easy to read from a distance

AT A GLANCE

Guidelines for a Designing a Poster

- Be selective in the information you include; integrate key points related to background, method, data, and your analysis or argument.
- Put the poster's title, authors, and academic affiliation at the top.
- Avoid visual clutter; consider using white space to offset various elements, including tables, figures, and written texts.
- Arrange materials in columns or around a central visual anchor.
- Avoid long passages of texts.
  - Include images, charts, and graphs as modes of visual persuasion.
  - Make sure your poster is readable from a distance; size your fonts accordingly.
- Always check with the conference organizers for their specific guidelines.

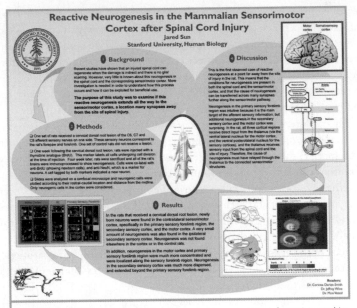

FIGURE 8.15 This poster by Jared Sun combines engaging information graphics with a concise overview of his project.

- Clear hierarchies of information
- Concise written content paired with compelling images
- Signposting involving both numbered sections and arrows
- Concise but specific discussion of research

When you create your own poster, keep in mind the fundamental elements for poster design described in the At a Glance box on p. 333. By following these guidelines, you can create effective public displays of argument that are consistent in format and easily understood by audience members.

Developing a Multimedia Presentation

In today's increasingly tech-mediated environment, multimedia presentations have become very popular in both academic and professional contexts. As with the other types of arguments we've discussed so far, consideration of the rhetorical situation (such as the concepts of audience, purpose, and persona) can help focus the task. If you think of all the different presentations you've encountered in school or everyday life, from an engaging TED talk, to a professor's lecture, or even a guest speaker at a school event, it becomes clear that each adapted their presentation to suit their particular rhetorical situation. Steve Jobs, for instance, perfected a particularly powerful and unique presentation style for his MacWorld presentations (see Figure 8.16). With his trademark black turtleneck and jeans, his emphatic hand gestures, his direct, plain style of discourse, and his skilled use of multimedia support, he was recognized as one of the most persuasive public speakers of the early twenty-first century. You, too, can carefully construct your presentation to be a powerful visual and verbal argument.

Your first step involves assessing the rhetorical situation. Ask yourself:

1. What format will my presentation take?
2. Who is my audience?
3. What is my purpose?
4. What persona do I want to convey?
5. What supporting materials do I plan to use?

Once you've completed this preliminary brainstorming, you can attend to the three components of a presentation: oral argument, multimedia support, and delivery.

Oral Argument   At the heart of any presentation lies the oral argument that supports it. In order to transform your research argument into one that you can present orally, you need to follow a process of *selection, organization,* and *translation* outline earlier in this chapter.

Selection: In most cases, you'll need to cut down the sheer amount of material you can convey; for instance, if you have 15 pages of written argument, it would probably take 40 minutes or more to read your words out loud. In fact,

FIGURE 8.16 Steve Jobs, co-founder and former Apple CEO, presenting a new product at MacWorld 2008.

AT A GLANCE

Key Steps in Transforming Your Research Argument into a Presentation

- *Scope.* How do I convert 10, 15, or even 20 pages of written argument into a 5-, 10-, or 15-minute oral presentation? Answer: Selection.

- *Content.* How do I reframe the content so that it makes sense to my audience? Answer: Organization.

- *Style.* How do I change the written word to a spoken, visual, and digital medium? Answer: Translation.

most of us speak for longer than we realize, so always plan for a shorter presentation time than what you actually have allotted. This means making hard choices about which subset of your research or argument you'll share with your audience.

Organization: As you transform your research into an oral presentation, you have an opportunity to reorganize your written argument to meet the expectations of a listening audience. You might for instance, begin with your conclusion and then convey the narrative of your research. Or you might want to show your visual evidence fist, ask questions, and then provide your thesis at the end. In other words, your presentation doesn't need to be a miniature version of your written argument. Be innovative, and think about what structure would be most effective for your audience.

Translation: You might find the most challenging step to be translation; for many rhetoricians, it can be difficult to **translate** your writing from text meant to be read to text meant to be heard. To do so, examine your language, assessing the length of your sentences and the complexity of your diction. Make sure to avoid jargon and to define any terms with which your audience might not be familiar. Lastly, add clear signposting (words and phrases like *first, second, third, for example, in conclusion*) to clearly indicate your structure to your audience. Listeners also respond to humor, direct address, familiar examples, and even questions. Attending to how to transform your argument in this way – for a listening audience – is key to laying a solid foundation for your presentation as a whole. Be sure to draft a formal script for your translated argument; even if you end up using it merely as notes, the process of writing out your argument completely will ensure that you give careful attention to the structure and style of your oral argument.

Seeing Connections
For an example of translation between oral and written forms, see excerpts from Nicholas Christakis's academic journal article and TED presentation in Chapter 3.

Multimedia Support   Once you've drafted your script, you can consider what types of multimedia would best support your argument. We use the word "support" deliberately. Any time you consider incorporating multimedia into a presentation, be sure to keep in mind the following: these multimedia components are *secondary* to your argument. It's the argument itself, not the technology, that should drive the presentation.

There are a range of options available to today's presenter: PowerPoint, Keynote, Prezi, or Google slides; film or audio clips; screencasts; projection of digital images; even, in some cases, live Web browsing or video conferencing with guest speakers. Many factors will influence your choice of multimedia, including your access to technology, the capabilities of the room in which you are presenting, the requirements of your presentation assignment, and your own technological expertise. However, you might also consider the choice of multimedia as a rhetorical one:

A **slidedeck** has been the standard mode of information display for many years. It is designed to showcase your material in a linear format, allowing you to clearly organize your ideas and to distill your points into "power-points" designed to persuade.

A **prezi** presents a creative alternative to the traditional slide deck, allowing for increased customization and a linked or non-linear structure.

A **whiteboard**, though often considered as "old school," can provide a versatility missing from slides or prezis in that it allows you to showcase process by creating notes on the spot to underscore points as you present.

There is no one set of rules for developing effective multimedia support, although, in general, you may find it helpful to remember that your slides or accompanying visuals should be designed to aid the audience's under-standing of your argument, not to provide you with notes for your presentation. You may find it helpful to keep these suggestions in mind:

- Use purposeful visuals, not clip art
- Plan to spend time discussing the images you use as visual evidence
- When using a film or audio clip, be selective in how much to show so it doesn't overwhelm your presentation
- Don't put too much text on each slide or frame or rely too heavily on bullet lists
- Use animation to stagger the amount of information you present to your audience at any one time
- Keep fonts consistent in style, size, and color, to avoid distracting the audience
- Break complicated ideas into multiple slides or frames
- Use clear, interesting headers to help visually structure your argument
- Tie your slides together with a visual theme or template that, if possible, reflects the content of your topic
- Include sound effects and animation rhetorically and sparingly
- Give a handout with full quotations or infographics as necessary

The most important thing to remember as you develop your multimedia support is that it should function not as a *script* for you to use, but rather as a *rhetorical act of persuasion* that should engage your audience.

Delivery   The last component of a multimedia presentation that you should attend to are components of the live delivery. Indeed, delivery is so important that, when asked which three of the five canons of rhetoric he considered the most valuable to successful public speaking, the Greek orator Demosthenes replied, "delivery, delivery, delivery." When considering delivery for contemporary multimedia presentations, we point to many of the same elements that classical rhetoricians focused on as well.

- **Voice**: pitch, tone, loudness, softness, and enunciation
- **Embodied rhetoric**: use of the body, posture, dress or outfit, appearance, mannerisms
- **Gesture**: use of hands to communicate or punctuate information
- **Pacing**: speed of words, visuals and argument; use of strategic pauses
- **Visuals**: interaction with visual support
- **Style**: inclusion of elements such as repetition, allusion, metaphor, stories, personal narrative, and jokes

As you can see, many aspects of delivery resonate with our previous discussions of oral argument and multimedia support: delivery itself is the performative element of the presentation, the way in which you draw together the different components of your argument and *deliver* them to your audience.

As you craft your own presentation, remember the old adage, "Practice makes perfect." Peer review and revision are as important to your presentation as collaboration on drafts and revisions are to your written work. They enable you to anticipate problems and harness your creativity as you shape your ideas into a memorable, moving, and persuasive form of rhetorical communication.

THE WRITER'S PROCESS

In this chapter, you've learned how to design and produce your texts in ways that meet your purpose and match the expectations of your audience. Often this means knowing, understanding, and adhering to conventions set forth by a community of scholars, readers, or writers. This is the case for the document design of your research essay, cover page, abstract, and bio. At other times, this means exploring innovative approaches to design in multimedia contexts. All modes of design depend on your rhetorical expertise in choosing a level of decorum, in knowing what strategies best work for your situation, in deciding on your medium and your format, and then in having these choices support your purpose in designing your work. By examining academic essays and a variety of multimodal arguments, you have seen that the rhetorical principles of audience, argument, form, and purpose carry across diverse media. With the ever-changing features of modern media, you have an increasing number of choices for designing arguments with purpose, power, and creativity. It's time now for you to make your contribution. Start brainstorming your ideas, and begin to design your own argument.

WRITING ASSIGNMENTS

MyWritingLab

1. **Write an Analysis of a Multimodal Argument.** Select an argument (a YouTube video blog, a work of graffiti art from a community center, a parody poster from a campus organization, for instance) and using the strategies developed in this chapter, analyze how it uses style and design elements to construct its argument. Use the checklist below to help you with this process.

   - **Argument:** What is the text's topic? What is its argument? What evidence is used to support the argument? What is the rhetorical stance and point of view on the topic? What role does verbal, visual, or multimedia play in persuasion in this text? Are words and images complementary or does the argument work primarily through one means?

   - **Audience:** Whom is the argument intended to reach? What response seems to be anticipated from the audience? Sympathetic? Hostile? Concerned?

   - **Medium:** Is the medium used appropriate for the argument and its target audience? What type of interaction does the medium create with its audience?

   - **Form:** What are the specific characteristics of the medium? Consider layout, images, style, and font. How are these elements organized?

   - **Purpose:** What is the purpose in presenting the argument to the audience in this design? To move them to action? Inform them? Teach them? What type of decorum or style (grand, middle, or plain) is used to realize this purpose?

2. **Design Elements to Accompany Your Final Essay Revision:** Write an abstract and bio for your research paper. Adhere academic document design. Post all your documents online as a showcase of your work as a writer and researcher.

3. **Visual Argument:** Create a photo essay based on the argument from your research paper or as part of an independent project. The images you use in your photo essay may be from your paper, or you can use a completely new set, particularly if you did not use images in your original essay. Your argument may mirror that found in your research paper, or you may focus on a smaller portion of your overall argument. The style, arrangement, medium, and rhetorical strategies of your photo essay should match your audience and your purpose. Include written text in your photo essay strategically. Once you have finished, write a one-page reflection on the strategies you used in this project.

4. **Multimodal Argument:** Transform your written essay into one of the creative formats you've learned in this chapter: try creating an op-ed, a Website, an online film, a visual collage, or text combining multiple modes, such one that uses words or audio strategically as part of the text's persuasive power. If using audio, match your images to a recorded argument. Alternatively, combine visual images with a soundtrack, and post your work on a Website that you design; pick your music carefully, and time each image to match a particular mood or moment in the music. If you are transforming your essay into a short online film, modify your organization, arrangement, text selection, and even order of images to accommodate this shift in medium. Once you have finished, write a one-page reflection on your work.

MyWriting**Lab** Visit Ch. 8 Designing Arguments in MyWritingLab to complete the Writer's Practices, Spotlighted Analyses, and Writing Assignments, and to test your understanding of the chapter objectives.

CREDITS

Images

Chapter 1

p. 1: Thomson Reuters.

p. 3, Figure 1.1: Mike Luckovichy, Editorial Cartoon used with the permission of MIke Luckovich and Creators Syndicate. All rights reserved.

p. 5, Figure 1.2: K. Clare Conrotto

p. 5, Figure 1.3: Christine Alfano

p. 6, Figure 1.4: Fernando Veludo/epa/Corbis

p. 7: Lunsford, Andrea.

p. 8, Figure 1.6: phdcomics.com

p. 9: Bitzer, Lloyd

p. 10, Figure 1.8: Cagle Cartoons, Inc.

p. 11: Lucas, George, Star Wars Episode IV, Disney.

p. 13: McCloud, Scott, "Understanding Comics".

p. 15, Figure 1.10: Bramhall, Bill, "I Can't Breathe", December 4, 2014 © Daily News, L.P. (New York). Used with permission.

p. 18, Figure 1.12: Clay Bennett Editorial Cartoon used with the permission of Clay Bennett, the Washington Post Writers Group and the Cartoonist Group. All rights reserved.

p. 19: McCloud, Scott, "Understanding Comics".

p. 27, Figure 1.14: Markstein, Gary, "Domestic Violence", September 12, 2014. Reprinted with permission by Creators.

p. 29, Figure 1.15: Cagle Cartoons, Inc.

Chapter 2

p. 43, Figure 2.1: JEWEL SAMAD/Getty Images

p. 45, Figure 2.2: Anheuser-Busch/Splash News/Corbis

p. 46, Figure 2.3, LEGO Juris A/S

p. 48, Figure 2.4: Bank of America

p. 56, UF2-A: Library of Congress, Prints & Photographs Division, [LC-USZC4-4440]

p. 58, Figure 2.6:Juan Carlos/Bloomberg/Getty Images

p. 66, Figure 2.7: Hugo Ortuño Suárez/Demotix/Corbis

p. 67, Figure 2.8: Natan Dvir/Polaris/Newscom

p. 75, Figure 2.9: Advertising Archives

p. 75, Figure 2.9: The Coca-Cola Company. Advertisement for Coca-Cola entitled "Coca-Cola goes along" and accompanying marks of The Coca-Cola Company. Used with permission.

p. 77, Figure 2.10: Richard Levine/Demotix/Corbis

p. 77, Figure 2.10: Cindy Ord/Getty Images

Chapter 3

p. 89, Figure 3.1: Eric Gay/AP Images

p. 92: Cicero

p. 93, Figure 3.3: Margaret Bourke-White/Masters/Time Life Pictures/Getty Images

p. 94, Figure 3.4: Library of Congress, Prints & Photographs Division, [3b06165r]

p. 94, Figure 3.5: Library of Congress Prints and Photographs Division[LC-USZ62-95653]

p. 97, Figure 3.6: Todd Heisler/Polaris Images

p. 98, Figure 3.7: Library of Congress Prints and Photographs Division

p. 98, Figure 3.8: Library of Congress Prints and Photographs Division

p. 99, Figure 3.9: Library of Congress Prints and Photographs Division

p. 99, Figure 3.10: Library of Congress Prints and Photographs Division

p. 114, Figure 3.14: Susan Walsh/AP Images

p. 119, Figure 3.16: The Columbian, September 2, 2005.

p. 119, Figure 3.15: From Anchorage Daily News, September 2 © 2005 McClatchy. All rights reserved. Used by permission and protected by the Copyright Laws of the United States. The printing, copying, redistribution, or retransmission of this Content without express written permission is prohibited.

p. 122, Figure 3.17: Library of Congress, Prints & Photographs Division, [0007q]

Chapter 4

p. 136, Figure 4.1: Alexandra Fischer

p. 138, Figure 4.2: Hoover Institution Archives

p. 140, Figure 4.3: Library of Congress, Prints and Photographs Division, LC-USZC4-5603

p. 145, UnFigure_4a: Palczewski, Catherine H. Postcard Archive. University of Northern Iowa. Cedar Falls, IA.

p. 145: Palczewski Suffrage Postcard Archive. Courtesy of University of Northern Iowa.

p. 149, Figure 4.6a: National Archives and Records Administration

p. 149, Figure 4.6b: Archive Images/Alamy

p. 149, Figure 4.6c: Library of Congress, Prints and Photographs Division

p. 149, Figure 4.6d: Gianni Dagli Orti/The Art Archive at Art Resource, NY

p. 149, Figure 4.6e: Library of Congress, Prints and Photographs Division

p. 151, Figure 4.7: Alexandra Fischer

p. 151, Figure 4.8; Alexandra Fischer

p. 151, Figure 4.9: Lalo Alcaraz

Chapter 5

p. 166, Figure 5.1: Nevada Wier/Corbis

p. 167, Figure 5.2a: Nigel Cattlin/Alamy

p. 167, Figure 5.2b: Paul Abbitt/Alamyp.

p. 167, Figure 5.2c: Danita Delimont/Alamy

p. 167, Figure 5.2d: Tom Wood/Alamy

p. 169, Figure 5.3: Steve Bronstein/Stone/Getty Images

p. 177, Figure 5.5: US Army, Getty Images

p. 183, Figure 5.7: National Institutes of Health

p. 185, Figure. 5.7: Copyright EBSCO Publishing, Inc. 1999. All rights reserved.

p. 195, Figure 5.8: Vincent Chen

p. 197, Figure. 5.9a: Ryan O'Rourke

p. 197, Figure. 5.9b: Ryan O'Rourke

Chapter 6

p. 211: Zoe Saldana/Everett Collection

p. 212, Figure 6.1: AF archive/Alamy

p. 219, Figure 6.4a: Everett Collection

p. 219, Figure 6.4c: Everett Collection

p. 219, Figure 6.4b: Zoe Saldana/Everett Collection

Chapter 7

p. 265, Figure 7.1: Justin Cone

p. 283, Figure 7.2: Christine Alfano

p. 283, Figure 7.3: Christine Alfano

p. 291, UnFigure_07a: Daniel Shim. "Wasabi-Boy No Engrish" video screen shot. Used by permission.

Chapter 8

p. 296, Figure 8.1: DC Vote

p. 315: Body Shop Mission Statement

p. 316: Roddick, Gordon quoted in Body Shop publication "Our Agenda", 1996.

p. 316: Roddick, Anita speech at Academy of Management, Vancouver, August 1995.

p. 319, Figure 8.7: The Advertising Archives

p. 319, Figure 8.7: **Moms Demand Action**

p. 320, Figure 8.8b: Christina Alfano

p. 320, Figure 8.8: Konstantinos Moraiti/Fotolia

p. 321, Figure 8.9: Chris O'Brien

p. 322, Figure 8.10a: Chris O'Brien

p. 322, Figure 8.10b: Chris O'Brien

p. 322, Figure 8.10c: Chris O'Brien

p. 323, Figure 8.11a: AP Photo/Farah Abdi Warsameh

p. 323, Figure 8.11b: Ulrich Doering/Alamy

p. 323, Figure 8.11c: Richard Lord/Alamy

p. 325, Figure 8.12: Screencapture, Eric fought against cancer, www.causes .com. Reprinted with permission.

p. 327, Figure 8.13: Screencapture, Visual Rhetoric of Protest, http://miranda rose.wix.com/marchon-washington.

p. 332, Figure 8.15: Dennis Schroeder/NREL/U.S. Department of Energy

p. 334, Figure 8.16: Jared Sun

p. 335, Figure 8.17: Paul Sakuma/AP Image

Text

Adbusters, "Create your own print ad", https://www.adbusters.org/spoofads/printad.

Baker, Chris,"Is Darth Disney Destroying Star Wars' Expanded Universe?" Wired, June 12, 2014. Copyright Conde Nast. Used with permission.

Barry, Doug. Excerpt from "Refreshing Tide Commercial Manages Not to Rely on Goon-Dad Caricature for a Change" by Doug Barry. March 15, 2013. Copyright © 2013. http://jezebel.com/5990826/refreshing-tide-commercial-manages-not-to-rely-on-goon-dad-caricature-for-a-change. Used with permission of Gawker Media.

Batouli, Ali. Reprinted with permission.

Bitzer, Lloyd, This paper was presented as a public lecture at Cornell University in November 1966 and at the University of Washington.

Bogost, Ian, Persuasive Games: The Expressive Power of Videogames, excerpt: 334 words, © 2007 Massachusetts Institute of Technology, by permission of The MIT Press.

Christakis, Nicholas A. M.D., Ph.D., M.P.H., and James H. Fowler, Ph.D, "The Spread of Obesity in a Large Social Network over 32 Years", New England Journal of Medicine, July 26, 2007.

Christakis, Nicholas. "The hidden influence of social networks." TED talks, May 2010. Copyright © 2010 TED Conferences, LLC. Used by permission of TED.

Christakis, Nicholas. "The hidden influence of social networks." TED talks, May 2010. Copyright © 2010 TED Conferences, LLC. Used by permission of TED.

Conrotto, Clare, "Dialogue of Sources."

Conrotto, K. Clare, "I'll Have the Lies on the Side, Please". Reprinted with permission.

Conrotto, K. Clare, "Salvador Allende's government in Chile in the 1970s". Reprinted with permission.

Conrotto, Kim Clare, "Sugar: The Hidden Drug."

Curtis, James C., "Dorothea Lange, Migrant Mother, and the Culture of the Great Depression", Winterthur Portfolio, Vol. 21, No. 1 (Spring, 1986), pp. 1–20, The University of Chicago Press.

Diamond, Matthew, From No Laughing Matter: Post-September 11 Political Cartoons in Arab/Muslim Newspapers.

Dunn, Geoffrey, "Photographic License", © San Luis Obispo New Times, January 17, 2002. Reprinted with permission.

Fehr, Molly, "Inspiring Nazi Germany". Reprinted with permission.

Gerrig, Richard J. and Zimbardo, Philip G. PSYCHOLOGY AND LIFE, 2012. Pearson Education.

Giménez, Andrés de Rojas, "May the Force be with…Mickey Mouse?" Used with permission of the author.

Horsey, David. "Obnoxious Freedom", LA Times, January 9, 2015. © Tribune Content Agency, LLC. All Rights Reserved. Reprinted with permission.

Kemp, Raymond, via Twitter, October 30, 2012. Reprinted with permission.

Light, Jennifer S. "When Computers Were Women." Technology and Culture 40:3 (1999), 455–483. © 1999 by the Society for the History of Technology. Reprinted with permission of Johns Hopkins University Press.

Martel, William C., "Ban on Photography Military Coffins Protected

INDEX